# WORDS, NOT SWORDS

*Gender, Culture, and Politics in the Middle East*

miriam cooke, Suad Joseph, *and* Simona Sharoni, *Series Editors*

# FARZANEH MILANI

# WORDS NOT SWORDS

**IRANIAN WOMEN WRITERS AND THE FREEDOM OF MOVEMENT**

Syracuse University Press

Mohamad El-Hindi Books on Arab Culture and Islamic Civilization are published
with the assistance of a grant from the M.E.H. Foundation.

∞ The paper used in this publication meets the minimum requirements
of the American National Standard for Information Sciences—Permanence
of Paper for Printed Library Materials, ANSI Z39.48-1992.

For a listing of books published and distributed by Syracuse University Press,
visit our Web site at SyracuseUniversityPress.syr.edu.

ISBN: 978-0-8156-3278-8

**Library of Congress Cataloging-in-Publication Data**
Milani, Farzaneh.
Words, not swords : Iranian women writers and the freedom of movement / Farzaneh Milani. — 1st ed.
p. cm. — (Gender, culture, and politics in the Middle East)
Includes bibliographical references and index.
ISBN 978-0-8156-3278-8 (cloth : alk. paper)
1. Persian literature—Women authors—History and criticism.   2. Persian literature—History
and criticism.   3. Women authors, Iranian.   4. Muslim women in literature.   5. Purdah
in literature.   6. Social control in literature.   7. Women in literature.   8. Women in motion pictures.
9. Women and literature—Iran.   10. Feminism and literature—Iran.   I. Title.   II. Title: Iranian
women writers and the freedom of movement.
PK6413.5.W65M55 2011
891'.55099287—dc22          2011005040

*Manufactured in the United States of America*

*For Faridoun and Paulo,*
*my guardian angels,*
*and*
*For Julia, Georgia, Leila, and Luca,*
*my sunlight*

FARZANEH MILANI is the author of *Veils and Words: The Emerging Voice of Iranian Women Writers* (1992) and the translator, with Kaveh Safa, of *A Cup of Sin: Selected Poems of Simin Behbahani* (1999). She has published more than one hundred articles, epilogues, forewords, and afterwords in Persian and English. She has served as the guest editor for two special issues of *Nimeye Digar* (a Persian-language feminist journal), *IranNameh,* and *Iranian Studies.* She has written for the *New York Times,* the *Washington Post,* the *Christian Science Monitor, Ms. Magazine, Readers Digest, USA Today,* and National Public Radio's *All Things Considered.* She has presented more than 150 lectures nationally and internationally. Former director of Studies in Women and Gender and current chair of the Department of Middle Eastern and South Asian Languages and Cultures, Milani is professor of Persian literature and women's studies at the University of Virginia in Charlottesville. She was a Carnegie Scholar (2006–2007) and McAndless Distinguished Chair at Eastern Michigan University for 2010. Past president of the Association of Middle Eastern Women Studies in America, Milani was the recipient of the All University Teaching Award in 1998 and nominated for the Virginia Faculty of the Year Award in 1999.

*My poems are my swords.*
—SIMIN BEHBAHANI, "Swords"

*Everyone has the right to freedom of movement.*
—UNIVERSAL DECLARATION OF HUMAN
RIGHTS, ARTICLE 13

# CONTENTS

# ACKNOWLEDGMENTS

Some of the finest expressions of Iranian artistic talent do not carry the name of a creator. There is great wisdom behind this deliberate refusal to credit a single artist for an artifact. Scheherazade, the ultimate storyteller, inserted with infinite acumen a disclaimer at the very threshold of each story. Following the enigmatic "There was one, and there wasn't one," she added: "Other than God, there wasn't anyone." The framing sentence, the paradox, and proviso at that magical moment of creation, when the storyteller becomes the literary equivalent of the Creator, provides an apologia and a justification. It also acknowledges the implicit distance between the artist and the art. It permits at the same time as it asks for permission and in the process recognizes the elusive, tantalizing, and collective nature of creative power. Couched in the totality of that couplet is the implicit idea that before the vast immensity of the previously created, the storyteller's role carries little authority.

I have accumulated several debts over the years and benefited from the guidance and scholarship of many family members, colleagues, friends, and students. They have led me in new directions and helped me explore and expand my views. Their insight, their much appreciated counsel, and their generosity of spirit is woven in the warp and woof of this manuscript.

I have been the lucky beneficiary of Bahiyyih Nakhjavani and Kaveh Safa's infinite magnanimity, profound intellectual acuity, and expansive vision. They have read and reread several versions of each chapter, helped me to hone my arguments, and led me to rewarding destinations. I could not have hoped for a reader more learned or scrupulous than Shahla Haeri, who suggested important changes and improvements. My good friends and colleagues Rae Blumberg and Zjaleh Hajibashi read the whole manuscript and offered invaluable comments and astute criticisms. Ruhi Ramazani and Nesta Ramazani never tired of listening, enlightening, and encouraging.

Friends and colleagues have supported this project in numerous and various ways. I am especially grateful to Afsar Adl, Heidi Akbarzadeh, Fati Aman, Negar Azmudeh, Hanadi Al-Samman, Homa Arvand, Amin Banani, Homa Bahrami, Mitra Bakhsha, Michael Beard, Janet Beizer, Charlotte Crystal, Farideh Farjam, Jessica Feldman, Michael Fisher, Cassandra Fraser, Mahdokht Guilani, Faezzeh Ghadiri, Scott Harrop, Bob Hueckstedt, Deborah Johnson, Mahnaz Kousha, Ann Lane, Parviz Mafi, Negar Mahmoodzadegan, Nahid Massali, Jila Malekzad, Mary McKinley, Deborah McDowell, Mahvash Milani, Romak Milani, Kenny Morrata, Barbara Noland, Jean Nylan, Pari Nikpey, Jahan Ramazani, Vahid Ramazani, Caroline Rody, Zahra Shadman, Chahla Shafiq, Fatemeh Shahidi, Lisa Spaar, Parvaneh Uskowi, Elizabeth Thompson, Denise Walsh, Sheida White, and Rina Williams.

Several colleagues granted me the privilege to discuss the findings in this book in workshops, talks, and conferences and to benefit from their own scholarship and that of engaging audiences. I have also benefited from the dedication and brilliance of several research assistants—in particular Elizabeth Walsh and Marie Ostby.

Mary Selden Evans, always welcoming, always wise and committed to excellence, is the proverbial angel at a university press. With the help of Kelly Balenske and Lisa Kuerbis, she shepherded this manuscript through various phases and permutations. Annie Barva is the ideal copy editor, unintrusive but eagle-eyed.

This project has been supported by several summer grants from the Office of the Vice Provost for Research and the Dean of Arts and Sciences at the University of Virginia. A University Seminar Teaching Award, a sabbatical leave, and a fellowship by the National Endowment for the Humanities availed me of concentrated time to devote to this project. The publication of *Words, Not Swords* was made possible in part by a grant from Carnegie Corporation of New York. I am especially grateful to Patricia Rosenfield and her effortless grace and genuine commitment to accessible, jargon-free scholarship.

My father, Mahmud Milani, and my mother, Zinat Shadman Milani, devoted their lives to the education of their children. No words can express my love for them or my admiration and gratitude for their many silent sacrifices. From my earliest memories, my brothers—Hossein, Hassan, Abbas, and Mohsen—have been a source of delight and unconditional love. Their kindness, their intellectual sustenance, and their unwavering support have nourished me and my work in innumerable and various ways. My love for them, like my debt to them, is enormous. I thank my lucky stars for having friends like them.

My son, John Faramarz, and my daughter, Farnaz, have convinced me that miracles do indeed happen. Since the magical, mystical moments of their births, they have been my companions, my teachers, my muses, my wings. With their spouses, Justine and Leo, they have thrown open the gates of my life to perennial sunlight.

Versions of some chapters of this book have been previously published, and grateful acknowledgment is made for permission to reprint. A shorter and slightly different version of chapter 6 appeared in *Iranian Studies* 41, no. 1 (Feb. 2008), edited by Farzaneh Milani, reprinted with permission. A shorter and slightly different version of chapter 8 was published as "On Women's Captivity in the Islamic World," *Middle East Report* 246 (Spring 2008) 40–46, by Farzaneh Milani, reprinted with permission.

I am also grateful for permission to quote from the following books: Anna Akhmatova, excerpts from "A voice came to me" from *Complete Poems of Anna Akhmatova*, translated by Judith Hemschemeyer, edited and introduced by Roberta Reeder, copyright © 1989, 1992, 1997 by Judith Hemschemeyer, reprinted with the permission of Zephyr Press, www.zephyrpress.org; *The Conference of the Birds*, Farid Ud-Din Attar, translated with an introduction by Afkham Darbandi and Dick Davis (Harmondsworth, UK: Penguin, 1984), reproduced by permission of Penguin Books Ltd.; *Tahirih, a Portrait in Poetry: Selected Poems of Qurratu'l-'Ayn*, Tahirih Qurratul'Ayn, edited and translated by Amin Banani, with Jascha Kessler and Anthony A. Lee (Los Angeles: Kalimat Press, 2005); *Neghare-ye Golgun* (Blood-Colored Designs), Simin Behbahani (Los Angeles: Ketab, 1998); *Collected Poems, 1912–1944*, Hilda Doolittle, edited by Louis L. Martz (Manchester, UK: Carcanet Press Limited, 1984); and *The Tragedy of Sohrab and Rustam*, Abol Qasem Ferdowsi, translated by Jerome Clinton (Seattle: Univ. of Washington Press, 1987).

I gratefully acknowledge the original publishers of *The Shahnameh of the Persian Poet Firdausi*, Abol Qasem Ferdowsi, translated by James Atkinson, Esq. (London: Routledge, 1976).

# PROLOGUE
## *"Yeki Bud, Yeki Nabud"*

"Yeki bud, yeki nabud": Iranian stories always begin with this paradoxical phrase, which simply means, "There was one, and there wasn't one."[1] Throughout my childhood, this phrase was my passport to an enchanted world of wonder and mystery. Like the word *abracadabra*, it had incantatory powers: now you see it, now you don't. It is so, and it is not so. Maybe, and then maybe not. Like dreams, like the unconscious, like nature in its infinite glory, "yeki bud, yeki nabud" was a tangle of competing viewpoints, expansive enough to accommodate seemingly contradictory claims. It was a warning at the threshold to all stories that there is always another story, another side to the story, that truth is elusively mutable. In its succinct yet economical way, it was a reminder that every story is the ghost of the life that inspired it. It celebrated the birth of one while mourning the death of the other, acknowledging the complexities of life and of its telling. It embraced paradoxes, destabilized certainties, allowed opposites to live in perfect harmony. It declined to choose one side over the other and greeted all moments that defied classification. It refused to be immobilized in certitudes, immured in dogmas, bound by judgmental pronouncements. "Yeki bud, yeki nabud" was a warning at the threshold of all stories that the mind creates its own elaborate, self-serving fictions. Bedazzled, I would throw open the gates of my eyes and ears and witness the birth of a charming world. On the wing of words, on the magic carpet of stories, I would journey to faraway lands, inaccessible places, spaces of boundless possibilities where everything sounded real but was beyond my everyday reality.

Before I knew it, childhood and its tantalizing tales came to an end. Chasing new dreams and different stories, I left my home country, and, ironically, it was by leaving Iran that I became an Iranian. Uprooted and transplanted, I looked every which way for a sense of familiarity and belonging. I needed something solid to hold on to—some familiar signposts, a lasting fixture in the ceaselessly changing landscape of my immigrant life. I gradually adopted Iranian literature as what I would later call "my surrogate home" in my book *Veils and Words: The Emerging Voices of Iranian Women Writers.*[2] It became my accessible consolation, my perennial and portable garden. I put down roots in it and turned it into a place to grow in. Every time I opened its gate, a familiar scent wafted out of it, a scent of home, a scent of effortless belonging, of childhood and its memories. I soon found myself drawn increasingly to the works of Iranian women writers. Against the advice of many and after having completed a substantial amount of research on Flaubert and his search for the ideal woman and the right word, I eventually chose for my dissertation topic the study of Forugh Farrokhzad (1935–67). Many well-wishers, including some of my teachers, were genuinely concerned about my professional future. They wanted to know why I was switching from a world-renowned author to an obscure woman poet from Iran. They argued, with conviction and concern, that an Iranian woman writing her dissertation on another Iranian woman from a feminist perspective was triple professional jeopardy. More than three decades later and with the benefit of hindsight, I consider that choice to have been a turning point in my life. Since then, the study of Iranian woman writers has flourished. Several books and countless articles are now available inside and outside Iran. This book builds on this scholarship and is deeply indebted to it.

At the time I was writing my dissertation in the late 1970s, however, precious few books were devoted to Iranian women, let alone Iranian women writers. Although women writers had elicited widespread attention inside Iran, there was no detailed treatment of the critical issues raised by their writing. One of the exceptionally few single-authored books I could find that was devoted in its entirety to an Iranian woman poet was published in 1977. In 140 long pages, the author, Fazlollah Garakani, argued with astonishing confidence in *Tohmat-e Sha'eri* (Accused of Being a Poet) that no woman, in particular one such as Parvin E'tessami (1907–41), who in his view was "kind of ugly, timid and cross-eyed," could possibly have produced such a masterpiece as the collection of poems attributed to her.[3] Not even Farrokhzad or, for that matter, any Iranian woman, writer or otherwise, had full-length biographies devoted to them at the time. As for autobiographies, I could barely find any. Highly controversial singer-dancer

Banu Mahvash and well-known political activist Malakeh Eʻtezadi had published their highly unconventional life narratives. Although Princess Taj al-Saltaneh's memoir, which was written in 1924, preceded the latter two books in terms of the actual date of composition, it was not published until 1982.[4]

Farrokhzad, however, was an exception. She had constructed her artistic universe around the individual and the individualizing perspective and had produced poetry more autobiographical than had ever been attempted in Iran. She unsurprisingly had become a figure of intense controversy. Criticized for her "exhibitionism," accused of self-absorption and promiscuity, she had elicited scandalized attention and voyeuristic fascination. With her reputation tarnished, her pioneering contribution to Iranian literature trivialized, she began to react more and more bitterly to the sensation-seeking interest in her personal life, an interest that all too often replaced the more serious attention that her work deserved. In sharp contrast to her poetic candor and perhaps as a reaction, she showed a progressively more pronounced aversion to giving even the scantiest biographical data on herself and dismissed all personal questions. Shortly before her untimely death at the age of thirty-two, when, in a radio interview, she was asked to talk about her life, she rebuffed the question altogether. "Good heavens!" she protested. "Discussing this seems to me a rather boring and useless task," proceeding instantly to discuss her poetry.

Finding biographical data on this most autobiographical poet proved not to be an easy task. The circumstances of her life were not of much help to me either. Farrokhzad was not granted any academic recognition in her short lifetime. She was never appointed as a poet in residence or a distinguished visiting professor in any institution inside or outside the country. She was never awarded honorary doctorates. She was never asked to deliver a series of lectures, temptingly entitled "Farrokhzad on Farrokhzad," in which she would delineate the magical transformation of a living woman into beautifully crafted and composed words. No university, no library or research center, no family archive housed her papers, letters, unpublished poems or manuscripts. Farrokhzad did not keep a journal, at least not any that we know of. Although she was a prolific correspondent, the overwhelming majority of her letters was unpublished. I did not have at my disposal tapes of her therapy sessions, records of her hospitalizations, or stacks of letters safely tucked away in some attic. My plan of amassing information through interviews was also thwarted at every turn. Various men who claimed to have been her lovers were all too eager to share their real or imagined experience, but those closest to the poet either refused to be interviewed, declined to answer "personal" questions, or thought it not proper to talk about the private life of a deceased person. When, with great anticipation and joy, I met one of the most influential men in her life, Ebrahim Golestan, he was quick to ask why instead of her biography I did not consider writing a cookbook in English. "Persian cuisine is exquisitely delicious," Mr. Golestan told me with great relish and conviction. "Imagine what a contribution such a book will be."[5]

I did not want a keyhole view of Farrokhzad's life, nor was I interested in turning into what Janet Malcolm calls a "professional burglar, breaking into a house, rifling through certain drawers," and triumphantly bearing my loot away.[6] If Farrokhzad was so reticent about sharing biographical information, I asked in the introduction to my dissertation, who or what gave me the right to invade her privacy? Switching from poet to poetry, from biography to autobiography disguised as literary criticism, I opted for an analysis of Farrokhzad's work. With passion and urgency, I portrayed her as a woman who refused silence and exclusion. I saw in her art my own skirmishes as an immigrant and characterized it as a struggle against cultural conventions. I argued that her poetry demonstrates a refusal to be confined within familiar boundaries, certainties, and norms, while revealing simultaneously a sense of homelessness, exile, and homesickness. Farrokhzad's poetry, I concluded, personifies both the pleasures and the agonies and anguishes of mingling the old and the new, the familiar and the unfamiliar.

Frustrated with the result of my interviews, trained to collect factual documents and surviving evidence, incapable of living with the anxiety of ambiguity that my research had generated, I settled for the easy way out. Wrestling with my biographical conundrums and let down by my failure to write Farrokhzad's biography, I found myself more and more fascinated by the openness and transparency of American culture.[7] The first entry in my diary upon arrival in the United States in December 1967 was the observation that there are no walls around the houses; I now took this absence of walls as a metaphor for the refreshingly upfront nature of verbal and nonverbal codes of communication in America. I was delighted to see self-narration as an acknowledged right of all Americans— in fact, a favorite pastime. I had never seen so many people eagerly recount their lives in books and magazines as well as on radio and television, in films, and in therapy sessions. Month after month, year after year, life narratives were in high demand and on best-selling lists. Considering autobiographies as the ultimate form of unveiling and a literary misfit in a culture that idealizes women's public anonymity, and viewing Iran as an essentially self-effacing culture, I chose the veil as the new topic for my research.[8]

All the major events of modern Iranian history—from the Babi movement in the mid–nineteenth century and the 1905–11 Constitutional Revolution to the 1979 Islamic Revolution—had featured veiling/unveiling as one of their central concerns. Now presented as religious reform or as a sign and symbol of the birth of a new religion, then clothed in the language of nationalism and its need to emancipate half the population—at times part and parcel of the aspiration to modernize Iran, at other times the trope and the icon of all that needed to be preserved and reinstituted as well as a rallying point in anti-Western struggles— the issue of the veil was taken up by both Iranian men and Iranian women, religious and secularist, young and old. For more than a decade, I studied the cultural and literary significance and consequences of the veil. I concluded in *Veils and Words* that the veil is a cultural phenomenon connected to such issues as boundary maintenance, social distancing, and notions of privacy. In a veiled society, I stated, women are not the only ones veiled. The concrete, the specific, and the personal also are veiled. Communication is veiled. Words and feelings are veiled. In such a society, I argued, walls abound; dissimulation conceals heretic tendencies; houses become compartmentalized into inner and outer areas; abstractions supplant concreteness; elusiveness substitutes for precision; art becomes impersonal.

The central argument of *Veils and Words,* however, revolved around Iranian women's literary output. I claimed that the veil had covered not only Iranian women's bodies, but also their literary voices. The norms and values that regulated women's physical concealment, I surmised, applied equally to their voices. Women's self-expression, either bodily or verbal, was thus covered by the material veil and its verbal counterpart, a contrived form of silence. Exposure of either a woman's voice or body was considered a transgression, outside the bounds of allowable discourse. I explored ways in which women poets and prose writers escaped the censoring of their culture and transcended the limits placed on their bodies and their voices. I chronicled the many internal and external hardships women have faced in their efforts to counter verbal exclusion, to unveil their bodies and their voices. To explain or, rather, to explain away the unparalleled thriving of postrevolutionary women's literature in spite of obligatory veiling, I conveniently reasoned that the veil has developed new connotations of its own quite different from the traditional notion. This new veil, I contended, no longer segregates: it now serves as a means of desegregation; it is an assertive refusal to withdraw from the public arena or mixed gatherings. It covers women's bodies, but not their voices.

Why, then, consider the veil as the focus of my critical inquiry in a study of women's integration in Iranian society if it is cause and effect, sign and symbol of both segregation and desegregation? If one does not have to be veiled to be confined and silenced, or, conversely, if a woman can be veiled but also desegregated and voiced, why then consider the veil my critical paradigm? I did not ask this question. Nor did it occur to me that perhaps the veil was a convenient cover to avoid addressing more fundamental issues. It took me years to realize that physical confinement—not the veil—was the foundation of women's subordination in Iranian society and the source of their literary quasi-invisibility. It seemed to me that I needed to reach beyond the confines of the veil if I wished to assess fairly women's vital integration in the public scene in general and in the literary arena in particular. I also began to see that other kinds of veils and walls existed. Many times, with eyes wide open, I stumbled over those walls and veils. Heaven knows how often, I ploughed right through invisible fences and found myself trespassing on someone else's privacy. I asked indiscreet questions, volunteered imprudent answers, looked too closely when I should have averted my eyes, listened with rapt attention when I should have pretended not to hear, offered advice when none was solicited. This lesson was brought home to me one hot summer day in 1982, when I took my five-year-old daughter, Farnaz, to the Santa Monica beach.

On that fateful summer day, Farnaz and I found ourselves a little spot, spread our towels, and enjoyed our picnic lunch, caressed by the generous ocean breeze. The conversation of a half-dozen preteenage girls sitting next to us soon attracted my attention. One girl, swinging her long, blond hair across her shoulders, was accusing her friends. "You are all jealous because you did not get to massage him," she screeched. Two of the girls were totally unimpressed. "Eeeuuww," they shrieked in unison. "Gross," exclaimed another, making a perfectly round O with her colored lips. Wow! I thought to myself, my eyes bulging in disbelief. These girls are already fighting over boys—massaging boys, at that. I was fascinated and curious, too. Taking a big bite out of my cutlet sandwich, I became all eyes and ears. Following their verbal battle blow by blow, I found myself mesmerized, taking in every tidbit of information that further embellished and enlivened the story for me. I was about ready to ask my own questions and offer motherly advice when one of the girls, her dental-floss bikini matching the color of her lipstick, cupped her hand around her mouth and whispered something to her friends. They stopped talking and together gave me an angry look. I did not have a clue why they were upset with me. Devouring the last of my lunch, I continued eagerly to pursue the rest of their lively conversation. One of the girls, clearly irritated, looked me directly in the eyes. "Why don't you mind your own business," she blurted out. I was minding my own business, I thought. Worse yet, I felt cheated. Like a dream cut short by wakefulness, I was startled out of a living soap opera.

I came from Iran, where we keep concealed what we consider private. We imagine paradise as a garden protected by celestial walls. We portray Adam and Eve covered in the Garden of Eden and stripped naked upon expulsion as a punishment. In Iran, privacy is synonymous with enclosure. So anything not covered by a veil or not screened by a wall is considered public property. Every move, every utterance, every part of the body exposed, every loud conversation are fair game. Enter any Iranian's audio-visual field, and you might find yourself unabashedly scrutinized from head to toe. Your private conversation can be listened to, replied to, sometimes even challenged.

That sunny bright day at the beach, the American walls of privacy were invisible to me. I considered it my right to listen to the girls. I had no idea I was intruding. They were speaking loud enough for me to hear, and I thought it was my right to listen in. With a stunning self-righteousness, with my accent and all, I began to lecture them: "If you don't want me to listen to your stories, then stop talking so loud." I was about to teach them a lesson or two in social protocol and caution them against massage-seeking boys when my five-year-old daughter intervened. Born and raised in this country, Farnaz was already aware of invisible walls of privacy. Mindful of open yet protected spaces, she dragged her mother to the welcoming sea.

I did not realize privacy has different meanings and parameters and can be guarded without perceptible walls and veils. My acclimatization to American society taught me that life, like truth, is covered with numerous visible and invisible veils. There is always another veil to rend, another curtain to part, another layer to discard. The real veil, I had to acknowledge, is the one that clouds minds, cloaks words, envelops transparency, hides us from ourselves and from facts. As long as I fixated on the literal veil, so long as I fixed my attention on a woman's body or face instead of on herself, I concluded, I would never cast aside fixed ideas. Despite all the controversy surrounding the veil, despite all the justifications or indignations it has aroused, the irony is that the veil continues to mask the woman beneath it. It definitely had kept me focused on appearances and away from underlying structures and patterns. I eventually had to stop fetishizing the veil and admit that "open" societies, even compulsively self-narrating cultures, have their own walls, their own veils, their own codes of silence. Open about certain issues, these societies consider certain other topics off limits. I finally had to admit to myself that the mind creates its own elaborate, self-serving fictions; that we reveal and conceal the truth of ourselves in the poems we craft, the stories we spin, the life narratives we produce; that biographies and autobiographies are not only means of self-expression, but also invisible walls we erect to protect the unsaid and the inadmissible. Like houses without walls around them, the chosen privacy of life narratives is protected.

The book you have in your hands thus revises the central thesis of *Veils and Words*. It reaches beyond the perennial veiling/unveiling debate and engages the issue of freedom of movement. My thesis is simple: a woman not only needs a room of her own, as Virginia Woolf remarked in her seminal work *A Room of One's Own*, but also the freedom to leave it and return to it at will. A room without that very right is a prison cell; a house without it turns into house arrest. The unconditional, untainted, and unrestricted right of entry and exit is a basic individual right. It epitomizes in its embodied form the capacity for exercising and enjoying an elemental sense of self-propelled, self-willed, self-choreographed freedom. Denial of free movement through incarceration, institutionalization, sex and race segregation, like forced movement—refugees driven from their land, dissidents exiled from their countries, prisoners marched to their execution, women traded around the world in sex trafficking, homelessness in an increasingly claustrophobic urban landscape—deprives human beings of the integrity, boundaries, and control of their bodies and denies them autonomy and authority. With the advent of modernity, with the increasing access to motorized mobility, freedom of movement has become even more vital and more valued, so much so that its denial has become the modern instrument of punishment. Consider the current multiplication and expansion of prisons.

The privilege to enjoy self-directed movement, the power and the prospect to pick up and go as one pleases and to return without incurring any penalties, has not been a "right" granted Iranian woman for centuries. Recognized as a masculine prerogative, this privilege has been denied them in the name of religion, chastity, class distinction, beauty, safety, and anatomy. It is only during the past 160 years—the time span covered in this book—that Iranian women have renegotiated boundaries and emerged increasingly as a moderating, modernizing force. They have reconfigured the boundaries, hierarchies, and relations between the sexes; impacted the allocation of power, space, and resources; challenged patterns of male domination and female subordination; stretched fields of action and imagination; expanded women's range of work and leisure activities; increased their direct participation in decision-making processes and posts; amplified their social relations; and impacted their position within the family, the state, and ultimately the international community.

Iran is a land of paradoxes. It has a mercurial political climate and is in the midst of sweeping cultural transformations and profound intellectual ferment. It is one of the world's oldest civilizations and has one of the world's youngest populations. In the crowded streets of its major cities, Calvin Klein jean ads compete with portraits of turbaned clerics. And surely no one can accuse the Islamic Republic of intolerance toward its contradictions, particularly when it comes to its treatment of women. Iranian women can vote and run for some of the highest elected offices in the country, but they must observe an obligatory dress code. They can drive personal vehicles, even taxis and trucks and fire engines, but they cannot ride bicycles. They are forcibly separated from men into the back of buses but can be squashed in between perfect strangers in overcrowded jitney taxis. They have entered the world stage as Nobel Peace laureates, human rights activists, best-selling authors, prize-winning film directors, and Oscar nominees, but they cannot enter governmental offices through the same doors as men. It is this complex mixture of advancement and setbacks, protest and accommodation, resistance and acquiescence, innovation and tradition, that reflects most accurately women's lives in Iran today. Yet for decades and prior to the highly contested June 12, 2009, election, only one side of this ongoing battle—the side that reflects a static image of victimhood and immobility—has dominated America's imagination and most of its best sellers about Iran.

Focusing on both sides of this ongoing struggle, I explore two competing narratives of womanhood that exist side by side in Iran. Women are oppressed by restrictive laws and male-centered interpretations of Islamic Scripture. They are also the most vibrant forces of change. And women writers have been and continue to be at the forefront of this conflict. Breaking the spell of their textual quasi-invisibility coincidentally with breaking into the public sphere, they have made the circulation of their bodies and their voices central to their artistic universe. Metaphors of containment—walls, veils, imposed silences, fences, cages, blind windows, closed doors, and bars—coexist in their works side by side with the desire to sprout wings, fly, flee, run, dance, sing through their texts, bear witness to the hitherto unspoken, and push boundaries into the unsaid and the forbidden. By refusing to focus solely on one side of this equation or to reinforce the veiled/unveiled, East/West divide, I examine how freedom of movement allows women—whether they are veiled or unveiled—easier access to centers of power, facilitates the exercise of legal and economic rights, permits the pursuit of a variety of careers in the public sector, promotes their integration into the literary arena, and sanctions the development of a civil society.

Relying on the wisdom and experience of thousands of storytellers over hundreds of years, I thus begin my tale of Iranian women's physical and literary desegregation with "yeki bud, yeki nabud."

WORDS, NOT SWORDS

# INTRODUCTION
## *Keeping Women in Their Place*

Women no longer know their place, and they have disoriented us men, too.
They are taking our place everywhere: in the universities, the ministries, on
the streets. Wherever you turn, there are aggressive women ready to push
you aside. You are lucky if they don't trample you under their feet.
> —IRANIAN TAXI DRIVER, in Haleh Esfandiari,
> *My Prison, My Home*

[T]he writer on the move is the avatar of literary modernity.
> —GILLIAN WHITLOCK, *Soft Weapons*


### ISLAM AND SEX SEGREGATION

In the political history of contemporary Iran, doubts about modernity, change, and relations with the West have often been projected upon women's bodies and the space they occupy. Muslim clerics, revolutionaries, royalists, rightists, and leftists all have at times considered the "public display" of a female body a flag, a badge of national honor, at other times an emblem of collective shame—now a shortcut to modernity, then the symbol of a lost order. The 1979 Islamic Revolution in its early days—like the Taliban in Afghanistan, the military junta in Sudan, the Islamic Salvation Front in Algeria, and the ruling elite in Saudi Arabia—wanted to "purify" public space in the name of Islam by clearing out women. Thousands of women were coerced into early retirement; many lost their jobs; many were forced into exile. Women were segregated in mosques, schools, universities, beaches, and buses. They disappeared as entertainers and singers. They faded away from the silver screen. Women's place, it was argued, was not public but private, not out in the streets but inside the home.

1

Does Islam advocate the confinement of women? If so, why were women a vital presence in the early Muslim communities, active in mosques as well as the battlefields? Why and when did male theologians find it necessary to ground codes of masculinity, femininity, and honor in the exclusion of women from the public sphere? Which Islamic texts or injunctions, if any, are the sources of such prohibitive laws? From all available accounts, women fared better in the early years of Islam than in later periods. They were a vital presence in the early Muslim community, involved in daily decision-making processes and public debates. A whole chapter in the Qur'an is titled and devoted to *mujadilah*, "the woman who argues."

Successive generations of male theologians, however, ordained the exclusion of women from public debate and the public sphere. They interpreted the Qur'anic injunction restricting women from going out for the purpose of wanton display (verse 33:33) to sanction women's increasing immobilization, instructing them not to leave their delineated spaces altogether. Gender boundaries were thus institutionally solidified, separating the worlds of men and women. The shaping of the legacy of Prophet Mohammed's youngest wife and daughter of the first caliph, Abu Bakr, is a telling illustration of women's shrinking role and space within Islam. Like many other women, Aisha (d. A.D. 678) played a significant role in the early Islamic community. Titled "Mother of the Believers," she was a woman in whose presence the Prophet received many revelations. She was a major source of hadith literature—the sayings and deeds attributed to Prophet Mohammad. She accompanied her husband in the battlefields. She commanded armies after his death. Beginning in the ninth and tenth centuries, however, a shifting Islamic self-definition and communal identity manipulated the construction and representation of her persona. Later theologians elaborated on two events, the accusation of adultery levied against her and the "Battle of the Camel" (which took place at Basra in Iraq in A.D. 656 between the fourth caliph, Emam Ali, and Aisha, who was mounted on a litter on a camel and commanding an army of men), in order to draw the same conclusion: had Aisha remained within the house rather than been riding on a camel, had her physical mobility been closely monitored, carnage and disruption within the Islamic community would have been prevented.[1]

The story of Aisha and the camel is not only about what was going on fourteen centuries ago. It is still relevant to debates regarding appropriate spaces and roles for Muslim women. For instance, when Fa'eza Rafsanjani, the daughter of the then-president Akbar Hashemi Rafsanjani, was running for a seat in the Iranian Parliament in the 1990s, the opposition to her election revolved around versified slogans such as "Aisha rode a camel / Fa'eza came on a motorcycle," or "Aisha rode a camel / Harlots ride motorcycles." During her campaign, Rafsanjani argued there was nothing un-Islamic about women's motorcycle riding. A group of ayatollahs, however, denounced bike or motorcycle riding as un-Islamic and sexually provocative. No less an authority than Iran's supreme leader, Ayatollah Seyed Ali Khamene'i (1939–) proclaimed: "Women must avoid anything that attracts strangers, so riding bicycles or motorcycles by women in public places involves corruption and is forbidden."[2]

Since women's freedom of movement was seen as the cause of *fitna,* chaos and disruption, sex segregation was implemented with increasing conviction and rigidity. For instance, Mohammad al-Ghazali (A.D. 1058–1111), one of the most renowned and celebrated Islamic scholars, argued in two works, *The Revival of the Religious Sciences* and *The Counsel for Kings,* that women should stay at home and avoid going out often; should visit neighbors only when absolutely necessary; should remain in their homes unless given permission to leave; and, if given permission to leave, should take only deserted streets and back alleys, avoid marketplaces, and make sure strangers do not hear their voices.

The cultural significance of an increasingly more rigid separation of men's and women's spaces was multiple and varied. It consigned power, control, visibility, voice, and especially mobility to one social category—men—at the expense of the other—women. It not only separated the worlds of men and women unrelated to each other by marriage or blood, but also created hierarchies across this divide.

## THE POLITICS OF CONFINEMENT

Gender apartheid, however, is more than a religious ordinance. It is related to such mundane matters as power, domination, and exclusion. If not sanctified in the name of religion, then it has relied on physiology, chastity, safety, beauty, and patriotism to restrict women's mobility. To focus narrowly on religious justification for sex segregation obscures the problem's embedded nature in social structures. Indeed, easy access to the arena of the "public" was denied Iranian women before the advent of Islam, even though Islam helped intensify and institutionalize it. Moreover, notwithstanding their differences, religious minorities living in Iran imposed, even if to different degrees, segregating regulations on women. In addition to divides defined by class, religion, and ethnicity, there existed for Iranians, regardless of their faith, another division of the social order, one based on sex. This axis, around which society was and to a certain extent continues to be organized, kept the world of men and women apart. By whatever name it was called—*andaroun* (the inside, the inner, the indoor), *zananeh* (women's space), *chahar divari* (the four walls), or *harem* (forbidden, private space)—it controlled women's freedom of movement.

In a sex-segregated society, the degree of man/woman interaction and intermingling remains almost the same for both sexes. However, whereas men enjoy their freedom of movement, women's access to the public domain is closely monitored and curtailed. Fatima Mernissi ends her delightful autobiographical novel *Dreams of Trespass: Tales of a Harem Girlhood* with reference to this "cosmic frontier" that "splits the planet in two halves. The frontier indicates the line of power because wherever there is a frontier, there are two kinds of creatures walking on Allah's earth, the powerful on one side, and the powerless on the other." And how does one know on which side one stands? The answer is "quick, short, and very clear: 'if you can't get out, you are on the powerless side.'"[3] This restriction placed on half the population subordinated women in multiple ways. It excluded women from certain crucial political activities. It confronted them with difficulties in fully exercising their legal economic rights. It prevented them from pursuing a variety of careers in the public sector. It denied them admission to public educational institutions and seminaries. It did not let them enjoy equitable health care with men. It hampered their artistic potential and did not allow them to develop their talents in public forms of art.

A fair distribution of space is cause and consequence of an equitable distribution of rights, liberties, and privileges. Denial of free movement curtails a woman's bodily expression, inhibits her verbal self-expression, frames her representation. It is the foundation upon which sex discrimination is built.

For centuries, masculinity and femininity were designed and defined in relation to space in Iran. Mobility was a desired trait in men; in fact, it was a prerequisite of virility and manliness. Men were engaged in activities outside the house in the public sphere of politics and the marketplace. They were the legitimate wanderers. It was as if the public square belonged to men and men belonged to the public square: *mard-e meydan*. Femininity, in contrast, was guaranteed and defined by enclosure. It revolved around domesticity: *zan-e khaneh*. The ideal woman was expected to remain in her "proper place." For her, mobility was denigrated, rejected, warned against.

One of the most compelling justifications for sex segregation in Iranian society has been the belief that sexual desire is easily stimulated in both sexes and if unregulated can cause social mayhem and disorder. In order to channel sexual conduct properly, various physical and symbolic barriers were created between the two sexes. To protect the integrity of the male line of descent, women's sexuality was closely monitored and contained. Key cultural concepts, none of which has an exact equivalent in the English language—such as *gayrat* (honor, machismo), *nejabat* (purity, decency), *namus* (chastity, reputation), and *hojb-o-haya* (modesty, shame)—came to govern daily life and commerce between the sexes. The development of each of these concepts revolved around women's sexual integrity. The virginity of unmarried girls, the fidelity of married women, and the sexual abstinence of widows and divorcées were symbols of communal dignity. Such a strong emphasis was placed upon confining and controlling women's sexuality that rape, a violation perpetrated against a woman, was at times considered a powerful tool of revenge and intimidation against the men of the rape victim's family.

Throughout this history of gendered control and discrimination, women's chastity has been inextricably linked with space. Mobility has often been associated with chaos and the opportunity for sexual promiscuity in women. The terms *kiabangard* (vagabond), *velgard* (vagrant), and *harja'i* (belonging or existing everywhere) are synonymous with prostitution when applied to women. If a woman dares leave her socially designated path, if she abandons her fenced-off space, she is branded a *streetwalker,* a universal term of disrespect for women "out of bounds." *Gomrah kardan* and *az rāh be dar bordan*, synonyms for "seducing," are space related and have the word *rah*—"road," "path"—incorporated in them. Leading a woman astray is equivalent to her indiscriminate mixing with men and sexual misconduct. The veil, the most conspicuous expression of sex segregation, like the hymen *(parde-ye bekarat),* is perceived to be a physical impediment, an obstacle to men and women's sexual temptation. This preoccupation with women's freedom of movement—its religious underpinnings, its sexual overtones, and its long-term social consequences—has marked Iranian culture from classical times until today.

An important caveat: idealized, gendered allocation of space was never fully actualized. Individual women and at times groups of women resisted it, opposed it, and even transcended it. Older women, deemed asexual, were allowed greater physical mobility, as were young girls before they reached the age of puberty (nine years). Women of the lower classes as well as rural and tribal women could ill afford to observe ideals of segregation as a matter of financial survival.[4] Instead, they were granted expanded usage of some "public" spaces by necessity in order to earn and maintain a living. Unlike men, they still could neither freely travel nor freely linger in the streets and the public square.

## ON MOBILITY AND LITERARY MODERNITY

Finally, in the mid–nineteenth century, prompted by religious reform movements, encouraged by forces of modernity, exasperated by the injustice of sex segregation and the cultural, political, and economic damages perpetrated by it, Iranian women and men began to argue against it. Some women used all their ingenuity to transgress limits and access forbidden territories, and some men helped them to do so. Women began to appear more frequently in public places. With their sporadic but vital activism in religious movements, continued by their active role in the Constitutional Revolution of 1905–11 and the 1979 Islamic Revolution, and leading to their mass participation in the Green Movement, women increasingly made their public presence felt and demanded the social expansion of their rights as citizens. Women writers, who felt the compound brunt of gender apartheid on both their bodies and their voices, were and continue to be at the forefront of this desegregating, civic movement.

Women's progressively more unfettered and uninhibited liberty to step out from behind any real or figurative "private" space was a vital catalyst in Iranian modernity in general and in Iranian literary modernity in particular. It brought women from behind walls and veils into open and public spaces. It ended the privatization of the female voice in the realm of home and family. It desegregated a predominantly masculine literary tradition by including women as producers, consumers, and objects of representation on an unprecedented scale.

In his book *The Art of the Novel*, the Czech writer Milan Kundera contends that "the founder of the Modern Era is not only Descartes but also Cervantes."[5] Kundera, like many others, considers Cervantes's masterpiece the first modern novel for a variety of reasons. As he points out, *Don Quixote* (1605) explores the "wisdom of uncertainty," "tolerates the essential relativity of things human," "discovers multiple perspectives," decomposes "the single Divine truth into myriad relative truths parceled out by men." Above all, the novel dispatches its central character, a knight errant, accompanied by his faithful sidekick, Sancho Panza, to explore the world. Don Quixote does not leave his village to go on a pilgrimage; he is not fighting a war, conquering an enemy, capturing a city, earning a living. Equipped with no single truth to guide him, he "set[s] off into a world that opened wide before him," free to go out and come home as he pleases.[6] Shaped by the romances and the tales of chivalry he had read, he believes he "must wander through the world, on probation as it were, in pursuit of adventures." So he takes up his lance and his shield and leaves his village.[7]

Is it possible to pinpoint such a defining moment for literary modernity in Iran? Can it be done without subscribing to binary modes of thought that detect and reify a reductive correlation between Western modernity and Eastern tradition, pitting one against the other? Many scholars have listed the shapers and markers of literary modernity in Iran: among them are democratization of authorship, readership, and themes; the birth of the novel; the introduction of free verse; the widespread launch of literary criticism; the vernacularization of the written language; the broad growth of the printing industry; the switch from oral tradition to print culture; the expansion of the communications media; the introduction of the camera, photography, and cinema; the adaptation to national and international pressures; and the impact of Western literature.

I believe Iranian women's desegregation, not unlike Don Quixote's mobility, heralded the dawn of a new era in Iran. It reorganized the visual scene of Iranian modernity and remapped the country's cultural, political, and literary geography. My intention here is not to glorify the perpetual change and dislocation, the alienation and fragmentation, the dizzying speed, hurried impatience, uprootedness, and instability of modern life. Nor do I want to suggest that women's integration into what can be loosely termed the "public" is necessarily a linear progression synonymous with liberation. I do suggest, though, that political and economic domination is largely founded upon the control of space, the geopolitics of location.

Although men have been ahead of women in their mastery of speed, (through horses, chariots, bicycles, cars, motorcycles, planes, and space shuttles), freedom of movement is considered one of the most essential rights of a modern citizen, just as curtailing it is a grave punishment. It should not surprise us then that in his groundbreaking book *Discipline and Punish: The Birth of the Prison,* Michel Foucault compels us to think about the widespread appearance of the prison as a modern form of punishment, one that has shifted the locus of punishment from death and torture to mechanisms of immobilization. "From being an art of unbearable sensations," observes Foucault, "punishment has become an economy of suspended rights." Incarceration, which occupies such a focal place in modern penal systems, is based on a number of "constraints and privations, obligations and prohibitions."[8] Prisons place offenders in enclosed and partitioned cells, depriving them of a range of personal rights, the most basic of which is the right to freedom of movement.

In *The Gender of Modernity,* Rita Felski ponders, "How would our understanding of modernity change if instead of taking male experience as paradigmatic, we were to look instead at texts written primarily by or about women?"[9] If we were to look at texts written by Iranian women during the past sixteen decades, if we were to focus on their experience as paradigmatic, then we would have to identify the subject of physical confinement as the central concern of their lives and the most recurring theme of their writing. If we were to engage the issue of gender as a critical category, it would no longer be possible to disregard, push to the margins, or relegate to footnotes women's vital contributions to Iranian modernity. More important, it would no longer be possible to get entangled in the perennial veiling/unveiling debate. Exceptions aside, veiling has overshadowed substantive studies of Iranian women and dominated mainstream political discourse regarding women inside and outside of the country.[10]

### THE VEIL: A MODERN FETISH

It is hard to imagine a symbol more potent, more contentious, more politicized in our times than the veil. It has grown so dense with meanings and interpretations, so frequently discussed in the media, so thoroughly abused by ideologues from across the political spectrum that it is almost impossible to discuss it for what it really is.[11] An emblem now of piety, then of backwardness; a badge of nationalism, then of domination; now a piece of clothing voluntarily adopted by women, then a dress code imposed upon them by force, the veil has accommodated itself to a puzzling variety of ideologies, situations, periods, and places. Viewed as an anachronism, it has often been considered the last barrier between the past and the present, between victimization and liberation. Perceived as a source of respect and protection, piety and pride, beauty and privilege, it has been regarded as a badge of Islamic identity.[12] Whether framing a woman's head and covering the hair wholly or partially (head scarf), cloaking her from head to foot (*abaya*, chador), providing a tentlike cover (burka), or being combined with a separate piece to hide the woman's face *(neqab);* whether made of cotton, linen, or silk, plain or embroidered, colored or not, gauzy and translucent or heavy and opaque, the veil is now the decisive mark of the difference between Islam and other religions.

Although there is great debate surrounding the origins of veiling, there is no doubt that the custom dates back to antiquity. In the beginning of its history, the veil, it seems, was a mark of distinction reserved for women of the court and high aristocracy. It was a voluntary retreat from public life, intruding gazes, unwelcome attention. The Persian term *chador,* the form of veiling prevalent in Iran, means "tent," in reference to the pre-Islamic practice of moving wealthy women around in covered sedan chairs. In fact, veiling was considered such a privileged prerogative of the elite that at times marginalized groups, ethnic minorities, slaves, and prostitutes were officially discriminated against by being prevented from veiling.

The veil, however, was institutionalized through sharia, the canonical law of Islam. Muslim women, according to the Qur'an, should cover themselves modestly. "And say to the believing women to cast down their eyes, and guard their private parts, and reveal not their adornment save such as is outward," instructs the Qur'an, discussing veiling in general terms and not establishing the limits and details of covering. Remarkably, unlike the Saudis, the Taliban, and the Islamic Republic, who punish unveiled women in the name of Islam, the Qur'an does not specify any penalty for a woman who is not veiled. The assumption that a woman's garment should cover her body, excepting her face and hands, and be loose fitting enough to conceal her figure is an interpretation of this verse, albeit one confirmed by the consensus of many religious authorities. Yet the great disparity of religiously acceptable clothing in the Islamic world at large proves the viability and possibility of varying interpretations of the Qur'anic injunction. Over time, the veil extended its semantic and legal fields and implications along different dimensions. Its use trickled down from high aristocracy to lower social strata. It became mandatory, migrated from urban centers to rural and tribal areas, took on new symbolic connotations, and became synonymous with women's segregation. It was a reminder and a visual proof that the public arena is a masculine territory. If a woman needed to trespass in that male domain, she had to cover herself by her veil and carry her segregation around with her. The nebulous term *veiling* became a rallying cry behind which was hidden the desire to keep women confined to the domestic sphere. The identity of a virtuous Muslim woman was to be sealed in secrecy, her individuality hidden in anonymity. This new development proved to be most detrimental to Muslim women, who slowly but surely found themselves clad in their immobility.[13]

Although the terms are often used interchangeably, *veil* is different from *hijab,* which means "curtain" and has a spatial dimension. The veil can operate as a sign and symbol of sex segregation or, conversely, as a means of desegregation.[14] A woman can be veiled but not segregated, or she can be unveiled yet immobilized and denied her full freedom of movement. Veiling is a context-bound institution. It is neither monolithic nor homogeneous. It cannot be understood without taking the issues of time, place, class, gender, space, and in particular power into account. Just as an "Islam" unified in its practices, policies, and goals has never existed, neither has a conveniently typical Muslim Woman. One out of every five women in the world today is a Muslim woman, a ratio that is projected to be one out of every four by the year 2020. The veil, which has no single definition, rationale, objective, or reception, can neither be the quintessential marker of such a large and varied group of people nor have a fixed meaning.

For well more than a century, the decision to wear or not to wear a veil has been central to discourses of modernity and countermodernity in Iran. Its elimination or reinstatement has been used as a shortcut to secularism or an attempt to restore a lost religious order. As a border marker, it has been viewed as the visual symbol of a society protecting its tradition, its independence, its faith. Governmental decrees have both required and outlawed the veil. Politicians have spoken for or in opposition to it. People have been killed fighting for or against it.

In neighboring Turkey, soon after the proclamation of the republic in 1923, Mustafa Kemal Atatürk became the first leader in the Islamic world to abolish the veil. Although Atatürk did not take any legal action against the veil, half a century later Turkey's military government banned it in public places. Women who disobeyed the law were punished. Some government employees lost their jobs.

An elected member of Parliament who insisted on wearing a scarf was prohibited from serving her term. Several university students who wore head scarves were arrested or prevented from taking their exams or expelled.[15]

In January 1936, following Turkey's example, Reza Shah Pahlavi (reigned 1925–41) ordered the mass unveiling of women in Iran regardless of their age or personal preferences. Law enforcement agencies were directed to tear veils off women's bodies. Welcomed by many women, this compulsory unveiling horrified others who opposed the royal decree. The latter group organized sit-ins, started hunger strikes, refused to leave the sheltering privacy of their homes or veils. Some, bundled up and put in a sack, braved the streets on the shoulders of their sons, brothers, or husbands. Others left the country, preferring exile to unveiling. Oddly enough, this hypersurveillant marking of the female body as a civic project, a prop in a bit of political theater, was considered a sign of modernity.

Compulsory unveiling could not and did not achieve its intended goal.[16] In due course, some women appeared in public with their veils on, and, finally, the ban had to be rescinded five years later, in 1941. Those women who continued to veil, however, found themselves looked down upon and humiliated. What was once a signifier of modesty, piety, beauty, and distinction soon became synonymous with backwardness, poverty, religious obscurantism, and forces of darkness. And then, in a complete reversal of the 1936 unveiling act and with the same perfect disregard for women's personal preferences, the Islamic Republic reinstated the veil in the early 1980s, less than five decades after its official banning. All women, including visiting non-Iranians and religious minorities within Iran, had to cover their hair. Even if we assume Islam requires Muslim women to veil themselves, why enforce the edict on non-Muslims?

Considering itself the owner or at least the major shareholder in the bodies of its female citizens, the Islamic Republic further politicized the veil and turned it into a sign of the reconstruction of an Islamic identity at the national and transnational levels. Once again, women—this time, the unveiled ones—were ordered off the streets. As the protected core of the community, women's veiled bodies came to represent society's symbolic attempts to protect its tradition, independence, dignity, faith, and honor. By making women's mandatory veiling the emblem of the Islamic Revolution, however, women paradoxically were brought to the center stage of world attention and made the object of the global gaze—a decisive act of unveiling.

Women were also inadvertently given greater power by being turned into bearers of highly politicized meanings nationally and internationally.[17] Consider the issue of makeup in Iran today. In the postrevolutionary Iranian political theater, colors are as pregnant with meaning and intention as they have ever been. Women have found ways to use colors to express their individuality, defy authorities, display ideological identities, and invoke political coalitions. Colors signal the space between autocracy and democracy. During times of political tolerance, they blossom on women's faces and nails—the only parts of a woman's body that need not be covered according to the obligatory dress code. They pale during times of political repression and disappear temporarily when reaction collides with reform, only to resurface yet again with baffling speed and with a bit more intensity, a bit more brightness.

Notwithstanding all the energy spent on imposing or opposing the veil, in spite of all the controversy surrounding it, despite all the justifications or indignations, the irony is that the veil has continued to limit our ability to see through to the woman beneath it. It has fixed our attention on her covered body or face, her beauty or absence of it, her rights or dearth thereof, the threat she poses or the threat she avoids. It has concentrated our attention on the body, but it has veiled us from the history of veiling, its significance in Judaism and Christianity, the larger implications of the institution for society as a whole and for men in particular. The veil can cover a thousand and one meanings, but it can never be outworn. Nor can it be permanently or wholly stripped. Ironically enough, the obsession with the veil has also covered a most vibrant force of change shaking the foundations of Islamic societies: women with or without veils.

As improbable as it might seem today, there was a time when women's veiling was not an indicator of difference, a banner separating Muslims from non-Muslims, the East from the West, the traditional from the modern, the oppressed from the liberated.[18] The conflation of the institution of veiling with the identity of Muslim women and subjugation is, historically speaking, a rather new phenomenon. None of the Muslim women protagonists in European medieval and early Renaissance literature—and there are many of them—was identified by the veil.[19] Some Jewish and Christian women did not let their hair loose, either. It was capped, wimpled, covered. Orthodox Jewish women's covering of their hair by a wig and wearing of long sleeves, long skirts, and thick stockings today resemble the codes of Islamic modest dress. In I Corinthians, St. Paul enjoins women to cover their hair when they pray.[20] As a matter of fact, "to take the veil" had a clear Christian connotation and referred to "becoming a nun." So, too, most pictorial and sculptural depictions of the Virgin Mary represent the Madonna with covered hair. The image of the veiled woman as the prototypical Muslim Woman is a by-product of modernity.

Don Quixote, the first modern novel, is significantly also the scene of the first appearance of a veiled Muslim woman, Zoraida, in Western literature. The Muslim woman subsequently and increasingly came to be depicted as a captive of her faith and her veil. Appearing and reappearing in paintings, novels, and films as well as on television screens, in advertisements, on the covers of books and journals, in the pages of newspapers and magazines, and even in such unexpected media outlets as Playboy, Penthouse, and Hustler, this veiled Muslim woman appealed and repelled all at once.[21] She represented the exotic, the erotic, but also the failed modern citizen, the unmodern, the immobilized. She personified a real prisoner with no recourse to justice and due process of law, and her veil was at odds with the yearning for mobility and transparency; it flattened out feminine individuality and was viewed as a lack, an absence, a prison. "These phantoms that now roam the streets of Kabul have a terrible time avoiding bicycles, buses and carts," remarks Latifa, the pseudonymous author of My Forbidden Face. "This is not a garment. It's a moving prison," she concludes.[22] "A woman in a Burqa is more like a live body locked in a coffin," observes Zoya, another pseudonymous author of a life narrative.[23]

Soon after the emergence of Cervantes's Zoraida on the Western literary scene, harem—an extension of the veil and its architectural double—became a locus of fascination as well. The word harem, which came to be understood as a domestic penitentiary, tellingly did not enter the English language until 1634. Seraglio, a derivative of the Persian word saray, meaning "a palace," was earlier used for women's quarters.[24] Demoted from a palace to a prison, that forbidden space came simultaneously to represent incarceration and sexual abandon. It warded off as it seduced. It appalled as it lured. Within its all-encompassing boundaries, sexual fantasies of all sorts took flight, and it captured the imagination of writers, painters, photographers, and eventually filmmakers.

The emergence of this sartorially and spatially trapped woman in Western literature coincided with a time when work spaces and living spaces were becoming more differentiated in Europe and the ideology of a "public sphere" for men

and a "private sphere" for women was gaining ascendancy. Even as more Western women found themselves thus constrained, the sex-segregated space of the
harem symbolized an absolute loss of freedom of movement that appeared worse
in comparison. The Muslim woman, even if embellished with a certain charm
and allure, was invoked in order to demonstrate denial of civic freedom. She was
an expression of the conflicts and ambivalences engendered by the processes of
modernization, a projection perhaps of suppressed European self-doubt and self-
criticism. "There is no denying it," states Reina Lewis, "as a topic, the harem sold
books. From the eighteenth century on, whether you wrote about living in one,
visiting one, or escaping from one, any book that had anything to do with the
harem sold. Publishers knew it, booksellers knew it, readers knew it and authors
knew it. . . . They cannily entitled their books with the evocative words 'harem,'
'Turkish,' 'Arabic' or 'princess,' and pictured themselves in veils and *yashmaks*
[the type of veil worn by Turkish women] on the front cover."[25] "How much suffering" has been inflicted upon women, asks Orhan Pamuk in *Snow,* "by turning
head scarves into symbols and using women as pawns in a political game?"[26]
Significantly, though, "when asked what they resented most about their own societies, a majority of Muslim women polled" in 2006 did not even mention the
issue of veiling. They "said that a lack of unity among Muslim nations, violent
extremism, and political and economic corruption were their main concerns.
The *hijab,* or head scarf, and *burqa,* the garment covering face and body, seen by
some Westerners as tools of oppression, were never mentioned in the women's
answers to the open-ended questions, the poll analysts said."[27]

### THE TURBAN, NOT THE VEIL

And yet for most of the veil's history, it was the turban rather than the veil that
symbolized Islam. For centuries, the turban was a badge of Islamic identity and
the signal vestment of the Prophet Mohammad. "To put on the turban" developed into a synonym for conversion to Islam. The Prophet Mohammad was
called "the Weaver of the Turban." The turban, or its Arabic equivalent, *imama,*
does not appear even once in the Qur'an, nor is wearing a turban a religious duty
in Islam. It was recommended, however, by the Prophet Mohammad, who is frequently quoted in the hadith literature as saying, "My community shall not fall
away so long as they wear the turban." He identified this headgear as "the frontier

between faith and infidelity," a symbol of honor, dignity, piety, and purity, "the crown of the Arabs." According to a number of authoritative Islamic narratives, all major male religious figures, beginning with Adam, were turbaned. So were the angels. Islamic painting abounds in depictions of angels, prophets, kings, religious figures, political dignitaries, and ordinary people wearing the turban. Their turbans come in different fabrics, colors, shapes, styles, and sizes. They have long or short trailing ends. At times, they are works of art in themselves, adorned with jewelry, decorated with feathers, embroidered with peacocks and ostriches.

The turban, like the veil, predates Islam, and, like the term *chador,* its linguistic root is traced to Persian. The words *sarband* and *toulband,* the latter eventually metamorphosing into *turban,* mean "a sash wound around the head." Mentioned more than twenty times in the Bible's Old Testament, the turban was a symbol of prophecy among the Israelites. "He set the turban on his head; and on the turban, in front, he set the golden plate, the holy crown; as Yahweh commanded Moses" (Leviticus 8:9). The turban is also closely associated with and held sacred in Sikhism, a monotheistic religion founded in the fifteenth century. Indeed, many turban wearers in the Western world today are neither Muslim nor Arab. They are male Sikhs.

In modern times, however, some politicians within the Islamic world spoke out against the turban or outlawed it altogether. They rejected it as an emblem of religious, political, or scholarly distinction and viewed it as a sign of reactionary obscurantism—an obstacle to modernity. In 1925 and 1928, respectively, Mustafa Kemal Atatürk and Reza Shah Pahlavi banned the turban in Turkey and Iran. Men who refused to shed it were punished. Massive and at times bloody protests ensued in both countries. Many men, especially the clerics, defiantly refused to unturban. They viewed the prohibition against the turban as blasphemous and irreverent as the unveiling of women. Some unyielding clerics, such as my maternal grandfather, ultimately received a special dispensation from the government to continue wearing their turbans.[28] Soon after the 1979 Revolution, this previously outlawed headpiece became the hallmark of the Islamic Republic of Iran. White and black turbans, the latter reserved for male descendants of the Prophet Mohammed, appeared in large numbers in mosques, presidential palaces, the House of Representatives, governmental offices, universities, and even on television screens. In Afghanistan, the last official edict of Mullah Muhammad Omar, the leader of the Taliban, required all men to wear their turbans straight on their heads. The first collective protest of Muslim detainees at Guantanamo Bay, Cuba, revolved around the freedom to wear turbans.

In recent decades in the West, the turban would appear only occasionally and often as the villain's headgear of choice in popular books and films. For instance, the grand vizier in the blockbuster animated movie *Aladdin* wears a turban. So does the villain in *The Electric Company,* a popular educational television program for children. Quirinus Quirrell wears a purple turban in the international publishing sensation *Harry Potter and the Sorcerer's Stone,* where it seems to be a symbol and generator of his nastiness. When in an interview the author, J. K. Rowling, was asked why Quirrell was "the bad guy instead of Snape," she replied, "Because I know all about Snape, and he wasn't about to put on a turban."[29] The cataclysmic events of September 11, 2001, brought this once tepid interest in the turban to a boil. Although none of the nineteen hijackers wore turbans, although all of them were smooth-shaven, close-cropped, bareheaded men in Western clothes, the turban became once again the defining feature of the Islamic world and associated with terrorism. John Cooksey, a U.S. Congressman from Louisiana, called the turban "a diaper on the head." In a radio show, he announced that should he encounter a diaper-headed guy on a plane, he would need to have him "pulled over."[30] He was not alone in his indictment. Indeed, some airline passengers were not allowed to be on the plane and wear the turban at the same time. A few who attempted to board planes wearing turbans were pulled off their flights. Others found it preferable to give up on air travel for a while. Much to their surprise and dismay, even non-Muslim men who wore the turban found themselves the target of anger. One man paid with his life for wearing a turban. A gunman mistook a Sikh for a Muslim and shot Balbir Singh Sodhi dead at his convenience store in Arizona in mid-September 2001.

Once again the turban became a badge of Islamic identity, a flag separating "us" from "them." Defending it, revering it, wearing it, like criticizing or disrespecting it, became highly politicized. At the heart of the violent and even deadly fury identified by Danish prime minister Anders Fogh Rasmussen as Denmark's worst international crisis since World War II was an offensive representation of the turban in 2006. The twelve controversial cartoons depicted the turban twenty times, focusing on it more than any other sign or symbol. In them, the turban is conjoined with the sword or with its modern, more deadly counterpart, the bomb. It is the symbol of terrorism.[31]

CRISIS OF MASCULINITY

Ironically, as Iranian women were being identified increasingly with the veil in the West, inside the country more and more of them were leaving their homes and reshaping traditionally masculine spaces. Their appearance in public provoked mounting confusion, even national anxiety.[32] Many writers, philosophers, and social critics lamented the breakdown of the moral fiber of society. A woman parading in the streets became the emblem of threatening changes, a favorite goblin. She was vilified and labeled a "Western Doll." The ills of society were blamed on her implicitly and at times quite explicitly. She personified the pollution of native and authentic culture. This made-up doll, masked and disguised, was viewed as the potential or actual fifth column, a tool of imperialist conspiracies, the primary accomplice of the superpowers that exploited Iran. Considered a fatal threat to Iranian culture, she was accused of national and sexual infidelity.

With gusto and passion, many writers, philosophers, and social critics wrote about this mutant character, this bad imitation of the West, this unauthentic replica of traditional Iranian women, this hybrid. She personified the painful loss of Iranian cultural identity. Hard to control, hard to define, and worst of all hard to immobilize, this "made-up doll" became the emblem of threatening changes in the social organization of space and gender relations in Iran. She disturbed "natural" gender categories and territories. She challenged the very integrity of the privileged term *masculine,* defined traditionally by its mobility and in opposition to femininity and feminine domesticity. Blurred now was the boundary between masculine and feminine, and blurred with it, too, was any sense of stability.

The rupture of tradition proved to be more visible and least tolerable in the area of women's mobility. This new woman strolling the streets, many argued, brought about the degeneracy of Iranian culture. "Westernized" and "half naked"—that is, unveiled—she was portrayed as sexually promiscuous, open to alien "penetration." Her "uncovered" and hence "uncontained" body became synonymous with licentiousness. Violated and violating simultaneously, licentious and also easy prey to the licentiousness of others, she became the paradigm of Iran, the endangered motherland. Many Iranian men began to perceive themselves as the emasculated sons who could no longer protect or control their women.

The panic over reduced masculine powers took several shapes and forms. Persian narratives of a few decades before the 1979 Revolution are saturated with the theme of imperiled manhood. A sizable body of literature decried the "dishonored man," the soft male, the womanly man. It lamented the sharp corrosion in the old and cherished ideals of masculinity. From Muslim clergy to secularist writers to politicians and scholars, men and women alike warned against this unfortunate decline and decay. Two of the most highly acclaimed masterpieces of modern Persian fiction, *Buf-e Kur* (The Blind Owl, discussed more fully in chapter 2) and *Shazdeh Ehtejab* (The Prince, published in 1969), focus on the crisis of masculinity.[33] Written by two of the most influential Iranian novelists, Sadeq Hedayat (1903–51) and Hushang Golshiri (1938–2000), respectively, both novels depict with great precision and perception, boundless angst and elegance, their male protagonists' traumas of transition and tormented souls. The two men oscillate between infantilizing love and intimidated hatred for women, and the books portray them as madonnas and whores, mistresses and maids. Both novels are tragic in their intensity, melancholic in their depiction of male impotency, modern in their focus on introspection, cyclical time, multiple perspectives, shifting identities, and changing definitions of masculinities and femininities. Both revolve around the issue of space, in particular women's newly found self-assertiveness, access to education, and, above all, freedom of movement and men's agonizingly ambivalent feelings toward this unfamiliar and independent kind of woman.

*The Prince*, set in the early twentieth century, is a hall of mirrors. Underneath this intriguing play within a play, Golshiri weaves together a number of themes central to his literary enterprise: ceremonial masquerade; the complex relationship between fact and fiction; the thin divide between reality and illusion; the symbiotic bond between subjugation and domination; the shifting lines of power; nostalgia for a bygone era. The Prince, the title character, is the locus classicus of incompatible aspirations and conflicting desires. He is locked into tragedy, dying a slow and lonely death from tuberculosis. Gone is the pomp and glory of his ancestors. And gone with it, too, is the traditional social organization. He is married to a woman who wants to become the architect of her own identity and fate, a bespectacled beauty who carries a book with her every time she appears in the pages of the novel, a reader of texts who is curious about the past and declares with much pride and confidence to her bewildered husband, "I wish to purloin your books."[34] She embodies for him the promise but also the threat of a quickly changing world.

The Prince is rendered effectively impotent by the woman he admiringly loves and bitterly hates, a woman who has rearranged her priorities, reordered her values, acknowledged the failure of the status quo to satisfy her. Dressed in lace, elegant, and self-reflective, she, book in hand, claims her intellectual independence and refuses to submerge her voice or vision in conventions or collective aspirations. Subverting the Prince's authority and control, she is a real challenge to his sense of *mardaneghi* (manliness). She calls it into question deliberately; she challenges it to prove itself repeatedly. She looks down at him "through the thick glass of her spectacles" (22), compares him to his forebears, and never tires of reminding him that "truly, not a grain of your forefathers' Magnificence has come down to you" (26). The balance of power between husband and wife seesaws dramatically, but the abuse and the lack of communication remain constant.

To control his unconventional wife, the Prince eventually reduces her to a veritable prisoner. If he cannot fully incarcerate her in domesticity, if he cannot control her mind and keep her away from her books, he can physically detain her in a cage. And he does so at great cost to himself. He changes their domicile and buys a house surrounded by walls. "The walls were high," says the Prince, "I had to search hard to find this house" (136). He disconnects the telephone lines (104). "When he goes out, he locks the door behind him" (96). "He never leaves the house unlocked, with its high walls" (108). By the end, his wife conveniently dies of consumption.

Filled with nostalgia for a more familiar and coherent world and worldview, incapable of defining or containing the woman he loves, torn by contradictory and mutually exclusive aspirations, the Prince resorts to a theater of the absurd. He dresses his maid in his wife's lace dresses, adorns her with his wife's jewelry, applies the same makeup on her face, and forces her to impersonate her mistress by abusing her physically, verbally, and emotionally. He also forbids her to wear his wife's glasses, and as soon as she starts to read his wife's books, he burns all of them ceremoniously. At the end of the novel, we find only a battered maid imprisoned in a house with high walls and locked gates; Morad, the wheelchair-bound driver; and the Prince, sitting as "motionless as his own armchair" (21).

Hedayat and Golshiri were not alone in their depiction of male impotency. In his pioneering book *Possessed by Western Culture*, published in 1947, Fakhr eddin Shadman, a prolific writer, portrayed a pathetic image of effeminate Iranian men. In *Persian Requiem*, published in 1964, Simin Daneshvar, the most popular

Iranian woman novelist at the time, mourned the "castration" of Iranian men. In his controversial short story "Dandil," the eminent playwright Gollam-Hossein Sa'edi portrayed the impotence of Iranian men to protect Iranian women.[35] And in his highly acclaimed and controversial book *Westomania* (also translated as *Plagued by the West* or *Weststruckness,* 1952), Jalal Al-e-Ahmad bemoaned the loss of Iranian manliness. "The west-stricken man is a gigolo. He is effeminate. He is always primping; always making sure of his appearance. He has even been known to pluck his eyebrows! He places great importance on his shoes, his clothes, and his home."[36] This object of ridicule and derision has made "way for the arrival of the women's caravan," bemoans Al-e Ahmad, and he is not one to welcome it. "What have we really done?" he asks in desperation. "We have simply given women permission to display themselves in society. Just a display. That is exhibitionism. We have placed women, who are the protectors of tradition, the family, the bloodlines, and the generations in a position of irresponsibility. We have brought them into the streets, to exhibit themselves, to be without duties, to make up their faces, to wear new styles every day and to hang around."[37] A new term gradually gained currency and widespread usage: *zan zalil,* shortened to ZZ, a "henpecked man," a diminished man dominated by a woman. A man not man enough.

Not only were fictive characters denounced as being unmanned, but so too were prominent political figures. Mohammad Reza Shah Pahlavi (reigned 1941–79) described his own prime minister, Mohammad Mossadeq, as a person who "cried like a woman and indulged in hysterical tirades." Prime Minister Amir Abbas Hoveida was denigrated as effeminate. The escape from Iran of Abolhassan Bani-Sadr, Iran's first president, and of Massoud Rajavi, the Mujahidin's leader, allegedly covered by veils has been used time and again to show not only their cowardice, but also their effeminate nature. The shah himself was not spared from such allegations. A book titled *Ernest Peron, the Husband of the Shah of Iran* typifies his enemies' attempt to portray him as lacking "manliness."[38]

A society characterized for centuries by its glorification of masculinity was witnessing a crisis. The implications and ramifications of this challenge remain to be fully analyzed and understood. But as gender categories eroded, the desire for a more familiar, reassuring lifestyle intensified. As notions of masculinity were further challenged, the need to accentuate the differences between the sexes increased, and veiling became essential to the articulation of manhood. As a system of visual communication, the veil expresses gendered identity unambiguously. It evokes femininity and creates an essential woman who is presumed to be different from men. The veil is a distinct, almost theatrical visual emblem. It separates rather than unites the sexes. It dramatizes and polarizes the differences between men and women. It is a defining female garment. A veiled woman makes a man, any man, appear more masculine by contrast. Mandatory veiling beginning in the early 1980s, in other words, was not only symbolic of the attempt to free the country of alien ideologies, establishing women's independence from Western domination or styles, but also a deep-seated desire to define gender boundaries between the sexes within Iran. It was meant to reconstitute and reestablish the lost or, rather, the "natural" order, accentuating the differences between men and women and, more important, their respective spaces.

And yet the clock on women's freedom of movement in Iran was not to be turned back. Iranian women refused to disappear from the scene. The eight-year war with Iraq, as the Second World War had done in the West, pushed a larger number of women out of the home to earn a living. The more traditional women were paradoxically encouraged to take on public responsibilities and move outside the framework preordained by their cultural roles. As Nikki Keddie writes about Iranian women thirty years after the Islamic Revolution, "The very efforts of the government to involve women in defense during the Iran-Iraq war, to educate girls at all levels, and, after 1989, to promote family planning and reduce births helped awaken many girls and women to new ideas. Women also increasingly resisted reversals in women's rights. What were formerly only elite ideas about gender and women's rights spread to the popular classes, sometimes in the form of what has been called 'Islamic feminism.'"[39] Several women began to give gender-egalitarian interpretations of the Qur'an. The Islamic Republic's earlier avowed interest in purifying public spaces of women proved indeed ephemeral. The presence of women as teachers and students in institutions of higher education (including technical and vocational schools), the sharp increase in their literacy rate, their attainment of leadership positions, their active participation in nongovernmental organizations, their vigorous involvement in various forms of art, politics, and sports are unprecedented in Iranian history. Rooted in decades of struggle for gender equity, these consequences are partly unintended, the collateral benefits of certain policies of the Islamic Republic.

Here are some facts and figures. Women's life expectancy in Iran has increased from 64.3 years in 1990 to 71.9 years. Although the Islamic Republic proceeded quickly to lower the age of marriage to 9 for girls, the real median age of marriage for women is 24. The fertility rate has dramatically decreased from 5.62 percent in 1990 to 2.33 percent. Girls' attendance at elementary school is at 94 percent. And gender disparities do not increase in institutions of higher education. In fact, 64 percent of all students admitted to Iranian universities now are women.[40] Iran is finally taking gender into account in order to promote equal opportunity for all: some members of the Parliament are suggesting affirmative action for men.

The literary scene provides another telling example of women's historically unmatched discursive participation in the public domain. Not only is there a strong and vital tradition of women writers in Iran today, but there is also a record number of books by women or about women. There are more female film directors in Iran today than in the previous one hundred years put together. With twenty-three million Internet users and an amazing 7,100 percent rate of growth in the number of users between 2000 and 2007, Iran has the fastest-growing number of Internet users in the Middle East.[41] Here, too, women play a most active role in the Iranian cyberspace and blogosphere. And on August 27, 2006, the most far-reaching campaign ever undertaken by Iranian women was launched. The Campaign for One Million Signatures, a nonviolent civil-society initiative and a collaborative street-based enterprise, is challenging discriminatory laws against women.

Let me hasten to add, though: despite these statistics, the Islamic Republic of Iran is surely no utopia for women, and gender inequities are facts of everyday life. Women lack an equitable political representation. The highest government offices in the land are monopolized by men. The Supreme Leadership, the presidency, and membership in the Guardian Council, the National Security Council, and the Expediency Council do not include even a token woman. Although an increasing number of women nominate themselves for presidential elections, so far all have been disqualified by the Guardian Council, made up of a group of men who have the unlimited authority to reject the credentials of any candidate regardless of gender.[42] The most notable and the longest-running women's magazine *Zanan* (Women) was shut down in February 2008. Women are segregated into lower-paying and lower-prestige occupations. They have higher unemployment and lower participation in the labor force. Textbooks for elementary and middle schools are often gender biased. The muezzin who makes the call to prayer at fixed intervals from sunrise to sunset is always a man. It is thus always a man who saves Muslims from one of the most dreaded sins in Islam: forgetfulness.

On a legal level, women and men do not share equal status. A boy becomes a man at the age of fifteen, whereas a girl becomes a woman at the age of nine. This makes her eligible for adult punishment at an early age. Women are barred from being or becoming judges. Some theologians argue that women do not possess the right qualifications for such a task. They are presumably too emotional and too kind-hearted, and, above all, they lack the logic and level-headedness of men. In most legal cases, the testimony of two women counts as the equivalent of one man. Furthermore, there is a dramatic rise in marital infidelities, the divorce rate, the prevalence of prostitution, and drug addiction as well as an alarming increase in the number of suicides and self-immolation among women.[43]

## TWO COMPETING NARRATIVES OF WOMANHOOD

For centuries, the Iranian nation was made up of two societies—one male, one female—separate and unequal. In part one of this book, "A Legacy of Containment," I look at the social implications of sex segregation in a society in which the right of place depended on anatomy and argue that gender relations, a culturally defined and historically situated system that regulates male/female relationship, has revolved around the issue of space in Iran. The study of gender relations has only recently emerged as an analytical category in the field of Iranian studies. Although essentialist accounts abound, often written from a male perspective and represented as divinely ordained and immutable order, few systematic explorations of the social, institutional, and linguistic dimensions of gender relations have been undertaken. To my knowledge, none has addressed the issue of space and mobility. The findings presented throughout this book are indeed exploratory and often tentative. I am interested not only in manifestations of gender inequity, but also in its causes. For instance, although I believe women's relative lack of economic power is an important determinant of gender inequality, I want to know how it was imposed on women. In the first two chapters of part one, I focus on how rules of segregation are simultaneously adhered to and subverted in classical Persian literature and Iranian cinema. I examine issues of women's representation as well as their entry onto the written page and the silver screen. In chapter 2, "The Bonds of Beauty," I analyze the intersection of feminine beauty and restrained mobility, the erotics of passivity in Iran and across cultures. Why, I ask, are static women—the sleeping beauties—lauded, whereas those who are on the move—the flying witches (always portrayed as women)—are vilified? More suggestive than exhaustive, this chapter discusses disparate moments and regions and various beautification practices out of their historic and cultural contexts.

In an article published in 2006, Azar Nafisi, the author of the best-selling *Reading Lolita in Tehran*, writes: "This is a good time to show our appreciation of that other hidden and confiscated Iran through reading and celebrating its best and most trustworthy representatives: its poets and writers."[44] Part two, "Wings and Words," is a celebration of an important component of "that other hidden and confiscated Iran." Iranian women writers, who have refused to disappear from the public scene, are among some of the most influential figures in contemporary Iran. They have produced a radically dissenting and questioning body of writing with a momentum Persian literature has never before experienced. They have attained unprecedented stature at a level previously reserved only for male writers. Although they have not achieved the level of international recognition they deserve and exceptionally few translations of their works are available in English, and even though they are conspicuously absent from world literary anthologies, they nonetheless have produced an impressive body of literature and are considered a most threatening emblem of change to all stripes of extremists. The four chapters of part two are dedicated to them. In particular, this section focuses on four seminal women poets and writers who build their literary universe on spatial metaphors of movement and containment. The legacy of Tahirih Qurratu'Ayn, Forugh Farrokhzad, Simin Behbahani, and Shahrnush Parsipur to the world of letters has been as extraordinary as their defiance against the age-old patterns of gender apartheid. Tahirih, who rejected sex segregation and celebrated freedom of movement (and of conscience) in the mid–nineteenth century, is being accorded recognition as the symbolic mother of the women's movement in Iran. The twin themes of flight and captivity are presented as the central tropes of Forugh Farrokhzad's poetry. The candor and courage of Simin Behbahani—the Gypsy poet—has made of her a symbol of resistance and integrity inside and outside the country and has given Iran a female national poet for the first time in its glorious literary tradition. And Shahrnush Parsipur proves that issues of containment and crossing are central to women's artistic universe and the central trope of their writing.

In part three, "Prisoners Awaiting Liberation," I shift the emphasis from an exclusively Iranian perspective and concentrate on how Iranian and Muslim women are reduced to stereotypes in the West. The problem with stereotypes is not that they are totally false. There is usually an element of truth to them. The problem is that they are arrested representations. They are fixed. Frozen. Dehumanized. They are immobilized, caged images of a reality that is perpetually moving and shifting. In chapter 8, I consider the birth of a new literary subgenre—the hostage narrative—and the portrayal of Iranian women as the ultimate prisoners in a giant gulag the size of Iran. Hostage narratives, I argue, generalize and simplify, flatten and fix, rather than specify and expand. They present women in the role of victims and effectively dismiss their contributions to Iranian culture in favor of a master narrative of oppression and irrelevance, entrapment and imprisonment. Intentionally or not, they perpetuate a legacy of silence and insignificance where there is in fact a resolute struggle for freedom and expression. In this chapter, I examine the allure of captivity as a literary theme and the explosion of life narratives written in English and addressed to a Western audience in which the figure of the Muslim Woman is represented as the victim of an immobilizing faith, the captive of a multigenerational army of male prison guards. As an expression of the conflicts and ambivalences engendered by the processes of modernization and the expansion of the prison industrial complex in the West, the emergence of this stereotype in literature, I conclude, is closely connected to the social drama unfolding within Western societies.

It has been difficult to limit the multiple inferences and wider associations of this subject. Paradoxical as it may seem, the topic of women's mobility cannot be contained within a single faith, culture, or literature. Its varied implications, particularly as related to women's lives, can be discovered across a diverse range of genres and themes. In classical as well as contemporary literature and in cultural as well as political attitudes, one finds variations of this theme across the world. The unnerving similarities of attitudes, applications, and approaches to this question of keeping women "in their place"—the congruence in imagery, metaphor, and interpretation when it comes to this desire—is indeed astounding. True to its name, freedom of movement is a theme that crosses all frontiers, ignores all formal boundaries, breaks all kinds of taboos, dissolves the conventional distinctions of geography as well as history, of high and low culture, of academic scholarship and popular journalism, of race, religion, and even international relations.

In the course of my researching and writing this book, the subject has literally run away with me.

Some of my most trusted colleagues advised me to avoid "opening up a can of worms" by launching into these widely diverse reflections on the fear of women's unrestrained mobility, however closely related they might be to my central theme in this book. But try as I might, the theme has refused to be restricted and confined to Iranian culture.

Although I have been unable to pursue all of the related themes in depth, I have found it both worthwhile and necessary to make connections, suggest parallels, and invite comparisons wherever possible between the central topic of freedom of movement as practiced in Iran and some of these seemingly peripheral themes, between the inequitable distribution of space in the Islamic world and elsewhere. My objective has been twofold. First, I want to trace the fascinating trajectory of Iranian women's increasing presence in the public arena—a radical development that has shaken the very foundation of Iranian society. Second, I also aspire to challenge the hierarchies of cultural norms, which divert attention from key issues in the control of women globally. I hope I have shown that a book about women's mobility in Iran is closely related to other topics such as the social and sexual underpinnings of foot binding in China; the marketing history of the Barbie doll worldwide; depictions of idealized feminine beauty in children's literature, popular fiction, and films of mass entertainment in the West; and even the symbolism and subversive powers of the figure of the female Gypsy and the witch.

Every book, like a door, can open in two directions. It is my hope that this book invites readers into the house of Iranian culture and literature, welcomes them, and leads them out again, through courtyards and private chambers, beyond high walls and hidden gardens to the wider world we all share. I hope readers will accompany Iranian women out of their previously walled-in spaces and roles into new territories and ask why, in view of such a dazzling sense of movement, the dominant image of them in the United States is that of virtual prisoners. Why is the reality of women's lives in Iran—so defiant, so vibrant, so subversive—overshadowed by the image of a captive trapped in the dark dungeons of fanaticism and autocracy? To what shall we attribute this perceptual dissonance? Are Iranian women the abducted daughters, the incarcerated girls, the invisible women they are portrayed to be popularly, or, to the contrary, are they the formidable civic power this book reckons them to be?

# PART ONE

# A Legacy of Containment

# 1

# ENCLOSED BODIES, TRAPPED VOICES, FRAMED IMAGES

## *The Poetics of Sex Segregation*

Polish your mirror, and perhaps that sublime beauty from the regions of mystery will shine in your breast—just as it did for the prophets. And then, with your heart illuminated by that splendor, the secret of the beloved will no longer be concealed from you.

—ABDOL RAHMAN-E JAMI, *Yusuf-o-Zulaikha*

Oh, if a tree could wander
and move with foot and wings!
It would not suffer the axe blows
and not the pain of saws!

—JALAL AL-DIN RUMI, translated by Annemarie Schimmel

### THE BLANK PAGE, THE LOST WORDS

Sex segregation has had a powerful impact on Iranian literature. It has shaped the language, the themes, the plots, and the systems of literary representation used by men and women over the centuries. While the veil, a portable wall, concealed women's bodies, silence and erasure, which are literary veils, disguised women's voices and images in the great works of literature in Iran. Rules of modesty not only minimized physical contact between the sexes but also forbade aural and visual contact in works of art as well. In other words, the norms and values that regulated women's physical movement applied equally to the circulation of their voices and their images—inhibiting these powerful transmitters wherever women were concerned.

29

Literature exposes women to public scrutiny. It allows them to establish communication with the outside world. It transports them as readers, writers, and protagonists from a private arena into the public sphere. It allows them to travel far and wide, confounds gender boundaries, integrates the sexes, blurs the boundaries between private and public. Even if not in its production, then certainly in its reception and consumption, literature is a public art. Small wonder then that for centuries Iranian women were denied easy access to the power and privilege of the published word. Principles of modesty substantially reduced their roles and their presence on the literary scene, suppressing them for the most part both verbally and visually. Theirs was a "private" world, where self-expression was confined within a delineated space. For almost ten centuries, literature possessed a predominantly masculine character in Iran.

By focusing on how rules of sex segregation manifest themselves in classical Persian literature and how these rules are simultaneously adhered to and subverted, I examine in this chapter how gender and space intersect in Persian literature. How, for example, was it possible to reconcile the demands of good storytelling, especially where love stories were concerned, with the need to restrict women to the private domain? How was a love scene transformed into literature and thus brought out of the private and into the public domain without compromising the lovers, especially the woman involved? Did the assertive, lustful, and "exposed" heroines of classical Persian literature—and there are many of them—violate sexual and textual proprieties, and, if so, did their irreverence elicit any outrage or penalty? How did their narrators/creators negotiate, revise, and suspend cultural conventions so that neither poet nor protagonist would be punished for traditionally punishable freedoms? Although I concentrate on literary conventions in this chapter, I do not believe creativity to be the prerogative of the literate or the literary elite only. On the contrary, I consider "private" forms of art, such as storytelling, carpet weaving, sewing, needlework, knitting, and cooking, among many others, to be just as important as "public" artistic expression. Orally transmitted stories are as important as published novels; lullabies are as significant as poems. My primary focus here, however, is the written literature alone.

To ensure woman's chastity, her voice was kept out of circulation in Iran. In fact, silence became the verbal extension of chastity, a token of a woman's inaccessibility, an important component of her charm and her allure, a criterion of her beauty. A woman's voice was considered part of her *awrat* (sexual organs).

Thus sexualized, it had to be controlled and contained. If a woman allowed her tongue to move about freely, she became *zan-e zaban deraz,* a babbler, a tattletale, a chatterbox, a nag, a gossip. She was called *kowli, saliteh, pacheh var malideh:* a gypsy, a shrew, a virago. The Persian language has a rich supply of epithets reserved for a garrulous woman, one with a wayward tongue. Conversely, the expression *sangin-o-samet,* which means "solemn and silent" and is still in use to this day, defines an ideal woman as one who is self-effacing rather than self-promoting, enclosed rather than exposed, mute rather than vocal.

It is hardly surprising, then, that it has been difficult for women writers to flourish in such a cultural context. With the female ideal perceived as silent, it has not been easy for women to appropriate a public voice without being condemned for doing so. In a world where women were kept under close surveillance, domesticated, tamed, and hedged about, publishing has been construed a masculine prerogative. In this climate of suppression, only a few women have managed against all odds to subvert the system and nurture their creative talents. Most have remained silent, at least in the public arena. Some have had to entrust their words to the wind, the river, patient stones, blank pages, buried papers. Leili, the famed but ill-fated lover in the legendary love story of Persian literature, laments this verbal erasure. Comparing herself to her voluble lover, she deplores the silence imposed upon her. Majnun, she says, "is a man. I am a woman. . . . He can talk and cry and express the deepest feelings in his poems. But I? I am a prisoner. I have no one to whom I can talk, no one to whom I can open my heart: shame and dishonor would be my fate."[1]

### THE CAUTIONARY TALE OF A LOVE-STRUCK FOOL

A woman's chastity, which was established and thereafter assured by means of her inaccessibility, imposed all manner of limitations on literary men as well. The idealized invisibility of femininity extended beyond women as artists to women as objects of literary art. Not only female authors but also female characters were expected to respect the codes of sex segregation. As a consequence, the male authors of Iranian love stories, who of course could not excise women from their narratives, had to follow a stringent code regulating gender relations. The story of Leili and Majnun itself, which is considered to be "the most popular romance in the Islamic world," versions of which "appear in prose, song, and poetry in almost every language within the vast area stretching from the Atlantic Ocean to the Chinese border,"[2] served as a warning and a model to all would-be authors. It was a manual on how women should be protected from exposure not only in public life, but also on the page.

The plot of *Leili and Majnun* revolves around the madness of a certain poet named Qais, who has fallen passionately in love with his childhood classmate, Leili. Intoxicated with love to the point of insanity, Qais—whose nickname, "Majnun" (the Mad One), reveals his condition—cannot even begin to conceal his love.[3] He sings of his boundless passion for Leili in endless poems and shares his praise of her with perfect strangers, anyone who is willing to listen to him. As a result of these insolent declarations of love, this reckless indiscretion of passion, and his violation not only of the social formulae but also of the poetic and rhetorical conventions governing lyric poetry, Qais is separated and prevented from marrying Leili. He has unveiled her verbally, and her father is livid with rage against him. "Not a wind passes without uttering my daughter's name," he laments in furious dismay. "Shall I sit with a vile versifier?" he asks. He accuses Majnun of having "sullied my good name—and his own. There is not one corner in the whole of Arabia where my daughter's name is not bandied about on everyone's lips—and I should give her to him who is the cause of all this? My name would be infamous for ever." To protect his reputation, Leili's father is willing to go as far as to kill his own daughter. "I swear to God that I would rather cut off her head with my own hands and feed this moonlike bride to the dogs—to save my honor and to live in peace."[4] Stricken with sorrow and heartsick, Majnun leaves the society of men to live with the wild animals of the desert.

Majnun, whose poems are not only his only source of consolation but also the cause of wonder and enchantment to all who hear them, is plagued by his talent. His disregard for sanctioned generic practices is both evidence of originality and proof of folly. His cure—poetry—becomes his curse. By breaking the covenant of privacy and secrecy and by breaching the rhetorical conventions governing lyric poetry, he loses both the woman he loves and his sanity.[5] In his own words, "No veil covered my secret, no ruins offered me a hiding-place for my treasure; that is why the world could rob me of it."[6]

Unlike Majnun, however, the authors of classical love stories—and there are many of them—did not abandon the commonly accepted literary norms of the time. On the contrary, they devised ingenious strategies and invented clever literary devices to circumvent traditional spaces and to transcend the culturally defined boundaries imposed on a sex-segregated society without openly violating them. They found ways to reconcile the exigencies of a compelling narrative with the social proprieties expected in their culture. As a result, they not only avoided Majnun's tragic fate but created a celebrated literary tradition. In the process, they produced a range of strong women protagonists, with key roles and strong characters, who demanded space and attention, who could not be silenced, who refused to be erased, marginalized, or exiled and thus left their mark on the Persian literary tradition and culture.

## INGENIOUS STRATEGIES

The overwhelming majority of women protagonists who populate the pages of Iranian classical literature are circumscribed by poetic conventions that reflect the real world outside the walls of literature itself. Although the narratives in which they appear expose them to the "public" eye of general readership, the fictive world they inhabit forces them to defer to the generic constraints of a "private" world more suitable to women. In a famous scene in *Shahnameh* by Abol Qasem Ferdowsi (935–1020), which has been illustrated in miniature paintings innumerable times, Tahmineh, while professing her love and devotion to the hero Rustam, is quick to remind him of her chastity:

> Outside these walls, there's none who's looked on me
> Nor has my voice been heard by any ear
> From everyone have I heard tales of you—So wonderful they seemed to me
>     like myths
> I'm yours now should you want me. And, if not
> None but the fish and birds will see my face.[7]

Tahmineh's double message of chastity and sexual passion combines both the fears and the fantasies of her male readers as well as of the author himself. It allows Tahmineh to be simultaneously exposed and covered by the fictions of privacy within the narrative world. Her passion is all the more appealing because of her modesty. Shirin, the well-educated, independent, resourceful, and fearless protagonist of another popular romance, is also the idealization of womanly chastity. Although dressed like a male warrior, she rides toward Iran in search of her beloved prince; she also swears "by the seven heavens, that even if she wept tears of blood for love of Khosrow, she would not be his until she was his wife."[8] In other words, she proclaims that she is abiding by the ideals of chastity imposed on women at the very moment that, astride her horse, she is violating them.

None of these heroines is the "spoiled" goods of another man; none has been involved in a previous carnal union. Virginity is presented time and again as a "jewel" sought by men, a "pearl" pierced by men, a "treasure box" appropriated by men. It is a "seal of God" and an absolute prerequisite for most heroines of classical Persian literature. To qualify for such high standing, even previously married women have to be "cleansed" of any physical trace of earlier sexual experience. They have to be virgins. And lo and behold virgins they become. Zulaikha, for instance, has an intact virginity even after years of marriage.[9] When she enters the nuptial chamber of the man she loves, Yusuf finds, to his absolute delight, that his bride's "jewel box" is still untouched. Zulaikha is not an isolated case. Though married twice before, Vis is also a virgin when she is united with Ramin.[10] In the words of Fakhr ed-Din As'ad Gorgani (eleventh century), Vis's creator-narrator, "the seal of God" was "yet intact upon her." Not that Zulaikha or Vis and many others like them have a renewable virginity. They do not. But for a variety of convenient reasons, their marriages are never consummated. Zulaikha's husband is conveniently impotent; Vis's first husband goes to war before consummating his union, and the second one becomes impotent thanks to the nanny's machination and potion. "As he pranced in the lists of happiness," Gorgani tells us about Ramin's nuptial night, "he put the key of desire in the lock of happiness: his delight in the lover grew the more when he saw the seal of God was as yet intact upon her. . . . He pierced that soft pearl of great price; seduced a saint from her virginity."[11] Hymen restoration, it seems, is not the purview of plastic surgeons only. Iranian poets have been performing them for centuries.

These authors' ingenuity is indeed boundless; the narrative strategies they use, which allow them simultaneously to preserve and expose the ideal of womanhood, are brilliant and diversified. Some writers, for instance, imported their heroines from foreign lands. Shirin, the lofty heroine of Abu Muhammad Nezami Ganjavi's (1141–1202) *Khosrow and Shirin*, is from Armenia; in the same work, Maryam, Khosrow's first wife, is Byzantine. Zulaikha, the determined and lustful heroine of *Yusuf and Zulaikha*, is from the West. In the medieval popular romance *Amir Arsalan-e Rumi,* Farrokh Lagha is the daughter of Petros Shah-e Faranghi (King Petros, the European). The female protagonist in the story *Sheik San'an* by Farid al-Din Attar (1142–1220) is Christian, and the protagonist of *Vis-o-Ramin* is Zoroastrian. By having a foreigner or a member of a religious minority at the crux of the love story, the authors of these works allowed themselves a certain leeway when it came to "exposing" her to the public eye.

Equally inventive is the fashion in which women and men meet and fall in love. Some see a portrait or have a vision of the other; Shirin sees Khosrow's picture and falls in love with him, and Zulaikha glimpses Yusuf for the first time in her dreams. Others hear rumors about the beloved: Rudabeh and Tahmineh in *Shahnameh* listen to others speaking of their lovers, Rustam and Zal, and the beautiful maiden Bazigha, from the highest rank of an ancient line, hears a description of Yusuf and at once feels irresistibly attracted to him. These women's ears fall in love before their eyes, hearts, and souls do. In the words of Abdol Rahman-e Jami (1414–92), "Sight is not the only way that love finds into the heart: it often happens that this blessing is born of the spoken word, and that the echo of beauty entering the ear robs heart and soul of peace and reason."[12] This is certainly how Khosrow falls in love with Shirin. His grandfather, who visits him in a dream, tells him about her beauty: "You shall have Shirin, your destined love, whose sweetness and beauty will sustain you all your days."[13]

Dreams continue to function as pretext for love or union in the contemporary period as well. Consider the marriage of Ayatollah Ruhollah Khomeini. According to Geraldine Brooks, "Ruhollah, an impoverished clerical student from the dusty village of Khomein, had been twenty seven when he asked for the hand of fifteen-year-old Khadija Saqafi." Her father, a prominent ayatollah, "didn't think much of the match. But Khadija felt differently. She had glimpsed her suitor when, wrapped in a chador, she brought him a glass of tea. She convinced her father to agree to the match after relating a dream in which the prophet proclaimed Ruhollah from Khomein was destined to become a great religious leader."[14]

## WORDS IN THE WIND

In addition to dreams, rumors, and portraits, Iranian writers have also relied on winds to serve as go-between in their love stories. Generally speaking, winds have played a significant role in Persian literature, just as they have loomed large in Persian culture. They are discussed in terms of their damaging or beneficial functions in affecting the weather, stirring up storms, moving the clouds, causing sandstorms, and bringing on rain or drought. They have also been appreciated for their transportation of seeds as well as for their scattering of scents and perfumes and their ability to stir up the dancing of spring and autumn leaves. In classical medicine, too, which stressed both physical and mental health, winds and breezes occupied a privileged place.

But this fascination with the wind in particular and with the wafting of breezes in general has gone beyond the mundane, the medical, the botanical, and the meteorological. It has permeated Iranian literature as a trope in the work of some of its best-known authors, such as Gorgani, Ferdowsi, Jami, and Nezami, among others. The wind's power to transform has allowed poets to contemplate the mystery of change. Its speed has personified the transitory nature of life. Its association with movement has inspired the possibility of crossing boundaries in both literal and metaphoric ways. The wind overcomes all obstacles and hindrances; it trespasses all man-made barriers and overleaps all walls. It migrates hither and thither with impunity and cannot be contained either by veils or stones. As a result, it has become a vital metaphor of mediation in several Iranian love stories, performing indispensable tasks and functions. It is a collaborator, a fellow conspirator, providing lovers with much-coveted glimpses of the beloved.[15] Ramin, the protagonist of *Vis and Ramin,* is one of the many beneficiaries of this subversive generosity. Had it not been for the wind, he might not have met his beloved Vis. "A fresh spring breeze arose," according to Gorgani, "and stirred the curtains on the litter one by one. It was as if a sword had been drawn from the scabbard, or as if the sun had come out from behind a cloud. The face of Vis came out from behind the veil and Ramin's heart became its slave at one glance."[16]

The wind and its attendant breezes have also served as confidants and messengers for women in classical Persian literature. Because it was not acceptable, let alone encouraged, for women to declare their passions in public and to do so was associated with promiscuity, women—at least the respectable kind—did not address romantic or sexual issues openly. In the rare instances when a woman was driven to do so, she betrayed her passion allusively, elliptically, camouflaging her desire behind accepted poetic formulas, veiling her ardor with metaphors and her infatuation with symbols. Shame, dishonor, even death awaited those who spoke publicly of love. So women talked to the wind and the breezes. This element served as their intermediary, delivering their confidential tales of love from heart to heart, door to door, author to reader. The recipient of a woman's passion was thus nobody and everybody at the same time.

Leili, knowing full well that it is improper for her to articulate her love publicly, entrusts the tale of her love to this sole and privileged audience.[17] Even Zulaikha, the passionate woman who seizes every opportunity to be united with the man she loves, is marked by her silence in the public arena. "Dear wind!" she says. "You that rise at dawn and shed musky fragrance on the bosom of the jasmine, and cause the moist tresses of the hyacinth to caress the petals of the rose; you that shake the tiny, bell-like leaves hanging from the branches, and make the trees sway with their feet rooted in the soil: you that carry messages between lover and beloved, soothing their distressed and agitated hearts! In all the world there is no one more doleful and desolate than I am. Console my afflicted heart, and help me to bear my bitter sorrow." And if not with the wind, Zulaikha vies with the Nile in communicating her passion to the river itself. In the words of her most admiring creator, Jami, "her lips, bud-like, had the seal of silence upon them. . . . For months, for years even," Zulaikha divulges her love to no one. She "would tell the flowers of her secret love and the burning grief in her heart. Sometimes she would rush like a torrential stream, head-long to the Nile to pour out her sorrows."[18]

### READERS AS PEEPING TOMS AND EAVESDROPPERS

Another fascinating device deployed by writers who were seeking ways to overstep the social and cultural bounds of a sex-segregated society was the figure of the peeping Tom. Voyeurs are among the most common characters not only in Persian miniatures, but also in Persian romances. Male readers and narrators often find themselves occupying the role of voyeurs, peering into a cloistered space that is simultaneously near and distant, sheltered and exposed. The heroine remains in this protected space, and poet and readers alike are allowed, through narratological ploys, to contemplate her activities there. The heroine thus is covered and discovered all at once. The "inner sanctum," though pierced by literary devices, remains intact within the framework of the story. There is all the pleasure of perpetual virginity in the experience. Although the reader and the poet have both entered into the private world of the heroine, they are kept at a safe distance so that she can become visible without being violated. It is made abundantly clear that this private space is inaccessible to the public within the fictive setting.

The rhetoric of inaccessibility seems to stimulate the desire to transgress sacrosanct boundaries all the more, though. Some of these voyeuristic scenes have become favorite motifs in Iranian pictorial arts. One popular theme depicted by various artists shows Khosrow watching Shirin bathe in a stream. Khosrow watches Shirin, and the viewer looks at Khosrow watching a naked Shirin. Believing herself protected and unaware of any peeping Toms, Shirin disrobes before she suddenly notices a man staring at her. At that moment, two things happen simultaneously: Shirin covers her nakedness with her long, flowing hair, and Khosrow averts his gaze. But the watcher who never stops staring is outside the frame.

Readers and narrators often share the role of the voyeur or the eavesdropper in romantic Persian narratives. Jami's seemingly obsessive effort to keep Zulaikha's declaration of love invisible and inaudible is a good case in point. Leading Yusuf to a labyrinth, Zulaikha seeks out a secret alcove in it, behind many hidden doors and numerous locks and bolts. It is only when they reach the deepest recess of this private space that she attempts to seduce him. "The eloquent narrator of this mystical tale now reveals that when they reach the seventh chamber, Zulaikha utters a cry of distress from the depths of her soul and begs Yusuf to step into her magnificent sanctuary!" Leading Yusuf into "that delightful apartment," Zulaikha "locked the door with an iron bolt and a golden chain. It was an inner sanctum, closed to all outsiders: not even her friends had any hope of access to it. There was only room in it for lover and beloved—the beloved's cheeks glowing with bewitching coyness, the lover's heart beating time to the melody of passion, the way wide open to voluptuous, soul-inflaming desire."[19]

In the seventh chamber of the gilded palace, which Zulaikha has had to spend "gold and silver by the camel-load" to construct, and behind several doors locked with iron bolts and golden chains, we reach the dramatic heart of the story and find ourselves at a nodal point in the unfolding saga. This moment contains the potential of the whole relationship. Tempted briefly, Yusuf eventually chooses to leave. We see him exiting the sanctuary not with the resplendent blush of postcoital bliss, but angry and harassed. He "ran as fast as he could. Each door opened in front of him, without any need for a key: the bolts simply flew aside." Poor Zulaikha! Even her locks and bolts are no good and serve no end! Although the author conspires with Yusuf and lets him run through all those elaborately locked doors without any need for a key, he cannot escape the reader. He is at the mercy of the ultimate voyeur who has entered the labyrinth with him and penetrated the private space from which he has fled.

This game of concealment and disclosure, of speaking within earshot of others and eavesdropping on them, of crossing boundaries and entering a private space "closed to all outsiders," is exquisitely tantalizing. It provokes the desire in both protagonist and reader to hear and see more and more. It invites the gaze and fantasies of the voyeur in and out of the tale. It satisfies as well as provokes his/her illicit pleasures of penetrating a forbidden, private zone. And it transforms the women's quarters—that mysterious space, that erotic arena—into a place of sexual fantasy. Most important, for the purposes of this argument, it does so without ever compromising the heroine, who conforms to the strictures of sex segregation within the framework of the tale itself even while seducing the reader to breach them. Both poet and reader penetrate the "interior space" of women's quarters without violating the laws of sex segregation. Desire is thus aroused and simultaneously controlled and circumscribed by cultural and literary conventions. Impervious to peeping eyes and listening ears, the sexually assertive, self-willed, and uninhibited women in these classical Persian tales are protected from being promiscuous by means of literary devices.

## NANNIES AS FIGURES OF MEDIATION

Even when the reader and narrator do not assume the role of voyeur or eavesdropper in these stories, they can always rely on the figure of the nanny to lead them into forbidden territory. This stock character appears with fascinating consistency in almost all love stories in classical Persian literature.[20] The term *nanny* used here is a generic term referring to all kinds of maidservants, slave girls, attendants, ladies-in-waiting, matchmakers, nurses, and wet nurses in these tales.[21] The differences between them are less significant than the traits they share in common as far as the politics and poetics of sex segregation are concerned.

Nannies operate on different levels and serve several indispensable functions in Persian romances.[22] They cross the lines of demarcation between inside and out, between right and wrong, between what is permitted and what is not. They articulate the forbidden, transmit messages across the sexual divide, challenge cultural barriers, and create a space of possibility by mediating between lovers.

They serve as go-betweens, bridges, and intermediaries between the text and its readers, too. These nannies' good and bad counsel, curiosity, interference, and disregard for sacrosanct boundaries are essential to the unfolding of many classical plots in Persian literature. Such masterpieces as *Bakhtash and Rabieh, Bijan and Manijeh, Khosrow and Shirin, Rudabeh and Zal, Rustam and Tahmineh, Farhad and Shirin, Vis and Ramin,* and *Yusuf and Zulaikha* depend on this literary device. Even such popular romances as *Amir Arsalan-e Rumi, Darab-Nameh, Eskandar-Nameh, Firuz Shab-Nameh,* and *Samak-e Ayar* rely for their resolution on the heroine's having a nurse as her "double." According to William Hanaway, the heroine and her nurse together create a set of "pairs which form fully rounded characters, each half being incomplete itself."[23] The desires of one cannot be fulfilled without the assistance of the other. It is only in *Leili and Majnun* that the nurse plays no important role. But then love is never consummated in this most popular love story, which paradoxically is more about separation than union.

The most important function performed by the nanny is that she allows the reader to gaze upon a cloistered space and hear a private conversation that would otherwise be inaccessible. In fact, readers borrow the nanny's ears, eyes, and feet to enter into the women's quarters; they need her to enter into the minds and hearts of its residents. The heroine, whose absence from and silence in the public arena must mark her out and distinguish her from all other women, can nevertheless talk in private to her nanny, confide in her, within the enclosed enclaves of the women's quarters. The nanny thus becomes her conduit to the outside world. She also serves as the readers' contact with the heroine's confined space. She therefore reinforces the public/private divide even while breaking it.

In one of the most beautiful love stories in Ferdowsi's *Shahnameh,* Rudabeh, upon hearing a description of the hero Zal, falls madly in love with him. She summons her nanny, confides in her, and asks her to unite her with the man she so desires. Only through the nanny's textual mediation do we learn of Rudabeh's secret love. "To you alone the secret of my heart / I now unfold; to you alone confess / the deep sensations of my captive soul," she tells her nanny.

> I love, I love; all day and night of him
> I think alone I see him in my dreams
> You only know my secret—and now
> soothe the sorrow of my bursting heart.[24]

Less constrained by laws of segregation, nannies have easier access to the outside world. Neither entirely inside nor quite outside the walls that separate public from private, they move freely between the center and the margins, between the male and female spaces. They are border transgressors who slip in and out of forbidden places; they are messengers, advisers, buffers, officers of misrule. Their lower social status and in some cases their age afford these women a certain mobility denied to the highborn. Heroines, whose restrained mobility is the prerequisite of their charm, borrow their nannies' voices, eyes, ears, and feet to communicate that charm and be charmed in turn.[25]

At the level of plot, the inimitable nanny is a strategist who is well versed in guile. She uses all her tricks and ingenuity, of which she seems to have an abundant supply, to bring the lovers together. She has "the nature of a fox in devising cunning ploys."[26] Satan often looks like an amateur beside her. She arranges secret meetings; she concocts love potions, magic recipes, aphrodisiacs; she induces impotence in pesky and expendable husbands. Unruly woman that she is, she also lies, cheats, steals, falsifies, and withholds vital information with impunity. She fulfills her mission to bring the lovers together with utter resourcefulness. Zulaikha's nanny enumerates her extraordinary powers. If the girl's lover were an angel from the heavens, she tells a distraught and almost deranged Zulaikha, she would be able to invoke him by "praise and prayer to come below." If he were "a son of the fairies of the woods and the mountains," she would be able to conjure him up with "an incantation." And if he were a "mere mortal," then she would make sure Zulaikha would be able to have joy of him, "be his mistress, not his slave."[27]

Not only the nanny herself, but many of the other characters in these stories and even the narrator himself acknowledge her amazing capacity for subversion. "You," Vis tells the nanny, "know more spells than any; you can likewise contrive remedies; you have a store of more than a thousand spells; all your thoughts are ordered and collected; nothing emanates from you that is not worthy of approbation; there is none so clever as you. At the moment of speech you have great lore in words: at the moment of action you have much store of talent." Even the craftiest characters in Persian literature can rarely match the nanny's creative intercessions. Her powers are quasi-magical. "By contriving men," Vis admits, the nanny can "turn mills towards the wind, uproot the river bed, entrap birds from the heaven, bring fish out of the sea, lure raging lions to the trap, tie up wild elephants in chains, tempt snakes out of their holes, make them lame and playful by spells, cut a passage out through adamantine rock and level Mount Qaf to the plain."[28] Within the context of these romances, the power of the nanny seems to be limitless.

Nothing can stop her, for example, in her mission of uniting the lovers. In one farcical scene, the nanny slips into bed with the heroine's husband, King Mowbad, so that Vis can be with her lover. The man is presumably too drunk to know the difference between his young wife and her old substitute. In the morning, though, as he lifts the nanny's wrinkled hand to his lips, a bamboozled Mowbad realizes what has happened. Incredulous, he "thunders like a cloud from the rage in his heart. He grabbed the hand of that witch and said, 'What demon are you that are clasped in my embrace? Who threw you into my arms?'" Meanwhile, Vis, who had been "lying lip on lip, face on face" with Ramin all night long, returns just in time to save the day and the trapped proxy. "You have hurt my hand from clutching it and pressing it so," she says coyly to the angry husband, "take the other hand for a time and then take it where you will." "When the King heard the voice of the idol-faced beauty, he was unaware of her redoubtable ruse. He let fall the nurse's hand and released that harlot from the net of shame."[29] Although it is Vis who spends the night frolicking with her husband's brother, it is the nanny who is called a "witch" and a "harlot." In the narrative world, the nanny fulfills the role that the poet rejects for his heroine and protects her from the very punishment she provokes, both freeing her and enforcing the conventions of her confinement in the process. The nanny aids in preserving the privacy and secrecy of the heroine's misdeeds, thus veiling them from public knowledge and shame. Only the reader, like God and the narrator, sees all.

### GUILE: THE MOBILITY OF THE TRAPPED UNDERDOG

In a sex-segregated society, it is ironically the woman's space that is inviolable, not the man's. Whereas women, albeit covered in their veils, have access to a man's world, men do not enjoy reciprocal rights of "intrusion" in the women's quarters. In this protected and forbidden space, women exchange ideas freely, joke and share gossip with abandon, tell stories, relish rumors. They play music and games, they dance, they offer and receive advice and support, they develop tactics and invent strategies, and above all they discuss men. This exclusively female space symbolizes a formidable source of power in a sex-segregated society. The power is hidden, invisible, subversive, but its tentacles are long, its impact deep. No wonder it mystifies those who are barred from it. No wonder it scares men. Fearing this power, men try to prevail over it. "The whole Muslim organization of social interactions and spatial configurations can be understood in terms of the woman's . . . power to deceive and defeat men, not by force, but by cunning and intrigue," writes Fatima Mernissi (under the pseudonym Fatna Saba). "The social order then appears as an attempt to subjugate her power and neutralize its disruptive effects."[30]

Persian literature, like Persian culture, illustrates the way in which men engage continually in devising defensive strategies to protect themselves across the sexual divide. They advise each other again and again to keep a check on women lest they lose control over them, to watch what the women do lest they take over. They view all womankind as manipulators, potential aggressors whose attraction is irresistible and whose power to deceive is limitless. It seems that women's guile, unlike their bodies and voices, cannot be put under lock and key. It refuses to be neatly segregated or restrained. It slips out of the women's quarters, trespasses over walls, reaches past veils, and penetrates through the silences.

When women deploy guile, they are portrayed as dangerous emotional manipulators. When men use it, they are considered clever; their ruses are perceived as signs of imagination, mental agility, creativity, and intelligence. In the former case, guile expresses the feline manipulation of the powerless; in the latter case, it reflects the strategic brilliance of the powerful. Although some of the most popular heroes of Persian literature and folklore—such as Rustam, Yusuf, Khosrow, and Ramin—frequently rely on tricks, they are never presented as liars or crooks. Their cunning is usually admired and is a sign of their wisdom. Iranian heroes have never hesitated to use trickery. "The ability to trick the enemy," according to Dick Davis, is one of the overt values promoted in *Shahnameh*. As a matter of fact, "the epithet of one of the heroes is the equivalent of Odysseus' 'guileful.'"[31]

Such Iranian heroes, however, are not presented as run-of-the-mill crooks. Their cunning is not portrayed as inherently masculine, but it is often justified and even valorized. In other words, although trickery is a trait associated with the deceiver, a man may need to keep its arrow in his quiver to use in cases of emergency. And if in these rare cases men are portrayed as guileful in the negative sense, the reader is reminded that guile is not part and parcel of *mardaneghi* (manliness). When Jami recounts Yusuf's brothers' plot to kill him, to "deceive their father," and to plunge recklessly "headlong into the well of calamity, without ever considering the depths of their treachery," he is quick to meditate on the manliness that is presented as the contrary of fraud. Unlike these atypical villains and ill-doers, "Javanmardan," the manly men, he interjects, "are free from the bondage of self and guile."[32] In referring to Sohrab's tragic death, scholar Islami Nudushan acknowledges that "the father had to resort to tricks and deceitfulness, even to lies, to kill his own son. This is indeed the only shameful blemish that stains Rustam's long and illustrious life." Rustam's guile, in spite of its tragic consequence, is not equated with that of all men all the time. It is presented as an isolated event, an anomaly of sort, an antithesis of manliness, an aberration in the hero's otherwise "illustrious" life. "Rustam," proposes Nudushan, "kills his own son acting out of guile rather than manliness."[33]

*Qayd,* the Arabic and Persian word for guile, and its numerous synonyms, although not gendered words, are frequently "feminized."[34] It is often associated with the natural or at least the socialized woman. For centuries, men, such as the two mythic kings in the frame story of *One Thousand and One Nights,* have come to the frightening realization that even the jinns are powerless before womanly guile. Together they have screeched in anguish: "Allah! Allah! Women's guile is great."

The reiterated indictment of woman as cunning is a token of the pervasiveness and deeply ingrained nature of this attitude. An example can be found in 'Aziz of Egypt, the husband who decries his wife Zulaikha's deceitful nature. He reproaches her treachery bitterly: "I should have known that this was one of your tricks," he says in anger. To be fair to him, what else can one expect a cuckolded husband to say when his wife has fallen in love with his slave? But the accusations do not stop there; the poet, Jami, substitutes all women for this particular woman and continues smoothly, "Truly, female guile is heartbreaking."[35] There is no shortage of such authorial interventions in Persian literature. After portraying Sudabeh as a vindictive and wicked stepmother whose mind is "a mass of jostling schemes," Ferdowsi, in the midst of the heartrending legend of Seyavash, takes a moment to remind his readers that Sudabeh, in fact, is no exception to the rule: "All our privations come from women's wiles," he says. "And if you hear this story to the end / You'll see it's best that you believe this fact."[36] Superimpose the traits of one woman upon any woman, and you will find another latent example of womanly guile ready to be yanked out of the closet.

The wily female characters of Persian literature have their counterparts in religion. In Zoroastrianism, Jahi, better known as Jeh, manages to trick even Ahriman, who, after lying prostrate for three thousand years, shatters the existing ideal order.[37] Eve is treated not much better than Jeh. As the temptress and the seducer, Eve is viewed as the prototype of womanly guile. She carries the burden of responsibility for tricking Adam and causing their subsequent expulsion from paradise. Mother of humankind, she also becomes the mother of their misery. Eve is remarkably exonerated from sole culpability in the Qur'an, though. Adam and Eve are tempted together and partake of the forbidden fruit together.[38] Satan murmurs suggestions to them both, and "So the two of them ate of it."[39] Disobeying the divine commandment, they both are equally responsible for their fall. Tempted together, they are equally guilty of sinning; both are equally punished by God, and both are equally forgiven when they repent. Eve is thus neither the first sinner nor the eternal deceiver. And yet, despite being vindicated by God in the Qur'an itself, Eve is nevertheless held accountable in popular narratives in Iran. She is traditionally blamed for cajoling her husband and remains the schemer, as have her daughters for generations.

Summarizing this catalog of blame in an interview, Mohammad Reza Shah Pahlavi told a bewildered Orania Fallaci, "All I can say is that women, when they govern, are much harsher than men. Much crueler. Much more bloodthirsty." He then proceeded to cross continents and centuries, transcend geographical and temporal boundaries, and generalize from references to a few women in the world of politics to all women at all times and all places. "I'm citing facts, not opinions," he continued confidently. "You're heartless when you have power. Think of Catherine de Medeci, Catherine of Russia, Elizabeth I of England. Not to mention your Lucrezia Borgia, with her poisons and intrigues. You're schemers, you're evil. All of you."[40]

It is not only men—kings, writers, clerics, philosophers—who equate femininity with trickery. The accusation materializes in other unlikely places and through the mouths of women themselves. "A woman doesn't have to tell the truth," writes gender-bending author Shahrnush Parsipur in her novel *The Dog and the Long Winter*, "because she is a woman. That is her nature."[41] Even the iconoclastic Forugh Farrokhzad, who challenged feminine definitions and spaces, speaks of feminine deviousness in the poem "Confession." Moving with fluid ease from the particular to the general, from a personal confession to a collective trait, she refers to the female capacity for treachery.

> O, don't ever believe
> My heart is one with my tongue
> All I said were lies, a pack of lies
> I never told you what I desired.

Later in the same poem, she reiterates the age-old association of guile with women: "Surely, you have heard it / Women say yes in their heart but have no on their lips," she warns. "They never reveal their frailty / They are secretive, reticent, guileful."[42]

The feminization of guile is, of course, not unique to Iranian culture. The wiles of women are notorious worldwide. In the words of Aristotle, women are "more jealous, more querulous, more apt to scold and strike, more void of shame and self-respect, more false of speech, more deceptive."[43] Lady Murasaki dedicated a whole chapter of one of Japan's earliest and greatest novels to the "wiles of women."[44] Rousseau believed that "this peculiar cleverness given to the fair sex is a very equitable compensation for their lesser share of strength, a compensation without which women would be not man's companion but his slave."[45] Mary Wollstonecraft observed in A Vindication of the Rights of Women that servility in women produces a propensity to "govern their tyrants by sinister tricks."[46] And Maureen Dowd of the New York Times more recently maintained that "women have learned, through long years of being subordinated to men in the workplace, to use their wiles and wits to maneuver past eruptions of male libido."[47] Whether guile is viewed as the essence of womanhood or as an acquired trait or necessary strategy, it is feminized.

## POLARIZED NOTIONS OF WOMANHOOD

Regardless of whether this subtle tool is defined as admirable or reprehensible, it has been honed and fully developed by the figure of the nanny in Persian literature. The nanny has always known what Machiavelli only confirmed: that guile is the ultimate means of maintaining covert power. In the segregated world of

Persian romances, it is inevitable that no love story can unfold in a culturally acceptable way without the nanny's guile. Acting as a mediator between the lovers and, more significantly, between the reader and the text, the nanny claims some of the traditionally masculine privileges by wandering back and forth between the two separated worlds of men and women. She also intervenes between two opposing, almost irreconcilable concepts of femininity. Fraudster that she is, she is assigned the role of the counterideal woman: the heroine's double, her shadow, the personification of her sinful and lustful side. She forfeits her personal identity, security, and reputation for the heroine and her love story.[48] Even as the narrator uses the nanny to tell his story, however, she ironically has to endure his sanctimonious protestations that she is a witch, a guileful harlot, a wicked transgressor, a trickster. In spite of all her mistreatment and unkind neglect, she utters no recrimination. As soon as her services become redundant and her presence superfluous, she graciously disappears from the text and the plot like snow on a sunny winter day.

Authors of classical Persian romances relied on a phalanx of nannies because without them the binary notion of womanhood as simultaneously good and bad could not be sustained. Nor could the status quo, which requires that a woman remain inaccessible and seductive at the same time.

These clever, mobile women, these boundary crossers who serve as guardians of the very system from which they tempt us to escape, are replete with paradoxes. They express all the contradictions within a sex-segregated society. Although they often sanction and sometimes even promote disobedience and temporary immunity from traditional rules of modesty, they also help to preserve and to reiterate the prevailing norms. They honor the system even as they betray it, offering a safe haven to both heroine and reader from the very dangers they instigate. They mock even as they reinforce, reinscribe the accepted codes of behavior as they resist them. They are consequently symbols of both power and powerlessness and, as such, become an expression of and a safety valve for the inconsistencies within the system.

Although Persian romances subvert social conventions, they ultimately uphold gendered allocation of space. They may suggest ways of breaking the codes, but they neither challenge nor reject gender relations. They do not question the existing arrangements between the sexes. In fact, they maintain the traditional divisions of space in sex-segregated societies, upholding the idea of a private sphere for women and a public sphere for men. The license accorded to nannies in classical literature thus did not undermine the status quo, but merely allowed the authors of romances to make use of class and age differences to normalize gender transgression and to explore and portray passionate relationships.

The plausibility of the plot is therefore dependent on these women's mobility. In the long run, however, their powers are relative and their deployment merely utilitarian. They are vulnerable to the author's infinite narrative power. All these romances ultimately reinscribe the centrality of the heterosexual couple. Marriage provides the narrative closure for the vast majority of them, and modesty and domesticity remain the central tenet of their dominant value system. Even such lustful women as Zulaikha and Vis are transformed and become embodiments of the "sin" that must be subjugated to the penance of restrained sexuality. However subtle and resourceful the nanny, therefore, the future of all these heroines lies within well-defined walls. Whatever boundaries may have been broken, whatever heresies these subtle mediators might have committed over the course of the plot, the end is always orthodox. Despite the heroines' trespasses, domesticity is the destiny of the overwhelming majority of Persian heroines. Their love affairs are simply interludes in the dominant theme of marriage.

And the nanny knows it. No matter how influential she is, no matter how indispensable to the plot, she is aware that at the end of the day she is perfectly expendable. And, indeed, she is often discarded quite unceremoniously; she is snuffed out and eradicated from the story rather callously. One might even argue that the nanny is mistreated from the get-go.

To start with, she is unindividuated, commodified: she is lumped in with a large and anonymous mob of nannies in Persian literature and merely reduced to her literary services. She often doesn't even have a name. The need to identify her as a character is overshadowed by her function. Her label fixes her in a system of relationships in which her role rather than her individual distinctiveness is what matters. Once this role has been performed and she has played her part, she is dropped from the story. Once her mission is fulfilled, her existence is unimportant and her history unrecorded. She has no other function except to be a go-between, and when this role is no longer necessary, she can be disposed of with ease. What eventually happens to this messenger and facilitator of love, we do not know. As soon as she becomes superfluous to the plot, she disappears into silence and oblivion, exiled from the text and the story.

Perhaps the erasure of the nanny from the narrative is the price she has to pay for having redeemed women from silence and invisibility. Perhaps another intermediary is needed; perhaps an ultimate go-between is required if the nanny herself is to be redeemed. Only the reader's imagination can intervene to save her at this point. But perhaps her final scheme is to survive between the lines in spite of her forced banishment from the official narrative. Although the writer has maligned, neglected, and finally disposed of the nanny in this uncaring fashion, she is not going to vanish from the text as easily as may at first appear. She is not going to lend credibility to the story and then quietly slip out of sight and mind. She is forevermore the third party in classical Persian romances and as such is indispensable to anyone who wants to write about love in a sex-segregated society.[49]

Just as Eve's presumed guile allowed Adam to discover his virility, the nanny's guile and creative mediation allow authors to achieve their literary goals. Although she remains the treacherous saboteur of morality, in none of these stories does she derive any benefits for herself. Her interferences are not in the pursuit of financial gains, material advantages, or job promotions. She does not serve her own self-interest. And in spite of often being subjected to harsh criticism, embarrassment, harassment, and even beatings, she is a fascinating character in her own right. Her subtle attempts to mingle categories and to cross the rigid divide of gender suggest—even if with tongue in cheek—that change is necessary in gendered categories and spaces. Whether motivated by devotion to the heroine or by some unacknowledged resistance within her own psyche, the nanny is a brave, adventurous, and quick-witted woman. She is an explorer who ventures into forbidden territories, creating literary, sexual, and textual possibilities. She is the worldly-wise woman who is more interested in mediation than in wars, in conflict resolution than in fighting, in love than in separation. Viewed from this perspective, the nanny is wise rather than sly, altruistic rather than cunning, an enabler rather than a cheat. As the ultimate mediator, she reminds us that the line of demarcation between craft and craftiness, between art and artifice, can be a thin one indeed. More important, perhaps, she registers in her own special way the futility of polarized perspectives and divided spaces.

# 2

# THE BONDS OF BEAUTY

*Immobilizing the Ideal Woman in Iranian Literature*

What is this, behind this veil,
Is it ugly, is it beautiful?
——SYLVIA PLATH, "A Birthday Present"

We were revisionists; we revised ourselves.
——MARGARET ATWOOD, *The Handmaid's Tale*

## REGULATING WOMEN'S LOOKS

In the sweltering heat of a summer day in Tehran in 1989, a female member of the morality police stopped me even though my hair was covered by a large head scarf and my body was cloaked in a long, loose tunic. Having returned home for the first time after the revolution, I did not fully grasp the strictness with which the new dress code was imposed on women, nor did I understand the power wielded by these arbiters of women's behavior and appearance. I did not know that such inquiries, like the one she was about to make, were not to be taken lightly. So when the woman looked me directly in the eyes and contemptuously asked, "Why are you wearing makeup in public?" I told her I did not have fresh makeup on. Proud of my answer and oblivious to the gravity of the situation, I also shrugged my shoulders with reciprocal contempt.

I knew Islam allowed—in fact, encouraged—women to beautify themselves, especially for their husbands. I instinctively had taken refuge in that prerogative, not knowing other women had used the same trick before me. Primed by her previous experiences, my interrogator leaned forward, gesticulating furiously. She adjusted her chador with her left hand, showed more of her angry face and long

50

teeth, drew a crumpled tissue paper swiftly from her pocket, brought it to her big mouth, and spat on it unceremoniously. Like a deer paralyzed by the glaring headlights of a speedily approaching car, I was stunned. All I could do was to follow the movement of her hand. Not knowing where exactly that soggy piece of tissue was going to land, I watched as she brought it up to my face and proceeded to scrub my cheek. I was drenched in disgusted rage and sweat. Had it not been for my father's intervention and his pleas on my behalf, I could easily have landed in jail, my crime glowing red, like fresh blood, on the tattered tissue paper.

Since the 1979 Revolution, accounts of harassment carried out against women in Iran are abundant. From essays such as "Lipstick Politics" and "Lipstick Revolution" to books such as *Lipstick Jihad,* there have been numerous reports of such incidents on the streets of Iran.[1] With varying degrees of intensity, women are humiliated, flogged, jailed, and treated like criminals for wearing makeup in public or for violating the obligatory dress code. Worse yet, their criminalization is turned into a spectacle in order to control the streets and to instill fear in those women who do not conform to the Islamic Republic's gendered disciplinary apparatus and step out of its firmly guarded boundaries. And yet the Qur'an does not contain a single verse suggesting a penalty—whether corporal or spiritual, public or private, celestial or terrestrial—for a woman who refuses to veil herself. As a matter of fact, if there were any prohibitions imposed on women in the early decades of Islam, it was to prevent marginalized groups, slave girls, and prostitutes from wearing the veil, which was considered a mark of distinction.

Since the mid–nineteenth century, the female body has been increasingly used as a battlefield, a metaphor, an emblem by one Iranian government or political movement after another in the name of Islam or nationalism, modernity or tradition, freedom or security, piety or progress. Each regime in turn has sought to impose its ideology on the people by means of its own ideal image of womanhood. Ironically, as a result of Iran's mandatory unveiling act of 1936, women were humiliated, harassed, bullied, and denied the right to enter public streets if they did not take off their veils. Women who resisted the ordinance had their veils yanked off and cut to pieces in front of their terrified and humiliated eyes in the streets. This public and at times brutal unveiling of women was viewed as an indispensable reformatory program needed to discipline proper and properly attired modern citizens. In speech after speech, Reza Shah Pahlavi and his all-male cabinet reiterated the narrative, blaming the veil as the cause of women's oppression. They portrayed its wearers as obsolete, uneducated, and embarrass-ingly backward obstacles to modernity. Confronted with the mandate to remove their veil, stigmatized and bullied for wearing it, women were denied access to the streets. Soon after the establishment of the Islamic Republic of Iran, women began to be punished for being unveiled or "improperly" veiled. The veil has been deemed necessary for building a harmonious social order built on "equal" but "distinct" rights. It has been elevated as a symbol of religious piety, an icon of purity, moral salvation, and political self-determination. It has been turned into the flag of an Islamic utopia.

Regardless of one's personal view about the veil, it is important to ask why women's appearance in public has provoked such extraordinary reactions in this country over the past century and a half. Why, during a period that has witnessed at least two revolutions, undergone as many coups, given rise to the tumultu-ous birth of two religions (the Babi and the Baha'i faiths), most of which have unleashed bloody social upheavals in their train, has the veil assumed so much significance? Why has the attempt to "restore order" revolved around women's looks and the space they occupy throughout this time of chaos and change? Instead of relying on education, persuasion, and, more important, respect for individuals' personal choice, why has one government after another spent so much effort, so many resources, and such a flood of words and laws to enforce a rigorous dress code on women in the streets?

Both the shah's unveiling decree and the ruling clerics' reveiling laws have been imposed on women. This fact alone betrays much about the country's politi-cal culture. Although many outspoken and enlightened individuals—male and female—have spoken out against such coercive measures, the ingrained gender hierarchies that dominate Iranian society have not facilitated a radical trans-formation in the country's public policies. The veil has continued to maintain a strong grip on the collective psyche and people's imaginations. What it conceals and what it reveals, when the female body is exposed and where, by whom, and why are questions that still raise intense emotions.

## BORDERLESS PURSUIT OF BEAUTY

The uproar over women's appearance in public can be viewed as one conflict among many shaking the foundations of the Islamic world in general and of

Iran in particular. It can be interpreted as a calculated scheme to fight against all reform movements that advocate women's basic human rights. It can be analyzed as the conflict between the forces of modernity and the forces of countermodernity, the push-and-pull syndrome of a society undergoing profound change. It can quite simply be described as a straightforward power struggle between monarchical and clerical rule, on the one hand, and the people's will, on the other. In the West, however, the mandatory unveiling act has often been deemed as a progressive act, whereas the compulsory reveiling has been vilified and condemned for a wide variety of reasons. Nancy Etcoff, for instance, sees the latter as a confirmation of how "Islamic countries like Iran" deny women even "the power of their looks." The author of the best-selling *Survival of the Prettiest: The Science of Beauty* voices a widely held opinion when she denounces the veil as a barrier to women's desire to be beautiful. Arguing that beauty is "one of the ingredients" that goes into a woman's "natural power base," Etcoff invites her readers to "consider societies where women have the least power and freedom—Islamic countries like Iran, for example. Women there are veiled and covered from head to foot. That is how the men control them, by denying them access to the power of their looks."[2]

In contrast, Deborah Rodriguez, the author of another best-selling memoir, who founded and taught in a beauty school in post-Taliban Afghanistan, acknowledges the centrality of women's beauty in that country. "In Afghanistan, a beautiful woman is worth her weight in gold," she writes in *Kabul Beauty School*. Rodriguez holds that "except for during the Taliban years, female beauty has always been treasured in Afghanistan. Beauticians have always had an important and honored role in enhancing beauty—especially during the parties and gatherings surrounding a wedding." Even under the Taliban's rule of terror, women jeopardized life and limb to operate and visit beauty salons. But Rodriguez sees a darker purpose to the practices of beautification in this Islamic country. Far from being a means of power, Afghan women's desire to be beautiful is, for her, just another indication of their collective victimhood and lower status. Unlike Etcoff, who defines beautification as women's desire to gain access to their "natural power base," Rodriguez sees it as a limiting factor, a constraint in the lives of Afghan women. Although women spend hours trying to enhance their appearances, "paradoxically," she notes, "this has to do with the lack of value that women have in this culture" rather than with accessing their "natural power base."[3]

Beautification practices can clearly be acts of defiance and subversion as much as mechanisms of social control and docility. They can empower and disempower women.[4] They can generate rewards and incur liabilities.[5] From the first face decoration to brass coils placed around necks to wooden plates inserted into lips; from excised or reconstructed genitals to mutilated feet and high-heeled shoes; from chadors and *abayas* to bikinis and power suits; from surgical scalpels to laser beams; from herbal formulas to dolphin fat, silicon, and Botox—the pursuit of beauty has transcended religious and geographic boundaries. From tribal Africa to Sung China, from ancient Egypt to imperial Iran, from modern-day New York to twenty-first-century Buenos Aires, the female body has often been subjected to discomfort in a bid to conform to ideals of beauty. Women have had their bodies pierced, tattooed, pinned, tucked, toned, trained, implanted, concealed, exposed, reconstructed. And today, thanks to cosmetic and medical advances, "not one part of a woman's body is left untouched, unaltered. No feature or extremity is spared the art, or pain, of improvement. From head to toe, every feature of a woman's face, every section of her body, is subject to modification, alteration."[6] The female body has become more and more malleable—"cultural plastic," in the words of Susan Bordo.[7] And it is a journey without end: even the most beautiful woman can become even more beautiful.

Iran is no exception to the rule, and Iranian women, like women elsewhere, are in search of a more and more accessible but less and less attainable beauty. In spite of the Islamic Republic's draconian measures to regulate women's looks, Iran is now considered one of the plastic surgery hubs of the Middle East: "Tehran has become the nose-job capital of the world, with 70,000 rhinoplasty operations a year."[8] Women reshape and resculpt their bodies in unprecedented numbers.[9] They have also turned the obligatory dress code into a fashion statement, a spectacle, a colorful theater staged on the streets for all to watch. With highlighted hair cascading from beneath their colorful scarves, their faces and nails, which need not be covered, made up with a vengeance, mandatory yet stylish tunics, many women have given beauty and makeup political meanings. This concern with female beauty, even if taken to new heights now, is nothing new in Iran. "For centuries, a woman's beauty has been an essential component of Iranian culture," notes *New York Times* reporter Elaine Sciolino. "'Kill me, but make me beautiful,' one Iranian proverb goes. 'The beautiful face soothes the tired heart and opens the closed door,' goes another."[10] Feminine beauty is one of the centerpieces of attention in Iranian literature, painting, and philosophy. On the one hand, it has served as a metaphor for and a "testimony" to divine beauty; on the other hand it has been seen as proof of the illusory temptations of the physical world. Its transitory and ephemeral nature has been praised and blamed, lauded and lamented. Literary metaphors describing attributes of beauty abound in classical as well as contemporary Persian literature. Fatema Soudavar Farmanfamaian tells us that one nineteenth-century author, "Sharaf al-Din Rumi, enumerates [these metaphors] in fully nineteen chapters, each of which is devoted to a specific part of the face or body."[11]

## THE BEAUTIFICATION OF FEMININE IMMOBILITY

Beauty is a cultural construct and lies in the eye of the beholder. Standards of beauty are subjective and historical; they change from one person to another, from one era to another, from one place to another. But, interestingly enough, despite all the personal, geographic, and historical variations, the aesthetic sensibility of Iranians, like that of many other peoples, has often equated feminine beauty with enclosure and constrained mobility. For centuries, the ideal woman maintained a closed-in existence that did not intrude or merge with the outside world. She was a person of minimal transactions, contracted to a narrow space. She covered her body, guarded her honor (and that of her family), controlled her desires, averted her gaze, measured her words, and remained in her proper place. She conducted herself with quiet poise and in a dignified manner. The movement of such a woman, like her voice, is controlled, confined, contained. She erects visible and invisible walls of separation around her by limiting her contact with the outside world. She has *hojb-o-haya* or *sharm*, which, as Salman Rushdie puts it, is a "short word, but one containing encyclopedias of nuance," covering the spectrum from shame to "embarrassment, discomfiture, decency, modesty, shyness, the sense of having an ordained place in the world, and other dialects of emotions for which English has no counterparts."[12]

A woman who has *hojb-o-haya* maintains distance. When in public, she claims as little space as possible. Head lowered, shoulders hunched, neck stiff, eyes modestly cast down, she blurs the outlines of her body and squeezes herself into a narrow space. She sinks into anonymity, disappears into her own shadow, fades into the background, remains silent, becomes generic. Walking in small and measured steps that do not give her body the right to stretch out in space, holding herself close so that her hands do not swing freely in the air, she is the epitome of grace and poise, an aestheticized and eroticized image of self-containment. Classical and modern Persian literature abounds in eulogies about such a woman. Amir, the male protagonist in Shahrnush Parsipur's novella *Women Without Men* echoes an age-old model when he defines his ideal mate as "excessively beautiful"—that is, a woman who is "gracefully silent, withdrawn, reserved, kind, industrious, diligent, modest, chaste, solemn, and neat. She wears her *chador* and when in public always casts her eyes down. She blushes all the time."[13]

Many of the synonyms for *beautiful* in the Persian language do not focus solely on a woman's exterior and appearance. *Maqboul, jamil, zibandeh,* and *shayeste,* among many others, are terms richly infused with the expectation of compliance with the norms. The equation of feminine beauty with modesty, moral rectitude, inner strength, diffidence, discretion, and inertness is not unique to one protagonist or one period or genre. Major and minor, male and female, young and old writers and poets have paid their tribute to a nonthreatening, nonaggressive, static sort of feminine beauty. Little wonder, then, if for centuries the veil was considered a mark of gentility, refinement, chastity, purity, and class distinction; it indicated respectable femininity, noble class, refined culture, moral superiority, and immaculate beauty.[14] It was not necessarily the expression of a loss of power, a deficit of control, or a denial of the body. Nor was it driven solely by religion, much less by a uniformly Islamic edict. The Old Testament includes the veil among its list of such ornaments as bracelets, earrings, rings, nose jewels, perfume boxes, and girdles. As a punishment for the haughtiness of the daughters of Zion, the Book of Isaiah warns against the loss of these fineries. If women do not behave themselves, the Lord will take away "the mirrors, and the fine linen, and the turbans and the veils" (3:16–23).

### LIKE A PEARL IN A SHELL

Graffiti, billboards, and propaganda posters around Tehran and other Iranian cities declare that a woman modestly covered is like a pearl within a shell. She is the pearl, the veil her shell, her protection, her passport to becoming a treasure and being treasured. Although the Islamic Republic is turning an aesthetic predisposition into a political mandate, the fact remains that a properly covered body has been invested for a long time with the notion of the cherished and the beautiful in the moral sense, whereas "nakedness"—that is, not being fully covered—has been seen as a sign of moral laxity, rampant sexuality, and unattractiveness. Consider clothing. The function of dress in Iran is not to display the body, but to cover it. In Persian, the verb *pushidan*, "to dress," does not mean to decorate and to adorn, but "to cover up" and to "conceal from view." Perhaps it is the allure of the hidden or "contained" body that conveys the illusion of beauty to the viewer; perhaps whatever is half seen is perceived as infinitely more attractive (and more threatening) than what is fully exposed. Perhaps this particular form of appeal, which depends largely on suggestion, inference, implication, and the power of the imagination, is a necessary means of implicating and engaging the viewer's interest. Perhaps the tension, the creative substitution, the active expectation and engagement on the part of the observer, without whose participation beauty cannot be said to exist at all, is precisely what creates desire.[15]

Whatever the reasons—and there are many of them—being covered is not only a sartorial expression of the ideal of Iranian womanhood (and manhood), but also the ideal state in Islam. According to the Qur'an, Allah is covered not with one veil, but with many. The Ka'bah, the house of God in Saudi Arabia, is veiled, draped with a cloth (Kiswah) on which are embroidered verses from the Qur'an.[16] Prophet Mohammed, according to the Qur'an, is "wrapped in his mantle" (74:1). The Islamic paradise is an enclosed garden surrounded by a wall of celestial mountains. Adam and Eve's bodies, in their prelapsarian state, are covered in the Islamic Eden. According to the creation story in the Qur'an, it was only after disobeying God's commandment that the primordial couple were punished by being stripped naked and expelled from paradise. Verse 115 of chapter 20 reads: "He brought your parents out of the Garden, stripping them of their garments to show them their shameful parts." And again, chapter 27, verse 7, proclaims: "Children of Adam! Let not Satan tempt you as he brought your parents out of the Garden stripping them of their garments to show them their shameful parts." Nakedness was therefore a divine punishment, which might explain why the revered historian Abu Jaffar Tabari (838–923) believed that even the snake, which was originally a "covered" and "four-legged splendid riding animal resembling the Bactrian camel,"[17] was punished for his deceitfulness by being condemned to slither away "naked," on his belly.

The long-term consequences of this equation between preciousness, elegance, beauty, and the veil can be seen in a variety of cultural contexts in Iran, from literature, cinema, and architecture to gait, gaze, and body language; it is reflected in methods of communication and in rhetorical devices; it is expressed through aesthetic and erotic sensibilities. The veil has become far more than a piece of cloth covering a woman's body or face in this culture. "Iranian art is far more concerned with covering and concealing things than revealing them," says film director Bahram Beiza'i.[18] "I want to create the type of cinema that shows by not showing," he states elsewhere. "This is very different from most movies nowadays, which are not literally pornographic but are in essence pornographic, because they show so much that they take away a possibility of imagining things for ourselves."[19] Even objects are not immune to the sweep of this propensity. Houra, one of the protagonists in the 2000 movie *The Day I Became a Woman* by a female Iranian director, Marzieh Makhmalbaf, captures this notion in a nutshell when, after a shopping spree, she objects to the purchase of a "transparent" glass teapot. It is the one item she wants adamantly to return. Why? Because "the teapot is naked, exposed, and thus shameless."

### THE PROMISE OF AN ENCLOSED GARDEN

Persian literature, like Persian cinema, is full of mysterious enclosures, hidden pleasure gardens, and promises concealed behind walls. In story after story and poem after poem, we see how the veil clasps the body close, only to unwind again, concealing and revealing simultaneously, lending an aura of mystery and promise to its wearer. Even some of the most steadfast opponents and self-proclaimed enemies of the veil, who view it as a cultural obstacle to social transformation and modernity, still deploy it for such seduction purposes.

One such example is an untitled poem by Iraj Mirza (1874–1926), well known for his scathing, antiveiling stand at a time when condemnation of the practice from every point of view was in no short supply. This much anthologized 127-line poem relates a satirical, quasi-pornographic tale of a chance encounter between a man and a veiled woman. It begins with the sensuous description of the woman's body undulating beneath the veil as she walks down a bustling street. The narrator is enticed by the mystique of the veil, now inviting, now forbidding, now revealing a teasing glimpse, now coyly concealing. His eyes, like a movie camera, record a series of stolen peeks, snapshots seen beneath the veil of parts of the woman's body: her lips, a corner of her cheek, the curve of her chin.[20] She is tantalizingly out of reach and seductively available. Her veil blocks and invites his gaze, repels and excites him at once.

Although the man is the observer, the woman is the one who decides what he will see. He is the voyeur, but she commands the illusions she gives him. She knows her power to provoke, to stimulate, and to arouse. She choreographs her seducer's imagination. Sure enough, unable to control himself, he, like a robot, approaches the veiled woman's shimmering, fluid figure. He pretends he has a message for her from an unnamed source and manages to lead her from the public street into his private chambers. And once there he attempts to seduce her with nuts, poetry, and flattering compliments. "God has created feminine beauty for the eyes of men," he tells her, using the age-old clichés of seduction. "Roses are not harmed by the nightingale's lament and love," he adds, with bland self-assurance. Although he identifies himself with the nightingale's boundless love, not for her the passive reticence of the rose. She has stepped off the street and entered the walled confines of his rooms for his sake, not hers; he is the one who needs the protection of this enclosed world to seduce her openly. But her condition remains unchanged off the street as well as on. She is unrelenting, at least for now. She rejects the man's impotent attempts at persuasion. She holds fast to her chastity as well as to her veil, rejecting his entreaties in no uncertain terms. "Get lost," she tells him, boasting of her inaccessibility. "My brother-in-law was desperate to see me unveiled," she says smugly. "My husband didn't allow him."[21]

The man is persistent in his attempts, however. Ignoring the woman's moral harangue, he approaches nearer, playfully squeezing her arm. To his surprise, she does not resist or fight him off. He continues his advances with increasing boldness till they are finally making love—she with no less enthusiasm than himself. Although she proves to be a woman of "easy virtue," she manages never to let go of her veil, keeping it wrapped tightly round her. In this scene of seduction and passionate lovemaking, it is not quite clear which the man enjoys most: "penetrating" the veil or the veiled woman. "Hold on tightly to your veil," he commands his partner, who is in his view "sweet as sugar and candy."

The nameless woman may keep her body veiled with willful consistency, but the poet unveils her on the page. He gives a detailed and graphic description of her body, using progressively lewder language to do so. The earlier suspense created by his rhetorical dance of the Seven Veils is followed by a veritable orgy on the page as the explicit nature of Iraj Mirza's vocabulary breaks all visual and textual taboos. But despite lavishing his verbal dexterity on the sexual encounter, the poet offers his readers precious little in the end besides anatomical details. The man is totally cheated of knowing this woman who holds on to the veil before, during, and after sex. His ignorance of her identity when she leaves him is a stark irony.

There is a dramatic shift of tone in this poem when the lovemaking ends. The narrator's pornographic fantasy is transformed into a lecture about hypocrisy when the woman leaves him and goes back to the street. The lascivious seducer metamorphoses into a pontificating moralist. Although he is hardly the best person to discuss the theme of chastity and has few qualifications to be the arbiter of sexual morality, he condemns the woman who clung to her veil with such tenacity and accuses her of outright depravity. There is no hint in his self-righteous tone or in the conclusions he reaches about the woman's lack of virtue concerning his own role or responsibility for this state of affairs. There is no admission either that he may have felt cheated in the end.[22] Once she steps out of the room, the woman becomes hideous in the poet's eyes. The postcoital transformation from beauty to ugliness is radical. Although the woman was the epitome of loveliness before, when she was veiled "from head to foot" in the street, after sexual conquest in the privacy of the bedchamber, she becomes a "loulou," the hideous cannibal monster invoked by adults to scare children. She is a "ghoul-e biyaban" (devil of the desert), "karih" (hideous), a "shalgam dar jawal" (turnip in a sack), and a "boghcheh" (walking bundle). Like "all veiled women," whom the poet condemns outright, she comes to epitomize the worst attributes of ignorance, backwardness, ugliness, and sexual permissiveness.

But Iraj Mirza does not stop there. In the second half of the poem, he reverses the traditional association of feminine beauty with enclosure. Although he sustains the longstanding binaries (pure/tainted; saintly/tempting; virtuous/wicked; beautiful/ugly) and the expectation that women should be chaste and beautiful in order to please men remains as binding for him as ever, and though he does not challenge gender relations within the family or in society at large and continues to consider men's looks and chastity as irrelevant, he reconfigures standards of beauty and desirability. They are no longer a function of space and segregation. Iraj Mirza refuses, especially in the second half of the poem, to perpetuate the mystique of concealment and immobility as a prerequisite of feminine beauty and chastity. In step with new tastes and "modern" values, he wants women to be socially active, to pursue education and professional employment, to mingle with men.

## NOSTALGIA FOR SLEEPING BEAUTIES

But once women entered the public scene in increasing numbers in the mid–twentieth century, a new discourse on beauty began to take shape. To the society's traditional sector, the rupture of tradition was most visible and least tolerable in the area of women's increasing presence in masculine territories. Traditional-ists opposed desegregation on all levels and lamented women's abandonment of their divine duties within the family unit. Even the educated elite, who con-demned the subjugation of the female sex and denounced women's oppressive condition, seemed to have had a hard time sharing the public space with women. "So we really have given women only the right to parade themselves in public," wrote Jalal Al-e Ahmad in his much acclaimed and controversial 1952 book *A Plague from the West.* "We have drawn women, the preservers of tradition, fam-ily, and future generations, into vacuity, into the street. We have forced them into ostentation and frivolity, every day to freshen up and try a new style and wander around."[23] Parading in public, being ostentatious and frivolous, wearing makeup and gallivanting around town? Is that what desegregation was all about? What about women's expanded work and educational opportunities, their increased sense of self-empowerment, their access to new forms of mobility and subjectiv-ity? Oddly enough, at the time he wrote this book, Al-e Ahmad was married to Simin Daneshvar, Iran's foremost female novelist, an accomplished translator, and a much-beloved faculty member at the University of Tehran. Integration had allowed this highly talented woman to gain higher education; to move from Shi-raz, where she lived, to the capital in 1942 in order to enter Tehran University, the premier institution of higher education in the country; to earn a doctorate in literature in 1949; to develop her artistic potential; to fall in love with a man of her own choosing (Al-e Ahmad and Daneshvar met on a bus) and to marry him rather than a suitor chosen by her family; to be a breadwinner; to travel to America on a Fulbright scholarship for two years; to study creative writing at Stanford University, unaccompanied by her husband; and to produce masterpieces of modern Persian literature. This impressive list of accomplishments hardly qualifies as vacuous and inconsequential activity, as frivolous and ostentatious wandering around.

Al-e Ahmad was not alone in condemning "parading" women. There are numerous other examples. 'Ali Shari'ati, for example, who believed that in an earlier "Iran a woman was like a prisoner who had no access to schools, libraries, or to the public domain,"[24] called contemporary women "Western Dolls, empty inside, made-up and masked." He saw them as "a hodgepodge kind of women, assembled in local industries with a made in Europe sticker."[25] In his eyes, these mechanical dolls, these hybrids, were worthless, useless, senseless slaves of commercialism and consumerism, concerned only with their appearance. They personified the painful loss of cultural identity. Hard to control, always on the scene, they were the emblem of threatening changes in the spatial organization of gender relations in Iran. They disturbed "natural" or "divinely ordained" gender categories and challenged the very integrity of the privileged term *masculinity*, defined traditionally in its opposition to femininity. Blurred now were familiar boundaries, and blurred with them, too, was any sense of stability and comfort. Shari'ati and Al-e Ahmad's nostalgia for a past when authentic feminine identity and space were not compromised, when women were not parading in the streets, exemplifies the sense of loss that permeates the works of many mid-twentieth-century Iranian writers—men and women alike. Writers again and again depict this westernized woman as half naked, unrecognizable in her mask of makeup, and sexually promiscuous. An earnest expression of this bereavement can be seen in books written by a highly acclaimed fiction writer in contemporary Iran, Sadeq Hedayat (1903–51).[26]

Women are central figures in Hedayat's writing. Whether it is to admire them, to criticize them, to fantasize, demonize, abandon, or domesticate them, by whatever name they are called—lovers and muses, mothers and wives, sisters and daughters, young and old, rich and poor, literate and illiterate—he portrays them as either angelic or demonic. They are either statuesque women, doll-like and lifeless—literally sleeping beauties—or footloose and fancy-free women, loose-tongued and shrewish. Hedayat's ideal women owe much of their charm and allure to their inaccessibility, asexuality, and, above all, immobility. Although they are by no means alike in character or personality, there is a fundamental similarity beneath their many external differences. From the elusive "ethereal girl" in *The Blind Owl* to the statue/lover in the short story "The Doll behind the Curtain"—both carried around in coffinlike suitcases—to the many idealized heroines of pre-Islamic Iran, such as Parvin in *Parvin, Sassan's Daughter,* Shahrnaz in *Maziar,* Golshad in "Mongol's Shadow," all live in a state of suspended animation. They are passive, nonthreatening, silent, undemanding, and immobile—in fact, so immobile that they are throughout the story either in a state of enchanting sleep or dead, asleep forever. The counterideal women are conversely hard to pin down or carry in a suitcase. In their bearing, their physical and verbal demeanor, and the space they occupy, they transgress the permissible thresholds of a closed and closed-in individuality. Although more human in the sense of being less abstract and less symbolic than the ideal and idealized women, they are fickle, rapacious, guileful, and consumed with greed, lust, and an unquenchable appetite. Their desire, sexual or otherwise, like their body, refuses to be contained and controlled. Lakkateh in *The Blind Owl,* Robabeh in "The Legalizer," Alaviyeh Khanum in "The Pilgrimage," Zarrin Kolah in "The Woman Who Lost Her Man," and Aziz Agha in "Search of Mercy," to name only a few, lack a sense of dignity and devotion, honesty and decency, but, above all, they are hard to fix spatially and to confine within familiar boundaries.

Throughout his literary career, which covered a span of almost a quarter of a century and encompassed a wide array of genres and styles, Hedayat found his society stifling. Refusing to glorify or neglect what he saw as vile and cowardly, he portrayed with contempt a world pushing both women and men toward mediocrity and triviality. Refusing to adulate his characters of either sex, he believed both had lost spiritual integrity and had reached a high level of self-indulgence and hypocrisy. If he described many of his female characters as manipulative, uneducated, superstitious, unreliable, and mischievous, he did the same to many of his male protagonists as well, characterizing them as "shameless, stupid, and rotten."[27] If he called some women *lakkateh*—bitches, angels of death—he nicknamed some men *rajjaleh*—riff-raff, rabble, mouths "from which a wad of guts hung out" and connected "with their genitals."[28] The cheap lust of these unsavory characters, their graceless copulations, their banality and insincerity tormented and alienated Hedayat to a point where he felt trapped among "a tribe of brazen, money-grabbing blustering louts, sellers of conscience, hungry of eye and heart."²⁹ Disappointed and dissatisfied with the society around him—its corruption, its cruelty and perfidy—he sought and found his utopia in pre-Islamic, Zoroastrian Iran.³⁰ He criticized Islam as the corruptor of Iran and the oppressor of its women. As far as he was concerned, "Every aspect of life and thought, including women's condition, changed after Islam. Enslaved by men, women were confined to the home. Polygamy, injection of fatalistic attitude, mourning, sorrow and grief led people to seek solace in magic, witchcraft, prayer, and supernatural beings."³¹

To portray these two antagonistic worlds, however, to express his love of one and disgust for the other, Hedayat relied mainly on female protagonists as signs and symbols of pre- and post-Islamic periods. He chronicled two distinctly different periods in Iranian history by characterizing them through the presence of two types—two mutually exclusive images—of womanhood. His favorite heroines are the reincarnation of the memory of a bygone epoch, a fantasy of the Persian past, a personification of their creator's romantic pride in the Zoroastrian era. They are impossible in their perfection, unearthly, apparitions who materialize in a fleeting ecstatic moment, only to disappear quickly in the next. They are motivated by high ideals, know how to rebel against the aggression of the invading Islamic faith, assert their autonomy and independence through strife or suicide. Quite the reverse, the counterideal women have Islam, as Hedayat saw it, written all over their body and soul. They wear the veil, pray, fast, and deceive. And deceive they must in order to survive in their morally bankrupt society. Their victims are betrayed and disillusioned men, who try hard to fathom the underlying motives behind whatever women say or do, endlessly swinging between groundless suspicions and justified ones. These two archetypal women—the child-woman and the vamp, the virginal girl and the available slut, the victim and the evil-doer, the madonna and the whore—populate Hedayat's works and coexist side by side in the pages of his masterpiece *The Blind Owl*.

A haunting tale, this seminal novel is the ramblings of a sensitive man driven to isolation, opium addiction, and eventual madness and murder. He is a man torn between the past and the present, ambivalent toward sexuality, incapable of reconciling love as a factual experience and love as an imaginative ideal. In desperation, he builds a dream world that is closer to his needs and values. "I hope to create from the resources of my mind a drug which would soothe my tortured spirit."³² This imaginary world depends for its existence on the author's glorification of and reliance on the past: "Perhaps for the very reason that all the bonds which held me to the world of living people have been broken, the memories of the past take shape before my eyes" (52). The two unmistakably opposite women in *The Blind Owl*, too, belong to these two different universes. The anti-heroine, the "Bitch," is a "woman, whose face still bore the tooth marks of the old odds-and-ends man in the square" (116). Later in the novel, the reader learns that between his teeth, the old odds-and-ends man recited the "Arabic verses of the Koran" (116). Lakkateh prays in Arabic and wears "a cloak" (115), which Hedayat views as a strictly Islamic imposition.[33] Her counterpart, the ethereal girl, is unveiled and sports a pleated dress that reveals "the lines of her legs, her arms, her breasts—of her whole body" (20). "No," laments the narrator, "no, this was not the same person as I had known." He has a point. Although the two women share overlapping physical characteristics (both have Turkoman eyes and the same slim, misty body; both share the habit of biting the nail of their index finger; the mouth of each tastes like the stub end of a cucumber, acrid and bitter), one is a woman of yesteryear, the other is contemporary.

The ethereal girl, who is "one of the old inhabitants of the ancient city of Rey" (67) and whose portrait is painted on an "ancient vase," is buried on the bank of the Suran River. Lakkateh falls in this same river in her childhood. "Once when I was running after the bitch on the bank of the Suran her foot slipped and she fell into the water. The others pulled her out and took her behind the cypress tree to change her clothes. I followed them. They hung up a woman's veil as a screen in front of her" (79). Lakkateh's emergence behind the veil marks the end of her childhood. Refinement and love give way to frivolity and vulgarity. This veiled woman, this daily torment, "a solid woman with a head full of commonplace, practical ideas—a genuine woman" (115), is not the ethereal girl, who "no longer belongs to this mean world" (4). Ten times throughout the novel, Hedayat refers to the Suran River. As Elton Daniel aptly observes, this repeatedly mentioned river has "mystified many readers."[34] The historical novel *Parvin, Sassan's Daughter*, I believe, demystifies this recurring motif, which is key to understanding the metamorphosis of the ethereal girl into the Bitch. It is alongside this river in the region of Rey, writes Hedayat, that the last vestiges of opposition against the invading Arab army were demolished. It is alongside this river that Hedayat's highly idealized heroes and heroines of the past were defeated. "Iranians fought courageously till death," he proclaims with a mixture of pride and sorrow.[35] For him, the Suran River is the last bastion of opposition against Islam. It invokes the Iranians' heroic struggle and resistance, but also their downfall.

Innocence and beauty sink in the Suran River, and in their stead rise vileness and repulsion. The ethereal girl of *The Blind Owl* falls into and disappears in the Suran River, and in her place appears Lakkateh. From then on Lakkateh is no longer an object of love; she is a ruthless persecutor of it. Unlike the ethereal girl, who epitomizes purity, authenticity, gentleness, solace, and pride, Lakkateh is phony, lascivious, aggressive, and involved in all manner of dalliances. She has "lovers right and left" (65). Whereas one is a slender and frail madonna, a sleeping beauty who never talks and barely moves throughout the whole novel except when she is carried around in a coffinlike suitcase, the other is a "sorceress" (67) who commandeers the space. If one is a somnambulant companion or safely dead, the other is animated by an uncontainable will to move.

Although Hedayat lamented women's confinement to the home and blamed it all on Islam, his own ideal heroines live in gilded cages or coffins. Their freedom to roam at will is not only disagreeable and unattractive; it can also lead to their murder. Consider, for instance, a short story titled "The Doll behind the Curtain." Its central protagonist, a university student named Mehrdad, does not dedicate his love and devotion to the utopian heroines of the past, but to a statue. He is captivated by a mannequin in a store window in France while he studies there.[36] He purchases what he thinks is "not a statue at all," but rather "a woman, an angelic woman smiling at him" (130). Upon his return, he arrives in Tehran with three suitcases, "one unusually large, resembling a coffin" (134). It carries the mannequin. He hides his doll behind a curtain in his room. "At night, when he returned home from work, Mehrdad locked his door, turned on the phonograph, poured himself a glass of wine and drew the curtain aside" (135). For hours, he would look at his motionless damsel. Sometimes he would step forward and caress her "hair and breasts" (135).

Meanwhile, Mehrdad's fiancée, who feels neglected and jealous, begins to imitate the doll. She makes "herself look as much like the statue as she could. She had her hair colored and styled after the statue's. She made herself a dress just like that of the statue and bought shoes of the same style" (135). One night, Mehrdad "arrived home rather late, drunk out of his mind. He turned on the light, drew the curtain aside, took out his bottle and switched on the phonograph. He had a couple of drinks one after the other, sat on the sofa directly facing the statue and stared it right in the eye" (136). In his customary fashion and "after a while, he stood up, took a few steps towards the statue and began to run his hand over its hair, neck and breast" (136). Something is wrong; something does not feel right to the puppet master. "Suddenly, as if his hand had touched a red-hot iron, he pulled it away and stepped back. Was this real?" Mehrdad throws himself back on the sofa and to his horror "noticed that the statue was moving in calculated steps towards him." As the statue moves closer and closer, "Mehrdad made a motion to run away, then paused momentarily. He had thought of something. He put his hand in the pocket of his pants, took out the revolver, and fired three successive shots at the statue. There was a shriek and then the sound of the statue hitting the ground. Petrified, Mehrdad bent over and raised the head. This wasn't the statue." The woman rolling in her blood was his fiancée, the walking doll, the woman in motion.

### DAINTY STEPS: FROM CINDERELLA TO BARBIE

The aestheticization of women's restrained mobility is not confined to one author, one period, or even one country. Different cultures have restricted women's freedom of movement in different ways and to different degrees. Some practices and institutions readily reveal the desire to contain women; others are more subtle, less visible. Symbolically speaking, the very emblem of femininity, the Mirror of Venus (♀), identifies women with beauty and stillness, whereas its counterpart, the Weapon of Mars (♂), is an arrow soaring toward the sky. The female symbol is tied to the ground, trapped in a hand-held mirror, whereas the male icon is in motion, unattached, looking upward.[37] By contrast, why is the figure of the female witch, often viewed as the epitome of ugliness, portrayed as flying on a broomstick? Unlike many "beautiful" women in fairy tales or the sleeping beauties, women witches disregard prescribed boundaries. They fly around and transform the very symbol of their domesticity into a magical vehicle able to carry them to "forbidden" places. Condemned for their mobility, they are also locked into their unsightliness.

Although it is hard to propose common criteria of ugliness, images of women witches are a good place to start. For instance, women witches are often portrayed as old and infirm. They are often lopsided with asymmetrical right and left sides of the body, the spacing and shape of facial features (eyes, eyebrows, nose, mouth) and placement of body parts (ears, breasts, arms, legs). With their green skin, warts, long and crooked noses, wild and frizzy hair, wrinkles and all, women witches whiz around in their frumpy black gowns, and, in sharp contrast to Cinderella and Barbie, expose big, flat feet.

Other than the symbolic, there are also significant true-life examples for comparison—such as foot binding, practiced for centuries in China.

The origin of foot binding, like that of veiling, is surrounded by legend and ambiguity. According to Maxine Hong Kingston, the author of *Woman Warrior*, the practice grew out of the fear of women's growing power.[38] Others believe that palace dancers, renowned for their exquisite toe dancing, originated the practice in the late tenth century during the Sung Dynasty (960–1279). They compressed their feet into special shoes to make them look smaller and stronger.[39] This practice, like veiling, soon spread from the imperial courts to the high aristocracy and upper classes and then to the middle and lower classes. It gave rise to more direct anatomical attempts to control or create female beauty. With increased popularity, the deforming/shrinking procedure became more extreme until the rarely attainable three-inch feet became the ideal. In point of fact, a practice that was voluntarily adopted by women dancers to increase their agility and to give their feet extra support (perhaps in the same way that modern-day ballerinas use toe shoes) led to the virtual disappearance of women dancers in the long run.

A whole body of knowledge developed around the size and shape of women's feet. "One fact is quite clear," notes Feng Jicai in the preface to *The Three-Inch Lotus*, "it would take two or three days to go into a discussion, even a brief one, of the care, rules, knacks, criteria, techniques, attainments, cultivation, and unique and secret methods related to foot-binding."[40] Causing great pain—"a pair of tiny feet, two jugs of tears," as the popular saying went—foot binding modified a girl's body.[41] Although there was no single, standardized method, it was usually around the age of six or seven that girls had to undergo this beauty treatment. After some preliminary preparations, the toes, except the big one, were curled tightly under the sole of the foot, and the heel was forced downward and forward. A long bandage was wound over the compressed foot. It was gradually tightened until the desired size and shape was achieved. In the case of fully bound feet, the instep was virtually shifted. It was as if high heels were made out of rotting flesh, dead skin, and dislodged bones. To keep the foot in shape, the bandaging had to be kept throughout a woman's life.

Bound feet were considered not only beautiful and elegant objects of aesthetic pleasure, but also a mark of gentility, refinement, chastity, purity, and upper-class distinction. They were called "golden lotuses"—"golden" because so highly prized, "lotuses" because unsullied even in swamps. It was also believed that women tottering on tiny feet develop a "willowy," "lotus" gait, which tightened pelvic muscles. Given such aesthetic, moral, and sexual valorization, it is not surprising that mothers bound their daughters' feet. "If you care for a son, you don't go easy on his studies; if you care for a daughter, you don't go easy on her foot binding," advised one popular saying, equating the importance of boys' education with girls' foot binding. "A mother could not love both her daughter and her daughter's feet at the same time," recommended another. Beauty contests were held in some parts of China to choose the tiniest and most perfectly proportioned feet.[42] Like Cinderella, the winners were handsomely rewarded.

Foot binding, like veiling, cannot be reduced to any single cause or effect. There are different kinds of foot bindings and different degrees as well. As Dorothy Ko demonstrates in her comprehensive history of the custom, "Each woman with bound feet lived in a complex world, each facing a changing constellation of motives, choices, sufferings, and rewards."[43] Yet among its numerous causes and effects, foot binding also reduced the parameters of a woman's universe by hampering her freedom of movement.[44] The contraction of women's space is clearly expressed in the following two adages. "Bound feet, bound feet / past the gate can't retreat," says one. "Why must the feet be bound?" asks the other. "To prevent barbarous women from running around," goes the answer.[45] The propaganda songs popularized during the eradication of the practice at the turn of the twentieth century also capture the incontrovertible interconnectedness between foot binding and mobility: "Big sister has big feet; / See how fast she walks the street! / Little sister has tiny feet; / with each step she sways complete."[46]

Dorothy Ko rejects the premise that "footbinding kept women in the house by crippling them." Such a thesis, believes the author of *Cinderella's Sisters: A Revisionist History of Footbinding*, "is a distinctly modern theory that gained currency during the anti-footbinding movement. . . . The logic of the construct and its premise that mobility is desirable are modern biases."[47] Indeed, the valorization of mobility and its recognition as the right of all citizens, in particular men, is a modern phenomenon. However, controlling women's freedom of movement has been means and symptom of social domination in patriarchal orders.

It predates modernity. Surely several dynamics were at play in the institution of foot binding; a woman hobbling about with hesitant, wobbly strides moved about less freely than a man with his natural feet left intact. Foot binding polarized the sexes and set them apart by accentuating their visual or symbolic points of differences and levels of mobility. As Patricia Buckley Ebrey remarks, a woman with bound feet "would move about less, sitting rather than standing, staying home rather than going out. With less exercise, she would be softer, more languid. . . . For women to be smaller, softer, more stationary, and more languid would of course enhance the image of men as larger, harder, more active."[48] A woman with bound feet made a man look more masculine in comparison.

Even today, dainty feet are a key criterion of some beauty icons. Cinderella, the princess of all fairy tales, owes her ascendancy from rags to riches to the fact that her tiny foot fit snugly into the delicate glass slipper. She becomes queen because her feet are smaller than all others. In unsanitized versions of the tale, when the prince or his representative brings the slipper to Cinderella's house, Cinderella's cruel stepmother has her daughters butcher their feet. "Cut off your toe," she tells one, handing her a knife. "Cut off your heel," she tells the other. She is quick to remind her daughters-turned-surgeons, "Queens don't need to walk." Unsurprisingly, some of the oldest written versions of the Cinderella tale were produced in the middle of the ninth century in China—contemporaneous with the beginning of foot binding.[49] Barbie, too, a space-age fertility goddess,[50] the world's most popular toy,[51] the icon of beauty, has exceptionally tiny feet. At human scale, she would wear a size 4 or 5 toddler shoe. Forever arched and pointed, often on high heels, her feet look like they have been bound. Not only do they stand out against those of her previous boyfriend, Ken, in terms of size and shape, they are even smaller than the feet of Skipper, her younger sister, whose feet are flat rather than on tiptoe. Barbie cannot even stand on her own two feet. Whereas her looks, her nationality, her hobbies, her professions, her skin color, and her clothes have changed over the years, her abnormally small feet have essentially remained unaltered.[52]

Dainty feet continue to have a hold on popular imagination. They remain, albeit to a much lesser degree, a criterion of feminine beauty. Top models, who "are on average between five feet nine and five feet ten inches tall" and naturally have big feet, borrow, in a manner of speaking, the diminutive feet of "foot models," who have "size six (American) feet, with perfect smooth skin and perfect little toes."[53] And those women who do not sport "perfect little toes" squeeze them, as best they can, into uncomfortable shoes. Although articles of clothing have become for the most part more comfortable and movement-friendly, the same cannot be said about footwear. "In 1991, the American Orthopedic Foot and Ankle Society did a survey and found that 90 percent of American women wore shoes that were too small for their feet, and 80 percent had foot problems of one sort or another." Ill-fitting or high-heeled shoes can cause a host of foot and ankle problems, from pain, deformity, twisted ankles, sprains, and ulcer formation to calluses, bunions, and corns. "The World Health Organization has said that 80 percent of foot amputations could be prevented in part by wearing well-fitted shoes."[54]

It is not only Barbie's feet that are peculiar in their size. Her unrealistic measurements for breasts, waist, and hips, which would be 39 by 21 by 33 at human scale—her tiny waist, unnaturally narrow hips, and masculine, broad shoulders—make her a physical freak. With her slight 120 pounds (a good part of which must be concentrated in her abnormally large breasts), the perpetually youthful Barbie is the product of a time period obsessed with an unattainable ideal of female beauty. Barbie, who was originally modeled after a German sex doll, "Bild Lilli,"[55] is the role model to millions of girls throughout the world.[56] Even adult women emulate her. Consider Cindy Jackson, an American woman turned celebrity who takes pride in having spent thousands of dollars to undergo, at last count, twenty-nine operations to transform herself into a human Barbie doll. Jackson's autobiography is aptly titled *Living Doll*.[57]

The twenty-first century may be the era of expanded female presence and power. But greater opportunities for women have not prevented the culture of beauty from being stifling. Anorexia, bulimia, and an obsession with thinness and exercise seem to punish the female body for its desires, its appetites, and the new spaces it now occupies. They contain and control women's physical and social space. "Loss of mobility, loss of voice, inability to leave the home, feeding others while starving oneself, taking up space, and whittling down the space one's body takes up—all have symbolic meaning," states Bordo, "all have political meaning under the varying rules governing the historical construction of gender."[58] Women are prompted to defy the laws of gravity, to be thinner, trimmer, and younger looking, to pursue a never-quite-achieved kind of beauty. Perhaps that is what led Naomi Wolf, author of *The Beauty Myth*, to write, "More women have more money, power, scope and legal recognition than ever before, but in terms of how we feel about ourselves physically, we may actually be worse off than our un-liberated grandmothers."[59]

Wolf is not alone in her dire assessment of the situation. Mary Pipher writes in her best-selling book *Reviving Ophelia* that girls "are coming of age in a more dangerous, sexualized and media-saturated culture. They face incredible pressure to be beautiful and sophisticated. . . . As they navigate a more dangerous world, girls are less protected."[60] And Joan Jacobs Brumberg talks in her highly acclaimed book *The Body Project* about a disturbing crisis of confidence and the plummeting of self-esteem when girls reach adolescence. "By age thirteen," she tells her readers, "53 percent of American girls are unhappy with their bodies; by age seventeen, 78 percent are dissatisfied."[61] Demand for elective cosmetic surgery is steadily rising among teenagers who seek the plastic surgeon's scalpel in unprecedented numbers.

### FLYING AND BEAUTY

Beauty ideals, like clothing fashions, change, though with more difficulty. And there is now a competing narrative of women's beauty that is gaining more and more currency. This new definition of beauty supplants stillness with motion. Consider Spider-Woman and Wonder-Woman. Both are beautiful and have extraordinary powers and equipment, wings and self-powered flight. Even Jasmine, the daughter of the sultan of Agrabah, an imaginary Middle Eastern country in Walt Disney's animated film *Aladdin,* is both beautiful and airborne. At the beginning of the movie, the princess, beautiful and spirited, is portrayed in a familiar role. She is a "prisoner" who yearns to be free. "I have never been outside the palace walls," she announces with grief and regret. Like the genie trapped in the lamp, Jasmine is locked up. Identifying with her caged birds, she throws open the gate to their cage and frees them all, watching longingly as they fly away. Inspired by her birds, she flees her palace prison by climbing over the soaring walls surrounding the palace to find herself in the busy marketplace. She is delighted but unschooled in the rules of the bazaar where she is caught stealing an apple. That is when Aladdin, a "street rat," meets and falls in love with her. Coming to her rescue, he wins her heart and eventually her hand, which she had refused her many royal suitors to her father's chagrin. Jasmine has set her beautiful black eyes on Aladdin. The film focuses on what is so especially attractive about him through Jasmine's eye: he is leaping across the rooftops of Agrabah with gravity-defying agility. No less nimble than his chattering sidekick, Abu the monkey, he jumps, runs, scales the walls, swings from building to building, skims roofs and treetops, sprints, climbs, dives. He is king of the road and, thanks to his magic carpet, king of the sky as well.

Unlike the princess's many suitors, Aladdin is neither rich nor regal, neither educated nor princely. What he offers Jasmine, however, is what she desires the most and what no one else offers: freedom from physical confinement in her gilded cage. In fact, he seduces her with a ride. "Do you trust me?" he asks Jasmine, inviting her for a tour of the sky. "Yes," she says, and mounts his flying carpet. Whisking her away, Aladdin proudly tells her,

> I can open your eyes
> Take you wonder by wonder
> over, sideways, and under
> on a magic carpet ride.[62]

Together, they fly joyfully in freedom. No boundaries, no borders, no palace walls restrain Jasmine any more. Like Aladdin, she is free and mobile at last. Whereas Aladdin's tale, like Cinderella's, is a rags-to-riches story, Jasmine's tale is one from immobility to unconstrained movement, from confinement to flight. "Soaring, tumbling, freewheeling / Through an endless diamond sky," she tells Aladdin triumphantly, "I'm like a shooting star / I've come so far / I can't go back to where I used to be." The rewards of movement, first initiated by her, are many, including a freely chosen mate rather than an arranged marriage, and, more important, freedom from the forbidding walls that once circumscribed her life and future.

Flying beauties, it seems, are replacing sleeping beauties and ugly witches flying on broomsticks.

# 3

## PARDEH NESHIN, OR "SHE WHO SITS BEHIND THE SCREEN"

### The Spatial Politics of Iranian Cinema

Why did your daughter decide to uncover herself—does she want to become
a film star?

—ORHAN PAMUK, *Snow*

### A WOMAN'S PLACE

A synonym for the word *woman* in the Persian language is *pardeh neshin:* "she
who sits behind the screen."[1] The expression perpetuates, even linguistically, the
cultural ideal of feminine modesty and woman's absence in public.[2] Although
Persian is not gender marked, the term *pardeh neshin* is understood to refer to a
woman. It implies enclosure, invisibility, and immobility, all associations that are
inseparable from conventional definitions of femininity. Traditional propriety
demanded that a woman maintain public anonymity, that she not intrude into
or merge with the outside world. When in public, she was expected to keep her
transactions to bare necessities. She was to cloak herself by erecting visible as well
as invisible walls of separation around herself. She enveloped her body in a veil,
covered her voice with silence, controlled her desires, restrained her gaze. But
rules of modesty demanded more than a woman's self-effacing timidity or her
mere physical enclosure. They also prohibited visual contact between the sexes,
and this regulation extended into the realm of visual representation. Just as a
woman's body could not circulate freely in the open spaces, neither could her
image, least of all her moving image. Thus, when the cinema first appeared in

74

Iran, it posed a challenge to the norms and values that regulated woman's physical exposure.

Cinema is a voyage, a magic carpet. It not only lifts the actors on-screen but also sweeps up the spectators and transports them to faraway places. It confounds the boundaries of time and space, blurring the borders between the private and the public. Feminine and masculine territories overlap as the narrative unfolds and the actors perform under the viewers' gaze. Cinema brings men and women together as protagonists, acting partners, and audiences in the theater. Unsurprisingly, then, women's participation in this most public of all art forms in Iran had a tumultuous beginning. When cinema was first introduced, religious authorities condemned it as a vehicle of desegregation, capable of conveying women from their "proper place"—secluded in private homes and gardens, restricted in delineated spaces—and exposing them on the public stage. As a result, sex segregation has had and continues to have a powerful impact on the Iranian film industry. It has shaped narrative structures, cinematographic techniques, systems of representation, directorial practices, and viewing codes.

If sex segregation controls visual pleasures in Iran, how, then, did cinema there flourish so well as it has? How did Iranians involved in the film industry negotiate, revise, and suspend these restrictive laws regarding the public display of the images of women? How did they reconcile the traditional erasure of women from the public scene with their representation on the silver screen, which was considered a form of indecent exposure? And finally, how could women—who traditionally had to sit behind the screen—avoid compromising their integrity or violating gender considerations omnipresent within Iranian society during the acting, the filming, and the showing of films?

AN ARDUOUS JOURNEY

To begin with, women were barred from even entering movie theaters. Public spectatorship was a masculine prerogative, and cinemas were urban spaces permitted to men alone. Thrusting a woman into such a public space, even when fully covered, was considered a resolute act of desegregation. It took almost a quarter of a century for women to be allowed to sit in the company of men in movie theaters and more than fifty years for a Muslim woman to act in any film made in Iran.

The first movie theater opened in 1905 in Tehran, five years after Mozzafar-ed-Din Shah Qajar (reigned 1896–1907) introduced the cinema to Iran. It "was a long hall, its floor covered with cheap Persian rugs called *zilos,* upon which people sat as they did in the mosques." It also borrowed from a familiar art form, *naqali,* or public storytelling. "A man stood near the screen and explained the films for the audiences in much the same way that storytellers had been relating stories for centuries to people in coffee houses and *meidans* [squares]," explains M. Ali Issari. Not surprisingly, the first theater in Iran had a short life span. It was, as Issari attests, "closed after a month because of religious opposition to cinema and the political harassment of its founder. Two years later, other cinemas opened in the capital city, but they too were ransacked, looted, or closed down. The love of cinema, however, was not to be extinguished in the heart of Iranians. Supported by the government, movie theatres sprung up in major cities."[3]

For twenty-one years, these new entertainment centers, like coffeehouses, remained the exclusive province of men. "In its early years," writes Ja'far Shahri, the social historian of Tehran, "cinema was monopolized by young and single men because taking women and children along was considered a shame. From its inception, everyone was convinced that this Western phenomenon fostered promiscuity."[4] When women finally found their way to movie theaters in 1926, they had to attend screenings reserved especially for them. Single-sex cinemas for women—such as Khorshid, San'ati, and Zardoshtian—opened in Tehran soon thereafter. But from a business point of view, they were not profitable. Insufficient numbers of women were allowed out on the streets alone, quite apart from being allowed to enter movie theaters without a chaperone. So when one movie theater, San'ati, caught on fire, its owner, Khanbaba Mo'tazedi, argued "that the women would have felt more secure if they had been accompanied by their husbands or brothers when the fire broke out."[5] Mixed movie theaters eventually became a reality, even though to guarantee the separation of the sexes, men and women had to enter the theater through separate entrances and sit in different sections. In some theaters, women sat on one side of the aisle, men on the other; in others, the balconies were reserved for women, the downstairs for men. Only after the unveiling act of 1936 could men and women enter cinemas together and sit side by side in the dark.

OFF-SCREEN, ON-SCREEN, SCREENED IN

The greatest barrier, however, concerned the nature of the spectacle itself. Having gained access to one forbidden space—the movie theater—women had to pass through the silver screen itself to reach the next. It took much longer to go from sitting passively in front of the screen to moving back and forth upon it. The question of female actors proved very complicated and raised many dilemmas for directors and actors alike in a sex-segregated society. That a woman who is projected on the screen is neither eliminated from the public scene nor relegated to the domain of the private was explained to director Mohsen Makhmalbaf: "Once when we had asked some Afghan women to be in the film, their husband told us that he was too chaste to show his women. I told him that we would film his women with their burqas on but he said that the viewers watching the movie know that is a woman under the burqa and that would contradict chastity."[6]

Were men and women allowed to look at women as well as men in the dark space of the movie theater? And were male directors permitted to see, let alone train the eye of the camera on, the bodies of the women they were filming? Such questions, thorny as they are, lie at the root of the originality and creativity of Iranian cinema today. In fact, the history of women and cinema in Iran is not only about spatial control, but also about the ingenious and imaginative ploys used to subvert the strictures of physical confinement.

A scene from Mohsen Makhmalbaf's 2001 film *Kandahar*, set in Afghanistan, reveals the sorts of representational challenges that filmmakers face in a sex-segregated society. But it also displays the novel cinematic effects that result from their negotiations and their manipulations of these strictures. In the scene, the film's female protagonist, Nafas, is ill and in need of medical attention. Accompanied by a boy who serves as her guide and chaperone, she visits the office of the local healer. Covered from head to foot and fully hidden behind her burka, she enters the doctor's office and sits behind a curtain that divides the space of the humble clinic. Through the mediation of the young boy, she relays her ailment to the doctor. Because the physician cannot speak directly to Nafas, according to the rules of propriety imposed by the Taliban, he conveys his questions and instructions through her youthful chaperone as he examines his patient from behind a curtain, one body part at a time.[7]

Nafas is visible to the doctor in the story only in pieces, in fragments, through a hole. She is disembodied and reduced to body parts—now an eye, now an ear, now a mouth, now a nose—but thanks to the gaze of the director and his camera, spectators can peek behind the screen that conceals her from the physician. Within the framework of the fictive world, the camera allows us to penetrate a cloistered, private space inaccessible in reality. Although the doctor in the story is permitted to examine his patient only from the "male" side of the curtain, the spectators in the movie theater are allowed to go farther. Nafas is hidden behind the screen in the film itself, but she is exposed before the gaze of a whole audience outside it. The woman is thus revealed and concealed to us simultaneously. She is covered but not concealed, veiled but not secluded, hidden by one screen and displayed to full view on another.

A similar scene, with a visual impact equally cinematographic, can be found in Salman Rushdie's great novel *Midnight's Children*. Although appealing to the eye of the imagination rather than to a literal camera, it depicts the identical situation explored in *Kandahar*. In the course of the story, the narrator's grandfather, a young medical doctor who has just returned from Europe to India, is summoned to visit the ailing daughter of a wealthy landlord. Entering an ill-lit bedchamber, he is asked to examine her. As he looks all round the room, Doctor Aziz cannot locate the patient. "But where is she?" he finally blurts out, befuddled. "Ah, I see your confusion," says the father. "You Europe-returned chappies forget certain things." The proud patriarch is quick to remind the physician that his daughter is "a decent girl," one who "does not flaunt her body under the noses of strange men." This woman might be sick, but certainly she knows her limits. She does not step out of line. "You will understand," continues the father, "that you cannot be permitted to see her, no, not in any circumstances; accordingly I have required her to be positioned behind that sheet. She stands there like a good girl." Doctor Aziz cannot figure out how he is to examine an invisible patient. "You will kindly specify which portion of my daughter it is necessary to inspect," says the father. "I will then issue her with my instructions to place the required segment against that hole which you see there. And so, in this fashion the thing may be achieved."[8]

Given the limitations imposed on women's representation in literature and their participation in theater in Islamic society, what Iranian cinema has achieved is nothing short of phenomenal in retrospect. In a country where to this day no woman on record has acted in the Ta'ziyeh (an indigenous form of theater that mourns the martyrdom of Shi'ite imams, in particular that of Imam Hossein and his family), and in a culture where even the viewing of such sacred dramas is traditionally sex segregated and where women spectators not only have occupied seats separate from the ones the men sit in but have sometimes even been hidden from the men's view within the audience itself, it is all the more remarkable to find such a strong and growing female presence on the screen itself during the past two decades.

UNVEILED EYES

Cinema in Iran was a compelling force of social change not just in terms of gender, but also in terms of class. Movie theaters, for instance, not only threatened to mix previously cloistered women with strange men in the dark but also brought diverse ranks of society together. Tickets were not uniformly priced, but the Iranian government made a special point of keeping "prices low so that all segments of the population, at any economic level, might have access to this source of recreation."[9] Although those who could afford to pay more sat together in a special section reserved for them, the social elite and the rich nevertheless gathered with street urchins and the poor under the same roof.

Critics viewed this social fluidity and sexual osmosis with alarm; they saw the cinema as a place where moral propriety was being compromised, where promiscuity was provoked and the gaze corrupted. A direct correlation was established between the growing number of theaters in the capital city and "the increasing number of prostitutes in Tehran and its red-light districts."[10] It was inevitable, too, that cinema would be considered decadent, an instrument of westernization, a catalyst of corruption, a polluter of the innocent. The eye of the camera, the shared glance of characters, and the hypnotized gaze of the audience itself were viewed as equally sinful.[11]

Visual exchange, which defines cinema, is subject to an elaborate set of regulations for both men and women in Islam. Indeed, how "to look and how to be looked at are the object of a precise, meticulous apprenticeship that is an integral part of the socialization of the Muslim. To be a Muslim is to control one's gaze and to know how to protect one's own intimacy from [the gaze] of others."[12] And because in a system of gender apartheid restrictions are not on women alone, but also against heterosexual interactions outside of marriage, the degree of male–female interaction is limited for both sexes, albeit to different degrees. Whereas women are assigned a bounded space, men, whose physical mobility seems to be their divine right, are nevertheless confined and restricted in certain ways. For instance, they must prevent their eyes from journeying to religiously unlawful destinations lest they violate rules of modesty. The concern is not only the objectifying power of the masculine gaze, but also its sinfulness. Like women's bodies as a whole, men's eyes are not free to roam at will in a sex-segregated society.[13]

The chapter titled "Nur" (Light) in the Qur'an instructs men to lower their gaze and guard their modesty. The famous Muslim philosopher Abu Hamid Ghazali considered the sexual look "fornication of the eye."[14] If not controlled, suggested Sheikh Zabihollah Mahalati, another religious scholar, "it destroys the person who looked. It stimulates, it delights, seduces, and murders. It breaks hearts, brings tears to the eyes, and ruins families. It is the gaze that demoralizes, increases envy, and makes young people go insane."[15] And for Ayatollah Ali Moravveji, the forbidden look is one of "Satan's weapons. . . . It plants the seed of lust in the heart and causes social chaos."[16] So important is it to restrict and to avert the gaze that it has become a key criterion of moral propriety and even desirability in Islam. Observant Muslims—men and women alike—are expected to exercise strict control over their eyes. They must limit visual contact, especially with the opposite sex; they must exercise vigilance over where or what or at whom they look. Those with *cheshm-e darideh* or *cheshm-e hiz*—that is, the ones who have impudent eyes or the ones who are not disinclined to look or to be looked at—are disparaged for showing no sense of modesty.

For religious authorities who consider the gaze forbidden and sinful, it does not matter whether a look is direct or passes through another medium, such as film.[17] A book about cinema and Islamic jurisprudence published in 1999 equates looking at a woman's image with looking at her in real life: "Looking at a forbidden woman indirectly is subject to the same rules as looking at her directly. Just as looking directly at a woman is forbidden, so is looking at her indirectly. It is religiously unlawful."[18] This was one of the reasons why Iranian women were barred for decades from acting and why they were nearly eliminated from Iranian cinema in the 1980s, the first decade after the Islamic Revolution. Even now, early in the twenty-first century, there are still no unveiled women in Iranian films. Even when filmed in the illusory privacy of their fictive homes, where they are not expected to cover their hair, women have to observe mandatory veiling on-screen. The presence of the camera in any private space transforms it into a public arena.

In other words, filmed spaces, according to the laws governing the Iranian film industry, are public spaces. Wherever and whenever the eye of the camera is present, spectators can be assumed. The viewer's eye effectively corrupts the legitimacy of the scene. As a consequence, physical intimacy is unacceptable on screen. This is the case not only between couples who are "lawfully married" in the story, but even between male and female actors who happen to be married in real life and are enacting a scene in the privacy of a fictitious bedroom. Touching, kissing, hugging, and the holding of hands are forbidden actions. Shared glances are also prohibited. Unmediated romantic involvements are out of the question. Any expression of affection between men and women is banned. Even the on-screen depiction of the traditionally celebrated and demonstrative mother–son relationship is off-limits.[19]

A LONG ABSENCE

The initial absence of Iranian women from movie theaters in Iran was paralleled by their absence on the screen, too, in the early years of cinema. The first feature-length Iranian films made in the 1930s, some thirty years after the introduction of cinema there, included no women in the cast.[20] Typically revolving around male friendships and buddy relationships, they conveniently avoided the tricky problem of female representation. In addition, actresses, especially Muslim ones, were hard to recruit. The short movie *Haji Agha, Actor-e Cinema* (Haji Agha, the Actor of Cinema), made in 1934, revolved around this theme and relied on a non-Muslim woman to carry it out. The protagonist, Haji Agha, is a devout Muslim who does not want his daughter to act. In the course of the story, however, he is persuaded to change his mind, and by the time the film comes to an end, he has actually allowed his daughter to become an actress. But the filmmaker had to recruit Asia Ghostantin, an Armenian woman, to play the role of Haji Agha's daughter.

Women who were not Muslim offered film directors a nifty strategy for circumventing representational restriction in Iran. Like the authors of classical romances in Persian literature, they, too, relied on and made use of non-Muslim women. Asia Ghostantin, Linda Matavoosian, and Jasmine Joseph, all Iranian nationals but members of religious minorities, appeared in short feature films.[21] Then Abdol Hossein Sepanta (1907–69), the director and scriptwriter of *Doktar-e Lor* (The Lor Girl, 1932), convinced Sedigheh Saminejad (1916–97), the Iranian-born, Muslim wife of the producer's driver, to take the lead role in his feature-length sound film made in India. Saminejad was so reluctant to become an actress that she adopted a screen name, Rouhangiz Kermani. She acted as a Gypsy girl named Golnar (Pomegranate Blossoms). The film, renamed *Ja'far and Golnar* by Iranian viewers after the names of its two protagonists, was a great box-office success. Although no statistics are available on the number of moviegoers at the time, by all accounts this first Iranian talking movie was screened repeatedly for several years to great acclaim. According to poet Simin Behbahani, "A movie theater in Shapour Square in Tehran reran *The Lor Girl* a couple of months, year in and year out. . . . Even very old grandmothers saw this film."[22]

In the film, Saminejad's character, Golnar, earned her living by singing and dancing. Sepanta cleverly relied on the familiar figure of the Gypsy and fully exploited her subversive potential. Gypsies are familiar figures in Iranian art. They are often portrayed as people of adventure and romance, entertainers, exotic performers of music and dance. With a reputation for aggressive nonconformity and flagrant immodesty, they refuse to be "domesticated." They are wanderers who defy laws of segregation. For centuries, Gypsies were viewed as rebellious characters who called into question traditional ideals of domesticity. Their whole identity, most dramatically for women, was defined by their refusal to sit behind the screen and stay put. Small wonder, then, if the first Muslim woman to act in an Iranian movie assumed the role of a Gypsy.

Golnar, the beautiful, on-screen Gypsy girl who sings and dances in teahouses, delighted Iranian moviegoers.[23] But Saminejad, the real Muslim woman who had the audacity to flaunt her face without a veil, entertain perfect strangers, appear and reappear on the silver screen shocked them. Ostracized and isolated, she quit the cinema.[24] Years later, when she was asked how she felt about her acting role, she was unequivocal in her regret, identifying the experience as a nightmare. She referred to the insults directed toward her by family, friends, and the Iranian public. Unacknowledged as the pioneering woman she was, Saminejad died a bitter and lonely death.

A STAR IS BORN

Originally intended for the Iranian community in India, *The Lor Girl* eventually found its way to Iran, where its success was a pleasant surprise for its producer, the Imperial Film Company of India. According to a 1935 report by the Evening News of India, the movie "was made in Persian with the hope that it would appeal to the Persian, Parsi and Irani communities (Iranian Zoroastrians who migrated to India) in Western India. The film went well in Bombay, the Persian Consul became enthusiastic and the film was taken to Persia. . . . The idea of having films in Persian, instead of German and French (French and German film companies were doing practically all the business in the country) was so enthusiastically followed up that Bombay hopes to arrange to supply many more talkies to Teheran."[25] Encouraged by the film's instantaneous success, the Imperial Film Company decided to exploit the Iranian movie market and recruit more Iranian actors and actresses. An announcement was posted in Tehran. A daring young woman, Fakhr-ol-Zaman Jabbar-Vaziri (1912–2009), better known as Fakhri Vaziri, saw the flyer and was mesmerized by the prospect of becoming a movie star.

"One day on my way to school," Vaziri recounted to me in my interview of her in Maryland in August 1999, "I saw the public notice posted by Cinema Mayak announcing that an Indian film company was looking for actors and actresses to go to India in order to make Iranian movies. For a few days, I kept staring at that ad thinking lucky was she who got the role. I very much wanted to be the one." It took Vaziri a few weeks to take the bold move, unbeknownst to her parents, and to walk into the office of the recruiting agency. She recalls the details of that defining moment with perfect clarity. "The office was small and humble. A man sitting behind a desk asked me what I wanted and why I was there. I said, 'I'm responding to your billboard. I want to act in your films.' He sized me up with surprise and asked, 'Have you ever acted or been on stage?' I said never."

Vaziri might not have had any training or experience, but she was fearless, determined, and eager. The Imperial Film Company wanted to hire her. A few weeks later the Iranian director, Abdol Hossein Sepanta, contacted Vaziri's parents. As expected, he encountered severe opposition. "Neither my mother nor my father wanted their daughter to act in films," said Vaziri, "but I cried and cried and cried. I refused to leave my room for days. I even threatened with suicide." Meanwhile, a persistent Sepanta returned for another visit to Vaziri's family, this time accompanied by his mother, wife, and son. He promised Vaziri's parents that his whole family would accompany their daughter on the trip to India and that they would treat her like one of their own. With some cajoling, the reluctant parents finally agreed.

Vaziri's first film, *Shirin and Farhad* (1934), was a big hit. Long before the West became infatuated with Bette Davis's eyes, Vaziri's black, almond-shaped eyes captured the cinematic imagination of moviegoers in India and Iran. Another film company, the Krishna of India, commissioned Sepanta to make a film about Vaziri's eyes. Simply entitled *Black Eyes,* the film was released simultaneously in Iran and India in 1936. The *Bombay Chronicle* admired more than Vaziri's eyes and wrote, "The atmosphere of magic, romance and poetry, reminiscent of the Persia of the poets, conveyed by *Black Eyes* is, surely, one that would be more than appreciated in the homeland of Mr. Sepanta and Mlle Vaziri. And it is no prophecy to suggest that as a first pioneering venture, which is as much a social as artistic and economic revolution, their efforts will receive the wide response they deserve."[26] The *Times of India* identified Vaziri as an "accomplished and cultured star," with a "refined personality and dignified grace."[27] In Iran, the young actress, who had appeared unveiled on the screen two years prior to the compulsory unveiling act, became "the idol of millions of Persian movie lovers."[28]

Soon after the completion of her third film, *Layli and Majnun* (1936), Vaziri returned to Iran, married, gave birth to a son, and at the height of her career left the world of cinema definitively. Despite her successful career and the three films in which she had acted, Vaziri, like Saminejad, never appeared on-screen again. A few years later, in 1947, she came to the United States as a film reporter for the Iranian Department of Information and Radio, turning her dramatic skills to news and entertainment broadcasting. She joined the *Voice of America* as a radio commentator and worked there for nine years before taking a job at an insurance company in the 1960s. But no trace of her movies remains. According to an article in *Tavoos* in 2000–2001, "There are no existing copies of these films, at least not in Iran, and investigations into the existence of copies in Bombay have so far been inconclusive."[29] Recent studies of Iranian cinema in Persian and in English rarely mention the groundbreaking role of this pioneering woman, who traveled all alone and against all odds to India when she was still young and single and played the lead role in three of the first five Iranian talkies in the 1930s.[30]

The meteoric appearance of the first Iranian movie star was as short as it was swift. Indeed, for the next two decades acting remained an elusive male domain and was a career that was effectively closed to women. In her memoir *Persian Girls,* Nahid Rachlin chronicles the details of the relentless and passionate struggle of her sister, Pari, to become an actress and the adamant opposition she confronted from both social and parental authorities. Pari was a talented and movie-obsessed girl whose only dream was a career on the stage, an idea as unrealistic "as dancing a polka on the moon," according to a review of the book.[31] She had an album with a red leather cover in which she kept treasured photographs of "Elizabeth Taylor, Paul Newman, Marilyn Monroe, Kim Novak, Ava Gardner, Montgomery Clift." On the wall of her room, she had a poster of her favorite star: Judy Garland. But hard as she tried, Pari failed to convince her parents to let her act. Instead, she ended up "a virtual prisoner" in the house of a wealthy husband, who watched over her "like a prison guard."[32] The harrowing loss of her acting ambition led to depression and eventually to an early death that looked ominously like a suicide.

Non-Iranian actresses populated the screens of Iranian movie theaters for the most part. Some rejected them as the epitome of corruption and lasciviousness; many others admired them. In fact, to be a female "movie star" meant in the first place to be a Western actress. Shusha Guppy, who dedicates a whole chapter to movies in her memoir *The Blindfold Horse,* does not mention a single Iranian actress. "At school," she writes, "we collected photographs of film stars, male and female, in ornate albums. We gave them to each other as presents, with elaborate dedications written on the back. We compared our collections and vied with each other in their variety and richness." The impact of Western movie stars, however, went beyond the compilation of their photographs in cherished albums. They were also viewed as role models.

We each had our favorite stars and argued endlessly as to their respective merits, their beauty and skill. We emulated their hairstyles, their clothes, their expressions. Any resemblance to a film star, however remote and nebulous was assiduously cultivated, and secured the reputation of the lucky girl—or boy. Gradually and insidiously, the cinema changed the criteria of beauty: a girl was no longer considered beautiful because she conformed to the ideal depicted by poets, the Persian miniatures, the friezes of Persepolis, but because she looked—oh ever so slightly!—like Hedy Lamarr or Danielle Darrieux or Ingrid Bergman.[33]

It was not until the 1960s that a large number of Iranian women made their presence felt on the screen. Ironically enough, this wider representation coincided with the emergence of a dominant masculine archetype in Iranian cinema: a man whose honor was violated and who had to avenge the rape of a woman relative. It was as though the presence of women on screen could not be divorced from the threat they symbolized to society. According to Shahla Lahiji (writer, translator, director of Roshangaran publishing house, and recipient of the 2001 PEN/Barbara Goldsmith Freedom to Write Awards), "The appearance of [Iranian] women [in cinema] signaled the arrival of disaster and misfortune. The young girl was helpless and unable to defend her chastity and the honor of the family. Thus, men of the family, carrying knives in their pockets, would search the city to repair the torn curtain of the honor and chastity of the clan by piling corpse upon corpse."[34]

Lahiji has a rather dismal view of the early representation of women in Iranian cinema. She believes that with the exception of *Khesht va Ayeneh* (Mud Brick and Mirror, 1965) and *Shohar Ahoo Khanum* (Mrs. Ahoo's Husband, 1968), Iranian cinema during the 1960s offered an "insulting and distorted portrait of the Iranian woman." She claims that until the end of that decade Iranian women could not be depicted on screen except as hapless victims or would-be whores. "The life, suffering and joys of normal women, the housewives, women working on the farm, in factories, at schools and offices, physicians, nurses, poets, authors, lawyers, and university teachers engaged in living normal lives had no place in the Iranian movies. Iranian movies were empty of real women—and real men too. What was shown on the screen included pure fantasy of the cheapest kind, without any artistic or aesthetic value."[35]

Not surprisingly, the more conservative elements in Iran came to consider such depictions as proof of the West's decadent and corrupt influence on Iranian society. Ayatollah Khomeini, who linked cinema "with the onset of corruption, licentiousness, prostitution, moral cowardice and cultural dependence,"[36] was not alone in associating the growing representation of women on the Iranian screen with the decline of morality and the onset of venality. Every step forward in the emergence of women on the screen was followed by a seeming step backward, until the 1979 Islamic Revolution, which brought women's active participation in the cinema to a temporary halt. The republic offered several reasons for imposing so many restrictions on the representation of women. These reasons ranged from the need to establish Islamic order and to impose Islamic laws to the claim that such strictures were intended to "protect" women and to prohibit the exploitation of their beauty and the exposure of their bodies. Paradoxically enough, the theocratic government's main rationale for the specific policing of women's place on the screen and the control of the production and showing of films more generally recalled the official reaction to cinema in Iran eight decades earlier under the monarchy.

### HISTORY REPEATS ITSELF

First, just as in the early 1900s, movie theaters were torched as part of the revolution.[37] On August 21, 1978, the doors of Rex Cinema in the southwestern city of Abadan were locked. The theater was ransacked and set on fire. Some four hundred innocent children, women, and men watching the Iranian movie *Deer* (1975), were burned alive. Only a few, an estimated twenty to forty people, managed to escape through a roof exit. Following this horrific event, almost half of all theaters in Iran were destroyed—32 in the capital city alone, some 255 nationwide. Some of the theaters saved from fire "were divided in half, with one side reserved for men and the other for men with their families."[38] Iran's booming film business was soon nearly shut down. Many directors, producers, and actors stopped working altogether; some were banned from participation in the industry; others were imprisoned and even executed on charges of spreading corruption on earth; many chose exile and left the country. If present at all in films, women were given only minor roles. They had minimal presence and mobility. They often appeared in seated roles.[39]

There were different phases in the evolution of women's representation on the screen in the aftermath of the Islamic Revolution. According to Hamid Naficy, "During the first phase, immediately after the revolution (early 1980s), the images of unveiled women were cut from existing Iranian and imported films." This frequently had a negative impact on the coherence of the story, of course. "When cutting caused unacceptable narrative confusion," continues Naficy, "the offending parts were blacked out directly in the frames with markers. In local productions, women were excised from the screens through self-censorship by a frightened industry unsure of official attitudes and regulations regarding cinema."[40] Cinema during the early years after the revolution therefore often served to remind viewers of the real world outside its doors rather than offering them a story enacted on the screen. Instead of merely inviting the audience to follow the film, the theater experience highlighted for them everything that was being left out of film. This habitual reminder of a tantalizing reality shimmering behind the veil of illusion, of a political and religious world in stark contrast to the fictive one depicted on screen, was to have a dramatic impact on the quality and aesthetic distinction of Iranian cinema during the decades that followed.

The Islamic Republic quickly saw the benefits of using cinema as a tool to propagate its ideology. Once in power, it began to encourage and even support "Islamic filmmaking" as an antidote to what it considered un-Islamic and corrupt Western influence. Not only did the religious establishment condone cinema; it even came to praise it. Ayatollah Khomeini soon deemed this art form a necessary tool to educate the people.[41] In an important speech he delivered at the Behesht-e Zahra Cemetery outside Tehran, he reiterated his belief that earlier cinema was "a center of vice" but assured his audience that "we are not opposed to the cinema, to radio, or to television. What we oppose is vice and the use of the media to keep our young people in a state of backwardness." The ayatollah claimed that he had "never opposed these features of modernity in themselves." He stated, however, that when films were brought from Europe to Iran, they were "unfortunately" used not to advance civilization but to drag the country "into barbarism." "The cinema," he added, "is a modern invention that ought to be used for the sake of educating the people, but, as you know, it was used instead to corrupt our youth. It is this misuse of the cinema that we are opposed to, a misuse caused by the treacherous policies of our rulers."[42]

### THE DAWN OF A NEW CINEMA

The phenomenal replacement of antipathy toward the cinema with appreciation of it can best be witnessed in the life and career of Mohsen Makhmalbaf. In his early youth, Makhmalbaf had condemned cinema as un-Islamic, corrupt and corrupting. He had embraced the ideals of the revolution and had not only refused to see any movies until he was in his twenties but had even rebuked his mother for doing so. Finally, when he did "occasionally" go to the cinema with his family, he would argue with his mother "about whether her *Chador* was on right," telling her "she'd go to hell for going to the cinema."[43]

Given this austere history, it is all the more remarkable that Makhmalbaf should have emerged in more recent decades as a world-renowned, prize-winning director. A man who blamed his mother for going to the movies now has two daughters and a wife actively involved in directing films and winning international prizes for their work. But his career and that of his family merely parallel that of the whole industry. The most surprising consequence of the Islamic Republic has been an unprecedented flourishing of Iranian films. Iran is exporting not only a large number of its brightest students and scholars, its oil, its rugs, pistachios, and caviar, but its cinema as well. Film critic Donald Clarke writes, "Never before have so many distinguished directors emerged from one non-western nation."[44] Finding creative strategies to circumvent restrictions, relying on allegorical echoes rather than Western stereotypes, benefiting from the marvels of new technology as well as old and deep-rooted forms of indigenous art, the new wave in Iranian cinema has integrated the old and the new, the masculine and the feminine, the local and the universal. Like Persian rugs, Iranian cinema is homespun with simple yet striking patterns. Like Persian poetry, it is humanistic, elliptical, and self-reflexive. Like Persian painting, it is a rhapsody of colors and textures. Like Persian cuisine, it is improvisational and relies with intuitive precision and ingenuity on ingredients close at hand.

The gradual, ever-increasing presence of women as consumers, actors, directors, producers, and objects of representation in Iranian cinema has been its most surprising aspect in the past two decades. Banished from the screen during the early years after the revolution, many women took refuge behind the camera. They worked as assistant directors, stage managers, designers, editors, producers, costume designers, and scriptwriters. There are currently more women directors in Iran than during the previous one hundred years. But women have begun to reappear in unprecedented numbers in front of the camera, too. Resistance to their acting, which recalls the early years of cinema, is now unsustainable. In the past few decades, there has been a massive shift in public opinion regarding desegregation. According to Reza Tahami, "About one third of the four thousand people who have appeared in Iranian films in leading and supporting roles in the past sixty years or so are women."[45] This statistical shift is astounding.

Filmmakers, women and men alike, have negotiated successfully within the confines of the government's stringent censorship. Despite the limitations imposed on them, they have pushed the boundaries of sex segregation regulating cinema. "Like trapeze artists swinging back and forth without a net,"[46] they have shifted and extended the bounds of permissible representation. They have introduced onto the screen such previously taboo themes as family violence, men's unilateral right of divorce, arranged marriage, abortion, child custody, prostitution, infertility, polygamy, depression, prostitution, drug addiction, cross-dressing, and homosexuality. More important, they have directly addressed the issue of women's physical confinement. They have confronted the significance of who controls the space in which women move and to what ends.

### FATHER TURNED JAILER?

Forced immobility in every sense finds frequent and imaginative expression in Iranian movies. It is a central theme, a vital preoccupation, a commentary on a society that kept half its population contained in demarcated spaces for centuries. It is no coincidence that over the past few decades Iranian directors have focused consistently on compulsory exclusion. They have expanded the metaphoric frame of reference for captivity and produced several movies that are parables for any form of cloistered existence.

The genealogy of this thematic interest can be traced to the first major movie made by an Iranian woman: *The House Is Black* (1962), directed by the poet Forugh Farrokhzad. She was the one who filmed what others found taboo or at least distasteful. *The House Is Black* reflects a society in pain, controlled and restricted in a narrow leper colony, and, not surprisingly, this theme has resonated powerfully with other Iranian directors since the Islamic Revolution. For instance, *The Apple,* made in 1998, more than three decades after Farrokhzad's film, is also a meditation on freedom of movement as a basic human right. *The Apple* blurs the boundaries between documentary and fiction. The events retold on-screen are based on a scandal that shook Iran in 1997. Neighbors in a poor district in southern Tehran reported the virtual incarceration behind bars of twelve-year-old twin girls in the Naderi family home. The authorities intervened and removed the sisters, Zahra and Ma'ssoumeh, to the welfare agency. They agreed to return the girls to their home only after Gorban Ali, the father, and Soghra, the mother, promised not to lock them up again.

Samira Makhmalbaf, the then seventeen-year-old daughter of Mohsen Makhmalbaf, heard the story on television, was intrigued by it, and decided to make a film about it. She contacted the Naderi family immediately and persuaded them to play themselves in her docudrama. She moved in with them for eleven days. "I didn't take my camera and intrude into the family's privacy," said Makhmalbaf, "instead I generated an atmosphere of trust, in which we made the film together, collectively."[47]

*The Apple* does not have an intricate plot. A father, the sixty-five-year-old Gorban Ali Naderi, finds himself accused of having kept his daughters locked up since birth. To his mind, neither the high walls surrounding his house nor the gate leading to its courtyard nor even the iron-grilled entrance to the building is enough to protect his family from the neighbors' prying eyes. Gorban Ali's incessant vigilance and his obsessive ritual of locking and unlocking the doors to his house are equally ineffective. The walls are porous, the gates are not tall enough, the windows are far too revealing. As Iranians have reminded each other for centuries, "Walls have mice, and mice have ears." In the film as in reality, concerned neighbors eventually report the situation to the local social services office. News of the girls' imprisonment attracts great media attention. Feeling betrayed and exposed, a baffled Gorban Ali cannot understand what the pandemonium is all about. He has done what custom dictated, especially considering that his wife is blind and cannot look after their daughters.

The father-turned-jailer knows exactly why he caged his daughters: he was shielding them from the dangers of the outside world. He was guarding their honor and his own.[48] Gorban Ali knows he is not alone in his belief that girls are vulnerable and in need of cloistering. He has relied on the authority of successive generations of elders' advice and their books. He diligently carries a tattered notebook around with him in which he has written down the wisdom passed down from fathers to sons. He quotes from a parenting manual titled *Advice to Fathers*. "A man's gaze is like the sun," he recites with authority, "and a girl is like a flower. If the sun shines on her, she will fade. It is like putting cotton next to fire. The fire will consume the cotton." Gorban Ali has simply taken traditional recommendations to their logical conclusions.[49] If, as custom has it, the ideal woman is one who is *aftab-o-mahtab nadideh*—that is, "one who has not been glimpsed by the sun or the moon"—it is only appropriate for this devoted father to make sure his daughters do not set foot outside the house.

The social worker assigned to the case rejects Gorban Ali's logic altogether. She is convinced the girls' isolation is gender discrimination. She castigates the bewildered father for his suffocating love: "The problem is that Zahra and Ma'ssoumeh are girls. If they'd been boys, they'd play outside. They'd go out with you. They'd even climb walls." To confirm the truth of her statement, the camera zooms in on three boys who are playing on the wall of Gorban Ali's house. With a combination of cheerful glee and remarkable entitlement, they look into his small courtyard searching for a soccer ball that they have lost. Yet their behavior ironically vindicates Gorban Ali's position. "Didn't I tell you, ma'am, that I have to lock the door?" he retorts to the social worker. "The boys in the street throw their balls into our yard, they ring the bell and when they don't hear any answer they climb the wall and jump in. Now, tell me, please, if one of them were to harm my girls, what am I to do?"

It is easy to imagine how Gorban Ali might have been persuaded that his problem was not with his girls, but with the male prerogative to harm them should they come in contact with them, but he is unable to look at things this way. Because he cannot even imagine a situation in which boys can be kept home-bound and off the street, he is convinced his paternal duty is to imprison his daughters to "protect" them from harm. As far as he is concerned, men's freedom of movement is God-willed and everlasting rather than human improvised and contingent. Women's proper place, according to this loving jailer, is at home.

Contrary to Gorban Ali's deeply ingrained conviction, Zahra and Ma'ssoumeh change once they are finally liberated from their dungeon. They delight in their freedom. Holding a mirror in one hand and a comb in the other, first reluctantly and then with increasing delight, they wander up and down the alley. They commit all kinds of faux pas in the process. They take ice cream without paying for it, share it with a goat, and gradually venture farther and farther away from home. Wide-eyed, they find their way to the park, the playground, the market-place. A dangling apple held in front of them by a boy attracts their attention and appetite. "If you want an apple," he tells them cheerfully, "follow me." The two sisters tag along. When they arrive at the fruit market, they grasp a handful of apples.[50] With no previous contact with the outside world, they do not know they have to pay. Desire is not equated with money yet, and from their perspective an apple desired and accessible is an apple owned.[51]

The director Samira Makhmalbaf does not romanticize access to the outside world. Although she depicts the children basking in the sun and the sun shining on them, although she shows them blossoming rather than withering and expanding as their world expands, she does not flinch from showing what happens in the Naderi family. The children act in a strikingly unaffected fashion in front of the camera. Blind to danger and oblivious to fear, they display an astounding self-confidence. And the director is similarly nonjudgmental and sympathetic; she, too, is equally frank. She portrays the space within the house not only as a prison, but also as a nest. It is a space free from temptations, the hustle and bustle of the street, the cruelty of a world of commodities, markets, and money. But she does not flinch from showing that access to that world, no matter how flawed, is necessary for change and growth.[52] "I couldn't wait to start," Makhmalbaf said in an interview, "because I was sure the girls would change very quickly. And over 11 days of shooting they did develop a lot—you can see it on the screen. They go to school now; you wouldn't believe they are the same people. They weren't mentally retarded—they're so clever—just socially retarded because of having no communication with the outside world."[53]

*The Apple* brings into focus the role of forced immobility, the impact of visible and invisible caging, the warping and controlling of women's lives. It views stasis as the principal cause of lost autonomy and arrested growth. Although the line of demarcation between the victor and the victim, the tormented and the tormentor, the prisoner and the prison warden is not always clear in *The Apple,* the film's central metaphor—freedom of movement—is undoubtedly the visual and symbolic signifier of change. "What I noticed about those girls," says the young director, "is that the more they came into contact with society, the more complete they became as human beings. For me that became a metaphor for all women. The other women in the neighborhood all have bars in front of their houses. They're all wearing *Chadors.* They live in the same prison, just a little better."[54] Once *The Apple* was made and Makhmalbaf traveled with it to several countries, she extended the frame of reference of its symbolism to include women in other countries as well. "I found that everywhere women's prospects are worse than men's."[55]

For centuries, the liberty to roam at will has been a masculine privilege, even a cultural imperative. A stay-at-home man has been considered unvirile. He has been depicted as childlike and effeminate, worthy of ridicule and social scorn, like Hassan Kachal in the popular folktale of that name ("Hassan the Baldy"). This well-known story was adapted into a highly acclaimed movie and became the first Iranian musical in 1970. Directed by Ali Hatemi, *Hassan Kachal* begins with the agonies of a widow whose bald son does not want to leave home. Hassan is ashamed of his appearance and has become a recluse. He does not play with the neighborhood children. He does not climb trees or walls. He does not compete in games. Although there is no term for it in the Persian language, he is in fact a "sissy." His mother fully recognizes that her son, who is on the verge of adulthood, should not stay inside the house lest he become henpecked and effeminate. Thus, grief-stricken and desperate, she tries every trick she knows to persuade him to go out.

Hassan does not outwardly exhibit any characteristics that are even remotely feminine. Unlike his mother, he does not put on a scarf. He does not wear girls' clothing or makeup. He displays no female grooming habits, does not befriend girls, never plays with dolls, doesn't throw tea parties, doesn't even cry. In other words, his behavior in no way reflects the assigned gender roles: he is not "girlish." His one striking unmasculine trait within the Iranian context—the cause of his mother's great anguish precisely because it proves that he has failed to live up to the expectations of masculinity—is his physical immobility. He wants to stay cooped up in the house. He prefers the inside, a "feminine" space, to the outside, the place associated with men. This trait is the only one that is inconsistent with his gender identity and gendered performance. To his mother's unending chagrin, Hassan has voluntarily and foolishly relinquished his innate right to roam the streets.

Finally, in her desperation to lure him out, the mother resorts to a ruse. She places red apples between his bedroom and the outside door. Hassan is tempted. He leaves the house, and his life is changed forever. He metamorphoses into a full-fledged man, falls in love with a woman who is incarcerated by a demon, liberates her, and marries her. With his masculinity secured, he lives happily ever after. So does his mother.

## THE THREE AGES OF FEMALE MOBILITY

Just as *The Apple* shows how Gorban Ali confined his daughters inside the house from birth, and *Hassan Kachal* depicts how Hassan's mother had to make him leave the house in order to make a man of him, *The Day I Became a Woman* (2000), the directorial debut of Marzieh Meshkini, focuses on the gendered allocation of space by rendering three stages in the Iranian woman's life. Although the veil, as an expression of sex segregation, is omnipresent in all three different yet interrelated episodes in this film, the theme of women's mobility emerges in them as the most serious threat to male-centered institutions and values. The first vignette equates a girl's puberty with her abrupt confinement at home. The last reflects on how old age restores mobility to a woman when it no longer serves much. And the middle film concentrates on the tropes of motion and containment during a woman's life when everything is most at stake.

In the first episode of *The Day I Became a Woman,* a mother and grandmother attempt to confine Hawa when she reaches puberty. The film begins with Hawa's ninth birthday. This is not an ordinary birthday for her; it is a rite of passage from childhood to the beginning of her youth. It is considered the onset of the age of *taklif,* which is the Persian word not only for menses, but also for obligations. From now on, Hawa (the Persian version of "Eve") has new responsibilities, new limitations, new liabilities in life. She has to don the veil, and, more traumatically, she has to relinquish her earlier free access to the street. "Starting today," her grandmother tells her, "you shouldn't go in the street and play with the boys anymore." Hawa is confused and annoyed. She doesn't understand the new restrictions. She has always played with her friend Hassan.[56] Why shouldn't she today? "Why was it OK for me to go out and buy ice cream with Hassan yesterday, but I can't do it today?" asks the baffled and irritated girl. "You weren't a woman yesterday. You weren't a grown-up. You're a grown-up today," explains the stern-looking grandmother-turned-warden. Yet the new little prisoner decides to negotiate the terms of her detention, as she will have to continue doing for the rest of her life. She was born at noon, and it is only eleven o'clock now, she bargains shrewdly with her mother and grandmother. She is granted one last hour to play freely in the neighborhood.

The last film, which deals with old age, looks at the question of female mobility from the other end of the spectrum. It shows an old woman, Houra, who, like the pre-nine-year-old Hawa, is free to roam at will. She is finally free of familial and marital obligations, but freedom has, alas, come too late. Houra, who has just inherited a sum of money and proclaims triumphantly, "Whatever I never had, I will buy for myself now," is in a wheelchair. Although she now has the material means to do as she wants, her mobility has been reduced to a wheelchair. Simultaneously mobile and confined in her own paralysis, she is trundled onto a beach, where she observes her newly acquired objects, including a vacuum cleaner that is used to suck up acres of sand. It is a powerful image of waste, futility, and loss that lingers with the audience long after the film is over.

The middle film in this cycle of three is the most interesting of all. It begins with a shot of a young woman who is participating in an all-women cycling tournament on Kish Island. Fully covered, Ahoo (which means "deer" in English) is speeding ahead. Her husband, her father, her brothers, and the village elders—all men on horseback—order her to get off the bicycle. First is her husband, who resorts to medical excuses. "You should not pedal with your bad leg," he shouts at her. Concern quickly turns into threat. "Didn't I tell you I'd divorce you if I ever see you riding a bike again? Get off the bike." But Ahoo pedals ever faster. The frustrated husband brings along the cleric who years earlier had officiated at their wedding. Mullah Osman tells Ahoo that the prospect of finalizing her divorce saddens him. "Get off the bike," he pleads with her gently and in an infantilizing tone. "Get off the bike, dear girl." But Ahoo prefers divorce to giving up biking and abandoning the race. The man who is now her ex-husband angrily shouts at her, "It's over. You can pedal all you want now." And she does with resolve and purpose—totally unrepentant and unperturbed. Marriage does not offer a happy ending for Ahoo. Traditional definitions of modesty and domesticity are not the central tenets of her life. On the contrary, she is willing to sacrifice all to pursue her path. The husband annuls their marriage, and the divorced Ahoo pedals on with even more passion and gusto than the married one. She picks up speed and focuses her attention and energy on the competition, on the road, on speed and motion.

Then her father and uncles suddenly arrive on their horses. They, too, do their best to persuade her to respect family honor and pride. They fail. Next the grandfather and the elders of the tribe show up. Pleas turn into threats, love into anger. The hectoring continues: "The devil be damned. Get off the bike. The honor of the clan is at stake," say the elders. An oblivious Ahoo pedals on. In fact, the more she is harassed, the faster she charges ahead. This time her two brothers show up on their galloping horses. They do not resort to medical excuses, advice, pleas, or words. They don't need to. They are strong and angry and know exactly what to do. They block her way like two bullies. As Constance Bacon writes, "In the end of the second segment, the tight framing of Ahoo on the bicycle allows the viewer an intimacy with her; we see her emotional struggle up close, we find ourselves almost out of breath along with her, and then, with the closing shot, the camera pulls away. And we see this violent clash from a distance."[57]

In the third episode of this film, two women show up on their bicycles and report on the consequences of Ahoo's story. "We were in a cycling competition," says one, "when something funny happened. Some girl was winning the race when her brothers showed up, took her bike and went away with it." Her friend adds, "She took a bike from some other girl who was too tired to continue the race, pedaled hard, and won the race." "No," rejoins the first woman, "someone else won the race. That girl was taken away by her brothers." Ahoo's fate is thus left open-ended, unresolved, but the significance of her struggle is unambiguous. Her longing to break out of the narrow space allocated to women and to break free of the customs, roles, and laws associated with it is clear.[58] Ahoo wants to move beyond the conventional frames established by her culture. She wants to be free. As a woman, she knows very well that the battle for freedom is being fought with the greatest intensity and the most passion on the grounds of women's mobility. In fact, Ahoo had to travel to Kish Island in the Persian Gulf to be filmed riding her bicycle. Women are not allowed to ride their bikes in Tehran. Offering certain liberties that the capital city does not, Kish is the only part of Iran where women are allowed to ride their bikes freely. Known for its cosmopolitanism, Kish is a modern city with many highways, towering apartment buildings, theme parks, and beaches. It is also famous for its bicycle paths, and this last distinction is not to be taken lightly.

Ahoo's strenuous efforts to ride her bicycle without permission or supervision symbolize an ardent desire to blur and destabilize sacrosanct boundaries. As a woman biker, she questions social assumptions, modifies codes of sex segregation, even questions government regulations. She refuses to maintain the distinctions between a private sphere for women and a public sphere for men. Her search for freedom of movement subverts all conventions. Rather than preserve the status quo, Ahoo disrupts it. She is an explorer on a bike; she ventures into forbidden territories. In *The House Is Black*, freedom of movement is asserted as a basic human right. In *The Apple*, access to the public sphere becomes a catalyst of change. And in *The Day I Became a Woman*, Hawa will do anything for even one hour more in the street, and Ahoo chooses mobility over domesticity because to give up such freedom would reduce life to a wheelchair in a desert of sand.

## CROSS-DRESSING AND CROSS-SINGING

Iranian directors have devised and deployed ingenious strategies in an effort to achieve a fundamental restructuring of the cultural landscape. Consider cross-dressing, for which there is no word in the Persian language. More than half-a-dozen movies produced in less than a decade deal with protagonists who move in and out of masculine and feminine roles and spaces. An even larger number of films allude to this practice. Although some of these films have been banned from the silver screen in the country, those allowed screenings have been box office hits. In addition, pirated copies of the banned films make the rounds in a flourishing Iranian black market.[59]

Iran has always had reasons for ritualized or occasional, isolated gender impostures. For instance, during the ancient Zoroastrian celebration of *yalda* (the longest night of the year and the beginning of winter) and *chahar shanbeh souri* (the last Tuesday of the solar year), men could masquerade as women by donning the veil. Furthermore, for centuries men dressed as female dancers and singers because women could not perform on stage in mixed gatherings; they acted as women characters in the Ta'ziyeh, an indigenous, Shi'ite form of drama; and on rare occasions they veiled themselves as a strategy for survival: to elude the enemy and to confound the foe. There are intriguing examples of cross-dressing in Persian literature and in *One Thousand and One Nights,* tales of restless lovers slipping into or away from women's quarters in disguise. Unveiling, however, was not tolerated for women even within the controlled setting of rituals. During *yalda* and *chahar shanbeh souri* celebrations, women could leave their homes and stroll outside in the city streets to listen to the conversations of random passersby *(falghoush),* but they could do so only if covered in their all-encompassing cloaks. The first words to reach their ears were then taken as predictions of events in their upcoming year. In the rare historical and literary accounts of transvestism in Iran, women disguised themselves in order to fight patriotic and religious wars.

In contemporary Iranian movies, men and women who cross-dress have different agendas. They often reject age-old absolutes, replacing them with ambiguous realities. By mixing traditional and rigidly differentiated categories, they reflect yet another aspect of the transformation that is shaking the foundations of Iranian society. Cross-dressers, especially women who dress as men, defy authority, evade the obligatory dress codes, run away from restrictive homes, seek jobs, roam the streets more freely, escape oppressive conditions, enter sports stadiums from which they are excluded even when they are fully covered from head to foot and willing to sit in segregated sections. The film *Offside* (2006) by Majid Panahi is a case in point. The movie centers on a group of young women who cross-dress to enter a masculine sphere: the Azadi Soccer Stadium. According to some unwritten postrevolutionary law, women are barred from entering the stadium either as players or as fans. Against the backdrop of a World Cup qualifying match—an actual soccer match between Iran and Bahrain—six young women masquerade as men to watch the game in the stadium. They wear men's clothing, cover their hair with baseball caps, and paint their faces with the color of the Iranian flag (green, white, and red). Although the camera follows the story of the six who are arrested for breaking the law and who are locked up in a makeshift prison, the viewers learn from them that many other cross-dressers slipped successfully into the stadium and escaped detection.

The veil has traditionally been synonymous with femininity and invisibility, its absence with masculinity and visibility. This dichotomy is so strongly imbedded in Iranians' collective psyche that certain contemporary performers do not even need to cross-dress for effect. They can depend on the Iranian beholder's imagination to supply the shock of implied transgression through a mere inflection of the voice, the barest hint of transvestism in song. One of Iran's top comedians, a sensation inside the country, is a perfect example of this trend. Dressed in a suit so that his rapt audiences cannot forget that he is a man, Hamid Mahisefat breaks into a falsetto, singing numbers that Iranian divas made popular before the Islamic Revolution or sing now in the Diaspora. He literally becomes a woman trapped in a man's body and attire.

There is, of course, nothing new about a man singing at high pitch. Castrati did it for centuries the world over. Iranian women's voices, like their bodies, have been banned in public for centuries, too. They were neither permitted to perform on stage nor sing in mixed gatherings until the twentieth century. The first concert held by a woman for a mixed-sex audience was at Tehran's Grand Hotel in 1924. In spite of death threats, Qamar ol-Moluk Vazirizadeh (1905–59) unveiled her voice, leading the way for other female singers to reveal their talents. Half a century later, however, when the Islamic Revolution banned women from singing in public, many of the country's great divas were chased into exile overnight.

Their recordings were destroyed, their voices were silenced.[60] Since then, none of these popular singers has been seen on state-run television; none has been heard on Iranian radio or appeared on stage. But a male comedian has begun to masquerade as these censored female singers before mixed-sex audiences.

What Mahisefat is doing is far more than cross-singing, however: he is daring to evoke the banned voices of women singers publicly and openly. And he is masquerading a woman's voice in a man's body. The irony is that although Hamid Mahisefat can cross-sing, at least for now, he cannot legally cross-dress. He has to depend on his audience to provide him with a woman's body. But he is not an isolated case or an aberration. He is part of a trend that is fundamentally remapping the political and cultural landscape of Iran. Cross-dressing, which is forbidden in Islam and is now illegal in Iran, has gripped Iranians' cultural imagination.[61]

More than three decades after the Islamic Revolution and in spite of mandatory dress codes for men and women, both veiling and unveiling have developed new meanings and implications. Nothing is exactly what it pretends to be. *The Circle* (2001) by Ja'far Panahi captures this redefinition of the veil. The central metaphor of this movie, which is a passionate and polemical protest against women's restrained mobility, is prison. The film begins and ends with locked doors and bars. First, the door of a maternity ward opens to herald the sadly announced and sadly received news of the birth of a baby girl. The bars of a jail close the film. The circle is complete, incarceration unending, almost inescapable. The circuit of a life is closed.[62] In point of fact, however, this film, which centers on prison, is almost fully shot on the streets of Tehran. David Denby astutely remarks, "I have never seen women move the way they do in the Iranian film, *The Circle*. On the busy streets of Tehran, four frightened women, veiled, dressed in black, rush distractedly from block to block, store-to-store, telephone booth to newsstand. They crouch at the side of cars to avoid the police, dart down alleys, flee from dangerous places with black chadors held over their heads, as if flying under dark wings."[63] Denby has a point. Chadors have become wings, means of flight, passports to enter previously inaccessible territories.

Veiling is no longer the equivalent of concealment in Iran, just as unveiling is not synonymous with disclosure. Instead, unveiling has now become a form of "veiling," a disguise, and veiling has mutated into a fashion statement, a spectacle, a colorful theater staged on the streets for all to see.

## COMPETING NARRATIVES
## OF MASCULINITY AND FEMININITY

The coexistence of this radical departure from deeply rooted assumptions regarding masculinity and femininity side by side with the frantic effort to hold on to them is a perfect metaphor for Iranian society today. It exemplifies the escalating push and pull between tradition and change, democracy and autocracy.[64] Take the veiled/unveiled antithesis that has typified traditional walls of separation in Iranian culture and has served as the visual marker and symbolic foundation of gender difference.

If, as F. Scott Fitzgerald once put it, "The test of a first-rate intelligence is the ability to hold opposed ideas at the same time and still retain the ability to function,"[65] then Iranian cinema is a first-rate intelligence. It is a testament to the intractability and inevitability of the deep-seated conflicts of a society in transition. The dialectic of revealing and concealing, private and public, travel and homecoming, movement and restraint is made explicit. The burning and ransacking of movie theaters that marked the beginning of the Islamic Revolution is as much a part of it as its attainment of one of the most globally appreciated form of Iranian art forms. Reflecting the complex and paradoxical realities of lives, cinema throws a vivid spotlight on the contradictions that are shaking the very foundation of Iranian society, especially where the lives of women are concerned. On the one hand, it portrays women as oppressed by restrictive laws, patriarchal norms, parents, and custodians of the status quo. With ingenious ploys, it informs the audience that on screen women are bound by stringent codes of cinematic modesty.[66] They cannot sing, dance, run, establish desirous or direct eye contact with men, openly express romantic love or lust. On the other hand, it depicts women as having agency, will, competence, courage, and aspirations of their own. They are far from being captives of conventional roles and confining interiors. Voluntarily or grudgingly veiled, they expand the range of action and imagination, proving to be central to the iconography of the new sociopolitical and artistic order.

Young, internationally acclaimed female directors and girls kept prisoner because of their gender live alongside one another. Women are forbidden to ride bicycles, but they drive cars with a vengeance. Moving cars have become iconic in many movies, and women drivers are central to the unfolding plots of numerous films in recent years. "In many of the recent family dramas," writes Najmeh Khalili Mahani, "the key to a brand new car serves the same romantic notion as a big diamond ring does in most Hollywood dramas."[67] Women's widespread use of cars as a means of mobility in a remarkable number of movies—*Two Women* (1999) and *The Fifth Reaction* (2003) by Tahmineh Milani; *Soorati* [2002] by Feyreydoun Jeyrani; *Ten* (2002) by Abbas Kiarostami; *The Iranian Journey* (2003) by Maysoon Panachi, among many others—contrasts sharply with an abundance of means of physical containment, such as walls, veils, curtains, bars, fences, and barbed wire, all designed to enforce women's immobility.

In spite of all the restrictions or perhaps because of them, women have invaded Iranian cinema, from which they were once totally excluded, even as spectators. What is truly astounding is their inspiring presence now after their earlier near erasure. Women are no longer consigned to absence or immobility, relegated to sitting behind the screen. On the contrary, they are on screen and involved in every aspect of filmmaking. For the first time in its seventy-six-year history, the Academy Awards honored an Iranian woman in 2004. Although actress Shohreh Aghdashloo did not win the much-coveted award for best-supporting actress—to the chagrin of most Iranians, who, regardless of their political affiliation, were rooting for her—her mere presence in the ceremony was celebrated as an accomplishment of great significance. Aghdashloo's nomination for her work in *House of Sand and Fog* not only acknowledged her powerful acting, but also uncovered a paradox. In her personal life, Aghdashloo is an assertive, articulate, and successful woman. Nadi, the character she plays in the film, however, is a submissive and subjugated woman who is caged in and suffocated by her domesticity. Together, actress and character capture the complex reality of Iranian women's lives. By honoring both Nadi and Aghdashloo, the Oscars portrayed Iranian women's victimization as well as their relentless resistance and hitherto unsung victories.

Today Iranian women are avid moviegoers, talented actors, prize-winning directors. They are actively present at the dawn of a new era in their country, an historic moment for an internationally acclaimed art form, the motion picture.

# PART TWO

# Wings and Words

# 4

# BADASHT AND SENECA FALLS

*Tahirih Qurratul'Ayn and Elizabeth Cady Stanton*

Ah! Alas, Qurratul'Ayn! You were worth a thousand Nasiru'd-Din Shahs.
—SULAYMAN NAZIF, "Passages from Nasiruddin
Shah ve Babiler"

She was not kneeling before him, as she should. She was not sitting with her
head bowed in his presence as might be expected of a daughter of the house.
She was pacing restlessly, back and forth, across the room. It was hard to
glare satisfactorily at a woman in constant motion.
—BAHIYYIH NAKHJAVANI,
"The Woman Who Read Too Much"

## WALLED IN ANONYMITY, VEILED IN AMBIGUITY

There are no photographs of Tahirih Qurratul'Ayn (1817–52), the Iranian poet who publicly unveiled herself in 1848 and was executed at the age of thirty-six in 1852, after almost four years of imprisonment in the city of Tehran. In mid-nineteenth-century Iran, the newly introduced art of photography was reserved for the court, and no official prisons existed for women anywhere in the country.[1] There was no need for them, really. Women were virtual prisoners, anyway, circumscribed in delineated boundaries, with every move under control. So no mug shots were needed, no wanted posters were required for this female who was under house arrest in the upper storeroom of the mayor's residence; not even any prison records were kept about this Iranian woman, who at the height of her intellectual and creative powers had been placed in solitary confinement in the capital.

There is, however, an image of Tahirih carved during her life and preserved against all odds in an unlikely place: the tombstone of her father-in-law, Taqi

Baraghani, in the private mausoleum of the family in the northwestern city of Qazvin. A carving on a tombstone, let alone an elaborate one that tells a story, is rare, if not unique in Iran. Pictorial representation is usually frowned upon for tombstones. More baffling yet is the scene depicted: a veiled woman, holding a piece of paper and half hidden by a curtain, looks on as two men, spears in hand, are stabbing a turbaned mullah in the back while he kneels down in prayer. Underneath this grisly image are inscribed the following words: "The martyrdom of Mullah Taqi by a Babi heretic."

Who is the "Babi heretic" charged with this dreadful murder? Why the singular reference when two men are clearly attacking the prostrate priest? Or is it the woman, rather, caught red-handed, who is being thus implicated? More important, who is the revengeful accuser absent from the scene but relentlessly pointing a finger of blame at this mysterious woman? She is covered in a chador and half-concealed by a curtain but is apparently overseeing and masterminding the assassination of Mullah Taqi Baraghani, the Friday Prayer leader of the city of Qazvin. The paper she holds is incriminating evidence against her, for it is clear that the woman's usurpation of the written word is as lethal as any assassin's dagger. The iconography of the tombstone seems to suggest that the death of the patriarch and the presence of a woman in a public place amount to the same thing.

That Tahirih had nothing to do with the murder of her father-in-law, other than perhaps predicting it, is a matter of historic record now. The real murderer, one Mirza 'Abdullah Shirazi, admitted his guilt and presented to the authorities the bloody dagger with which he had assaulted Mullah Taqi in the mosque in 1847 as he was praying. However, the person who commissioned the carving, the murdered mullah's son and Tahirih's estranged husband, Mullah Mohammad, remained unaffected by his wife's acquittal, even though it was approved by no less a personage than the king himself, Mohammad Shah Qajar (reigned 1834–48). He continued to hold her culpable or at least complicit in the killing of his father and had several other men tortured and executed in his unquenchable desire for revenge. Wrong but resolute in his allegation of homicide, he was nonetheless right in his recognition that the killing of his father was effectively the symbolic end to patriarchy in Iran, at least as he knew it. A new era was in the making: one in which women were no longer absent, one in which women could read and write and with daring insert themselves, body and voice, in the public scene. And yet, ironically enough, though driven by his wrath and despair to carve her guilt in stone, the angry husband could not allow his exwife to be unveiled or her name uttered in public. He labeled her a heretic, accused her of murder and mayhem, but made sure she was covered with a veil, concealed behind a curtain, anonymous. He refused her a personal identity even in this accusatory carving. This pattern of slander, erasure, and denial seems to have been set in stone—literally a tombstone—from that time on.

Even 160 years after her death, the mere recognition of Tahirih Qurratul'Ayn's existence and any discussion of her life and work are forbidden in her own country, but criticism and vilification are welcomed and in plentiful supply.[2] In rare instances when individuals acknowledge her contributions, they wrap her in anonymity, cloak her in ambiguity, veil her in allegory. Consider Sharnush Parsipur's masterpiece *Touba and the Meaning of Night* (1989), one of the classics of modern Persian literature.[3] The book covers almost a century of Iranian history, from the late nineteenth century to the 1979 Revolution, through the perspective and life of its title character, a woman named Touba. One might argue that this novel, like the carving on Mullah Taqi's tombstone, is the tale of the death of the patriarch and women's emerging public presence. The impact of this seismic change on men, women, and children is examined with precision in the novel. In fact, it is its central trope, an event that launches a sequence of events over the years and sets in motion the whole plot.

Touba's father, a man named Haji Adib, is a poet-scholar whose world of certitudes and absolutes has been shattered. "Something had been shaken in him," writes Parsipur, "just as it had the first time he had seen the globe." Haji Adib has come into contact with the new sciences and the "question about the shape of the earth continued to weigh on his mind." Although he had known that the earth was round, he wants to continue believing it was flat and square. This is more comfortable, more comforting. But the world around him is changing with relentless rapidity and circumstances are conspiring against his long-held and snug convictions. In particular, one "subversive woman" has unsettled his universe. Although she remains mysteriously unidentified throughout the novel, she had lived during Haji Adib's "childhood and created chaos and uproar." She had proven that women could think and reason in public. "It was rumored that she was a *harja'i* [a prostitute, a woman who was everywhere], but she was also believed to be a learned woman. There was so much controversy about her!" One man had told "his father with great enthusiasm that she was the messiah."[4]

A befuddled Haji Adib cannot reconcile the two extremes of admiration and condemnation, approval and disapproval, reserved for this enigmatic woman. But he is astute and observant enough to acknowledge, even if with pain and apprehension, that just as the world is no longer flat and square, everything around him is in flux and has taken a different meaning. Boundaries are no longer clearly delineated. Everything is in movement and not in its assigned place. Walls, veils, curtains, and previously drawn borders no longer enclose women. Like the round and rotating planet, women move about freely and refuse to be still. The genie is out of the bottle. And worse yet, women's physical mobility is accompanied by their entry into the forbidden fields of knowledge and jurisprudence. Two of Haji Adib's most solid and longstanding convictions, that the earth is flat and that women can't think, are thus shattered. To him, thinking, like roaming freely in the streets, is a male prerogative. "They think," he tells himself in a moment of lucid and intuitive leap of understanding. "Unfortunately," he realizes, women think. "Neither like the ants, nor like the particles of dust, but more or less as I do."[5] To his chagrin, he can see the ensuing change in the balance of power between the sexes. In response and before he dies, he makes sure to give his daughter a globe and teach her how to read. And Touba, like her unnamed foremother, the "subversive woman," becomes the harbinger of change, the emblem of a transformed cultural, political, and literary landscape. She goes on a spiritual quest, appraises traditional spaces, has ambitions beyond the domestic, and navigates uncharted territories. She becomes the iconoclastic heroine of a novel by an iconoclastic and talented writer.

This transformative moment is also central to Bahiyyih Nakhjavani's provocative allegory *The Saddlebag*, a novel published in the United Kingdom in 2000 and translated into many languages, but not Persian. It is about the impact of mysterious writings found in the desert by nine different characters in the course of a twenty-four-hour period in an unnamed country in the mid-nineteenth-century Middle East. In one of its chapters, a young priest who finds these scrolls is overwhelmed by recollections of a woman who had destabilized and upset the equilibrium of his life some years earlier and who had been the cause of his fleeing into the desert in the first place. He had heard her debate theological issues with the highest religious authorities and had listened in horror and fascination as she confronted them with arguments in a manner that was at once confident and eloquent, courageous and candid. "The young priest had attended some of this woman's classes," writes Nakhjavani. "They had caused him nights of feverish sleeplessness and furious mental strife. She sat behind a curtain and held sway over a room full of men by the power of her oratory alone. . . . When the young priest remembered it he still flushed to the roots of his scurfy hair and felt his limbs tremble beneath him, even though months had passed since the event."[6] As a result of this disquieting encounter, the priest is uprooted from home and family and drifts into exile, his beliefs shaken, his confidence destroyed, so unable is he to resolve the dilemma of whether to condemn or to accept this woman's words. He remains irresolute, a wanderer and simultaneously a prisoner trapped in the middle of the desert of his indecision. Given the novel's historic context and the description of the nameless woman, it is clear that this female orator is inspired by the historical character Tahirih Qurratul'Ayn.

Parsipur and Nakhjavani are two exceptional examples of the few writers over the past few decades who have dared celebrate this "subversive woman" who blazed the trail of change in nineteenth-century Iran. Although Parsipur clearly identifies many historic figures of the time such as kings, activists, and clerics, she had to leave unnamed this woman who is pivotal to the unfolding plot of her novel. Nakhjavani, too, who explores the life and times of Tahirih Qurratul'Ayn at even greater length in a subsequent work, *The Woman Who Read Too Much*,[7] chooses to deploy allegory rather than biography in each case. It is as though there is no way to speak of Tahirih Qurratul'Ayn, this woman who unveiled herself with such audacity in mid-nineteenth-century Iran, except in veiled terms.

## THE SKETCHY BIOGRAPHY OF A MUTANT WOMAN

So who is this woman whose name can barely be mentioned in her own country more than 150 years after her death? Who is this enigmatic woman extolled as a saint and denounced as a sorceress, praised as an exceptional woman and called a dangerous lunatic? Is she a martyr or a murderer, a heretic or a heroine? Is she the sign of the end of times or a female messiah? Is she "the first woman suffrage martyr,"[8] "the Persian Joan of Arc, the leader of emancipation for women of the Orient,"[9] Iran's "Florence Nightingale,"[10] or simply a crazed woman caught in the grip of her own lustful debaucheries, the victim of a self-destructive dream? From beneath the avalanche of sensational gossip, fragmented information, polarized adulation, and hatred that engulfs her, is it possible to unearth this woman who wanted to command her own destiny and write her own script? Is it impossible to evoke the life and times of this pioneering woman and not depict the fear and idolatry, the demonization and sanctification of her by her compatriots? To humanize a legend and show the realistic dimensions of a myth, is it not necessary to examine both extremes? Such seemingly irreconcilable opposites—witch and saint, villain and victim, martyr and murderer—considered with either wholesale slander or absolute worship by detractors or admirers, reflect reactions to a woman who was ahead of her time and hard to pigeonhole and categorize.

Tahirih Qurratul'Ayn was born Fatemeh Baraghani into a religious family sometime in 1817 in the city of Qazvin.[11] Despite this statement's seeming simplicity and brevity, there is no unanimity of opinion even on it. In fact, there is debate regarding both the name she was given at birth and the date of her birth. According to some sources her real name was Om-e Salmeh, Hind, or Zarrin Taj rather than Fatemeh, and, according to others, she was born in 1814 rather than three years later. This ambiguity illustrates the contradictory and complicated roles Tahirih has played in the Iranian society and psyche. The names Zakiyeh (Intelligent), Noqteh (the Point), Tuti (Parrot), Qurratul'Ayn (Solace of the Eye), Tahirih (the Pure One), Bent-e-Taleh (Daughter of Evil), Shir Zan (Lioness of a Woman), Khatun-e 'Ajam (Lady of Persia),[12] among many others, were foisted upon her during her life and after her death. She was and is too protean to fit under a single name or label.

Owing to the happy circumstances of her birth, and thanks to the character of her father, Mullah Saleh, who was a liberal and broad-minded scholar of the Qur'an, Tahirih received an education quite unusual and extensive for women of her time. Mullah Saleh, like his brother Mullah Taqi, was an influential *mojtahed* (high cleric) of his province. He became his daughter's first teacher, mentor, interlocutor, and admirer. Under his tutelage, Tahirih explored theology, Qur'anic exegesis, jurisprudence, and Persian and Arabic literature. Her father recognized and encouraged her insightful mind and allowed her, against all the protocols of the time, to participate in his classes and debating sessions from behind a curtain. And she did so with a vengeance. The ease with which she undertook theological argument, the power of her eloquence and expression in debate, the range of her inquisitive and searching mind, and her vast knowledge of Persian literature quickly earned her a reputation not only in her town, but in the whole country. "If only she were a boy," her father lamented, "she would have illuminated my house and come to be my successor."[13] In his wildest dreams or nightmares, Mullah Saleh could not have imagined the fame and notoriety his daughter was destined to acquire. Nor could he have fathomed the role she was to play in Iranian history and literature.

Tahirih lived at a time in Iran when women's reading was controlled, if not outright discouraged. Higher education and seminaries were barred to women. Their divinely ordained missions in life were marriage and motherhood, their place inside the house or in delineated spaces. Tahirih followed the custom and was married by arrangement to her cousin at the age of fourteen. The marriage took her to Iraq, where her husband, Mullah Mohammad, the son of her paternal uncle, pursued his religious education. While in Iraq, the couple resided in Karbala, the shrine city, for thirteen years, and Tahirih gave birth to two sons, Ibrahim and Isma'il. A third child, a daughter whose name remained unknown until recently, was also born during this period and a little boy in the early 1840s.[14] Though domestic quarrels clouded her marriage, the environment of passionate debate and exploration of controversial points of theology in Karbala inspired Tahirih. She discovered Shaykhism, a nineteenth-century heterodox school of Shi'ism, and possibly attended classes conducted by its leader, Seyyed Kazem Rashti.

Upon returning to Iran, Tahirih blossomed into an orator and a thinker in her own right. Like the Shaykhis, she had a strong messianic vision of the world and believed that a new era was in the making. Instead of challenging and discussing religious doctrines with her family, she now began to contradict them. Her reformist views clashed bitterly with her husband's orthodoxy. After the birth of her last child, she left her husband and family and, along with her sister and her brother-in-law, returned to Iraq in order to join the classes of Seyed Kazem Rashti, who in appreciation of her erudition had given her the title "Qurratul'Ayn." But by the time Tahirih reached her destination, Rashti had died. She stayed in his home and eventually took up his place, teaching his students from behind a curtain. Even today, no woman in Iran occupies such a position as she assumed in 1844—that of a teacher and a leader in a center of higher religious scholarship for men. Iranian seminaries were all-male bastions of Islamic learning. By being denied admission to these centers of Islamic education, women were in effect silenced in juridical deliberations. Their religious standing, like their legal and ethical rights, was determined without their direct participation in the debates. Important decisions were thus made without taking into account the necessity or even the validity of a female perspective.

Tahirih's father-in-law, her husband, and other members of her family blamed her book learning for the destruction of her domestic life. At that time, women were excluded from the public discourse. Even for the exceptional few who did attain higher education, the means of communication with the outside world was limited. If some daughters of clerics or the privileged classes were given an education, their expression of that knowledge, like their acquisition of it, was restricted to the private and familial domain. The power to interpret religious injunctions was the preserve of men; it remained strictly a male prerogative. But Tahirih refused to be pinned down within limits of propriety and the prevalent cultural norms for womanhood. She attended classes, studied at libraries, engaged in talks and debates, traveled extensively, and challenged openly and publicly some of the highest-ranking theologians and politicians of her times. She represented a break with the culture of segregation that kept the female body, voice, point of view, sensibility, and knowledge trapped in the private realm of home and family. She became a public scholar in both the spatial sense and the discursive sense. She addressed theological issues in the wider world rather than only speaking or writing on personal matters in private. She proved to the chagrin of many—represented by Haji Adib in *Touba and the Meaning of Night* and the young priest in *The Saddlebag*—that women could think, write, and reason like men both in public and for the public. By becoming her own woman, Tahirih authorized for herself a public life and an identity both sexual and textual. Her poetry echoes her objection to forced immobility:

Then how much longer must I be restrained,
My feigned indifference to you still maintained?
How long must agitation be contained?
A prudish piety, how long ordained?
My wares banned from the marketplace?[15]

Resistance eventually grew into overt rejection, and Tahirih stepped beyond the pale of Islamic and Shaykhi jurisprudence. She proposed a break with previous interpretations of religion and became one of the most influential and controversial figures of Babism (a religion that flourished in Iran beginning in 1844, claiming to override the authority of Islamic rules and regulations and eventually leading to the Baha'i faith), the only woman among its first eighteen disciples. Her fiery oratory, her knife-edged eloquence, her vast and radical knowledge, and her candor and courage captivated and shocked audiences. Because of her novel and threatening ideas, many considered her a troublesome heretic over-powered by satanic temptations. Because she was a woman and her resistance involved the rejection of both the veil and the old interpretation of words, her presence was inevitably perceived as having a licentious connotation. Tahirih proved to be a challenge even for the Babi disciples, including the most rebellious among them, who were nonetheless colored by cultural limitations and contem-porary ideas of femininity. They complained to the Bab (1819–50), the founder of Babism, in an attempt to protect their new faith from the threat of this interloper. But the Bab disapproved of the allegations of immorality against Tahirih. To the surprise of most and consternation of some, he defended her, telling his followers "to accept without questions whatever she might pronounce, for they were not in a position to understand and appreciate her station."[16] He bestowed upon her the title "Jenab-e Tahirih," His Excellency, the Pure One ("Jenab" is an honorific title, often reserved for certain classes of distinguished men).

Tahirih's second sojourn in Iraq came to an end in 1847, when, after having been put under surveillance for her activities for several months, she was deported from Baghdad. She was ordered to leave the Ottoman territory in the wake of the unrest she had provoked. At her departure, she was accompanied by some thirty Babis. Stories of her fame and notoriety reached Qazvin long before her, and when she finally arrived, her father and her father-in-law attempted to dis-suade her from her religious activities, demanding that she return home to her husband. Tahirih refused. The couple eventually were divorced. According to the laws, Mullah Mohammad had the sole right to divorce his wife. But from all available data, it is evident that Tahirih rejected reconciliation with her husband.

It was during this difficult time, when family quarrels infected the whole town and the population of Qazvin was caught in the heady polemics of reli-gious and domestic controversy, that Tahirih's father-in-law was found stabbed in the mosque early one morning. He died two days after the attack, in Septem-ber 1847, and his murder unleashed a veritable witch hunt not only in the city, but across the whole country as well. Tahirih, accused of instigating the murder, escaped from home and went undercover for almost a year. She fled from town to town, taking refuge in different homes and hiding places across Iran. Finally, in the summer of 1848, she traveled to the northern province of Mazandaran to attend a congregation of the Babis in Badasht. The convention was significant because no public claim had ever been made before it that the Bab was the inaugurator of a new faith. At Badasht, Babism was declared an independent religion. Tahirih herself was the one who announced this new revelation. The dawn of a new age was heralded by the startling unveiled and voiced presence of a woman in a male gathering.[17]

### A PRIMORDIAL SCENE

The majority of the men assembled in Badasht were scandalized by a woman's participation in a conference of men. When Tahirih stepped into the public tent unveiled, pandemonium ensued. Some men panicked. Others were startled, paralyzed, speechless. Enraged by her act and bewildered by her spectacle, some covered their eyes with their hands in order not to see her; several stopped their ears and left the scene rather than confront the blasphemy she posed. Many called her a crazy fool, a blasphemer, a heretic. One man even raised his sword against her. Another, one Abdol Khaleq Esfahani, feeling violated and distraught, directed his anger toward himself: "Aghast and deranged at the sight, he cut his throat with his own hands. Splattered with blood, and frantic with excitement, he fled away from her face into oblivion."[18]

It might be hard, more than a century and a half later, to reconstruct the emotions of those eighty-one men present at that meeting—to feel the shock, grasp the tension, experience the terror and turmoil and confusion they felt at this woman's entrance into their space, her face and voice so unequivocally uncovered. Nonetheless, this scene captures with dramatic intensity how traumatic the presence of a woman in all-male spaces could be so short a time ago in Iran. Theatrical representation and drama were brought together in this unforgettable scene.[19] It was the first time that a woman assumed a novel function, appropriating both literally and symbolically a hitherto male space. In Badasht, Tahirih became the main protagonist of a primordial scene that was to be replayed again and again in the pages of contemporary Iranian history.

In analyzing this historic event, most commentators, including myself in *Veils and Words*, focus on Tahirih's audacious unveiling. But Badasht was the locus of multiple novelties, the most important of which, I believe now, was space related. When Tahirih walked into a public congregation with her face and voice bared, when she inserted herself in these forbidden territories, she was not merely adopting a new sartorial facade. She was demanding integration in a segregated society. She was leaving her assigned space and appropriating masculine roles and territories. Those present were confronted by a stark choice; they had to decide between an old order and a new one, between including women in their midst or excluding them as usual. How were they to resolve these contraries? Who was right and who was wrong in these circumstances? The audience, in effect, became both spectators and participants in the resulting drama; they became witnesses of both Tahirih's act and their own reactions—horror, indignation, bewilderment, wonder, and acceptance. The scene bears all the characteristics of a morality play, its resolution all the elements of classical catharsis. As Tahirih lifted her voice above the uproar, as she began to speak to the young man who had raised his sword against her, the onlookers saw him gradually lower it before the challenge of her words. Was it possible that logic alone cowed him? It is hardly surprising that some interpreted the reconciliation between the main protagonists in this drama as nothing short of venal. It was inconceivable for certain of those present to imagine that this seemingly intractable opposition could be resolved except by a physical affair. Like players blamed for the action of a play, the principal actors in this primal scene were accused of immorality. The caravan of those assembled in Badasht was ambushed on its return to the capital. The sight of a woman in the company of nonrelated men on the open road was enough to symbolize all that was most decadent in Babism.

## UNCANNY ABSENCE

To better understand the reactions of the men present at Badasht, to better appreciate the significance of Tahirih's act, and to reconstruct the impact of her appearance and grasp the symbolic power of her appropriation of male space, we need to imagine what Iran was like in the mid–nineteenth century. We need to think, in particular, about the uncanny absence of women in that country's public spaces. This negative presence was like a black hole in the middle of society. Many Western travelers to Iran at the time commented on it. It was so glaring that a visitor could focus only on it. For instance, Lady Sheil, the wife of the then British ambassador, who stayed in Iran from October 1849 to April 1853, observed in *Glimpses of Life and Manners in Persia* about the welcoming ceremonies that took place soon after their arrival to the country, "It was difficult to say how many thousands of people had assembled, or what class of persons had not come forth to do honor to the Queen of England's representative. There were princes and priests, and dervishes, and beggars; there were Koordish and Toork horsemen of the tribes, and soldiers, and Ghoolams; in short there was everything and everybody, but there was not a single woman."[20]

Not a single woman in the midst of such a large gathering? Was Lady Sheil exaggerating? Where were all the mothers, sisters, wives, and daughters of the princes and priests, of the officials and dignitaries, of dervishes and beggars in the ceremony that the ambassador's wife had witnessed? One has to wonder how that physical absence translated itself into emotional configurations and what the consequences of that nonpresence might be on the mental cartography of a population. What sort of psychic space did these Iranian men inhabit, having been denied the sight of their mothers and their daughters, their sisters and their wives in the outside world? What did they think, how did they feel when a woman appropriated a public space as if she belonged there? To see her enter it on her own terms, to witness her choosing when and how and even whether she would leave it, must surely have been as destabilizing for them as to be told that the flat earth was actually round. No wonder Abdol Khaleq Esfahani attempted to slit his own throat when confronted with the dangerously mobile orator of Badasht.

If the ambassador's wife, like many others, was surprised by the absence of women in public places, one can only imagine how shocked Iranian men were who traveled to Western cities and found themselves surrounded by unveiled foreign women in the streets. The sight of female arms and faces bared to public view must have been traumatic. According to Mohamad Tavakolli-Targhi, "For the counter-modernists who wanted to uphold the Islamic social and gender orders, the European woman became a scapegoat and a symbol of corruption, immorality, Westernization, and feminization of power. In the Iranian body-politic the imagined European woman provided the subtext for political maneuvers over women's rights and appearance in the public space."[21]

Even a century later, the experience of Badr ol-Moluk Bamdad, a women's rights advocate and one of the first twelve women admitted to an institution of higher education in Iran, Tehran University in 1938, reveals that physical closeness and mingling of the sexes became the cause of bedlam. "While the girls had deliberately and prudently prepared themselves for entry," writes Bamdad, "the boys were completely disconcerted. For most of them, mixing with girls was something quite unforeseen. They therefore avoided talking to girls or even answering them, and if there was no escape they blushed from ear to ear and stuttered. At the lectures, wherever a girl sat the bench on each side of her stayed empty."[22] One has to sympathize with these bewildered men. Sex segregation creates boundaries for men, too, and the resulting mental restraints and constraints are not exclusive to one gender. As Fatima Mernissi writes, "The Moslem man had to be alert, on the defensive, with one eye on the *hudud* (boundaries) that hemmed in the women, the other on the frontiers of the empire."[23]

It is within this context of gender apartheid that Tahirih's actions ought to be analyzed. Although social movements, unlike pregnancies, cannot be traced back to a precise date or a single event, I believe that Badasht was a moment of iconic importance. A woman was recorded to have publicly refused to be silent and out of sight, to accommodate to injustice, to relinquish her rights as a citizen, to keep away from public discourse. It was a poignant moment that announced a challenge to the enforced spatial separation of men and woman. It was indeed an act of civil disobedience and of moral courage.

> Gatekeeper! Friends are knocking at the door.
> Open the door! Why not open the door?
> What is so wrong with letting them come in?
> Why must they wait in the dark corridor?
> How long do you think they can be patient?
> How long should they stay there and pace the floor?[24]

## 1848: BADASHT AND SENECA FALLS

The year 1848 was momentous in many corners of the world. A number of revolutions and social movements were to bring about radical change and remapping of the religious, political, and cultural landscapes in countries as diverse and far-flung as France, Rome, Hungary, and Brazil. Karl Marx published *The Communist Manifesto* in that year, and two explosive meetings marked a turning point in American and Iranian history. On July 19, 1848, Seneca Falls in upstate New

York became the location for the first women's rights convention in the United States; some 260 women and 40 men made their slow way on foot, on horse, and by wagon to the Wesleyan Chapel in order to begin a movement that was to shake the foundations of their society. Just two weeks before this historic gathering, in the small northeastern hamlet of Badasht in Iran 81 Iranian men and a lone woman were also making history. Even if the immediate effects of the conferences in Seneca Falls and Badasht were limited, the spark ignited at both events was not to be snuffed out. Indeed, the long-term impact of both events was profound and far-reaching within each of these two countries and abroad. The implications of these near-simultaneous happenings were great for both genders, but particularly for women, who were championing the right to be free verbally, physically, and legally. In addition, they demanded full access to the pulpit. So why does history today celebrate the significance of one of these events, extolling its role as the beginning of women's struggle for equality, recognizing it as the dawn of universal suffrage, but for the most part neglect the other? Numerous books, articles, and documentary films explore the importance of the Seneca Falls convention and the contribution of its principal organizers, but little is known about the Badasht conference.[25]

The Seneca Falls Declaration of Rights and Sentiments, modeled after the American Declaration of Independence, "protested women's inferior legal status and put forward a list of proposals for the moral, economic, and political equality of women. The most radical resolution was the demand for woman suffrage, a goal that would consume the women's movement for more than seventy years." Over the years and following the Seneca Falls convention, its organizers "actively supported dress reform and women's health issues, greater educational and financial opportunities for women, more liberal divorce laws, and stronger women's property laws."[26] Elizabeth Cady Stanton, one of the principal actors at the Seneca Falls convention, came to believe that the Bible had been interpreted to favor the subjection of women. In 1895, half a century after the convention, she published *The Woman's Bible*. Tahirih's gender-egalitarian intentions were filtered through religious intervention from the outset. Putting aside issues of theology, I wish to note here specifically the centrality of freedom of movement for women in both these events. As far as the Seneca Falls convention was concerned, women's access to the public arena was one of the gathering's motives and concrete goals. In Badasht, however, women's access to the public arena became the symbolic means by which other forms of emancipation were achieved or at least demanded. Whatever the obvious and far-reaching differences between these two events, it is the theme of mobility, expressed on the one hand literally and on the other though dramatic action, that is my concern.

In spite of their differences—and there are many of them—the two conventions shared many overlapping issues. Both challenged, in their different ways, inequalities in the distribution of space. Whereas the participants at Seneca Falls openly claimed that men and women were created equal and demanded individual freedom of choice, the Babis, who had gathered with the ostensible purpose of freeing their imprisoned leader, found themselves, through the dramatic action of the sole woman among them, claiming freedom of conscience and belief as an end to sex segregation. Whereas Cady Stanton and her colleagues questioned women's relegation to the home and to domestic tasks, demanding changes in women's religious, legal, and civic rights, Tahirih, by stepping across the boundaries of social and religious convention, dramatized the appropriation of public space and literally assumed the rights traditionally denied to her sex.

As surprising as it might sound today, women were "covered" in both societies at the time. In the young American republic and under the British common law, once women were married, their legal status was placed "under cover" according to the legal doctrine of *coverture (femme couverte)*. Under this cover or "protection," a woman's legal existence was turned over to her husband upon marriage. By law, he had the right of possession to his wife's property and wages as well as custodial rights. She was prohibited from owning or inheriting property. She could not sign contracts, serve on a jury, or testify in court. She had no control over the custody of their children. It may be a shock from our contemporary vantage point to imagine the constraints imposed on American women a mere 160 years ago.

But history leaves us in no doubt. As Andrea Barnes remarks, "Inheritance laws passed from fathers to sons, and marriage laws passed from fathers to husbands as if they were property. Children were the property of their father and belonged to their father in the case of divorce. Even the money or property that women owned independently before marriage became the property of the husband on marriage."[27] Norma Basch confirms that, according to the law, on marriage "the husband and wife were one person—the husband." As a consequence, a wife "could neither sue nor be sued in her own name. Theoretically, all of her personal property belonged to her husband: the management of her personal property belonged to her husband; the management of her real property came under his control; and she was restricted in making contracts and wills. If the legal oneness of husband and wife was a common law axiom, the legal invisibility of the wife was its corollary."[28]

The Declaration of Rights and Sentiments focused on women's invisibility upon marriage. It went as far as stating that man "has made her, if married, in the eye of the law, civilly dead. He has taken from her all right in property even to the wages she earns."[29] If not "dead," legally speaking, a woman certainly disappeared upon marriage. She became a "wife" or a "mother." Her identity was family bound. The advocacy for women's suffrage, therefore, was a radical proposal because, in Gretchen Ritter's words, *coverture* positioned women as "relational and dependent," whereas suffrage for women would allow them to move into the public realm of discourse legally and physically. The vote for women was radical precisely because, as Ritter puts it, "it threatened to change women from wives into persons. . . . Instead of the containment of women in the domestic sphere of home and family, they would be present in the public sphere of politics and commerce."[30]

Iranian women were also "covered," but in a different sense. They were segregated and as a result incapable of fully implementing the rights that were already granted them by Islamic law—rights such as owning property, signing contracts, and earning wages, including compensation granted for housework and nursing. They were also given the right to hold onto their maiden names, to inherit legacies, and to seek knowledge. The problem was that without freedom of movement none of these rights could be fully implemented. Although Iranian women enjoyed certain rights denied their Western sisters, they suffered some restrictions unfamiliar to American women. Whereas both were expected to remain silent in houses of worship, barred from the pulpit and public preaching, Iranian women were also hidden physically behind walls and veils, their bodies and voices associated with enclosure. Even if their spatial confinement afforded them a network of support, comfort, stability, and domestic power, it denied them easy access to the public arena. Men monopolized the public square. If a woman needed to trespass into that male territory, she had to carry around her a portable house in the form of a veil.

Owing to the inner dynamics of each society, the specificity of their cultural contexts, and the contrasting textures of their concerns, strategies, and alternatives, this theme was expressed in different ways. Whereas one wanted to amend the Constitution, the other questioned the interpretation of canonical Islamic laws as immutable and struggled to revise religious texts. Whereas the American activists wanted to change the terms of their social contract—to own property, to control their wages, to keep their maiden names—Tahirih, who enjoyed those rights, at least in principle, had to fight for the fundamental privilege of being seen and heard in public. By threatening the status quo, challenging gender hierarchies, and questioning the allocation of power, space, and resources, both conventions provoked daunting opposition and an avalanche of accusation, ridicule, and scorn. The Iranian experience, however, proved to be far more traumatic for the society and more perilous for its participants. Tahirih herself was executed four years later. Accused of being a heretic—a fate she shared with many men indicted for being Babis—she was sentenced to death by a government order in spite of the fact that according to Islamic precepts of apostasy a woman should not be killed but imprisoned until she regains her faith.[31]

## FREEDOM MACHINE

Although these two gatherings had very different political and theological aims, even though neither group knew of the existence of the other, and in spite of the fact that the subject of women's freedom of movement was not openly discussed in either Seneca Falls or Badasht, the underlying central theme of both events was the reallocation of space and the freedom of movement. Despite the differences in the two societies, women were excluded—albeit to different degrees—from the public square in both societies and in many others as well at this time. They were barred from most professions; they were often expelled from the public domain and discourse.

Tahirih, who had experienced gender apartheid firsthand, understood the value of the freedom of movement. She appropriated it as a right. Although she had inherited the old maps of sex segregation from her culture, she rejected them repeatedly through her actions, her poems, and her beliefs. Her participation in the Badasht convention was only one manifestation—a culmination—of this

rejection. Throughout her short and eventful life, she fought against the partitioning of space, against the limiting of movement of body, voice, and mind.
According to Peter Smith, she "defied and scandalized social convention with the
freedom with which she spoke and traveled."[32] The manner in which she chose
to live was in the end symbolic of her belief in change. She moved back and forth
tirelessly across a country difficult to traverse, across inhospitable terrain where
roads were for the most part nonexistent, across bare plains and desert wilder-
nesses, dry riverbeds, and mountain passes, traveling on horseback, jolted about
in a *howdah* (a covered seat) carried on the back of mules, in a caravan of pilgrims at the risk of bandit raids, from Qazvin to Najaf, Najaf to Karbala, Baghdad to Tehran, and Tehran to Mazandaran. She journeyed far and wide during
her brief life, transgressing physical, verbal, and theological frontiers at every
step. Uncompromising in her revolutionary demands, she placed her body and
her voice, her knowledge and her opinion in open circulation. She blurred the
boundaries in every sense.

The women attending the Seneca Falls convention, too, refused to remain in
their "proper place"—either physically, legally, or discursively. They wanted to
break out of the bounds of established spaces and conventional cultural frames.
They valued physical mobility and saw it as the means that would allow them
to travel to forbidden territories. Not surprisingly, suffragists and early women's
rights advocates knew immediately the liberating importance of the bicycle and
called it a "freedom machine." Susan B. Anthony was convinced that "the bicycle
has done more for the emancipation of women than anything else in the world."[33]
Predictably enough, when American women first began riding bicycles in the
nineteenth century, they were seen as threats to the social order, a provocation to
promiscuity. It was believed that riding a bicycle, like horse riding, could arouse
women sexually. Just as a woman had to ride side-saddle and seemingly one-
legged, perched modestly on the horse, she had to avoid pleasurable sexual contact with her bicycle saddle. Intriguing mechanisms were thus developed, and
women's bicycles were manufactured with holes in the seat.

### SINGING IN THE ARMS OF THE WIND

The image of a woman riding away from her walled-in enclave into the arms of
the wind is also central to Tahirih's life and poetry. Through words, rhythms,

and the restless pulse of rhyme, she feels the wind in her face, tastes it on her
tongue, chases it like a lover:

> I would explain all my grief dot by dot, point by point
> If heart to heart we talk and face to face we meet
> To catch a glimpse of you, I am wandering like the wind
> From house to house, from door to door
> From place to place, from street to street
> Separated from you, the blood of my heart gushes from my eyes
> In torrent after torrent, river after river
> In wave upon wave, stream after stream
> This afflicted heart of mine has woven your love
> To the stuff of my life strand by strand, thread by thread.[34]

The poet literally leaps into the arms of the wind to reach the wider world. She
escapes from the narrow confines of the Persian *andaroun* (women's quarters)
and flees the twisted alleys of an old Iranian town in order to traverse the seas
and oceans in search of her beloved. The wind becomes her freedom machine,
her speeding bicycle.

In this poem, her most anthologized, Tahirih becomes one with the wind.
In literature as in life, she abandons hearth and home and runs away from the
space socially prescribed to her. Although the poem is a meditation on the grief
caused by separation from her beloved, it is also a refusal to give in to despair.
Rejecting the feminine virtue of *soukhtan-o-sakhtan* (suffering and enduring
in silence), the poet calls out in all directions to the object of her desire. In her
search, she passes from one house to the next, from one alley to another, yearning for a glimpse of her beloved. Uninhibited by constraints, moving restlessly
from place to place, she refuses to be trapped by the stereotypes foisted upon
her by tradition and becomes her own public interpreter—an embodied voice
demanding sexual as well as textual recognition. She takes charge of her own
myth in this poem and harnesses the wind as an agency of search. This restless
movement, echoed by the repetitive pattern of doubled synonyms, phrase after
phrase, couplet after couplet, is fueled by such longing that it subverts the master
narrative of Tahirih's culture, which would keep women in their place; it bursts
the bounds of immobility and orchestrates a public image for the poetic persona,
which is at once ubiquitous and vocal. Although memorializing her grief in a

stark and self-assured language in this poem, she also celebrates her hard-won freedom to roam at will.

Tahirih's life was brief after her appearance at Badasht. She was arrested one year after her escape from Qazvin, ostensibly for collaboration in the murder of Mullah Taqi, and placed under house arrest in Tehran. Although the king charged that she be left alone and even indicated that she be granted her freedom, she underwent enforced reeducation and was finally condemned to death. When three Babi men made an attempt on the life of the king in August 1852, Tahirih shared the fate of many other men and women accused of heresy. Her execution, however, unlike that of men, did not take place in public. It was carried out at midnight, outside the city walls, in shrouded secrecy and enveloping darkness.

But the tales surrounding her death are as confused and conflicted as those about her life and differ in many details. How was she executed? And by whom exactly? Was she killed by soldiers under the orders of the chief of the armed forces, or was she finally strangled by a drunken slave? Was a handkerchief or a head scarf used to execute her? Was she garroted, or was she choked? The obsession with the physicality as well as the symbolism of her death is another characteristic of the uncertainty that abounds on the subject. Was she still breathing when she was buried under a heap of stones, or was her bruised and broken body already lifeless when it was flung into the well? Some of the popular fantasies are extravagant, a wild amalgam of the symbolism associated with Tahirih's life, an insistence on her sexual identity even in death. Was she choked with the green turban of another executed Babi who was alleged to be her lover or with a piece of silk that she had laid aside, like a bridal veil, for her martyrdom? The facts themselves are still in motion, even to this day, subject to repeated revision, open to renewed investigation. All that is known is that one summer's night in August 1852 Tahirih Qurratul'Ayn was taken to a walled garden outside the gates of the capital, strangled, and thrown down a well. She was buried in her best silk clothes beneath a heap of stones, lost to an early and cruel death.

### TAHIRIH AND THE CAMPAIGN FOR ONE MILLION SIGNATURES

Tahirih's story has become embedded in the cultural memory of Iran. She has inserted herself in its history forever. Although the truth of who she really was remains veiled, she has taken on a new life in the memory of her people and has assumed the dimensions of a legend, a mythic fantasy, a tale that both expresses her society's fears and symbolizes its unspoken longings. Despite the contradictory information about her and the conflicting interpretations of her work, she is undoubtedly a pioneering woman. Her struggle was not merely focused on personal growth and self-improvement, for she advocated structural and systemic change in society. Throughout her short life, she was passionately interested in women's issues. She created study circles for women. She taught illiterate women how to read.[35] She advocated the search for truth and justice.

> The search for truth shall drive out ignorance
> Equality shall strike the despots low
> Let warring ways be banished from the world
> Let justice everywhere its carpet throw
> May Friendship ancient hatreds reconcile
> May love grow from the seed of love we sow.[36]

Tahirih reconfigured the very definition of selfhood by stepping beyond the confines of her role. She denied men the monopoly of scriptural interpretation. In fact, for all intents and purposes, she joined the ranks of preachers when delivering sermons from behind the curtain, and when she walked into the forbidden spaces in front of them and violated the prescribed limits by taking off her veil, her own body dramatized the heresy of her beliefs. One might even say that she was at the forefront of a movement unlike any other in nineteenth-century Iran that raised these very questions for debate. She refused to be confined, no matter how gilded the cage. She rejected established patterns no matter how sacred. Her transgressions were multiple—religious, philosophical, verbal, sartorial, legal, and spatial—for she challenged the boundaries between what was feminine, private, emotional, static, and silent, on the one hand, and what was masculine, public, rational, mobile, and articulate, on the other. She did so repeatedly, in the face of every kind of opposition—familial, political, religious—and in spite of all sorts of difficulties, including slander, ridicule, neglect, and incarceration.

Her life story is thus an exquisite mix of triumph and despair: a narrative of ceaseless search, the tale of endless journeys, the map of an expedition toward an unfounded but ardently believed new world. She never saw that ultimate country toward which she had set her face and turned her eager steps. She never reached the land of her heart's desire, but she kept faith in it in spite of everything. Through all her losses, disappointments, frustrations, and deprivations, she remained stoic; she stayed sure and confident and, if legend be true, was characterized by a remarkable certitude till the very end. She never gave up her beliefs, her dreams, or her dignity. She was trampled to death, but her voice has miraculously survived, even though, as Amin Banani remarks, her "short and tumultuous life, the beleaguered circumstances of the Babi community, the clandestine handling of Babi manuscripts, the scattering of her possessions, and the hostility of her immediate family members, who may have destroyed or suppressed her papers—all these mitigate against any sense of assurance that we now have access to all the poems that she wrote."[37]

Like her carved image on a stone, however, some of Tahirih's poems have survived in most improbable places, such as the Campaign for One Million Signatures. This campaign is the most far reaching ever undertaken by Iranian women. This nonviolent civil-society initiative has chosen as its motto "Face to face, street to street." These inspiring words are borrowed from one of Tahirih's most anthologized poems.[38]

On August 27, 2006, following several peaceful protests, the Campaign for One Million Signatures was launched in Iran. As its name indicates, the campaign's aim is to collect one million signatures to protest discriminatory laws against women—laws regarding marriage, divorce, child custody, guardianship, inheritance, testimony in court, and civil compensation—and to demand their revision. More important, the campaign seeks to raise awareness and educate Iranians. To achieve this goal, three generations of secular and religious, rich and poor, married and single, rural and urban women and men have taken the campaign's message to the streets. They "fan out in ones and twos, to small towns and villages, going into shops, beauty salons, schools and offices, or stand at bus stops explaining 'face to face' how the Iranian interpretation of Sharia law is stacked against half the population. They ask men and women to sign the petition. Those who refuse are asked to take a leaflet detailing the manifold forms of legal discrimination."[39] As Noushin Ahmadi Khorasani, women's rights advocate and one of the campaign's organizers, notes: "Direct contact between equal rights defenders and other women's and citizens' groups will allow those involved in the campaign to identify the everyday concerns of women, especially their legal needs and problems. On the other hand, this direct contact will increase awareness among the general population about the inequities that exist within the law."[40]

Although the initial two-year time frame to collect one million signatures had to be extended, the physical presence of women in the public square and the challenge to discrimination against women in the public discourse is consolidated by the brilliant strategy of combining consciousness raising, peaceful civil disobedience, and education; adopting a street strategy; going from house to house, from buses and metros to beauty salons and workplaces and parks; and getting one signature at a time. Shadi Sadr, lawyer and journalist imprisoned for her involvement with the campaign, writes that Iranian women today "have imposed themselves on a male-dominated society which still believes women should stay at home. Perhaps nobody sees us, but we exist and we make our mark on the world around us. I assure you that if you look around carefully, everywhere you will see our footsteps."[41] Sadr is not exaggerating. If you look around carefully, you will see everywhere the footsteps of brave women who are struggling for their rights, and if you look even more closely, you will see that they are following in the footsteps of their foremothers, who fought before them.

# 5

# ICARUS REBORN

*Captivity and Flight in the*
*Work of Forugh Farrokhzad*

Why? Because she was the dew
Pristine. Suicidal.
Reaching for the sun.

—FORUGH FARROKHZAD, "A Bitter Tale"

Born of the sun they travelled a short while towards the sun,
And left the vivid air signed with their honor.

—STEPHEN SPENDER, "I Think Continually
of Those Who Were Truly Great"

## THE PRISONER WHO FLEW OUT OF PRISON

The gods and goddesses of the Greeks understood it well: prisoners learn how to fly.

According to the myth, Icarus was the son of Daedalus, the architect of the first labyrinth, the space of dead ends, winding roads with no beginning and no ends. In due course, though, the builder of the first prison became a prisoner himself. He was incarcerated with his son on Crete Island. To escape the waves, Daedalus created human wings for the two of them and counseled his son to avoid flying too high lest the sun melt the wax with which his wings were glued on or too low for fear that moisture would pull him into the ocean. Consumed by the love of beauty and freedom, summoned by the sun, an imprudent and daring Icarus glided overhead, soaring higher and higher, oblivious to his inevitable dive into the deep. And thus it was that a perfectly innocent prisoner became the

128

patron saint of all prisoners and all those who dare to soar.[1] Like Icarus, the Iranian poet Forugh-ol-zaman Farrokhzad (1935–67) kept her eyes on the sky and the gateless, inviting sun. Knowing but never fearing consequences and reckless, she refused to live under conventions of safety.[2]

Her first name, like many Iranian names, carries a meaning, "eternal light," and she was beckoned by the blazing source of light. The image of the sun is one of the most recurring motifs in the poetry of this gifted and influential literary figure of twentieth-century Iran. It appears and reappears ten times in her first poetry collection and even more so in the next four. In her fourth book, *Reborn,* two of the thirty-five poems are titled after the sun.[3] Seeking to be infused with energy, embraced by the clouds, touched by the breeze, she danced like a dervish, chased the winds, jumped over walls, darted on wings, journeyed to stars a thousand light years away.

> Look! See me scorched by the Star
> See me enveloped, fevered
> See me awash in the light
> Lifted to the stars
> . . . Look! How far I have come
> To eternity; to the Galaxies
> To the infinite.[4]

Acquainted with captivity, Farrokhzad never relinquished the desire to fly. Like the many birds that wing through her works—phoenixes, eagles, doves, crows, finches—she soared with the many pleasures of the sky. She disdained conventional strictures on women, from an early aversion to walls, bars, closed doors, shuttered windows, and cages to a perennial desire to fly and flow. Advocating reorganization of physical, discursive, and social spaces, she did not wish to stay in her "proper" place. She did not want to have her body, her voice, her gaze, her desire kept under lock and key, domesticated, tamed, or hedged in.

> Sheltered by the night
> I rush, clutching
> At the tail of every breeze
> To pour frantically
> My tresses in your hands

And I make you an offering
Of tropical flowers
From this green, fresh
Summer pasture.
Come with me.
Come with me to that star
A thousand years distant
From the congealment of dust
From the Earth's counterfeit measures
Come with me to that star
Where no one fears the light.[5]

Like Icarus, Farrokhzad refused to take the prudent middle course; to live a life disciplined by delineated spaces. Believing in risky ideals and bold dreams, she refused to live in a smug and secure world. "I have always sacrificed my calm in life to my adventurous nature," she wrote in "Confession," a short autobiographical story she published anonymously in *Omid-e Iran* magazine early in her literary career.[6] She pursued danger almost in a trance, throwing herself headfirst in harm's way.[7]

It is hard to imagine an Iranian poet more concerned with the issue of space than Farrokhzad. Her body of work can be seen as the chronicle of an explorer defying familiar frames and certainties. It is the roadmap of a relentless border crosser, the tale of a Gypsy living on frontiers. Taken as a whole, it is the account of a rich variety of real and metaphoric journeys. Stasis is its nemesis. "When water loses its flow in a lagoon," she believed, "It goes stale, stagnates, and sinks low / Its soul becomes a wasteland / Its depth a burial place for fishes."[8] She refused to remain typecast in any single role, ideology, political party, discipline, or relationship—that is, in any kind of bounded space—no matter how high the price of transgression.

Grant her forgiveness
She who dares forget
The painful bond between her being
And the still waters
And the hollow pits
She who foolishly imagines
She has the right to live.[9]

In one of her final poems, a short, haunting eleven-line obituary of sorts, she describes a vertiginous plunge into depression and despair. Though the desire to fly is still alive, physical death is close in the poem, and the vast blue sky is inaccessible. For Farrokhzad, it seems, stillness means death, at least death of the body.

> My heart is squeezed
> My heart is squeezed
> I go to the porch and with my fingers
> Caress the taut skin of night
> The lamps that connect are dark
> No one will introduce me to the sun
> No one will escort me to the celebration of finches
> Remember flight
> The bird is mortal.[10]

She took her own imperative to heart, and remember flight she did. Indeed, if the preservation of the Persian language and pre-Islamic history was central to the monumental national epic *Shahnameh* by Ferdowsi (tenth century); if mysticism inspired and informed most of the poetry by Jalal al-Din Rumi (thirteenth century); if love was central to Hafez, the master of Persian lyric poetry (fourteenth century); and if pre-Islamic Iran was the lost utopia for Sadeq Hedayat and nature pivotal to the poetry of Sohrab Sepehri (twentieth century), then in addition to love, which was a central theme for Farrokhzad, the relentless search for the open road, freedom, speed, and incessant motion was clearly fundamental to her work. In one of her most anthologized poems, "Only the Voice Remains," she asks six times in sixty verses: "Why should I stop?"[11] The rhetorical question, the poem's refrain, was the poet's most pressing concern in life.

As with Icarus, however, Farrokhzad's love of motion is only part of the story. The weightiness of the captivity she strained against all her life is what gives her explorations of flight poignancy and rich symbolic meaning. In her life as in her letters, poems, and films, from the beginning of her literary career to its tragic and abrupt end thirteen years later, the thrill of being free and fetterless was counterbalanced by an acute familiarity with feelings of containment. Running back and forth with her gaze fixed to the sky, she found her feet weighed down by attachments and rules, hampered by chains. The interconnectedness of freedom and flight is a theme that dominates her work. She felt bound and unbound simultaneously, captured and released at one and the same time. At one moment immobilized in a room, cocooned in a satin-lined box, trapped in a cage, contained in conventions, immured in a coffin, she was at the next moment awash in the light, lifted to the stars, in the company of birds and wind. Now hemmed in, besieged, locked in the cave of self, then circling, sprouting wings, reaching the sun. Images of stagnant waters, bottomless pits, hibernation, darkness, and death thus alternate in her poetry with metaphors of flowing waters, wings, open windows, fresh air, growth, and vibrancy.

Mobility might be the central trope of Farrokhzad's canon, but there is full awareness in her writing of its consequences. Once in motion there is no alternative for a displaced woman but dislocation, homelessness, and the sometimes devastating results of her own impetuous behavior. Even while she celebrates her autonomy and independence, she also mourns the resulting loneliness and isolation, and she is at the mercy of the pull and tug of these conflicting impulses. The parallel narratives of stillness and speed, of prison and escape together constitute the core of Farrokhzad's artistic universe. Her autobiographical poetry thus captures two poetic personae: one joyous and in flight, the other tragic and entrapped. One moment she is flying high: giddy with love and lust, alive with ecstasy, elated; the next she is suicidal—depleted, weeping, grieving with regret and remorse. A daring explorer of a public language of intimacy, she celebrates love and lust in her famous erotic rhapsodies but also repudiates physical and emotional intimacy in no uncertain words. Her long posthumously published poem "Let's Believe in the Dawning of a Cold Season" is in fact an obituary to love. "All my wounds are caused by love / love. Love. Love," she laments.[12] And the death of illusions is no less brutal, no less painful than the passing of the body. She hides herself in a room for week-long spells of depression, which are followed by joyful bursts of creativity and an even deeper reverence and appetite for life. In photographs of her, too, her face, as expressive as her poetry—portal to her candor—reflects her highs and lows, her joys and despairs. A single photograph occasionally captures both extremes, with her smile concealing the glitter of unshed tears.

Paradoxically enough, although the poet herself was torn during her life between the ecstasy of freedom and the despair of being chained, although she suffered as a human being from the often tragic consequences of these bipolar impulses that drove her to the heights only to plunge her into the depths, her art protects the reader from these two extremities. Seen as a whole, her poetic legacy presents us with a remarkable synthesis of the extremes. Her 130 poems refuse to reduce the world to binary opposites of captivity versus freedom, good versus bad, right versus wrong. Through the constant shifts of darkness and light, her work keeps us spellbound in a twilight zone, a place of overlapping shadows, linkages, porous boundaries. It depicts a world of complementary views and competing desires, a world built on moral ambiguity, the fusion of opposites, a synthesis of divergent views. The opening lines of Charles Dickens's *A Tale of Two Cities* capture with precision the paradox that she created through her poetry: "It was the best of times, it was the worst of times, it was the age of wisdom, it was the age of foolishness, it was the epoch of belief, it was the epoch of incredulity, it was the season of light, it was the season of darkness, it was the spring of hope, it was the winter of despair."[13]

Farrokhzad's poetry, like the responses it elicited, offers insight into the ethos of pre-revolutionary Iran. It explores some of Iran's internal conflicts, involving tradition and modernity, men and women, their relationships and gender roles, and the allocation of public and private space. In the early 1950s, when Farrokhzad began to publish her poetry, Iran was a politically polarized, culturally divided country. Seeking a shortcut to modernity, it heaved with rapid, violent change. The capital was ever expanding: a place where both women of fashion and women of tradition walked side by side through streets teeming with both cars and donkeys, bicycles and peddlers. It was a city at war with itself, suspended between the fourteenth-century Hegira and the twentieth-century Christian era, a city of mosques and cabarets, designer clothes and chadors. And Farrokhzad's poetry, which never succumbed to ideological fervor or political pressure, reflected the torments and triumphs, the fervor and folly, of a nation undergoing seismic changes. With a sensuous quality all its own, with its simple, unpretentious, lucid language, her canon is a metaphor for a culture in transition—one might even say a traumatic transition. It captures in the prism of a single woman's life what a whole nation was undergoing over the course of several decades. In the poem "I Pity the Garden," she even predicts a revolution that would shake the foundation of Iranian society.

All day long
The sounds of blasts and explosions can be heard
Instead of flowers

Our neighbors plant mortars and machine guns in their garden
And store gunpowder in their covered pools
And the kids in our neighborhood
Fill their backpacks with little bombs.[14]

This uncanny forecast of doom and destruction came at a time when the political leaders of the country believed they were forging ahead. No one at the time, inside or outside the country, foresaw a change of regime, let alone the end of twenty-five hundred years of dynastic rule and revolution. Who, then, was this rebel-poet-seer?

### A CAST OF DOLLS

Forugh Farrokhzad was the third child born to Mohammad Farrokhzad and Turan Vaziri-Tabar. Both her parents were oblivious to conventions, iconoclastic, with a penchant for outspoken simplicity. The father was a tyrant, and the mother a stickler for control, order, and cleanliness. Turan had refused the veil prior to the mandatory unveiling act of 1936 and fallen in love with her future husband, sixteen years her senior. She gave birth in rapid succession to seven children, of whom only three survived her. She died of a rare cancer of the tongue. Turan was an avid collector of dolls and wanted to be buried with her favorites. Her request was not granted. My poem "Cast of Dolls" captures the tragedy that visited the Farrokhzad family.

She had seven children
Seven beautiful, even if unruly children,
But Turan loved her dolls.
She had assembled them in her bedroom
Assigned each a special place
Given each the name and role she liked
Choreographed their lives.

Turan did not collect dolls
She adopted them.
It was sublime to wrap her arms around their wills
Direct their desires

Dictate their wardrobe
Design their future.
Their stillness brought her peace
Their unhurried patience unruffled her
Their consenting silence filled her ears with music
Their unaging presence comforted her.

Unlike four of her children
Turan's dolls never died on her.
They were her loyal companions.
So fierce was her attachment to them
So complete her devotion
She requested
To have mother and dolls buried together.

With her last wish ungranted
Turan died as she lived
She weeps in her grave.

Farrokhzad spent her early childhood years in the province of Mazanda-ran, bordering the Caspian Sea. When her parents moved to the capital city, she attended a coeducational elementary school in her neighborhood, and after graduating from Khosrow Khavar junior high school, she transferred to Kamal-ol-Molk technical school to study painting and sewing. She did not finish high school and at the age of sixteen fell in love with a neighbor and a distant relative of her mother, Parviz Shapour (1924–2000). He was a satirist and caricaturist eleven years her senior. In spite of vehement parental objections, she married him, and soon after their wedding, she accompanied her husband to Ahwaz, the capital of Khuzestan Province in southwestern Iran, where he was employed by the Ministry of Finance. Their only child, a boy named Kamyar, was born a year later. Kamyar was two years old when his mother began to publish her poems.[15]

## METEORIC ASCENT TO NOTORIETY/FAME

It was on September 24, 1954, that a short poem by an unknown woman barely twenty years old made literary history and caused a scandal. Published in a popular magazine, *Rowshanfekr* (The Intellectual), the twelve-line poem "Sin" heralded the awakening of a woman's sensuality.[16] The literary treatment of her extramarital affair titillated some readers and sent a chill down the spines of others. To the absolute delight of the magazine's editor in chief, Nasser Khodayar, letters poured in from all over Iran, some in support, but many in protest. Seeing the poem as an illustration of rampant immorality that needed to be dealt with lest it corrupt impressionable women, a number of clerics signed a petition condemning the author of such a poem and the magazine that had had the insolence to publish it.

Riveting narratives of female desire, even of adulterous affairs and sexual consummation, are in no short supply in Persian literature. "The greatest poets of Iran," comments Robert Surieu, "accepted and appreciated all the different forms of love, seeing in each of them a fresh means of fulfillment, no matter if they ran counter to the strict laws of morality or were exalted by the sublimity of their object."[17] So what was so scandalous, so dangerous, so threatening about this particular poem? At that time, according to the law of the land, a man could marry up to four wives. In addition to visiting prostitutes, which was his prerogative, he could also marry as many temporary wives as he wished. A woman had none of those options, and if suspected of adultery she could pay with her life for her sexual indiscretion. If her father, brother, or husband murdered her to redeem their tarnished honor, they were punished lightly, with a maximum of six months imprisonment, if at all.[18] "Sin" was violating moral, linguistic, and sexual codes and conventions.

Indeed, the poem seemed to have subverted power and propriety. It displayed female self-assertiveness rather than self-effacement. It abandoned the female body to pleasures that were forbidden and the pen to expression that was taboo. And it did so in the first-person singular, a combination that in its sensuous immediacy and autobiographical overtones shocked readers. The unabashed physicality of female lust was unsanitized by narrative strategies, uncontained by male authorship and authority. This was not the familiar male-speaking-as-female sort of story. It was not a man putting words in the mouth of his created, controlled character. It was not a figment of some creative mind's imagination. Nor was it the murmuring of a woman's forbidden desires in the privacy of an inner chamber, protected by tall walls, behind doors closed with seven locks. Heralding a radical change in the verbal and emotional space demanded by and allowed to a woman,

"Sin" celebrated female lust and loss of control. It introduced unmediated articulation of feminine pleasures and fantasies into Persian literature.

In this poem, a woman gladly proclaims her freedom to stray from the conventional paths of morality and pay for having done so. Instead of expressing self-denial, instead of agonizing about sexual repression, she gives voice to her bewilderment in the grip of physical desire and the consummation of her passion.[19] There are no locks in this poem, no indirection. There are no rhetorical devices, no euphemisms, camouflage, or other kinds of tactical maneuvering. There is no whining, either, no equating of love with frustration, no heartache, no mincing of words. The poetic persona speaks with naked candor; she looks her readers directly in the eye and shares with them an account of what she knows is a forbidden desire. She voluntarily makes a public confession of a crime for which the punishment was death.

> I sinned
> it was a most lustful sin
> I sinned in arms sturdy as iron, hot like fire
> and vengeful.
>
> In that dark retreat of silence
> I looked into his mysterious eyes
> my heart trembled restlessly
> at the pleading in his eyes.
>
> In that dark retreat of silence
> I sat, disheveled, beside him
> Passion poured from his lips into mine
> I was saved from the anguish of my foolish heart.
>
> I whispered the tale of love in his ears:
> "I want you, O, dear love of mine
> I want you, O, life-giving embrace
> I want you, O, crazed lover of mine."
>
> Passion struck a flame in his eyes
> the red wine danced in the glass

in the soft bed, my body
shivered drunk on his breast.


I sinned,
it was a most lustful sin beside a tremulous, intoxicated body
do I know, O Lord, what I have done
in that dark retreat of silence?[20]


The active agent in this poem is not the man. Nor is the woman repentant in the conventional sense. Unlike the slew of adulterous women in Persian literature, she undergoes no religious awakening; she is not led to the right path through marriage; she does not blame anyone other than herself; she does not conveniently die; she does not attempt or commit suicide; she is not punished by her creator—at least not yet! Her transgression is neither admonished nor short-lived. Quite the contrary, she refuses to adopt the mantle of victimhood or to chronicle a journey from sin to salvation, from innocence lost to innocence claimed. She calls herself a sinner but acknowledges publicly that something mysterious and pleasurable happened to her. She does not assign any responsibility or complicity to the lover, who remains unidentified to the end. She is a sinner but has no partner in sin. Instead of casting blame, she accepts it all, dramatizing and admiring his fiery arms, his alluring eyes, his tempting lips. She objectifies him in a moment of ecstatic abandon, praises his virility, portrays him as a physical creature made for her desires.

It is small wonder, then, if that short poem created such uproar and its author found herself at the eye of a gathering storm. The poem was a rupture from all that had preceded it. Although few data exist, it is safe to say that the narrating and the narrated "I" and the woman who wrote the poem were assumed to be one. They were viewed as reflecting one another. This interpretation was encouraged by the magazine's layout of the poem. To prove its "authenticity," to make sure readers understood that the story was real rather than fictive, that the voice was that of an actual woman, "a devoted wife and mother of a two-year-old son" no less, two pictures of the poet and her biographical sketch were included alongside the poem. The focus was on the marital status of the poet, whom the piece described as "a woman with disheveled hair and penetrating eyes." The larger textual and pictorial context in which the poem appeared, which was no less astonishing than the poem itself, gave it the aura of a testimonial, a report of sorts. At the time, some of the most famous Iranian poets and writers followed the established tradition of having pen names (Nima Yushij for Ali Esfandiari [1896–1960]; Omid for Akhavan Sales [1928–90]; Bamdad for Ahmad Shamlu [1925–2000]; Behazin for Mahmud Etemadzadeh [1915–2006]; Sereshk for Shafii Kadkani [1939–], among others). But Farrokhzad, who adopted "Bot Shekan" (the Iconoclast) for some of her prose writings, chose to break with this tradition and used no pen name for this poem or for any of her others.

"Sin" was a new literary and cultural adventure. And like most novelties, it was bound to be controversial. Outraged women and men heaped it with scorn. Farrokhzad rocketed to fame or, more accurately, to notoriety with the poem's publication, and in the process the poet of "Sin" became the sinful poet, a defiant woman frozen in a moment of admitted guilt and virtue lost. She would be remembered for her disgraceful public confession. If the poet accepted admonition for what she deemed unchaste behavior but defied gender roles and notions of virtue, many chose to focus mainly on the first part. In a way, they wished to tame a poem that was by no means a lesson in chastity or conformity into a cautionary tale.

Although Farrokhzad did not punish her poetic persona for seditious gender bending, society punished her. She was verbally lynched in the public square. Nasser Khodayar, the man for whom "Sin" was composed, began to publish a serialized story describing in minute and pornographic detail their love affair gone sour. Titled "Shokufeh-ye Kabud" (The Bruised Blossom), the "fictive" story was adorned by a pictorial sketch of the adulterous heroine. This woman had an uncanny resemblance to the poet of "Sin," published less than a year earlier in the same magazine. Farrokhzad's repeated pleas to Khodayar to stop the scandalous tale were rejected with matchless cruelty.[21] Her husband, Parviz Shapour, and her father, Colonel Farrokhzad, already angry with the publication of "Sin," were furious with this new, serialized humiliation. Their honor, they felt, was being repeatedly sullied, and there seemed to be no end in sight. Farrokhzad fell into a profound depression, attempted suicide, was taken to Rezai Psychiatric Hospital, given electroshock therapy, and released only after one long and agonizing month.

These were hard times for the young poet. Her marriage ended in divorce—an uncommon practice at the time. According to the first national census of Iran taken in 1956, only 4 percent of all women in the city of Tehran were divorced. As dictated by law, she lost the custody of her son, Kamyar, and was later deprived of even limited visitation rights with him. The pain of this forced separation never left her and is a central trope of her poetry to the end. A year later, when her first poetry collection was published, "Sin" was excised from it. The volume, though, begins and ends with direct and indirect references to the expunged poem. The introduction by Shojaeddin Shafa, a prolific writer and literary translator, as well as the poet's epilogue, which was deleted from later editions, refer to the eliminated poem without naming it.[22] Shafa begins his essay with reference to "a poem" he had "read less than a year ago in a magazine by a young and unknown poet." The title of the poem, the name of the magazine in which it appeared, the exact date of publication remain unidentified. Shafa, however, defends the right of a woman "to confess and depict her feelings candidly and openly. . . . And let's face it," he asks, "which one of us can deny having felt these unspeakable desires in our own hearts? In the words of Jesus, 'Let he who has no sin cast the first stone at the sinner.'"[23] In this case, however, countless verbal stones were thrown at the "sinner."

### NEW CARTOGRAPHY: TRAVELING ELSEWHERE

Barely twenty, shaken by her fragile health, botched suicide attempt, and psychiatric lockup, with her reputation tarnished, her marriage in flames, her love affair with Khodayar ended and then betrayed by him in print, the pariah among Iranian literati found herself surrounded by lingering rumors and spiteful gossip. Tabloids masquerading as literary journals and investigative reporters–turned–literary critics invented and reinvented her with abandon. They made no distinction between a woman's life and her art, between the poet and her poetic persona. But Farrokhzad was a born survivor. Her reserves of talent and energy were remarkable. Despite the public scandal and the private pain, she somehow managed to pull herself together and devote herself to the pursuit of poetry while developing new interests. To recuperate and regain her bearings, to get away from the tumult and restore her sense of self, she also decided to leave the country. So one hot summer day in early July 1956 (15 Tir 1335), she left Iran for Italy on a cargo plane. This was the first of many future trips inside and outside the country.

Farrokhzad went to Europe to start a new life and returned fourteen months later, her mind stretched and her capacities deepened. With a new surge of energy and independence, she challenged God, state, family, father, husband, lover, conventions, and gender roles in her poetry with even greater fervor. She also undertook a new literary enterprise for a woman. She published the travel narrative of her unchaperoned trip.[24] "Dar Diyari Digar" (Elsewhere) first appeared in an eight-part serial in the literary magazine *Ferdowsi* in 1957. With its unpolished prose style, "Elsewhere" is certainly not a work of literary distinction. It is, however, a document of great significance for the information it generates regarding a period in its author's life about which little is known. Featuring a young woman traveler, it is emblematic of a modernity associated with motorized mobility: planes, cars, trains.

"Elsewhere" begins with trepidation regarding the writing of a travel narrative. Is a fourteen-month journey worthy of recounting, ponders the author? Is her memory reliable, especially considering that she has lost her notes? Does she have anything new to offer her readers? she wonders. After questioning and validating the act of writing on such a subject, Farrokhzad proceeds to justify the trip itself. Hers was not an excursion for leisure or hedonistic gratification, she explains. It was for therapeutic purposes. It was prompted by the need for fresh energy and strength, for loosening constraining bonds and suffocating circumstances. It was a desperate search for breathing space, an escape from distress and discomfort. She had descended into such emotional chaos, she confides, that it felt as if she lived in a dark, dank cave. She needed to stretch her cramped wings, to find her way out of the murkiness in which she resided. She needed sunshine.

The space a woman occupied in the Iran of that time defined her. Given the strong cultural association between masculinity and mastery of the road, the image of an unescorted woman traveling abroad, surrounded by strangers in a foreign land, was hardly the most virtuous one. It invoked licentiousness and conjured menacing possibilities. It was a threat to the status quo, family stability, tradition. The first installment of the narrative was barely out before irate readers began to denounce its author as a pleasure-seeking hedonist. She was castigated for being a traveler, a female who had abandoned her proper place behind the walls of her family's home and had ventured into forbidden territories, foreign countries no less. How could an unchaperoned woman who escaped the controlling grasp of her family not be seeking illicit pleasures? Even the magazine's proofreader took the liberty of changing one of the author's statements from "My goal in going to Europe was not to see new things and seek more colorful pleasures and joys" to its exact opposite. Farrokhzad was outraged and complained about the distortion in the next installment. The man retorted with his own rebuttal in a footnote in the next installment, condemning the author angrily. "You have unjustly and unduly attacked me in this issue, blaming me for everything, Khanum-e Farrokhzad," he writes. "All the employees at the printing house are my witnesses. Some of your words and even sentences cannot be read by anyone. And as everyone knows, our employees, like pharmacists, are experts in reading illegible handwriting. I am quite willing to put your handwriting to a test. If anyone can read it without committing an error, then you are justified in your criticism."[25]

Ironically, *Elsewhere* is scarcely a page turner. Readers seeking descriptions of romantic adventures or sexual encounters would have been disappointed. It offers a series of personal reflections rather than a display of the illicit actions of a "sinful" woman. Claiming that geographic distance is a catalyst for change, providing a physical space for further exploration of the self and the discovery of new inner landscapes, it chronicles the development of a mind exposed to new places and new people. "I was happy to be a foreigner among Italians," writes the intrepid traveler. "This helped me better understand other people . . . and in the process I got to know myself better."[26] Portraying herself as the traveler of this internal journey, the storyteller of this tale, Farrokhzad created a narrative rich in self-revelation. She redefined herself, reimagined the world she lived in, celebrated the theme of growth and rebirth.

During her fourteen months abroad, Farrokhzad was not an accidental tourist. Instead, she explored the new places she was visiting with conscious determination. Stepping off the beaten track, she participated in the culture of her host country. Wandering freely in unfamiliar places, she treasured the many pleasures of a country that did not restrict her. Protected by her anonymity, she ventured into public places without fear or accountability. She lived under no self-imposed curfew; challenged the conventions of urban decorum; walked bare-footed; cavorted with a group of children; flung herself in the water, the breeze, the sand; strolled the moonlit back alleys; went on long, solitary walks in the dark. She visited public places—museums, beaches, parks, gardens. She traveled on streetcars, journeyed in trains, sailed on boats, rode on the waves of the sea, enjoyed water fountains whispering in the branches of trees. She received the sun in its full glory. And all the while, she listened carefully to the eloquent poetry of nature—the flowing water, the traveling breeze, the carpet of rustling, flaming leaves, the dancing clouds, the falling rain. It was a free space for her, this foreign land, and she felt caressed by its magnanimous beauty and its many surprises.

Traveling became very important for Farrokhzad. For the remaining ten years of her life, she would travel extensively. She went from Tehran to Mazandaran and Ahwaz; from Beirut to Rome, Munich, and Paris; on her return, from Tehran again to Esfahan, Mashhad, Tabriz, and Khuzestan; and finally to London again, Pesaro, and Berlin. She became a seasoned traveler in the course of her short life. These journeys—from one city to another, from one country to another, from one universe of definitions and meanings to another—stretched her mind to new dimensions.[27] Although they indicate a dizzying, dazzling mobility, they also bespeak a sense of homelessness, perpetual wandering, and exile.

### THE VOYAGER IN LIFE AND ART

Farrokhzad's travels were both literal and figurative. She crossed boundaries of all kinds. Disliking walls with a passion, she titled her second collection *Divar* (Wall) and never hesitated to express her desire to live in a more open society. "I wish I would die and be born again in a different world. . . . One in which no one erects walls around their houses," she confided in a letter.[28] Later in life she came to believe that this desire for a total absence of walls—both the visible and the invisible varieties—was no less unrealistic than the demand for full transparency. "The walnut sapling has grown tall enough / To explain walls to its fresh leaves."[29] Nevertheless, she continued to believe in the futility of building ever higher walls. History proved her right. Built at great cost, walls have provided real or lasting security neither for those who have raised them nor for those who have sought protection behind them. We need only to consider the Great Wall of China, the Berlin Wall, the high walls of Troy, and the Maginot Line in France to know that she was right.

In a culture of walls and veils, masks and masquerades, in a culture where keeping appearances, *hefz-e ab-e rou*, is a national pastime, Farrokhzad explored a language of openness and intimacy, thrilling in its directness, lush in its soul-baring intensity. Meditating on the nature of the self and its literary expression, she avoided cover-ups, Iranian conventions of decorum and good taste.

O! You, my poems
Rebellious flames of an afflicted heart
O! You, bitter complaints
Clear mirror of a restless soul
Escaping the body's prison
O! You, laughter of desire
Bitter tears
Ominous songs
Howls of pain
Tell my heart's tale.[30]

Telling her tale in free-floating speech, she focused on the concrete, the specific, the personal. The naked "I" of her poetic persona, with all its vulnerabilities, refused to be barred from the pages of her writing. She called herself a "sinner," a "disloyal wife," an "unworthy mother," even a "self-confessed harlot," but considered duplicity and hiding behind a mask an even bigger crime. Life, like writing, was not a matter of "fearful whispers in the dark." It was for her a matter of "daylight, open windows, and fresh air."[31]

Farrokhzad was horrified by the prospect of becoming a doll, an impersonator with a glitzy wardrobe and glassy eyes. She refused to be programmed, to provide cheerful and compliant responses, to live a life of elaborate pretense. In one of her most beautiful poems, "Windup Doll," she writes:

One can sleep for years and years
In a velvet box
Between layers of lace and tinsel
With a body stuffed with straw
With every squeeze of a shameless hand
One can declare, for no good reason
O, I am so very happy.[32]

Although she knew that words, like veils, both reveal and conceal, connect and divide, express and repress, she wanted to weave a different kind of cloth with her texts. She wanted to let her nakedness glitter "[l]ike fish scales in water."[33] She wanted to demolish as many walls as she could, discard as many curtains as possible, cast aside as many veils. She wanted to live and think outside the box. She wanted to be stripped "naked," undisguised, uncovered, although she knew full well that it was traditionally a source of shame in her culture. "I am naked. Naked. Naked / I am as naked as the pause in between words of love," she declared with pride.[34]

Uncovering her personal life, opening herself to the world, refusing to be commandeered by strings like a marionette, Farrokhzad launched a new space where readers—especially women readers—could give voice to their body and body to their voice. By presenting herself nakedly in her poetic voice, she subverted a whole way of living and thinking. She did not evade details or ambiguities, forbidden pleasures, or conflicting feelings. If, as William Butler Yeats said, "we make out of the quarrel with others, rhetoric, but of the quarrel with ourselves, poetry,"[35] she made little rhetoric and a good deal of poetry. She locked horns with what she considered her dark side, her demons, her wells of guilt, regrets, flaws. Rejecting a walled-in self-representation, a predetermined role, a limited and sanitized vocabulary, platitudes, and pronouncements, she created an oasis of the sexually, textually, and culturally forbidden. No wonder her work rocked the foundations of the walled and veiled society in which she lived.

Just as Farrokhzad wanted to explore the world, she also wanted to cultivate her artistic potential. Refusing to be locked into a single discipline, genre, or field, she studied sewing and painting. She wrote poetry, literary criticism, essays and short stories (some under different pseudonyms, others anonymously), and screenplays. With the help of her brother, Amir, she translated German poetry into Persian. She edited an anthology of contemporary Persian poems (which surprisingly does not contain any other female poet than herself, even though at the time of its publication Lo'bat Vala [1930– ], Simin Behbahani [1927– ], and Parvin Dowlatabadi [1924–2008] were published and acclaimed poets). She directed a prize-winning documentary film, and acted in films and on stage. She had many talents and believed in self-invention.

### THE LEPROSARIUM AS A PENITENTIARY

Soon after her return from Europe, Farrokhzad decided to be economically independent. Her ninth-grade education was not a great asset, nor could royalties from her writing—often a pittance—support her. To earn a living, to finally be able to afford a room of her own, she worked as a receptionist and filing clerk at the Golestan Film Studio. The owner, Ebrahim Golestan, a pioneering writer and film director, detected her talent and interest in the cinema and helped her achieve mastery over the form in a short period of time.[36] In July 1962, accompanied by Dr. Abdolhossein Radji, the devoted head of the Society to Assist Patients of Leprosy, the novice cinematographer went to the Bababaghi Leprosarium in northwestern Iran to explore the possibility of making a documentary about leprosy. Shocked by what she saw, she returned to the leprosarium three months later with a crew of five men. She lived for twelve days in this remote colony, twenty kilometers from the city of Tabriz, surrounded by rock-strewn mountain roads. She spent the first few days getting to know the colony's inhabitants. She wanted to learn about the reality of their everyday lives and, above all, to earn their trust and cooperation. And she did. While there, she also adopted a son, Hossein Mansouri, who now lives in Germany and has translated his mother's poems into German.[37] Unmarried at the time and without the familiar context of a nuclear family, she may have been the first Iranian woman to become an adoptive single parent—a role tragically cut short by her early death.

A film of exuberance and compassion, directed by a poet at the height of her imaginative powers, *The House Is Black* (1962) has great stylistic affinity to Farrokhzad's poetry. It is a heartfelt ode to all those who deviate from the norm. The socially rebellious director empathized with her subjects from the colony. Labeled the "poet of sin," she identified with innocent "sinners." Feeling confined within cultural, political, and familial structures, she understood their incarceration. As a member of the community of social outcasts, she knew exactly how it felt to be a misfit, an exile in one's own land. Grappling with suicidal depression, she appreciated the leprosy patients' struggle against a condition they had no control over. She, too, was waging a war for survival.

Although *The House Is Black* is, first and foremost, a film about leprosy, it is cinematically and aesthetically much more. It is a visual poem, a philosophical statement, a social commentary, an autobiographical sketch. Shot in stark black and white, only twenty-two minutes in length, it casts unflinching eyes upon ghastly scars, open sores and skin lesions, crippled hands and feet, stumps of fingers and clawlike toes, eroded nasal cartilage, and flaking skin. Yet in spite of its refusal to sugarcoat reality, the film never devolves into an exercise in morbid curiosity or humiliating pity. On the contrary, it celebrates perseverance and human dignity. The composition of each frame conveys a genuine reverence for the pride and self-possession of perfectly innocent people banished from society. Each scene, each glance, each cut humanizes these exiles, victims of circumstance, people under the medical sentence of incarceration.

Few diseases have been so dreaded as leprosy or so morally stigmatized over the centuries. Few patients have been so isolated, so anathematized as "lepers," few human beings so exiled from society as the victims of this disfiguring and painfully public disease. During the 1960s, there was a revival of interest in "leper colonies" in the West. Several programs came into existence at this time, especially in Europe, for the rehabilitation and destigmatization of patients of leprosy, some supported by the Catholic Church and others by secular organizations. Whether influenced by the civil rights movement in the United States, the students' movement in France, or even the Eichmann trial in Israel, which revived interest in the World War II concentration camps, the level of popular awareness regarding forced immobility was heightened at this time, and questions of human rights became a matter of paramount concern, especially among the younger generation. "Leper colonies" were another example of unjust and unjustifiable exclusion that should be eradicated. And Farrokhzad's film, released in 1962 and viewed by Western audiences in Germany, where it received an award a year later, was a pioneer in this regard.

*The House Is Black* refrains from traditional attitudes of finger pointing and frees leprosy from judgment. Refusing all metaphoric connotations of biological accident, rejecting all correlation between character and physical condition, between moral and mortal flaws, it considers leprosy for what it is, a medical conundrum. But Farrokhzad goes even further. She not only does not dwell solely on the malady per se but focuses her film on the exclusion imposed on patients of leprosy. Even the title of the film alludes to the setting rather than to leprosy or its victims. In the closing shot, a student is asked to make a sentence with the word *house* in it. After contemplating what to write, he finally turns to the blackboard and begins to scrawl across it with a piece of chalk. The camera tracks away from his impassive features and follows the progress of his hand. "The house is black," he writes painstakingly. The title of the documentary reflects Farrokhzad's principal concern. What has filled the young director with indignation, what has truly upset her, is the colony itself, this forsaken and walled community of the leprosarium, whose house is "black" in every sense.

Like her poetry, Farrokhzad's film never settles on a single meaning, never offers a single response. It presents the stark truth as both provisional and relative. It does not pit normality against abnormality, health against sickness, purity against impurity, beauty against ugliness. Although it is uncompromising in its portrayal of heart-wrenching conditions, it also registers moments of beauty and celebrates human dignity in the face of prejudice and adversity. It focuses on everyday activities: weddings, communal meals and prayers, children playing, women applying makeup, breastfeeding, and caring for their healthy children. It captures moments of ordinary human life—people dancing and singing and smoking and lounging on benches, soaking up the sun. Notwithstanding its grisly subject matter, *The House Is Black* is a monument to the strength of the human spirit, an homage to the courage of the human soul. Its message is survival, its style lyrical rather than documentary. It is an affirmation of the will to live and to be free. It is about resilience and the desire to rise above misery, to cling to liberty against all odds. Passion for life and its pleasures shimmer in it like rays of sunshine in a dark cave.[38] Living in close proximity to death, the inhabitants of the Bababaghi Leprosarium, like their director, are fiercely attached to life. Familiarized with the color of darkness, they seek out the sun.

### THE INDIGNITIES OF INCARCERATION

Farrokhzad's insights on captivity found expression in *The House Is Black*. The documentary was not shot in a prison; it did not portray guards or inmates, solitary confinement or escape attempts, guilty verdicts or convictions. But it is nonetheless a prison film. It focuses on a colony that is hidden in a faraway place, whose inhabitants have been exiled from society. Surrounded by big mountains, the leprosarium is fenced on all four sides and locked behind huge wooden gates. Its architecture speaks the language of containment and rejection. The film's poetry—visual and verbal—laments imprisonment.[39] The gentle voice-over of the director herself, which accompanies the images, is infinitely sad and dirgelike. "Our being, like a cage full of birds, is filled with moans of captivity," she says, standing eye to eye with the inhabitants of this forsaken colony, at one with them. Expanding the frame of reference beyond traditional definitions of incarceration, she transforms this leprosarium into an allegory for all forms of cloistered existence, all closed societies anywhere, all kinds of forced exclusion.

Farrokhzad never experienced imprisonment in the literal sense of the word, but the entire body of her work can in one sense be read as a prison memoir. In a letter to her husband, she wrote, "My soul, like a caged bird, is restless."[40] It is hardly surprising that she titled her first poetry collection *The Captive* and referred to herself as a prisoner to the end of her life. And she had good reason to do so. From all available accounts, this woman who was to explore forbidden places and utter forbidden thoughts had felt constrained from early childhood. According to her older sister, Pouran, their parental house "was a big prison with numerous cells. Although they were not wearing striped uniforms, the children had to sleep at a given time, wake up at a given time, eat at a specific time, and change their clothes on time."[41] Feeling confined within these oppressive familial structures, Forugh not surprisingly sought refuge in the arms of a neighbor and insisted on getting married at the age of sixteen.

Having fled from one prison, however, she found herself in another. Domesticity clashed with her yearning for freedom. She rebelled against the confining roles and spaces assigned to a wife and chafed at being denied equal rights with her husband. In her poems, she repeatedly chronicles the tangled emotions of a wife who feels locked up.

> I think about it and yet I know
> I'll never be able to leave this cage
> Even if the warden should let me go
> I've lost the stamina to fly away.[42]

Although she was deeply attached to the husband with whom she had fallen in love and married despite vehement parental objections, domesticity was like a chain around her restless feet. In one angry poem, she compares a wedding band to a "ring of servitude and slavery."[43] In another poem, published in the first edition of *The Captive* and deleted from later editions, she calls upon women to rise up. "Fight for your rights, my Sister," she recommends.

> Fight all those who want you weak
> All those who keep you in the corner of the house
> Through a thousand wiles and guiles
> Your angry complaints

Must turn into screams
You must break this heavy chain
To set yourself free.[44]

After only a year into her marriage, Farrokhzad became a teenage mother. Unlike legal fatherhood, which is based on the biological act of fertilization, motherhood is a privilege, not a right, in Iran. It has to be earned. Even though it is in giving birth that a woman becomes a "mother," to remain one she has to follow a stringent code of conduct and consider motherhood her sole mission in life. For instance, should a divorced mother remarry, she loses even her minimal custodial rights. The choices that faced Farrokhzad at this time were stark. Living in a culture that glorified motherhood as the sole calling of a woman, she openly expressed the urge to pursue art as a profession. Everyone around her reinforced the notion that women took naturally to homemaking and mothering, but she found herself committed to her art just as intensely.

As a consequence of her poetic aspiration and her sense of maternal duty, she was at war with herself. She was keenly conscious that her unadulterated devotion should have been reserved for her child and often asked herself if her forthright ambition to be a "great poet" was worth so much human suffering. Before Betty Friedan's revelation in *The Feminine Mystique* that "we can no longer ignore that voice within women that says, 'I want something more than my husband and children and my home,'"[45] Farrokhzad had articulated hitherto unexpressed frustration with domesticity and now with motherhood in her poetry. Although she wanted something more than husband and child and home, she loved them dearly nonetheless.

Her desire to reconcile the life of a fulfilled mother and a successful poet gave an anguished depth to her work.

If I wish to fly
Out of this dark, dank cell
What can I say to my weeping child?
O let me be . . .
I am a caged bird.[46]

She acknowledged in many poems that the artistic vocation was in conflict with the traditional feminine ideal. She depicted with much agony her failure to reconcile her life as a woman-wife-mother and her life as a poet. Yearning to be united with her biological son, she recognized the sacrifices extracted by this "blood-thirsty Goddess."

> Other than two tearful eyes
> What have you left me?
> O! Poetry, you blood-thirsty Goddess
> Stop. Enough sacrifices.[47]

Torn between creativity and domesticity, she decided to break with convention when she divorced. Despite being deemed a failure as a mother, she forged ahead and became a successful poet. Although she suffered from the loss of her natural rights and the disregard of her maternal instincts, she vociferously objected to these man-made laws and customs and resisted the narrow definition of motherhood. Treated in effect as an exmother, she attempted to transform the definitions of motherhood and expand the boundaries of family alternatives. For although Farrokhzad rejected the singleness of commitment asked of mothers, she never rejected motherhood itself. On the contrary, she celebrated it and mourned to the end of her life the many obstacles she confronted in her attempt to reconcile her creative potentials and maternal bonds. In an intense and agitated poem, "Green Phantom," written at the height of her fame, she portrays herself as a woman denied motherhood. Kept awake by the glaring eyes of a revealing and unkind mirror, the poetic persona weeps all day long and still cannot wash away the pain.

> All day, I cried in the mirror
> The spring had abandoned my window
> To the green phantom of the trees
> My body had outgrown
> The cocoon of my loneliness
> And the stench of my paper crown
> Had polluted that sunless world.

Here, in this mirror, in this poem, a woman, also a poet, complains about the impossibility of combining the joys and comforts of family life with the fulfillment of her artistic talents.[48] In the harsh clarity of her spring-filled mirror, nature's rejuvenation stirs in her the misery of being separated from her biological son.

Shelter me
O, simple women
Complete women
Women whose dainty fingers
Follow under the skin
The thrilling motions
Of a fetus
Women, in whose open collars
The air is always mixing
With the smell of fresh milk.[49]

### REMEMBER FLIGHT

After leaving her husband and her son, and having refused to be locked within the confines of a predetermined femininity, Farrokhzad withdrew into her art— her adopted faith, her shelter, her window to eternity. The last decade of her life was a period of intense and remarkable creativity. As exuberant and expansive in her poetic rhythms as Walt Whitman, as precise and infatuated in her choice of words as Gustave Flaubert, as candid and controversial as Sylvia Plath, as intense and suicidal as Anne Sexton, part Iranian, part universal, Farrokhzad became one of the most inspirational and provocative of Iranian women writers. She not only was driven by a poetic vision but wanted to weave life and poetry together, and to a large extent she succeeded.[50]

Her career came to an abrupt end with her death in 1967. She was at the height of her powers as a poet and only thirty-two years old. Dying as she lived— in motion—she, who loved the open road, was killed behind the wheel of a speeding car. The quintessential modern experience and the confluence of Forugh's love of travel, mobility, speed, independence, agency, and recklessness, a speeding car was a sad, but symbolic closure for a life torn between two contending desires for movement and stillness, flight and rootedness. As she had hauntingly predicted in one of her last poems, she was buried beneath the falling snow.

Perhaps the truth was those two hands
Those two, young hands buried beneath the falling snow
And next year
When Spring mates with the sky beyond the window

and cascades of saplings will erupt from her body
She will blossom, O my love!
O, my dearest only love.[51]


Ironically enough, despite being a maker of movies, a poet of motion, Farrokhzad has become fixed in her compatriot's imagination since her untimely demise, like the still image of the young Icarus who soared into the sky and melted in the sun. Never having experienced the ravages of old age even though she detected with alarm in her early thirties a gray hair here, a wrinkle there, she has come to symbolize eternal youth for Iranians, always defiant, always rebellious, always in love, even though at the end she was fully disillusioned with love.[52] The two subjects, gender and space, which she addressed half a century ago, continue to be among the most contentious in contemporary Iran today. Her words may not have changed the views of those who believed in traditional divisions between the sexes, but they have raised the discussion to a higher plane. Despite having been both maligned and admired during her lifetime, she has come since her death to inspire a large number of women and men who have rejected sex segregation. She has come to stand for a moment in the history of her nation that reflects the tensions and crises as well as the triumphs and joys that she faced as an individual.

Farrokhzad's work was and continues to be a double metaphor. It seldom leaves the Iranian reader impartial, evoking strong attraction or keen aversion, exaggerated hostility or exalted praise. Whereas some consider her a promiscuous woman, dangerous in her advocacy and her choices in life, love, and art, others see her as a cultural hero, a rebel in search of freedom. No matter how she is seen, her fame has grown consistently, especially since her death. She died at the heights of her powers, deprived of the possibility of further evolution both as a woman and as a poet—although, in her own words, in the "sanctuary" of her window, poetry, she is now "connected with the sun"[53]—so we will never know what further heights she may have attained or what depths she might have plumbed. And yet, in spite of her tragic and early death, until Farrokhzad no woman had reached that level of mass appeal reserved for male poets such as Ferdowsi, Hafez, Sa'di, Rumi, Attar, Nezami, and others, who have been revered as producers of a national scripture for centuries. As she herself attests, she planted her ink-stained fingers in the eternal garden of poetry.[54] Although her work was banned soon after the 1979 Revolution, she is now the Iranian equivalent of a rock star or guru or cult figure. In recent years, a whole industry has developed around her name, including poetry collections, books, movies, artworks, voice recordings, and documentary films. An icon-bashing woman has ironically become an icon herself. "Cascades of saplings" have indeed erupted from her ink-stained fingers.

# 6

# THE GYPSY POET

*Fluidity and Flux in the Poetry
of Simin Behbahani*

We wrote our books not with ink but with [our] blood.
—SIMIN BEHBAHANI, in Cynthia Haven,
"Iran's Leading Poet"

I am the gypsy, oh, yes.
Here there is no one else but me.
—SIMIN BEHBAHANI, "Gypsiesque (1)"

## A NATIONAL POET

A woman in her eighties, who gleefully calls herself "a seductive Eve" and brandishes a cup of wine in one hand and a red apple in the other, might not be the first image that comes to mind when we think about Iran today. But to understand the work of Iranian poet Simin Behbahani (1927–) is to understand better the paradoxical nature of contemporary Iran. Indeed, if Emily Dickinson so much identified with her community that she occasionally signed her letters "Amherst," then Simin Behbahani can sign her poems "Iran." In book after book, in one deeply felt poem after another, she has painted miniature portraits of her country over the decades. She has given voice to the yearnings of the Iranian people, chronicled their hopes and disillusionments, documented with pride and precision the heroic resistance and creative subversion of her nation and herself:

My country, I will build you again,
if need be, with bricks made from my life.

155

I will build columns to support your roof with my bones,
I will inhale again the perfume of flowers
Favored by your youth.
I will wash again the blood off your body
with torrents of my tears.[1]

In death-defying poems of wonder and mystery, Behbahani has offered a multilayered portrait of her nation from the street level up. With poignancy, passion, and a strong sense of purpose, she has written the history of Iran in the past few decades. It is the kind of history that is often unavailable in history books. She has captured the chaos and vibrancy of a culture in transition and of a country defining, undefining, and redefining itself. And she has done so with integrity and an ethos of respect for complexity and ambiguity.[2] Her body of work is the voice of a nation in search of itself. Hers is a poetry of immediacy and resonance, of hopes betrayed and renewed, of disillusionment and dissent. It is high art and popular art at the same time, accessible to the ordinary reader, despite its formal traditionalism, its encyclopedic breadth, and its many historical and cultural allusions, both local and global.[3] It is a quest for beauty and elegance, clarity and moderation through all the turbulence of war and revolution.

The history of Iran over the past century has been one not only of successive political and international crises, of kings assassinated, deposed, executed, and exiled, of hostages taken and a nuclear industry under development, but also of a literary renaissance. And Simin Behbahani is surely a renaissance woman. Within the net of her tightly woven words, she has captured the reality of the Iranian experience during one of the most challenging times in its history, proving that the darkest of nights can produce the most luminous of poets. In her lifetime, she has witnessed the coming to power of a new king, the nationalization of Iranian oil, a coup d'état, the White Revolution, the 1979 Revolution, the end of twenty-five hundred years of dynastic rule and the toppling of a monarchy, the establishment of a republic, the Cultural Revolution of the 1980s, an eight-year war with Iraq, and the trauma of various forms of repression and tyranny. In her own words, "Unbending and harsh rules, constant arrests, an atmosphere of fear and trembling, of terror and cold, repeated blackouts, selfless martyrdoms, shortages of food and fuel, closure of all universities, and the escape of fourteen year old boys from their homes to the warfront have created an intolerable situation."[4]

Committed to the truth and prepared to confront power in all its forms, Behbahani has produced some of the most enduring poems of contemporary Iran, such as "Wine of Light," "Camel," "My Country, I Will Build You Again," "A Man with a Missing Leg," and "Banu, My Lady." Her poems are memorized, put to music, quoted as aphorisms. They portray the everyday reality of Iranian life while reconciling political and aesthetic passions. Never one to wallow in bitterness or advocate revenge, Behbahani has always believed in the futility of fighting violence with violence and has taken refuge instead in the creative power of language. Never one to twist words to venal ends or sacrifice them to fame and fortune, she has fought a different battle, to protect the integrity of language. And her words have protected her in turn. In a way, they have become a living proof that although politicians come and go, governments are voted into office and chased out of it, the miraculous, triumphant, and regenerative power of a poet's words remain throughout it all.[5]

Behbahani's concerns are not limited to the local and immediate. She focuses on the central concerns of our time, one of which is war and peace:

My Lord, what kind of century is this
the introduction of which
is signed with bile and blood
Marked with shame and hatred?
In the fields of horror and war
it has spread its prayer rug in pools of blood
what hope is there for the people
of this Century?[6]

She laments: "The world is rife with injustice and oppression, with violations of human rights. A horror permeates my whole life: of dead men hanging; eyes gouged out; amputated limbs, and skulls and chests drenched in blood, crushed by stoning."[7] Refusing to turn her back on the specters of terror that she witnesses on every side, she dreads what is to come:

How can I believe
that death, dour faced
scythe in hand

waits on every corner? How can I believe
that the whole world is a wreck
and I am a wreck like the world
only more so?[8]

She also ponders the conflicts between the forces of extremism and moderation, repression and freedom, revenge and reconciliation, religious fundamentalism and political absolutism. She questions artificially drawn boundaries between East and West, between good and evil, even between elite and popular art. She blends profound sympathy for the individual with sharp criticism of ideology, ruthless condemnation of fanaticism, disgust with the caprice of the crowd. By combining love with loss, humor with horror, and by focusing on both the sublime and the mundane simultaneously, she offers readers a multifaceted, layered view of Iran. In her rainbow world of color and nuance, nothing is black and white except perhaps the black ink on the white page—as stark as blood on fresh snow.

Although prose fiction has rapidly replaced poetry as the most popular genre of literature in postrevolutionary Iran, Behbahani has attracted the attention and admiration of the reading public and the academy both inside and outside her home country. She has come to play the role of a cultural icon, a symbol of resistance. Consider this scene at a 2006 International Women's Day rally in Tehran, when riot police menaced the poet. Participants rushed from every side to protect her. One student in the crowd was crying out: "This is Simin Behbahani. If you touch her, I will set myself on fire right here!"[9] In more than a thousand years of Iranian literature, it is unprecedented for a woman to have reached this level of national recognition during her lifetime. Her eminence testifies to her years of hard work, her literary talents, her political uprightness, her candor, and her courage. But it is above all a confirmation of the pivotal role women play in Iran today as a result of the new spaces they have occupied and appropriated as their own.

### NIGHTINGALE'S FEVER

Though Behbahani's poems differ greatly from each other in their tone, their themes, and images, they share certain defining characteristics. They all show evidence of "Nightingale's Fever," a condition described by the Russian poet

Osip Mandelstam (1891–1938) and explored in a book by the same title. In that book, Ronald Hingley identifies Nightingale's Fever as an ailment that "will not be found in any medical dictionary, but its main symptom is easily described: an inability to stop singing regardless of the consequences."[10] Hingley could be describing Behbahani: she who has continued to sing regardless of consequences. And there have been many consequences, from the monetary to the political, from street harassment to court summons, from anonymous slander to official denunciation, from anxiety and suffering to censure and fear for her life. Her tongue and pen do not stop moving whatever the consequences.

In September 1996, she spent a night in prison. At the time of her arrest (along with some of her fellow writers—Mohammad Ali Sepanlou, Faraj Sark-ouhi, Houshang Golshiri, Roshanak Dariush, and Mehrangis Kar), she had been a guest in the house of the German Embassy's cultural attaché. No charges were filed against her, and she was set free the next day. She was, however, blindfolded and physically abused. As she recalls, "We were released the next morning. They led us out and dropped us in the middle of the street with our blindfolds still tied."[11] Despite this experience, the nightingale did not stop singing. No cage has cured Simin Behbahani. Her fever still rages.

In fact, Behbahani is the most prolific female poet in Iran. For centuries, it was difficult for Iranian women to express themselves in any artistic medium that required a high public profile, such as music, painting, sculpture, or drama. Poetry has been one of the few art forms available to them because it is so thoroughly integrated into the daily lives of Iranians and can be produced in the privacy of one's own home. It costs little or nothing to produce, does not require long periods of uninterrupted time or travel, is independent of actors, studios, theaters, and contracts. It is no small coincidence that women poets have been a presence for more than a thousand years of Persian literature, though their official literary output has not been that substantial. Only some of their poems have survived—at least in print. Indeed, it wasn't until the mid–twentieth century that a woman, Parvin E'tessami, published a collection of her poems. It contained 210 poems composed over twenty years. Only about 50 poems have survived from Tahirih Qurratul'Ayn. Forugh Farrokhzad published 130 poems in her short literary career. In contrast, Behbahani has published some 600 poems—a historically prolific achievement. By the early twenty-first century, she had published nineteen books of poetry; two collections of short stories; a memoir of her late husband, Manuchehr Koushiar; and numerous literary articles, essays, and interviews. She has translated a book from French into Persian[12] and composed about three hundred lyrics for some of Iran's most prominent singers. Though her body of work is impressive in its own right, her output is particularly noteworthy when one considers that Behbahani also was a married woman, a dedicated mother of three children, and a full-time high school teacher for twenty-nine years.[13]

Even as a child, Behbahani demonstrated a love of words and a talent for rhyming. She vividly recalls the end-of-the-schoolyear celebration at her kindergarten, which was run by American missionaries. She was to dance and act as a Yellow Rose and was dressed as one in a yellow organdy skirt with yellow ruffles. She was to recite: "I am a yellow rose, the sultan of all the flowers / The sultan of all the flowers." She was dissatisfied with the lines she had to say, however, and tried to rhyme them. So "even at that age, only two or three years old," she "had enough metrical sense to abbreviate Sultan."[14] A little more than a decade later Behbahani's poems began appearing on the Iranian literary scene with little fanfare. They were first published in literary journals in the late 1930s and early 1940s. Her first book, *Setar Shekaste* (Broken Sitar), was published in 1951 when the poet was barely twenty-four.[15] Ever since then she has been producing carefully crafted poems and developing a complex and distinct voice, at once traditional and provocatively contemporary. The "sultan of all the flowers" of yesteryear is the "sultan of the contemporary *ghazal*" of today.

### FELLOW TRAVELERS: BEHBAHANI AND AKHMATOVA

Despite her abundant contributions to Iranian poetry and her status as a most outspoken dissident voice of postrevolutionary Iran, this poet who is in some ways the equivalent of Anna Akhmatova (1889–1966), an influential Russian poet of the Stalinist era, has not been given due international recognition.[16] The parallels between the lives and the poetry, the impact and the sensibilities of these two women are tantalizing and beg to be explored. Their relationships with words, their representation of subjects and themes, the history and culture they each so candidly depict, the connection they so clearly feel with the sufferings of their countries, their resilience, their courage, and the iconic status each reached late in life—all call for comparison. So does the way they link art with history, private with public destiny, subjective tragedy with collective. Each is able, through a shared love of beauty, to forge new alliances between political opposition and aesthetic, moral, and semantic commitments.

Both poets' resolve not to leave their respective countries in spite of revolutions and repression is remarkable. Akhmatova saw many of her friends and fellow writers abandon Russia to its fate:

> A voice came to me. It called out comfortingly
> It said, "Come here,
> Leave your deaf and sinful land,
> Leave Russia forever."

Refusing to emigrate, however, she answers: "I covered my ears with my hands / So that my sorrowing spirit / Would not be stained by those shameful words."[17] Although Behbahani never rebuked her colleagues for leaving Iran (those who did include Lo'bat Vala, Yadollah Ro'yai [1931–], Nader Naderpour [1929–2000], Nassim Khaksar [1944–], Esmai'il Khoi [1938–], Gholam Hossein Sa'edi [1936–85], and Eslam Kazemiyeh [d. 1997], among others), she was deeply saddened by their exodus. In several poems, she reaffirms her own commitment to stay in the land of her birth regardless of the consequences. In fact, both Behbahani and Akhmatova were able to keep the frontiers open between home and exile by becoming a perpetual reminder of the possibility of return. As Behbahani notes, "Those of us who stayed in the country, putting up with all the hardships, have on occasion mingled our voices with the voices of our compatriots outside the country. On occasion, we have gone to visit them, conveyed a greeting or a message, and returned. Once, one such compatriot, showing enthusiasm for my visit and my poems, asked: 'Why go back? Stay here.' I replied, 'My cries have reached your ears from inside the country. I will go back to the same place to call out to you, 'come back.'"[18]

One of the reasons that Behbahani may not have received the international recognition she deserves is that much of her work, unlike Akhmatova's, is not yet available in English. Her words have not crossed that last important boundary of translation. Indeed, it is only during the past decade that her poetry has attracted some attention outside Iran. She has been nominated twice for the Nobel Prize in Literature (1999 and 2002). She has been the recipient of several international prizes, such as the Hellman/Hammett Human Rights Award in 1998; the Carl

Von Ossietzky Human Rights Award in 1999; the Latifeh Yarshater Book Award in 2004; the Freedom of Expression Award by the Writers Union of Norway in 2007; and the Bita Daryabari Prize for Literature and Freedom at Stanford University in 2008.[19]

## DESEGREGATING THE GHAZAL

Behbahani has transformed the *ghazal*, a traditional poetic form with deep roots in Persian literature, into something new. The *ghazal* is usually governed by strict structural rules. It contains seven to fifteen couplets and is characterized by a single rhyme pattern that holds each poem together. A rhyme appears in the first couplet (aa), and the second line of every ensuing couplet repeats this rhyme (ba, ca, da). Although the meter must be maintained throughout the poem, it can be chosen freely, but the unit of thought remains for the most part limited to the single line. With the birth of free verse, the *ghazal* became identified with the past. Some poets, including Forugh Farrokhzad, considered it antiquated, bloodless, even dead. Behbahani, unlike many of her modernist colleagues, however, never considered this odelike form to be antiquated. In an age characterized by a rejection of the old, on the one hand, and a nostalgic reconstruction of the past, on the other, she consistently challenged dichotomous views of tradition and modernity.

At the beginning of her literary career, Behbahani experimented with a variety of forms, such as rhyming couplets and free verse. Only eleven poems in her second collection, *Foot Prints,* forty in *A Lamp of Forty Lights,* and fifty-five in *Marble* are in *ghazal* form. But as time passed, the *ghazal* gradually became her chosen genre. Behbahani revolutionized its rhythms, its thematic range, and the directness of its expression. She created a new repertoire of subjects for this traditional poem and reversed the relationship within it between the speaker and the spoken to, the lover and beloved. Although she followed in the footsteps of the old masters of Persian literature by turning her hand to this classic form, she created new devices and techniques for it along the way. She adopted an autobiographical voice, used individual expressions, employed everyday speech, and accepted cosmopolitan openness and respect for pluralism in these poems. As a result, her poetry transcends the boundaries of the *ghazal* and expands them beyond traditional limitations of love. It invites recognition and expectation of the familiar while surprising the reader with improvisations and innovations of the genre. In dialogue with the past, it is neither overshadowed nor overwhelmed by the Persian literary tradition.

Throughout most of Iranian literary history, the *ghazal* has been defined as a masculine form. As most dictionaries and literary books affirm, a *ghazal* is a short lyrical poem in which a man writes about a woman or a feminized lover. For centuries, men wrote *ghazals*, and women listened to them, provoked them, inspired them, but rarely created them. Behbahani changed this age-old pattern. Many of her poems enact a reversal of such gender-bound representations, violating mores, power, and propriety. They subvert the very definition of the *ghazal* by placing a man at the poem's center, thus demanding a new emotional space for women. At the same time, they provide men with the possibility of being the desired object for a change. Men are unveiled in Behbahani's *ghazals*.

Although Behbahani has consistently resisted being pigeonholed and objected to being categorized as a "woman poet" or a "feminist," she has challenged some of the most hidden forms of gender inequality in her poems. This is all the more important because it is often the subtlest forms of inequality that are the most compelling and sometimes the most destructive. Invisible, unquestioned, they are taken for granted, perceived as "natural." These masked inequities are enacted on a daily basis in sexist jokes, blanket generalizations degrading to women, rationalizations of unwarranted antagonism, double standards regarding men and women, "scientific" theories supporting sex discrimination, implicit acceptance of gender imbalance, and the definition of certain literary genres as masculine territory. Behbahani disrupted these clichés. From the beginning of her literary career until now, she has contested intentional or unintentional misogyny, questioned stereotypes about women, challenged traditions, and, perhaps most radically, resisted gender apartheid in her *ghazals* by reversing sex segregation.

By desegregating this predominantly masculine form of literature, Behbahani has democratized the *ghazal* to an unprecedented scale. Through her work, women can now be the producers as well as the consumers of this literary genre; they can be its authors as well as its objects. The Iranian *ghazal* is no longer associated only with the names of men such as Rumi, Hafez, and Sa'di. A woman has finally joined the ranks of these masters of Persian literature and used this literary device to talk about women's love and passion, their insights and experiences and sensibilities. She has entered a previously all-male pantheon and left the gate wide open for others to come after her.

Behbahani has also taken this masculine genre and married it to a form considered a woman's province—storytelling. She has taken the classical literary language of song and adapted it to the telling of simple stories of domestic life, human pain, war and love, and loss from a woman's perspective. In other words, she not only has reversed the position of women in the *ghazal* tradition but has turned the song into a story for the woman to sing.

Storytelling has been a form of discourse integrated into the lives of women. It was a safe and domestic craft as well as a survival strategy: an outlet for pent-up emotions, an artistic arena for the expression of camouflaged life stories. Behbahani has elevated women's vernacular storytelling to the status of an established public discourse. In the tradition of her literary foremother, Scheherazade of *One Thousand and One Nights,* she tells her stories with courage, wisdom, fairness, playfulness, and narrative alchemy. Like Scheherazade, she focuses on the concrete as much as on the abstract, the particular as much as the general, the historical and the literal as much as the timeless and metaphorical. Her attention to intimate details of daily life protects her from making facile, sweeping generalizations, but in the course of creating these miniature portraits, she questions the existing order of things with emotional and intellectual acuity. She challenges the status quo and demands change even as she reworks the form itself. She utilizes the mundane details of daily life—presumably insignificant but always incisive— as a means by which to relay powerful sociopolitical messages.

In an animated theatrical style, she narrates the stories of a diverse cast of characters: a maimed soldier returning from the front; a poor gravedigger; a prostitute; a man whipped in the public square; a woman stoned to death; a spurned lover; a Gypsy galloping on a horse; schoolchildren executed by firing squads; a woman poet holding stars in her hands. Behbahani turns the *ghazal* into an autobiographical poem, and in a language dazzling in its directness and scrupulous in its attention to details she discusses, among other subjects, forbidden love, the anguish of a failed marriage, the fear of aging, the loss of peripheral sight, the experience of plastic surgery, the loneliness of widowhood, the despair associated with motherly love, and the loss of a grandchild to cancer. But her autobiographical references bear no traces of self-indulgence. Even her private tales avoid being solipsistic by being suggestive, rather, of the nation's fate. It is hard to think of many other contemporary poets who cover a similar range of topics. As Kaveh Safa astutely remarks, Behbahani "violates generic-thematic expectations; not only of the traditional *ghazal* but also in much of contemporary Persian poetry, which may be confined thematically less by manifest generic prescriptions than by the emotional, intellectual, and ideological predilections of individual poets and the times; not only by what she says in her works, by her thematic breadth, but by how she says them."[20]

A cycle of poems titled "From the Street" offers impressionistic sketches of the ordeal endured by people in postrevolutionary Iran. The streets are a theater of the absurd, and the poet is there to record for posterity the quasi-surrealist scenes of everyday life. Behbahani experiments with unpredictable themes and seeks inspiration in unusual places. In one poem, "From the Street / Number 3," a pregnant woman has to wait in line for rationed food for so long that she has her baby right there in line. As the poet tells us, amidst the pandemonium of an oppressively long line two women are conversing when suddenly one of them announces in panic that she is in labor. "Don't worry. Be patient / our turn will come soon / the count has almost reached two hundred," reasons the other, who does not want to lose her spot in the long line. By the time the two women reach the head of the line, a newborn infant is screaming. The mother, who weeps in pain mingled with joy, is busy negotiating: "Yes . . . but . . . can't you see," she quarrels, "I have become two persons now / and these rations are still for one."[21]

In another poem, "From the Street / Number 6," the reader is made to witness a woman being stoned for adultery. The poem begins with a straightforward account: "When the woman confessed for the fourth time / stoning her became necessary / as commanded by religion." But this is no ordinary execution. Despite the enthusiastic crowd of believers who have climbed the trees and rooftops to watch the scene of execution, something goes horribly wrong.

Her guard, enraged,
picks up a cement block
and smacks it on her head,
thus finishing the unfinished business.

In a distanced, ironic voice, Behbahani closes the poem with the image of the mutilated body of this woman, covered beneath stones and cement blocks but kept alive by an advocate who, like Antigone, is distraught and refuses to let her memory be buried, too. "Religion is catching up with the times. / At last death by stoning / has given way to death-by-the-cement block."[22]

## NO TWIG TO BEND

Besides feminizing the *ghazal*, Behbahani has widened its thematic concerns to include human rights. Although she has avoided involvement in party politics since the beginning of her career, Behbahani has shown deep concern for social and political issues. She has unfailingly advocated the rights of all individuals regardless of gender, class, religion, political affiliation, or ethnicity. Her concern for social justice, however, has become much more vocal since the 1979 Revolution. Rejecting any form of violence or discrimination, she has spoken at women's meetings, gatherings of the Association of Iranian Writers, sit-ins, International Woman's Day celebrations, and rallies against the government's treatment of dissidents. Given the harsh punishment carried out against political dissidents in Iran, several interviewers have asked her if she worries about the repercussions of her open criticism of the regime. Her trademark answer, as in this statement to Soheila Assemi, has been: "I am not out to overthrow any government. Nor am I a guerilla or a terrorist. I am the kind of person who tells the truth as she sees it. I am not scared, in the least bit, by the Islamic Republic either. If they wish to cut off my tongue or blind me, they are welcome to do so."[23] In her poems, too, she reiterates the same proud and fearless sense of defiance:

> I'm no twig to bend easily
> I am the tall, unyielding pine tree
> in me is the essence of resistance
> even if I am cut into pieces . . .
> let the willow tremble
> let the wind billow
> the shame of the wind and the willow is not for me
> I'm the tall unyielding pine tree.[24]

True to her motto, "to stay alive / you must slay silence,"[25] she has spoken out at great risk to life and limb. One instance of her courage and refusal to be censored occurred on October 23, 1997. Behbahani was one of the invited participants in a festival organized by the government in Tehran to celebrate "Woman's Day and national reconciliation." Her speech, however, was interrupted soon after she took the podium. She tried to continue, but she was not allowed to finish her talk. Her description of that day is harrowing: "The Ministry of Guidance invited me to read poetry in a hall large enough to hold 2,000 people. I pulled out of my purse the written text of a speech, which concerned the harassment, the censorship, the oppression that had been inflicted on Iranian writers for eighteen years." But she was only halfway through her enumeration of this persecution "when the microphone was cut off. I continued at the top of my voice. The lights were shut down. I walked farther upstage in order to use the light streaming through from the auditorium. The curtain was pulled down on me. I stepped in front of the curtain. It was the audience's exuberant show of support that saved me that day. . . . Later, I was threatened with death, and another round of vicious attacks by the media was set in motion yet again."[26]

Intimidation and the battle of nerves could not silence Behbahani. She read her speech in its entirety over the phone for one of the Diaspora radio stations the next day. It was picked up by other radio stations and broadcast widely. She also published the full text of her speech in several journals outside Iran.[27] In that speech, Behbahani described the day when the documents and the tapes of the Association of Iranian Writers were ransacked and piled like so much rubbish on the ground. She condemned the government's banning of books and names, the violation of civil and human rights, the prevalence of poverty and unemployment, the financial and psychological pressures on the Iranian people.

Lamenting the exodus of many fellow writers who had left the country because they feared persecution, Behbahani's speech continued to condemn the moral, sexual, ethical, political, and religious slanders foisted upon her and her colleagues. She openly grieved for all those

who had been crushed by hardships and died before their time. One such individual was Mehdi Akhavan-Sales, a political activist and poet, who could have enriched Iran's literary heritage for many more years. Others could not survive imprisonment. Sa'idi Sirjani walked into captivity on his own two feet and left in a coffin. Many died in mysterious circumstances with no official effort made to shed light on the cause of their deaths, such as Ahmad Mir'Alai, Ahmad Taffasoli, Ghafar Hosseini, and Ebrahim Zalzadeh. Some committed suicide: Ghazaleh 'Alizadeh, in Iran, and Eslam Kazemiyeh, in exile, in France.

Following a meticulous and disturbing list of inflictions imposed on Iranian writers and poets, bemoaning their sufferings and losses rather than reciting her poems, she asked: "What had we done to deserve such spiritual and material annihilation?" Her reply confirmed the heavy price paid by all those who wielded a courageous pen: "Now, scarred by years of suffering, by debilitating diseases and successive surgeries, by pressures of censorship and insults and threats to my freedom, I find my powers depleted and at their end." But in her customary steadfast fashion, she immediately added, "Fear is useless. It is vital to take on difficulties and obstacles, even at the cost of one's life. . . . Time is running out fast."

### THE SCRIBE OF A NATION
### THAT IS IN SEARCH OF ITSELF

Aspiring to live in a free society with respect for human dignity and freedom of expression, Behbahani has recorded the saga of a nation in search of liberty. Her whole body of work, especially her postrevolutionary poetry, is a chronicle of the struggle for freedom that has emerged from the wretched mess of revolution and the perils of war. Although she celebrated the Golden Age of pre-revolutionary euphoria, that brief, intoxicating moment when freedom seemed almost within reach, that "Spring of Freedom" in 1978–79 when change seemed imminent, she also recorded the brevity of its blossoming, the swiftness of its blight, and the rapidity of its death. Merciless vigilantes and bands of angry zealots sprang up like weeds after the rain in that parched land, and Behbahani did not hesitate to oppose them or write about them. She called them "Zahak," likening them to the archetypal tyrant, the king-turned-cannibal. She called them "domestic snakes" and "monsters" who leave trails of "plunder and intolerance" in their wake. She portrayed them as hoodlums and hatchet men who turned a season of hope into a time of terror and tyranny.

Although she was never influenced by the veering winds of political and ideological change, she rejected fear mongering and refused to be subjugated to manipulation. She rejected the equation of patriotism with silence, which she considered a form of tacit consent in the status quo. And because she did not like what she saw, even if it was sugar-coated as a struggle against "imperialism," "world arrogance," or enemies intent on derailing the revolution, she did not hesitate to protest:

Sing, gypsy, sing
in homage to being you must sing
let ears register your presence.
Eyes and throats burn from the smoke
that trails the monsters as they soar in the sky.
Scream if you can of the terrors of this night.[28]

Scream she did soon after the revolution, and she continues to make her voice heard today. Never waiting for the right time or the right place to exercise her freedom of expression, Behbahani openly criticized the new regime. And she did so consistently from inside the country, which is not the safest place for taking such a stand. Less than a month after the 1979 Revolution, she bemoaned the merciless cruelty that was visited upon the Iranian people in the name of justice. She condemned the major newspapers' front-page display of bullet-riddled bodies of officials of the previous regime who had been executed without trial or due process of the law:

I can't look: a corpse lies on the ground
its horrifying outline punctuated by bullets
the swamp bubbles that were his eyes
expelled from their sockets
emptied of all joy and sadness
separated from all hatred and love.[29]

Disillusioned by the revolution she had initially supported, Behbahani bemoaned the violence, the disruption of everyday life, the murder of beauty, the disappearance of the simple pleasures of life. Horrified by the wave of terror that followed, the kangaroo trials, the summary executions, the repression of the Kurds and ethnic and religious minorities, the spread of false accusations and vendettas and shameless opportunism, the reign of terror, she described Iran as

a "bloody house." Referring to "The House Is Cloudy," one of the most anthologized poems by Nima Yushij (1896–1960), considered by many the father of modern Persian poetry, she wrote:

> The house was cloudy once
> the house is bloody now
> such it was then, thus it is now
> . . . the old tiger drags the young gazelle in her blood
> the law of the jungle shames religion now
> youthful brides of crystalline bodies and arms
> have graves as nuptial chambers and earth as their pillows now
> you cut the diamond first, and then you destroy it
> pray, tell me, what kind of creed is this?[30]

Filled with anguish at the routine injustices perpetrated upon the Iranian people,
the steady arrests of those who dared oppose the new regime, and the mass exodus of artists, writers, and poets, she saw her hope disintegrating into misgiving
and doubt:

> Doubts, doubts, doubts at dusk
> when you can't tell wolf and sheep apart
> when a sickly, jaundiced, light
> has spread itself on the dirt of the threshold
> the gray line on the horizon:
> what is it blowing our way?
> Is this the lead of the lies of the night?
> Or the silver of the dawn's truth?
> Uncertain, full of dread, the traveler ponders
> at the threshold of his journey
> "shall I wait or begin?"
> With doubts settled in the shelter of the eyes
> faith will repudiate truth
> even if it shows its face.[31]

And then, as if these oppressive internal measures were not bad enough, in
October 1980 the first bombs exploded over the Mehrabad Airport, and the war

with Iraq began. Locating her poetry—and her life and death—squarely within the physical and spatial boundaries of the country, Behbahani mourned the bloodshed anew:

> We wished no war
> but here it is
> war; this inferno, this ball of fire
> "may there be no war" I had ventured
> but war is upon us
> oh, my homeland, I vow to you
> I'll be yours for as long as I live
> my poetry and passion and joy are all here
> my coffin and my grave shall be here too.[32]

Many gut-wrenching poems about war followed this earnest wish for more peaceful days. "The Necklace" is one such poem, composed in September 1988 and published finally outside the country in 1992 in a collection entitled *Paper-Thin Garment*. By crystallizing a mother's pain into art, "The Necklace" makes readers witness the nightmarish consequences and long-term implications of war. The poem features the mother of a dead soldier. Although guns, uniforms, and battlefields have no place in the poem, the reader experiences the full impact of the war in spite of these conspicuous omissions. The dead soldier's boots and his mother's wretchedness are all there are to see. The parameters of the battlefield have thus been stretched unbearably. Ironically enough, the poem so blurs distinctions that it articulates a new conception of war in which dead soldiers are not the only casualties and their mourning mothers become new kinds of combatants. Behbahani defines another kind of war here, one in which a corpse refuses to be buried and finds reincarnation in boots. Rejected by the earth, this grief-stricken mother can't even take refuge in death. She is condemned to live and carry her pain, like an excruciating necklace around her neck, a chain around her soul. Through her life, the death of her son is thus assigned a new meaning and a heartrending urgency:

> Anxious, agitated, sad,
> her face uncovered, her head unveiled,
> not afraid of arrest or policeman,
> oblivious to the order to "Cover! Conceal!"

Her eyes two grapes plucked from their cluster,
squeezed by the times to fill a hundred barrels of blood,
mad, really mad, a stranger to herself and others,
oblivious to the world, beyond being awakened even by the deluge,
a particle of dust adrift in the wind, without purpose or destination,
lost, speechless, bewildered, a corpse without a grave,
carrying around her neck a necklace of curses and tears,
a pair of boots tied together belonging to a dead soldier.

I asked her: What does this mean?
She smiled: my son, poor child, sitting on my shoulders,
hasn't taken off his boots yet.[33]

The poetic persona here refuses to be concealed behind walls. She will not be the mother whose suffering remains invisible behind the veils of war propaganda and religious slogans; she will not be a silent witness, a solitary mourner refused the right to grieve in public because her son has died a martyr. Defiant and distraught, she exposes her face, uncovers her hair, and displays around her neck for all to see these monstrous trophies of destruction. Her dead son's boots communicate her pain and grief to the entire world. She refuses to submit to forgetfulness. Nor will she "celebrate" her son's martyrdom as she is expected to do, weeping and sighing in private as the mother of a martyr should in such circumstances. Instead, she demands a communal mourning of this death.

As a way of redressing the unveiled woman's losses, the poet suspends the traditional conventions associated with the *ghazal* as well as the masculine discourse about war and gives voice to this woman in the street. In this way, both the inconsolable mother and the outraged poet appropriate the public arena; they transform a private grief into a matter of public concern. Both, like the dead boy, are casualties of the war and suffer as a result of this tragedy as they struggle against loss and amnesia. But neither of them suffers passively; neither is a mere observer of events. The mother carries the ghost of her dead son around her neck like a permanent albatross, and the poet relives the violence visited upon a demented mother. Behbahani will not allow the glorified language of martyrdom to divert the gaze from the brutality of war. In protest, she transforms her sorrow into moral indignation and powerful irony and re-creates the *ghazal*, her love poem, into a funeral song, an elegy for the living and the dead.

Although condemning war, Behbahani never belittled the men and women who sacrificed their lives defending their country. On the contrary, she celebrated their courage and patriotism. Calling it an "epic resistance," she depicted their valor with pride and admiration:

> O, History! Record this epic of resistance
> record the tale of this season of blood
> record the stone thrown by a sparkling child
> record the ax which was carried by a caring elder . . .
> record the shout of all those who cried out "Death or Honor"
> those who embraced death with courage
> O, History! Record it all; record it.[34]

And at long last, when the war ended after eight years and countless casualties, Behbahani wrote:

> Our tears are sweet, our laughter venomous
> we are pleased when sad, and sad when pleased
> happy when heart-broken, heart-broken when happy
> we wash one hand in blood, the other we wash the blood off
> we cry as we laugh at the futility of both these acts
> eight years have passed; we haven't discovered their meaning
> we have been like children, beyond any account or accounting
> . . . we wished for a war, it brought us misery
> now repentant we wish for peace
> we pulled wings and heads from bodies
> now seeking the cure we are busy grafting
> will it come to life, will it fly
> the head we attach, the wing we stitch?[35]

The war might have ended, but the difficulties of daily life continued in Iran. There were shortages of the basic necessities, repeated blackouts, inflation, and unemployment. Universities remained closed, and the invasion of all forms of privacy continued. There was a chain of repressive measures designed to silence dissent. In March 1981, Saʿid Soltanpour (1940–81), a member of the board of the Association of Iranian Writers, was arrested on his wedding day and executed.

The association was soon under attack, its documents, lecture tapes, and other materials confiscated. It eventually was shut down. Some of the writers and a few of their lawyers were imprisoned. Shahrnush Parsipur (1946–), a prominent novelist, was incarcerated without a charge or trial. Undeterred by the atmosphere of terror, Behbahani wrote:

> Dark, angry, Arabic script is the language of your violence
> soft and blue tile is the symbol of our compliance
> the bruise of your lash, fused with red blood
> has painted amazing flowers in blue and golden yellow
> monkeylike, you still bask in imitating Arabs
> what uncouth manners you have
> how fake is your mimicry.[36]

### LUMINOUS TALE OF DARKNESS

Behbahani details a deplorable catalog of punitive measures taken against dissidents. The violence she portrays is staggering: writers, poets, and journalists maligned, censored, isolated, abducted, incarcerated, mutilated, gunned down, exiled, executed. Although alarming, this list of atrocities ultimately becomes a declaration of victory. No matter how drab the reality, no matter how oppressive the circumstances—and the reality is drab, the circumstances are oppressive—optimism and a sense of resistance shine through her work and refuse to be extinguished. She does not give into silence or despair. Her poem "Banu, Our Lady" is proof of it.

On a Thursday evening, July 8, 1999, soldiers and vigilantes invaded a dormitory at the University of Tehran. It had been the first day of student protests against the new censorship laws and the forced closing of the newspaper *Salam*. The invaders attacked the students, beating many and throwing some out of the windows. The poem "Banu, Our Lady" is an expression of Simin Behbahani's outrage at this event (*banu* is a term of respectful address for women, here applied to one of the most beloved and respected women in Islam, Fatemeh Zahra):[37]

> Banu, Our Lady,
> this is my gift to you. Accept it.
> This said, he raised his offering
> and threw it down the stairs.

On the ground, the sacrificial victim
twisted with pain.
A stream of blood flowed from his fall.
Silence followed his screams.
A demon had made an offering,
and a person had ceased to exist.
Oh for the child lost so young!
A hundred times Oh for the old mother.

Banu, Our Lady, I dreamt I saw you
in the halo of the moon,
your face pale, your eyes red with sorrow.
In your arms you held two sons,
one perfect like the full moon,
the other radiant like the sun.
You sat beside the corpse,
your face still covered
by the dust of the road
your soul scalded by sorrow,
your heart weary of arrows.
You complained: O Justice! O Faith!
O, the shamelessness of the brute—
offering me a corpse
and asking me to accept it!

Banu, Our Lady, you shed a deluge of tears
over the man murdered by such ignorance.
You turned your silken robe into a shroud
to cover his body.

O, Banu, our guide! O, Banu, our savior,
O, Banu, unblemished! O, Banu, full of light![38]

At the root of Behbahani's rage in this poem is the ghastly travesty symbolized by an attacker who pushed a student to his death while invoking the name
of Fatemeh Zahra, the beloved daughter of the Prophet Mohammed. Behbahani
takes the sheer blasphemy of such an act, the unadulterated mockery of it, and

transforms it into a prayer. The sacred figure of Fatemeh is depicted with such dignity, the manner in which she responds to the brute attacker's invocation so charged with spiritual purity, that it is as if the act of flinging the victim to his death has been utterly reversed and cleansed of its original intent. By showing Our Lady Banu grieving over the body of the broken boy at her feet and tenderly covering him with her silken robes, Behbahani succeeds in turning the very flight of steps upside down and revolutionizing the axis of the world. The boy has been lifted up rather than thrown down by the poet's transformation of space.

ONE POET, MANY IRANS

Many writers have been silenced by such horrors, but just as many others, Behbahani among them, have angrily borne witness to the literal as well as literary suppression of their colleagues and innocent victims. It is this tension between forced silence and voiced protest, between acquiescence and resistance, that reflects the Iranian literary scene and Iranian society today, and Behbahani bears witness to both sides of this ongoing battle.

As a result, in her work—her poems, speeches, interviews, and prose narratives—she never depicts a monolithic Iran. The Iran she lives in, like the one she portrays, is a country in flux and constant motion, a country under threat of earthquake and upheaval, split between opposing visions of religion and conflicting variants of orthodoxy, fissured by the opposing ideologies of cultural Puritanism, pluralistic moderation, and democratic aspiration, cracked and divided by gender strictures and sex segregation. The Iran she knows so well is made of many Irans. It is a land that she herself has described as "blessed with millennia of written history and civilization; a land where Zoroaster once spread his message of good deeds, happiness, and light; a land where Cyrus once championed justice, freedom and humanity, where he inscribed in stone a foundation for the defense of human rights, attracting the admiration of men of judgment everywhere"; and at the same time a country forced to its knees by decades of abuse and exploitation. Once a "beacon to the world," it is "now infamous in the world's eyes for the lower depths to which it has sunk."[39]

Behbahani has never subscribed to absolutes; she has always resisted binary modes of thinking. The fluidity of her poems, the shifting of the genres and forms she has deployed, all reflect their hybrid content, their versatile worldview. The way she reconfigures the familiar boundaries bears witness to the elasticity of her mind. She never sticks to a fixed or rigid position. Her poetry refuses to be locked into narrow categories. Old and new, East and West, masculine and feminine, personal and collective, traditional and modern, art and history—all are woven seamlessly into the fabric of her work. She challenges hierarchies, interrogates relations between the sexes, and attempts to influence the allocation of power, space, and resources not only in literature but beyond. Her series of poems dedicated to Gypsies best exemplify this elasticity.

It is clear that Behbahani identifies with the figure of the Gypsy in her work. At the close of the first of a series of poems devoted to Gypsies, she writes:

I am the gypsy, oh, yes
here there is no one else but me
the gypsy's image is visible
as long as I face the mirror.[40]

This identification is fascinating in view of the common Iranian association of Gypsies with promiscuity, aggression, public presence, and an annoying surplus of feminine noise. Gypsies are frequently seen to be the source of antagonistic hubbub and loud commotion; they cause unnecessary uproar and disrupt the conventional norms. To say that someone is like a Gypsy, Kowligari, is far from a compliment in the Persian language, and to call a woman "Kowli" (Gypsy) is a downright derogatory remark. A Gypsy is believed to engage in a litany of undesirable behavior: she is immodest; she cheats; she steals; she lies; she robs; she sings and dances in front of perfect strangers. She is loud and unruly and shameless: she looks people directly in the eye and invites their gazes. She performs all sorts of petty crimes, and she is unrepentant. Worse yet, she claims as her unquestionable right unrestrained mobility.

To Behbahani, the Gypsy—whom she always portrays as a woman in her poetry—possesses the capacity to cross all limits and to resist all conventions. She cannot be pinned down and is free of all spatial constraints. She has a public presence and an identity that is not subject to any of the conventional boundaries. Rejecting geographic frontiers as well as traditional notions of femininity, neither submissive nor domestic, she abandons her "proper" place and invades the public arena of attention. Vocal rather than silent, transgressive rather than submissive, mobile rather than walled in, she challenges the prevailing values of the established order.

In our era of cultural dislocation and political wandering, in our world of universal exiles, refugees, and emigrants, the figure of the Gypsy can hardly be ignored. Although this border crosser has myriad guises and has appeared in various forms of art throughout history—from Miguel de Cervantes's novel *La Gitanilla* to Victor Hugo's *The Hunchback of Notre Dame*, from Georges Bizet's opera *Carmen* to Bram Stoker's *Dracula* and Gabriel García Márquez's *One Hundred Years of Solitude*—she or he has never before now presented such an unnervingly accurate portrait of our times. Gypsies were traditionally always considered the "other." The mass culture from which they were excluded and fled simultaneously dreads and admires them, despises and desires their imagined freedom. But behind their carefree lifestyles, so refreshingly autonomous, so romantically defiant, and so mobile, can also lie the harsh reality of homelessness, the misery of marginality, the grim limits of poverty, and ostracism.

Gypsies have been familiar figures on the Persian literary scene for centuries. Despite lacking any major claim to land, written tradition, or "political" voice, they have nevertheless been depicted as figures of magic, adventure, and romance. In older literary examples, they appear mainly as entertainers, exotic performers of music and dance. According to Ferdowsi in his monumental *Shahnameh,* they were first brought into Iran by the Persian monarch Bahram-e Gur, who asked the Indian king Shangul for dancers and singers. His request was granted by the dispatch of ten thousand Gypsies to the Persian kingdom.

However, the sympathy that contemporary Iranian women writers in general and Behbahani in particular show for the figure of the Gypsy goes beyond anything that might have been provoked by the experience of exile, either chosen or imposed. Nor can it be explained merely as the usual worldwide fascination with Gypsies as outlaws of society or as its entertainers, singers, and dancers.[41] Such a degree of preoccupation with this curiously liberating figure on the part of a poet is surely more than a mere interest in the exotic and the gothic, a puerile attraction to the loud or unruly, more even than an expression of the universal instinct to idealize or demonize. It is, I think, a culturally specific phenomenon. The Gypsies' sexually desegregated lifestyle and their exemplary mobility have a special meaning for women in a society in which sex segregation has been the ideal for centuries. It is to be expected that they would have an even more specific meaning for Iranian women writers and poets. These defiant figures' disregard for boundaries and their adventurous leap into the forbidden arena of public space hold wide-ranging aesthetic, political, and literary significance. Moving from one city to another, from one country to another, the Gypsy embodies motion in a physical and metaphorical sense. These seductive interlopers on the fringes of conventional society, unmindful of rules of modesty, unclassifiable in terms of identity, and ambiguous as far as gender is concerned, serve as ideal representations for the one who would break boundaries of all sorts.

Recognizing the recalcitrance of the Gypsy figure, Behbahani has deconstructed and then reconstructed this familiar image in her poems. This reconstruction is not about the taming of the shrew, the domestication of the wild, the containing of the otherwise uncontainable. Behbahani instead has infused the symbol of the Gypsy with new meanings, divesting it of its age-old connotations. She has revised it and reenvisioned it. In a clever inversion, she has portrayed the Gypsy as articulate rather than loud, autonomous rather than unruly, free rather than promiscuous, courageous rather than aggressive. She has celebrated rather than censured her, portraying her as a woman who challenges the traditional feminine virtues of domesticity, invisibility, submissiveness, silence, and immobility.

Like the Gypsy in her poems, Simin Behbahani rejects silence and stillness. She has raised the banner of poetic rebellion in spite of harassment, attacks, and death threats. Through her words, a nation has found its voice, can lament its suffering, and finally celebrate its hard-won victories. As a firm believer in the futility of violence and as an advocate for an Iran in which dissent is neither eliminated nor punished, she has relied on words to fight for justice and human dignity. For more than six decades, her allegiance has been to democratic principles; her perspective has been egalitarian, her worldview tolerant. Her voice—so eloquent, so hopeful, so defiant—accompanies political prisoners to their solitary cells.[42] It inspires those who share her ideals of beauty and elegance and her dreams for a better and more peaceful world. Even when the experiences described are harrowing—and there have been many—and even when the poem bleeds with sorrow and grief, the sheer persuasiveness of her images, the luminous telling of a tale of darkness, the boundless power of her words and their magical spell lift the heart, console the soul, and promise better days. May her message of beauty and peace, tolerance and social justice be carried across many languages, cultures, and continents.

# 7

# WOMEN ON THE ROAD

## Shahrnush Parsipur and the Conference of Female Birds

Completion of this road needs a man.

—FARID-UD-DIN ATTAR,
*The Conference of the Birds*

One path: a thousand lifetimes to fulfill.

—SHAHRZAD SEPANLOU, *Touba*[1]

How many roads must a man walk down
Before you call him a man?

—BOB DYLAN, "Blowin' in the Wind"

### DANCING IN CEMENT SHOES

I could not believe my eyes or my ears. The band was playing lively Persian music, and it was accompanied by the melodious voice of a woman. Rowdy customers had turned their glasses and plates into drums, their knives and forks into drumsticks. A sea of torsos swayed to and fro in harmony with the seductive rhythms. "Welcome to Shab Sara [House of Night] Restaurant," said the headwaiter, directing my friends and me to our reserved table. The House of Night would indeed be full of surprises that night in 2003, one of my most memorable experiences during that trip to Tehran.[2]

Was such public merrymaking finally possible in my country? I wondered. Were women allowed to sing in public now? I knew the "cleansing" process after the 1979 Islamic Revolution had purged Iran of all its women singers, driving

180

many into exile and others into silence. Dancing in public also had been banned. Even in private, it had been outlawed between the sexes. As we took our seats, though, I noticed with astonishment that the singer was sporting a moustache and trousers. "How ingenious," I said to my friends. Here was a woman disguised as a man in order to sing in public. Iran has a long history of casting men in women's roles and attires, so why not reverse the old order now? My friend, Mitra, quickly corrected me. "He is not a woman. There is a growing number of men who imitate women singers. Haven't you heard about Mr. Mahisefat?" I had not. "He is the absolute best, I wish you could hear him," she continued with excitement. "If you close your eyes and listen to him, you would never know he was a man. He impersonates Iranian female singers who are in exile now. Honestly, you can't tell the difference."

Postrevolutionary Iran has never ceased to astonish me, but I had not in my wildest dreams imagined this scene. I was filled with a palpable sense of danger, though. I was scheduled to leave Iran in two days, and I had no intention of getting into trouble. I wanted to stay away from the morality police, who could enter any house, march into any restaurant, crack down on any activity they chose to call "depraved" and arrest "corrupt" partygoers and merrymakers at the drop of the veil.

So I sat there, stiff-necked with anxiety, rigid with apprehension, trying to take up as little space as possible—to be invisible, really. With a scarf covering my hair, my shoulders hunched, my hands folded modestly on my knees, I must have looked like a statue in the middle of that raucous restaurant. People were in motion all around me. The cross-singer had roused his audience to frenzy. It was hard to know who were the performers, who the spectators. Women and men, young and old, tossed their heads gracefully from side to side. They lifted their arms, undulating from shoulder to shoulder, fluttering. Softly and sinuously, they rotated their wrists, their hands weaving, their fingers twirling and curling, twisting and turning. They were like birds poised to take flight!

The dance was improvised; it emphasized upper-body movements and a wide variety of facial expressions. Because everyone was sitting, no footwork was necessary. No flouncing, no jerking, no cavorting was needed. It was a dance without dancing. It was a movement within the music itself. The House of Night was a kaleidoscope of sensuality, color, and sound. Like everything else in Iran today, it demonstrated a creative mixture of subversion and subservience. Tied to their seats, women and men flapped their wings and soared.

It was hard to believe that these rhythms were not preplanned or coordinated, that this dance had not been choreographed, but everything was instinctive, spontaneous. The excitement was tangible. It was contagious. As the tempo grew faster, the music louder, and the crowd more aroused, the passion swept me away. My body began to pulse with the rapture of the beat. My arms lifted like wings. My shoulders rose and fell. Before I knew it, I began to sway with the other dancers seated and soaring around me.

My friends and I left the House of Night in the early hours of the morning. As we trooped out, we made sure our heads were properly covered.

### DANCING WITH WORDS

Women's literature in Iran today reflects the same atmosphere of constraint and self-determination, limitation and liberty, compliance and defiance as I had seen in the House of Night. It is a fusion of creative resistance and resistant creativity. On the one hand, it is the tale of women whose words have been censored and whose lives bear the scars of conflict and control. On the other hand, it is the saga of women who reject whispers behind tall walls by revolting against patriarchal authority, by refusing to be stopped by man-made rules and boundaries. The Islamic Republic in its early years clearly wanted to regulate literary activities and banned some prominent Iranian women writers and poets. In the short run, it succeeded in driving a number of women into silence or exile, but in the long run it has failed. The life and the literary trajectory of Goli Taraghi (1939–), one of Iran's most critically acclaimed and talented novelists today, is an eloquent case in point.[3]

Taraghi migrated to France soon after the revolution. In her own words, "I left Iran in 1979, the year of the Islamic Revolution, and settled in Paris with my two small children. I was naïve enough to think that the chaotic upheaval of the beginning eventually would settle into normal life, and I could return. The increased hostility of the government toward the intellectuals and the war with Iraq, which lasted eight years, forced me to stay longer than I had imagined." Those were difficult days for Iranians inside and outside the country. Although the Dr. Zhivago of the 1979 Revolution and the Iran-Iraq War remains to be written, surely the biography of those whose lives were disrupted or torn apart by forces beyond their control is a powerful indictment of wars and revolutions.

Taraghi had the means to migrate to France, but her life there was fraught with difficulties. For one, she "was educated in America and did not speak French," as she later recounted in the autobiographical short story "The First Day." She "had to start from zero." Moreover, "fear of an uncertain future, financial worries, being lost and homesick and many other problems, conscious and unconscious, all contributed to my nervous breakdown. I believed I could fight back personally. I underestimated the destructive force of the enemy. After a year of suffering, I was finally hospitalized in a psychiatric clinic."

Autobiographical narratives of mental illness, depression, and institutionalization are rare in Iranian literature, and Taraghi's wrenching description of her experience is unique. It proves the healing power of words and bears witness to her refusal to give in. "Taking the right medication restored my mental stability and helped me to overcome my dreadful anxieties, but what came to my rescue and pulled me out of the dark well of depression was the magical force of literature," she explained. In spite of the painful separation from her young children, her descent into silence and stasis, she eventually recovered. "I make a rope of words," she wrote in "The First Day," "and slowly pull myself up from the depth of darkness, from the bottom of the well."[4] She regains her health, or is it her command of words? Publishing in France and in Iran, she grew into a writer with an increasingly more complex and more provocative work, with a well-deserved international fame.

### THE PERILS AND JOYS OF WRITING

Taraghi's tale of literary success, following several years of silence and suffering, is not atypical. After a temporary lull in the early postrevolutionary years, Iranian women emerged with renewed energy. Their vigorous involvement in various literary genres, the unprecedented popularity of their works, their variegated themes and concerns and backgrounds are beyond comparison with any earlier period of Iranian literature.

The path to such unprecedented emergence has been strewn with difficulties, the cost of integration exorbitant. In fact, the whole tradition of Iranian women writers portrays the hazards and the thrills of writing in a literary scene dominated by men. On one hand, it is a tale of imposed silence, atrophy, tension, and paralysis; a saga of unfinished work, unrealized potential, blank pages. On the other hand, it is a chronicle of radical dissent, a testament to a presence asserted, a body reclaimed, a voice regained. The price pioneering women writers have paid for their transgressions during the past 160 years has been high. Tahirih Qurratul'Ayn was executed when only thirty-six. Parvin E'tessami died of a mysterious fever at thirty-four. Taj al-Saltaneh attempted suicide three times. Zand-Dokht Shirazi (1911–52), whose tragic life is immortalized in Simin Daneshvar's masterpiece *Persian Requiem*,[5] departed in her early forties, an early death caused by overwork and depression. Fatemeh Sayyah (1902–47) died of a heart attack at forty-five. Forough Farrokhzad lived a life marked by nervous breakdowns and attempted suicides. Mahshid AmirShahi (1937–), Goli Taraghi, Shahrnush Parsipur (1946–), and many others have written about their depression or attempted suicides. Mehrangiz Kar (1944–), Shahla Lahiji (1942–), and Shirin Ebadi (1947–) were incarcerated. Ghazaleh Alizadeh (1947–), disillusioned and embittered, hanged herself with colorful ropes in Javaherdareh village in Ramsar. Parvaneh Eskandari (1938–98) was cut into pieces in her home along with her husband, Dariush Foruhar (1928–98). No wonder Simin Daneshvar (1921–) proclaimed in an interview, "Let Simone de Beauvoir come and live for a year the life I live here and if she can still produce one line of writing I'll change my name."[6]

This catalog of depression, isolation, imprisonment, suicide, execution, and early death is indeed disconcerting. The decision to nurture their creative drive— or the "bloodthirsty Goddess," as Forough Farrokhzad called it—has been fraught with difficulties. Women writers have made many sacrifices. They have climbed steep paths. But they have also seen results and rewards. They have created a considerable body of literature in the past several decades, leaving a cultural heritage and launching a veritable renaissance.

Women now are publishing a record number of books in Iran—fiction, nonfiction, and poetry—creating a strong and vital literature in the process. It is exciting to see women moving into traditionally male literary genres. Today poetry is no longer the only literary genre open to women. For instance, women write some of the most interesting and provocative fiction in Iran. In fact, fiction is now their preferred medium. Although there have been women poets for millennia, going back to the very beginning of Persian literature, the first attempts at fiction writing go back only to 1930, when Irandokht Teymurtash published *Dokhtar-e Tireh Bakht va Javan Bolhavas* (The Ill-Fated Girl and the Unfaithful Boy).[7] Three years later Zahra Kiya brought out *Parvin-o-Parviz*

(Parvin and Parviz). From the 1930s to the 1960s, only about a dozen women—compared to 270 men—published works of fiction in Iran. The prominent novelist Simin Daneshvar reached widespread popularity during this period and produced her masterpiece, *Savushun*. By the mid-1990s, however, women dominated the fiction best-seller lists. The number of women novelists now is 370—thirteen times as many as ten years earlier and about equal to the number of men novelists.[8]

It is not only the number of women novelists that is significant, but also their widely different social, political, and religious backgrounds. The popularity of a large number of women novelists such as Simin Daneshvar, Moniru Ravani-pur, Goli Taraghi, Mahshid AmirShahi, Shahrnush Parsipur, Fataneh Haj Seyed Javadi, Zoya Pirzad, Farideh Golbu, Fariba Vafi, Shiva Arastui, and many others is particularly noteworthy. Novels by women often outsell novels by men. Whereas the average Iranian novel has a print run of about five thousand copies, several books by women have enjoyed printings of more than one hundred thousand copies. Fataneh Haj Seyed Javadi's novel *The Morning After*, an engaging and detailed portrait of love and loss published in 1995, has outsold every other work of fiction in postrevolutionary Iran.[9] Although these books' literary merit varies widely, the stories they tell resonate with an ever-increasing readership. They explore taboo topics such as family and gender relations, domestic violence, the difficulties of reconciling family commitments with artistic aspirations, mental illness, depression, the tyranny of older brothers, drug addiction, child custody, sexual relationships, the right to choose one's partner or lover, and the desire to be free and fetterless.

The same phenomenal growth can be seen in the number of women working as literary translators. Whereas in 1997 Iran had 214 women translators, the number soared to 708 six years later. According to a recent report released by the United Nations Commission on the Status of Women, women working in the Iranian publishing industry as a whole numbered more than 2,000 in 2003 as compared with 700 in 1997. The number of women publishers almost doubled in that six-year period as well, rising from 66 to 103. There is also an exciting new development outside the country. Iranian women writers in the Diaspora are producing highly acclaimed best sellers and attracting remarkable attention from mainstream Western media. Some diasporic authors have found a propitious market inside the country. For example, Homa Sarshar's biography of Shaʿban Jaʿafari, a controversial figure during the 1953 CIA–led coup in Iran, sold about seven thousand copies outside Iran.[10] Its publication inside the country was a big success. As a best-seller, it has gone through seventeen printings. The translated version of Firoozeh Dumas's *Funny in Farsi: A Memoir of Growing up Iranian in America,* written originally in English and published in the United States, went through six printings in its first year of publication in Iran.[11]

## I AM MOBILE, THEREFORE I AM

Assia Djebar (1936–), the celebrated Algerian novelist and film director, believes that "though it sounds surprising," she "would not have taken the path of literature" had her father kept her secluded "as a marriageable maiden," and if she had not "wandered passionately and anonymously through the city streets as a passer-by, an observer, a disadvantaged boy and, till the present day, as a pedestrian." To Djebar, this disguised boyhood "is the primary freedom—the freedom to move, to be underway, the ever surprising freedom to decide about one's coming and going, from indoors to out of doors, from the private to the public domain and vice versa."[12] "By hook or by crook," writes Virginia Woolf in *A Room of One's Own,* "I hope that you will possess yourselves of money enough to travel and to be idle, to contemplate the future and the past of the world, to dream over books and loiter at street corners and let the line of thought dip deep into the stream."[13] It is exactly this very theme of traveling, of loitering at street corners, that heralds the beginning of Iranian literary modernity. Mirza Saleh Shirazi's *Safar Nameh* (Travelogue) published in 1819 and Haj Zeynalabedin Maraghe'i's *Siyahat Nameh-ye Ebrahim Beyk* (The Travel Narrative of Ebrahim Beyk) (1894) are influential books in modern Iranian literature. Although it took women more than a century after the publication of Shirazi's *Travelogue* to publish their first travel narratives, the theme of traveling now fuels a significant number of their books. It is travel that enlightens characters' minds and begins their metamorphosis. It is the freedom to loiter at street corners that leads to their self-exploration.

This very concept of physical freedom is a central concern of contemporary women's literature in Iran. By desegregating themselves, Iranian women writers have envisioned a more integrated world by insisting on mobility rights. They have opposed segregation along gender lines in their personal lives and in their female protagonists' lives. Shiva Arastui (1962–), the prolific poet-novelist who has garnered a number of prestigious literary awards in the past few years, expresses this unparalleled and determined presence of women in the public square. "The narrator of my stories," she announces with great pride, "has been involved in a revolution; she has been a student, has attended the university, has been present in the streets with boys her own age at every step of the way, and has not found the time to stay inside the house. She wants to say: 'I exist.' She wants to say: 'I, too, am a human being.'"[14] If Descartes said, "I think, therefore I am," Arastui's narrator, like the protagonists of many other women writers, seems to declare: "I am mobile, therefore I am."

This broadened concept of physical mobility—this sense of entitlement, this conviction that a woman has the right to be in the public domain without being seen as a "streetwalker"—is revolutionary. Persian folklore and literature are full of men who have been seekers after truth, knowledge, or enlightenment. They are replete with male travelers, pilgrims, explorers, adventurers, trailblazers. They are packed with Sufi masters who provide their readers with a roadmap for spiritual illumination and rely heavily on the discourse of physical mobility. Yet rare are the women who claim the road. Even though Iran can claim the existence of remarkable women mystics, and the search for God and truth per se is nongendered, the language associated with the Sufi tradition is marked by gender apartheid.[15] Sufi maps for spiritual development and self-knowledge are for the most part written by men, for men, about men. And because a virtuous woman should not be out alone, just wandering, even the privilege of taking the "mystical path" remains the reserve mainly of men. Implicitly if not explicitly, the possibility to be out there in the wilderness of spiritual quest without permission or chaperon, without fear and without penalty, has been something open to men and closed to women for the most part.

## REMEMBER THE JOURNEY, THE TRAVELER IS MORTAL

It is hard to imagine many contemporary Iranian writers besides Shahrnush Parsipur whose works focus on women's freedom of movement more than do hers. It is equally difficult to find a writer whose life reflects, with more clarity and in a more condensed form, the two extremes of triumph and despair, joy and grief, so discernibly in the women's literary tradition. This most talented and prolific novelist has confronted horrific obstacles throughout her inspiring literary career but has never left the path of writing. She has suffered imprisonment four times for a total of more than five years before and after the 1979 Revolution.[16] She has endured ill health and repeated hospitalizations, long interruptions in her writing because of economic hardships and employment as a receptionist, typist, bookseller, editor, and government employee. She has faced self-imposed exile and submitted to separation from her only child, her son, Ali. In her own words, she "has always suffered as a writer in Iran."[17] Yet Parsipur has never succumbed to silence or put down her pen, and in the process she has produced some of the masterpieces of contemporary Persian literature. She has ten novels and collections of short stories to her name, a prison memoir, an anthology of articles and stories, and a children's story.[18] She has translated nine works from French and English into Persian and has published several literary essays in magazines and journals, both inside and outside of Iran. Writing has never been a hobby for her; it is, rather, a philosophical and spiritual quest, a necessity, a means of survival. It has been both her affliction and her cure.

Parsipur thinks and writes across borders. Few Iranian authors, male or female, have been influenced by so many diverse schools of thought. Although this intellectual globetrotting can pose a challenge to readers, she nevertheless seeks enlightenment in different cultures and religions, different schools of philosophy, and different branches of science. Her worldview cannot be confined to a single country or school of thought: East and West, Islamic mysticism and Chinese Taoism, astrology and physics, parapsychology and mythology are important to her and an organic part of her literary enterprise. Geographic boundaries, intellectual disciplines, religious elitism, and political correctness have never restricted her quest. She is not only familiar with masters of Persian literature such as Hafez, Attar, Rumi, Sepehri, Hedayat, and Farrokhzad, but also with the ancient Chinese philosopher Lao Tse, the early Spanish novelist Miguel de Cervantes Saavedra, the nineteenth-century Russian playwright Anton Chekhov, the American author William Faulkner, and the British novelist Virginia Woolf. She has read Charles Dickens's *Great Expectations* thirty-three or thirty-four times, the last time "in prison in the Islamic Republic," when she noticed that she "still loved it."[19] She has benefitted from the style of the Russian novelist Fyodor Dostoyevsky and from the narrative complexities of the Persian Sufi master Farid-ud-Din Attar. She has mixed the magic realism of Scheherazade of *One Thousand*

*and One Nights* with that of the Colombian novelist Gabriel García Márquez or the Argentinean writer Jorge Luis Borges. She has combined the insight of Eastern and Western writers with the boundless wisdom of her female forebears to produce stories all her own.

Born and raised in Iran, Parsipur traces this cross-cultural interest to her mixed ancestry: "Turkish, Persian, Tatar, and Indian."[20] As for her psychogeographical journey, she sums it up as follows: "It was Italy that mesmerized my childhood with its art and its perspective. . . . When I was ten or eleven, I was immersed in the mystique of the Algerian War of Independence. When I was 14, I was in love with Fidel Castro. And later on I was absorbed by Vietnam."[21] She recalls that while a youth she was given a copy of *I Ching*, the ancient Chinese classic text, also called *Classic of Change*, and believed she might be able to find the influence of that book on Islamic mysticism, thinking that its mysteries bore striking similarities to the mysteries of backgammon and chess.[22] To pursue these uncanny similarities over vast geographic areas and long stretches of time, she began to study the Chinese language and culture while a student in France more than thirty years ago.

Creating a magical, mystical backdrop to all her stories, Parsipur experiments with new styles. She mixes the familiar and the unfamiliar, the simple and the complex, the mundane and the fantastical. She blends history, folklore, and myth, the terrestrial and the celestial, the ordinary and the extraordinary, and leads her reader, like Alice, into a wonderland. In one of her stories, two murdered women, Satareh and Mariam, speak words of wisdom from beyond the grave. Their bodies lie underneath the earth, but their voices roam free, audible and lucid, above it. In another story, a young woman plants herself in the garden in order to become a woman-tree. In yet another, pregnant mothers breast-feed trees. The world created by Parsipur is home to the living and the dead, the natural and the supernatural. It is a place where animals, humans, spirits, and plants coexist and are in communion with each other. "The world of Parsipur's novels has a texture all its own," writes Abbas Milani, "and few Iranian modern writers have expected as much suspension of disbelief from their readers as Parsipur. Nevertheless, readers have not only understood her world, but have shown an affinity for it in record numbers."[23]

What characterizes Parsipur's body of work is its fluidity, its rejection of political or philosophical absolutes, its refusal to be confined within the familiar.

Her stories, like the wind rolling through fields of wheat, are hard to pin down. So, too, are her most memorable heroines—and she has created many of them. Just as the author allows herself artistic wanderings, she grants her female characters geographic wanderings. Much to the chagrin of those who believe in hiding women away, Parsipur's protagonists are always on the move, casting off the constraints of geography and insisting on their freedom to drift and stroll and travel. The theme of traveling is central to Parsipur's whole body of work. If Farrokhzad said, "Remember flight / the bird is mortal," Parsipur has repeatedly insisted on the importance of being on the road. In an interview I conducted with her in 1987, I asked what she would have done differently if she had been a man. Her answer was swift. "If I were a man," she said with conviction, "I would pursue particular kinds of jobs. I would become a sailor or a pilot. I would seek jobs that involve coming and going. Perhaps I would become a tourist."[24] Sailor or pilot she did not become, but she did choose "coming and going" as the central trope of her work.

Her heroines, like their creator, do not accept stasis of body or mind. They fearlessly confront and cross gender lines, test sexual and textual orthodoxies, reject the social order that would regulate their movement. Having reached a new level of awareness and self-awareness, they express and at times even fulfill the previously unexpressed and inexpressible. They roam streets, climb mountains, cross deserts, explore forests. They run in the rain, dance in unlikely places, refuse to confine their bodies or quiet their voices. They rest on the wings of words and travel far and wide.

But these women are surrounded by characters who think otherwise about how women should live. There is Amir, who believes "the house belongs to women and the outside world belongs to men," or Karim, who is convinced that "our ancestors knew it all too well that a woman's place is inside the house. If a girl leaves the house she will descend to the depths of corruption."[25] It is exactly this imposed apartheid that causes some of Parsipur's women to feel claustrophobic. Many of them feel overwhelmed by a sense of sorrow and confinement. They know that women have never been able to loiter aimlessly on street corners or to sit in the bazaars or teahouses; they "have not been able to look carefully at a butterfly, or to look at the wings of a cricket." Throughout their childhood, they "have looked at trees with envy,"[26] hoping that one day, perhaps only once, they might be able to climb a tree—any tree.

Parsipur does not adopt the stance of a detached documentarian. Convinced that "throughout history women have not been given the chance to think" or, perhaps more important, that women have not been given the chance to express their thoughts openly and publicly, she has chosen the moving, thinking woman as the central figure in her literary landscape. She has said repeatedly that "she writes because she has started thinking." These thoughtful and mobile women are the pillars of strength of all her books. In one sense, her work can be considered an extended biography of Iranian women whose lives have been transformed by historic events beyond their control, women who have witnessed the crumbling of their moral, ethical, and spiritual convictions and who have been driven from one psychic exile to another. But most of these women continue their search and never give up. Their voices echo in every one of her stories: "I wanted warmth," they cry out. "I wanted love; I wanted light, I wanted presence. I screamed, 'Why do you keep me at the bottom of the ocean?'"[27]

## THE EXILE OF THE FEMALE BIRDS

Parsipur's heroines bemoan the forced confinement of women and protest that "they have never passed through the seven cities of love," or "like the birds in *The Conference of the Birds* they have not climbed to the Ghaf mountaintop in order to see themselves in eternal mirrors."[28] This statement is a fascinating re-reading of a seminal Sufi text by the twelfth-century Sufi poet Farid-ud-Din Attar. An exquisite meditation on a symbolic quest for spiritual perfection and eternal beauty, *The Conference of the Birds* is an allegorical travel narrative.

A group of birds convenes to discuss finding their king, that legendary bird in Iranian mythology—the Simurgh. The Iranian phoenix is believed to live on Ghaf, the highest peak of the Alburz Mountains. The birds choose Hoopoe as their leader. He quickly proceeds to exhort the assembled birds to embark on this journey and at the same time to warn them about the difficulties of the road and about the tests and impediments awaiting them. If you are man enough, he challenges the birds with confidence in his voice and leadership, then fly and be a seeker after truth, knowledge, enlightenment, and the Simurgh. Many of the birds make excuses and decline to travel; others lose courage and falter on the way; still others fall by the wayside and cannot survive the arduous voyage. The majority never reaches the destination, and in the end only thirty birds make it to the Promised

Land. But the king they find on top of the mountain is not the one they expected. When they finally enter the gates of his palace,

> Then by reflection, the faces of the thirty birds of the world
> The face of the Simurgh found, from the world.
> When these thirty birds looked hard,
> No doubt about it, these thirty birds were that "Thirty-Birds".
> Themselves the complete Simurgh they saw;
> The Simurgh Himself was all the time the si murgh![29]

In Persian, *si* means "thirty" and *murgh* means "bird." *Simurgh* is a compound word, "Thirty-Bird," meaning "the phoenix." The thirty individual birds who made it to the mountaintop, then, saw themselves in the Simurgh's radiant face and realized that what they were seeking in distant places existed all along in every one of them: the Simurgh is the thirty birds. To reach that conclusion, to find their inner Simurgh, however, they had to face collectively the trials and tribulations of a difficult expedition.

One can read *The Conference of the Birds* as a Sufi text that maps out and popularizes the difficult journey of the human spirit in its search for God and truth. Women, however, are excluded for the most part from this trip. They are not the interlocutors of Hoopoe, the bird leader, or of Attar, the Sufi author. As a matter of fact, many lines make it clear that this voyage, this spiritual quest, this path toward enlightenment is meant only for men—manly men. This difficult path demands a manly man, suggests Attar. It is hard to argue that the author might be using the term *man* in the generic sense because the emphasis is repeatedly on the social construct of masculinity.

> When might life without the Beloved be of any use?
> If you're a man, bear not life without the Beloved!
> Completion of this road needs a man:
> Forfeiting life this Gate needs.
> Hands must be washed of life manly-wise,
> That it might be said, "you're a man of purpose."[30]

Female birds are not the pilgrims in this voyage of discovery and self-discovery, and Attar is not alone in keeping them from flying. The same absence is conspicuous in Iran's national emblem. Iran is home to 490 different species of birds.[31] Out of this rich and diverse flock, the nightingale has become a powerful metaphor not only for Persian poets, but for the country itself. Iran is known as the "Land of the Rose and the Nightingale." Every spring between late April and June, nightingales, migratory birds, return to Iran. This return coincides with their mating season and the blooming of roses. Edward Burgess, who visited Iran in the mid–nineteenth century, wrote that the nightingales "make such a noise as to be almost unpleasant. After a day or two their constant singing is nearly annoying. I recollect one which appeared to sing four and twenty hours almost without stopping in a tree close to my window." Tired of the lamenting bird's unreciprocated serenade, Burgess goes on to explain that "the Persians say the nightingales are in love with the roses, and that they sing to them until they lose their senses and being in a sort of singing rapture or stupor the cats catch them without much trouble. The love of the nightingale for the rose is the orthodox belief of the Persians, but I can bear witness to the fact, that their note is scarcely ever heard except in the rose season."[32]

Other than the implied consequence of love in this story—falling in a stupor and being caught without much trouble by predators—what is perplexing here is the fate of the female nightingale. Where is the female nightingale in this garden? Why doesn't the male nightingale sing her praise rather than that of this immobile and eternally reticent Rose? Why, contrary to Western literature (which nearly always portrays the nightingale as female), in more than one thousand years of rich Iranian literature have nightingales been assumed to be male? Although the rose is used as a metaphor for perfection and beauty, elegance, charm, and refinement, it is the nightingale that is invariably depicted as the active agent. Endowed with wings and gifted with a voice, he soars freely and serenades the rose.[33] His song is redolent with pain; the beauty about which he warbles is never without thorns. As for the female nightingale, her freedom of movement, like Attar's female birds, seems to be controlled and contained.

### THE CONFERENCE OF THE BIRDS REVISITED

Whereas the body of Parsipur's work can be regarded as a collective travel narrative, one of her most controversial books, *Women Without Men*, published in 1989, can be read as a modern-day, feminized version of *The Conference of the*

*Birds.* In this book, too, the path to liberation of the self is inextricably inter-twined with mobility, but women are not excluded from the journey. Here, too, the voyage is long and uncertain, the dangers many, but women don't lack wanderlust. If Attar addressed his audience and asked them to "be a man" and face danger bravely like a man, Parsipur addresses a desegregated audience and announces that women, too, are ready to face danger bravely like a woman. Her five woman protagonists, like the thirty birds, are empowered and transformed by their voyage to the garden. New vistas stretch out before their eyes as they soar through flight of imagination. And as Leonardo da Vinci said, "Once you have tasted flight, you will forever walk the earth with your eyes turned skyward, for there you have been, and there you will always long to return."

*Women Without Men* is a journey novel. It is the story of five women and one man explored through a multivocal narration.[34] The five female protagonists—an "old maid," two teachers, a widowed housewife, and a prostitute—feel con-strained by their roles and their spaces. They desire to be on the road, to be free, to come and go as they please, but they are denied that right. Even Zarrinkolah, the "streetwalker," is confined in a brothel. To free herself from bondage, she has to take refuge in the streets. The women manage to escape their confinement and transform their lives by trespassing into masculine spaces, by disturbing the age-old boundary lines dividing masculinity from femininity. They reject the exem-plary paradigms of ideal womanhood, venture out, and eventually find their way to a garden outside of Tehran, purchased by Farrokhlaqa, the widowed house-wife. She has "accidentally" killed her husband of thirty-two years by punching him and sending him down the stairwell. "Whenever he was in the house, she would lose her ability to move, and she would hide in a corner. She had a thirty-two-year-old habit of not moving. She had gotten used to immobility. She knew only this, and she knew it instinctively, that when Golchehreh [her husband] went out, mobility and happiness would come to her."[35] The husband's death/ murder translates into his wife's remorseless freedom and boundless mobility.

Parsipur, like Attar, knows that the road is strewn with hazards of all sorts; unlike Attar, however, she does not believe only manly men may travel it. She sends women on a perilous journey in search of self-knowledge and spiritual rebirth. All the women in the book, who were told time and again that "home is for women, the outside world for men" (28), have come to believe that domestic-ity traps and ensnares as it nurtures and protects. "I can't stay home any longer,"

Munis, the "old maid," admits to herself and to her readers with candor and courage, "but because I am a woman, I must stay home somewhere. I can make a
little progress, then get stuck in a house, then go a little further, and get stuck
in another house. At this rate I might be able to go around the world at a snail's
pace" (99). Munis wants to go to "India and China to see the world." Although
she knows the road is hazardous, the journey difficult, she has "decided to take a
risk and seek knowledge." She admits that "this is not a good time for a woman
to travel alone. She has to be invisible to travel, or just stay at home." She knows,
"it is natural that when you get on the road, you face danger. Either you're strong
enough to face danger, or you're not, and you return like a lamb to the flock" (96).

One of the reasons Munis is ready to take a risk rather than join the flock is
a deeply disturbing sexual revelation. For thirty-eight years, this "old maid" had
jealously "guarded her virginity" (29). In fear of tearing her hymen, called a "virginity curtain" in the Persian language—a spatial metaphor of enclosure—she
had not climbed trees, scaled walls, roamed about freely. Instead, like a moth
attracted to light, she had been irresistibly drawn to the window and to the world
beyond it. She had stood by the window and watched the forbidden outside world
throughout her childhood. "She recalled how she used to gaze longingly at the
trees, wishing, that just once she could climb one. But she never had, out of fear
for her virginity" (26). The image of virginity as a "curtain" that "can be torn"
(26) had confined her inside the house as a child. But then her twin convictions
that virginity is a curtain and that to protect it girls have to monitor their physical activities are suddenly shattered. Her friend Faezeh tells her that virginity is
not a curtain. It is something that starts "narrow and then it becomes wide" (26).
Munis is devastated. Confused. Betrayed. She "thought about how for thirty-
eight years she had been looking out the window at the little garden, assuming
that virginity was a curtain. When she was eight years old, they had told her that
God would never forgive a girl who lost her virginity. Now it had been three days
and two nights since she found out that virginity is a hole, not a curtain. Something inside of her had broken. She was filled with a cold rage" (29). Had she been
taken hostage by this curtain of virginity?

Fifty-six hours later, distraught by an existential shift, Munis jumps off the
roof into the street that had been denied her for so long. Privileged with a sympathetic creator, she is quickly resurrected. We, the readers, watch in awe as she
stands up and spends "a month walking the streets" (32). Her wandering leads

to self-knowledge and growth. When she returns, she announces with pride that she is "not the same person that I was before. Now I know a lot" (33). Her brother, Amir, however, thinks otherwise. He is convinced she has sullied his honor. He is furious. As far as he is concerned, she who walks the streets is a streetwalker. "You have destroyed our family's reputation," he cries out. "Now everybody and their cousin know that you are ruined" (34). First, he takes off his belt and beats her. It is not enough. To save his honor and protect her reputation, he kills her and buries her in the garden. But Parsipur will not allow her murder to remain concealed behind walls, shrouded in silence, hidden under the earth in an enclosed garden. She will not allow the story of this honor killing to vanish into oblivion. She defends Munis's right to life, liberty, and the pursuit of happiness and thus brings her back from death a second time—stronger, wiser, and capable of reading people's minds. From a woman filled with unspoken dreams and desires, Munis turns into a reader of other people's unspoken minds. She also develops new plans. To stop honor killing, she will found "an organization to prevent older brothers from killing their sisters" (48). More important, she will travel and discover the world around her. Accompanied by her friend Faezeh, she decides "to escape from the prison of family life" and "go on pilgrimages" (97). She leaves her home and the wife/mother/daughter/sister narratives by stepping outside familiar spaces and definitions. But as soon as she embarks on her pilgrimage alongside Faezeh, she is raped. Both women eventually find their way to the garden where all women converge.[36]

Women Without Men is a slim book with thirteen interwoven chapters. Each woman protagonist is allotted two chapters for her story. Three chapters in the middle of the book are devoted to the circuitous journey and its destination. They are titled "Two Girls on the Road," "Farrokhlaqa's Garden," and "The Garden." All the characters are urged forward by the need to find this walled, enclosed garden, at once a space of restraint and yet paradoxically a space of freedom as well. Here, women experience a sense of freedom and don't feel oppressed to the point of rebellion and tragedy. They turn the garden into a literary salon of sorts. They read each other's poetry, offer criticism, exchange ideas, reinvent themselves. They break out of the prisons they lived in.

If her protagonists escape conventional frames, Parsipur breaks away from the prison of "proper" language for a woman, established themes, conventional approaches, and familiar narrative structures. This enigmatic novella reveals that all borders and boundaries are porous, whether they are the borders between life and death, the borders between one story and another, or the borders between the "human" world and the natural one. The author cannot confine herself to a static vision of reality. She ventures into unfamiliar worlds, expands the boundaries of the real. One character has multiple lives. She becomes perfectly and fully alive after she throws herself off a roof, only to be murdered by her elder brother later and revived yet again. A second character, a schoolteacher named Mahdokht, is forced into ceaseless knitting by a brother who covets her artistry as casual presents for his family—the same brother, who, like Amir the sister slayer, has the power of life and death over his female sibling. Mahdokht is obsessed with her chastity but can no longer bear the burden of guarding her virginity. She thus plants herself in the garden by a running stream. Rooted in solid ground, she becomes the axis of the community gathered in the garden. She becomes a fertile virgin, a woman-tree. Her seeds, Parsipur tells us, will spread to the four corners of the universe. Mahdokht frees herself from linear time and, like nature, becomes cyclical. She maintains her sexual purity, yet is fruitful and multiplies, traveling all over the world as seeds.

Mahdokht's transformation, her emblematic blending of fertility with virginity, is a kind of fusion or interrogation of "male" and "female" paradigms in the image of the woman-tree: as a tree, she's rooted, but at the same time she is mobile through her scattering of seeds. Zarrinkolah transforms from a prostitute into a wife, a mother, and finally a lily—a symbol of chastity and perfection. First, she gives birth to a lily, and later, accompanied by the husband she has found in the garden, she sits on the lily and, whirling like a dervish, ascends to the sky to be absorbed by the welcoming sun. Her metamorphosis must also be an allusion to the contradictory symbolism (at once fertility and purity) of the lily in Greek myths, Roman legends, and Jewish and Christian traditions. That would be a deliberate irony, no doubt, given Zarrinkolah's background as a prostitute. Whenever metamorphosis occurs in *Women Without Men*—women changed into light, trees, winged creatures—their transformation is self-propelled, self-motivated, self-willed. Even if pressure from the outside world drives the change, it cannot happen without action by the women themselves.

The peculiar way in which the story ends refuses to idealize categorically the notion of "women without men." In reading about the different women's journeys, one might expect their paths to converge in some utopian apotheosis of freedom and happiness, which, given the book's title, would likely entail the exclusion of men. All five women become "women without men" in the sense that they do not need men to define themselves. But the women eventually get tired of or annoyed with one another after they live together for a while, and for a variety of reasons all except Mahdokht the woman-tree leave the garden. In other words, it seems to me that Parsipur is suggesting that happiness lies neither in the exclusion of men from these women's lives nor in the women's submission to the patriarchal codes of their society. And she seems to be saying as well that in fact the happiness or personal fulfillment that one achieves through freedom may ultimately be relative, a kind of compromise—neither intense happiness nor unmitigated unhappiness. She embraces the cultural tensions and social challenges of today with a breadth of vision that is neither nostalgic in its inspiration nor self-deludingly utopian in its resolution. This honest kind of ending resonates with Parsipur's statement that "if she desecrates accuracy and honesty, her 'pen will dry up.'"[37]

With her protagonists breaking out of their molds and freeing themselves from the prisons in which they live, Parsipur smashes through themes and language deemed "proper" for a woman. She constructs entirely new spaces within which to discuss taboo topics such as virginity, its relation with space, its use as a mechanism of sexual and social control, its direct correlation with women's freedom of movement. Talking about virginity per se is nothing new in Persian literature. Poets and preachers, fathers and brothers have paid their tributes time and again to this "seal of God," this "jewel," this "pearl," this "treasure box." They have made sure the "curtain" is delivered to its proprietor—the husband—intact. Parsipur inserts herself and her protagonists in that age-old male transaction. What is new is her treatment of the topic, her refusal to uphold the cult of chastity, her questioning of established norms and assumptions. She decouples chastity and space, redefines the hymen not as a "curtain" behind which women are kept immobile and "protected," but as a mere anatomical part of a woman's body. She commits a sexual heresy by refusing to imprison women behind one curtain in order to protect another curtain.

If *Women Without Men* is the tale of forbidden and circuitous journeys, if it promotes women's travel in spite of the hazards, it must redefine chastity as well. And it does. Herein lies the book's radical reappraisal of cultural and sexual norms. Every one of the female protagonists, each in her own way, meditates on attachments and detachments; on being elsewhere; on being displaced physically, metaphorically, or culturally; on being translated; on being transplanted. All these women break away from the family and the familiar, from convictions and conventions. Their saga is not only about departures and arrivals, but also about redefining the meaning of their lives. Their story not only charts the difficulty and the exhilaration of being on the road, but also presents it as a necessity.

Not surprisingly, this novella about breaking free from the bonds of traditional society—escaping from the prison of accepted language, loosening the chains of convention, releasing the ties of immobility—led to its author's imprisonment. Parsipur was incarcerated twice for the publication of *Women Without Men,* once in 1990 and again in 1991. Soon after her release from prison, she left Iran for the United States, where she now resides and defiantly continues to write.

The novelist who has devoted her career to the promotion of the freedom of movement has ironically also written the most heart-wrenching prison memoir. Prison, as Parsipur portrays it, can be figurative, meaning ideological inflexibility, political or philosophical absolutism, greed, bad habits, naive utopian thinking, sex segregation. It can also be "real," like the prisons in which she spent more than five years of her life, although she was never tried or officially charged with a crime. Parsipur decries all forms of "imprisonment," but she never confuses the figurative with the literal. She knows from personal experience that the two are not the same. Although she found her actual prison experience terrifying and empathizes with thousands who were incarcerated under the harshest conditions and later executed, she is nevertheless willing to discuss the creative strategies she adopted to survive. As Mohammed Al-Urdun summarizes in a 2007 interview, "She counts herself lucky however to have spent formative years with other intellectuals and fellow travelers and to have found the inspiration for [her novel] *Touba and the Meaning of Night.*"[38]

*Prison Memoirs,* published in Sweden in 1996, is a harrowing portrait of real incarceration, of life in various prisons in Tehran. It is nonideological and written from a humanitarian perspective. The memoir could have been produced only by a writer of Parsipur's sensitivities and talents, someone who had honed her craft through decades of creative writing and who had meditated on the concept of imprisonment in its various manifestations. Iranians have produced many prison memoirs, of varying lengths and from different political viewpoints, before and after the 1979 Revolution. But few of these narratives match

Parsipur's for its human insight, unflinching depiction of physical and mental torture, attention to everyday detail of life behind bars, and searing candor. She captures and reveals her prison experience with haunting precision.

This refusal to be hidden in the dark, enclosed within walls, silenced by segregation that most characterizes Parsipur's work is also the hallmark of women's postrevolutionary writing in Iran. Iranian women writers are transforming alienation into art, suffocation into sound. They are digging to excavate unwritten scripts. Whether by rewriting old texts or creating new narratives, whether penning poetry or prose, crafting fact or fiction, they are claiming the road to freedom for themselves and their female protagonists—not as trespassers or interlopers, but as proprietors and seasoned navigators; not with hesitation and uncertainty, but with resolve and authority; not in fear and anxiety, but with calm and confidence. The search for the mythical Simurgh is no longer a quest solely for male pilgrims. Women have taken to the road, knowing well that, as Fatema Mernissi puts it, "when a woman decides to use her wings, she takes big risks. . . . When a woman doesn't use her wings at all, it hurts her."[39] The journey to reclaim the inner Simurgh, as Fariba Vafi (1962–), one of the leading voices in Iranian fiction today, demonstrates in her award-winning novel *My Bird*,[40] is not easy. But despite the obstacles, women are on their way. And in the garden, the female nightingale, even if not soaring "above the level plain of tradition and prejudice,"[41] is finally singing. We can hear her and her song is music to our ears.

# PART THREE

# *Prisoners Awaiting Liberation*

# 8

# READING AND MISREADING
# IRANIAN WOMEN
# IN THE UNITED STATES

## On Abducted Daughters, Incarcerated
## Girls, and Invisible Women

The only thing that could ever straighten out this screwed-up country is an
atomic bomb! Wipe it off the map and start over.
—BETTY MAHMOODY, *Not Without My Daughter*

The great world is a complicated place. It is a world of weapons, to be sure,
but not all the weapons take the form of bombs, guns or other engines of
physical destruction. Some of the weapons are rhetorical, taking the form of
mythmaking and media domination.
—ROBERT SCHOLES, "Presidential Address 2004"

## FROM THE LAND OF ROSES AND
## NIGHTINGALES TO THE AXIS OF EVIL

One spring day in 1994, a day like any other, I was taken hostage by an image.
Wanting to strip the veil of its symbolic stigma, I had decided to teach my class
at the University of Virginia covered in a chador. The distance between my office
and the classroom seemed endless, and the familiar grounds of Thomas Jeffer-
son's academical village felt like burning coals under my restless feet. I looked
forward with great anticipation to a provocative discussion. I wanted to make a
point to my students that we needed to stop fetishizing the veil and go beyond
mere appearances. As I entered the classroom, I confronted a wall of shocked

silence. Half the class stared at me with incredulous eyes. The other half could not bear to look at me at all. I searched in every direction for a sympathetic gaze, a welcoming glance. None was forthcoming. I felt disoriented, like a cat without whiskers. After a seemingly endless pause, I finally asked why everyone was so silent. Not a peep. I repeated the question. No one was willing to volunteer an answer until suddenly one of the students, with shocked reproach, mumbled, "I'm scared. You might be carrying a gun under your veil." I was sure she was joking. To my chagrin, she was not. She was scared and serious, too. By donning the chador, I had ceased to be the teacher she knew so well. I had become a symbol for her, the gun-toting image of a menacing woman.[1]

I was unprepared for what transpired in that classroom. I knew my sudden transformation from an unveiled woman to one covered from head to foot in an all-encompassing cloak was a dramatic sartorial change. I expected my students to notice the difference and ponder the expressiveness of diverse styles of dress. I wanted them to consider the symbolism of the veil. I even expected them to voice some well-intentioned but pitying comments. Over the years, I had grown accustomed to my students' association of the veil with oppression and subordination. What I had not expected in the safety of my classroom was to be transformed into a security threat. With hindsight, I should have known better. I should have realized that the chador had become an emblem for the Islamic faith in the Western imagination and that Islam in general and Iran in particular had become associated with terror long before September 11, 2001.

Since the hostage crisis in 1979, Iran, once a valuable ally to the United States, has become an enemy, cast in the role of a major villain in the conflict between Western and Islamic civilizations. Starting in that year, Persians, praised in the Bible for freeing the Jews from their Babylonian captivity, came to be seen as captive makers. A country known for its long history, its authorship of the first declaration of human rights, its elegant and humane art and literature, and its hospitality was now branded a "rogue nation," a "challenge" to the safety and welfare of America. Persia, "the Land of the Rose and the Nightingale," had turned into Iran, the vanguard of an apocalypse of terror, on its way to become, along with Iraq and North Korea, one node in the "axis of evil."[2]

The history of this sentiment can be traced back to November 4, 1979, soon after the Islamic Revolution, when a group of militant students stormed the American Embassy in Tehran to take fifty-two Americans hostage for 444 days in violation of international laws.[3] In their wildest dreams, the hostage takers and their local supporters could not have anticipated the huge impact of their actions. The militant students were surprised to find themselves the object of infinite national and international attention. They were flattered to see their own images alongside those of blindfolded Americans blazoned around the world. They suddenly appeared on the front pages of major and minor newspapers, on the covers of leading magazines, on television screens, on T-shirts and banners, on posters on trees and walls, and in marquees on bridges.[4] An indelible sense of anguish etched itself into the collective memory of a justifiably outraged nation.[5] "America in Captivity" was the headline that captured the mood of a country in psychic pain.[6] President Jimmy Carter broke diplomatic ties with Iran, and freeing the hostages became a national mandate.

### RITUALS OF BOOK BURNING

Even as the temperature rose in America over this horrific violation of diplomatic protocol, the Iranian people also suffered. Within two days, the seizure of the American Embassy led to the fall of the first postrevolutionary prime minister, Mehdi Bazargan, who resigned in protest.[7] The event "hijacked" the consequential debate regarding the nature of Iran's future government, which was raging throughout the country at the time.[8] And in less than a month, it contributed to the ratification of a new Iranian constitution, which consolidated the rule of Ayatollah Ruhollah Khomeini and sanctioned his reign with an iron fist. The fist descended not only on the lives of the Americans taken hostage in their own embassy, but also on all aspects of Iranian lives, even in the privacy of their homes. It trampled basic human rights and choked dissent.

To the government's exasperation, Iranians raised their rebellious voices anyway. Many writers and poets articulated their pain and outrage publicly, believing with poet Simin Behbahani that in order "To stay alive / You must slay silence."[9] They lamented how every drop of freedom was squeezed out of their lives. They acknowledged the indispensability of resistance, of bearing witness, of safeguarding endangered civic rights. Believing in the ultimate triumph of language over the deepest despair, of light over darkness, they refused silence and erasure.[10] The metaphoric flames of blazing songs and poems rose in this place of darkness and chill.

But the literal image of books on fire developed into a refrain in Iran's early postrevolutionary literature or later recollections of those dark years. It was an expression of outrage at the ruling elite's aim to control the marketplace of ideas and words and images; at times, it was a defining moment in the lives of readers and writers. For Roya Hakakian in *Journey from the Land of No*, the scorching of her most precious belongings shapes the final pages of her memoir and marks the beginning of the family's migration to the United States. The adolescent Hakakian, coming home one moonlit evening to find her bedroom locked to her entry, senses something terrible is happening behind the closed door. As her mother pleads quietly, "Don't be upset," Hakakian shouts to her father inside to open the door. To her horror, she finds that "Father held a long wooden stick charred at one end" and "among the ashes, in the bonfire, my world was burning: my newspapers and magazines, my fifth grade appreciation certificate from the shah's minister of education. Underneath them, my weightier loves had settled: Albert's copy of *The Little Black Fish*, my records and tapes, signed copies of my favorite poetry books, my *Jane Austen Reader*, my hardcover Mikail Sholokhov's *And Quiet Flows the Don*, my leather bound Dostoyevskys—all burning to punish me for what should have never been a crime." As the young narrator kneels before the fire, she discovers her own diary and book of poems, "now only identifiable by their thick spines that had yet to burn." That is when the father announces solemnly and "faintly," as the last line of the text, "It is time we leave for America."[11]

Farideh Goldin's narrative begins, as Hakakian's ends, with her fifteen-year-old self awakening to the stench of smoke. Rushing to the kitchen, she finds her entire family—her mother, grandmother, siblings, uncles, and aunt—witnessing the burning of her book collection by her father. "He was throwing books in the fire," she writes with palpable pain, "my books, the books I had hidden underneath the bed, behind my clothes in the armoire, in the pocket of my winter coat."[12]

In Hakakian's closing scene and Goldin's opening lines, fathers commit to flames their daughters' most precious belongings to protect them. This is no ritual of book burning in the public square. It happens inside the house, where even ordinary privileges of privacy have become unaffordable luxuries. There are no more closets to hide in, no safe places to take refuge in. This is an era of strident state censorship and its attendant self-censorship. Terror has obliterated privacy, and reading, or at least certain kinds of reading, has become a crime. Inquisition of ideas and even feelings has extended its tentacles in all directions: in bedrooms and under beds, in closets and bookshelves, even in the pockets of winter coats.

## THE BIRTH OF THE HOSTAGE NARRATIVE

As new literary themes and concerns were arising within Iran, as the relationship between the United States and Iran shifted, so, too, did the way Americans and later Iranians in America wrote about Iran, its culture, its religion, and in particular its women. A new genre of books about Iran, which can be best described as "hostage narratives," began to emerge in the United States. Soon after the hostage crisis and partly in response to the American reading public's increased curiosity about Iran, a slew of books, written originally in English and tailor made for mass markets, were published and continue to be published. These often melodramatic, sensational books perpetuate misconceptions. Part reality and part imagination, they embellish engaging stories with a generous supply of intrigue and suspense. They promise to offer their readers an intimate glimpse of Iran, but they leave out inconvenient facts and historic contexts. By impact, if not intent, they promote stereotypes about Iranians, especially about Iranian women. Ostensibly championing women's rights, they actually denigrate Iranian women, belittle them, ignore their heroic resistance. They reduce these women's self-assertion to silent suffering, passive-aggressiveness, secret meetings with little or no consequence, cosmetic subversion such as revealing wayward strands of hair or wearing makeup in public. But even these paltry triumphs are contradicted by the books' overall message, which emphasizes again and again Iranian women's helplessness, their dependence, their invisibility, and, above all, their captivity by husbands, family, government, faith.

Whether intentionally or not, hostage narratives fan the flames of antagonism between the two countries and refresh the painful memory of a national trauma. Blurring the lines between fact and fiction, they are replete with selective clarity, careful details, and half-truths. Eleana Benador, president of the New York and Washington–based public-relations firm Benador Associates, captured the disinterest in truth when she readily admitted that "accuracy with regards to Iran is a 'luxury.'" She explained her unconcern with truth in haughty terms. "My major concern is the large picture," she announced when challenged regarding the veracity of statements made by her firm's associates. "As much as being accurate is important, in the end it's important to side with what's right. What's wrong is siding with the terrorists."[13]

It is ironic that although the physical captivity of the American hostages ended after 444 days, Iran is still held captive to its hostage-taking ordeal. Its image as a stagnant place dominates the media, popular films, and books. Time, it seems, has stopped in Iran, frozen in the hostage-taking days. Three decades later Iran still remains an abstraction and an enigma to many Americans. There are several reasons for this misreading of Iran. The United States and Iran have had no official diplomatic relations since April 7, 1980. There has been more than a quarter-century of hostility between the two governments. With numerous prohibitions on access to Iran, with travel and tourism virtually cut off, it has been difficult to see the country behind the headlines.[14] In addition to an absence of diplomacy and scarce cultural communication, there is also an alarming dearth of intercultural communication between the two countries, particularly in the realm of print media. Precious few books are translated from Persian into English. Hostage narratives fill this vacuum.

Although contemporary American literature as a whole has become less politicized, and as Sean Wilentz remarks, on the fiction side of best-selling lists "politics appears almost nowhere,"[15] many of the most popular books about Iran, whether labeled fiction or nonfiction, are handmaiden to politics. Consider the New York Times Best-sellers List, established in 1931.[16] Even though America was intimately involved with Iran (first through much-appreciated missionary work there and then in 1953 because of a covert CIA operation that toppled the elected government of Prime Minister Mohammad Mossadeq), no book about Iran appeared on the best-seller list during its first fifty years.[17] The hostage crisis quickly changed that. A slew of books were ushered into print with a fanfare of publicity. In less than two decades, at least five novels—On Wings of Eagles, Whirlwind, Sword Point, Shadows of Steel, and House of Sand and Fog—and three nonfiction books—Under Fire, Not Without My Daughter, and Reading Lolita in Tehran—scaled the much coveted Times list.

### PRISONERS AWAITING LIBERATION

In the unprecedented flourishing of writings about Islam in the United States in recent years, one category of books—life stories of women—has been the most popular, attracting the attention of politicians, publishers, the media, and the reading public alike. In an old narrative frame of captivity recast for the present-day reader, some of these memoirs and autobiographies portray the Muslim woman as a virtual hostage. She is the victim of an immobilizing faith, locked up inside her mandatory veil—a mobile prison shrunk to the size of her body.[18] She has no real voice or visibility, nowhere to escape to, no protection, no shelter, no freedom of movement. Captivity is her destiny.[19] Ayaan Hirsi Ali, the best-selling author of *Infidel* and *The Caged Virgin* whom *Time* in 2005 named among the one hundred people who shape our lives and whom the US-based international affairs *Foreign Policy* journal in 2008 ranked as one of the world's top-twenty public intellectuals, sums up this mindset when she describes Islam as "a mental cage," a set of "mental bars," and women as "trapped in that cage."[20]

The recent spate of memoirs and autobiographies involving Muslim captors and their native or non-Muslim victims puts a new and tantalizing twist on the familiar theme of women's captivity in the Islamic world. It is no longer mainly Western men who recount the tales of women's confinement, but women who relate them firsthand. As Betty Mahmoody (1945–), best-selling author of *Not Without My Daughter,* articulates succinctly in her endorsement of another run-away best seller, *Mayada, Daughter of Iraq: One Woman's Survival in Saddam Hussein's Torture Jail,* "It had to come from a native woman to be believable."[21] And authoritative and authentic these memoirs are considered to be. As Mary Wakefield notes, "It would be easier in some ways to ignore Ayaan Hirsi Ali, to label her as bonkers—but it would also be irresponsible. She's not just another hawkish hack, anxious to occupy the tough-guy media slot—she has the author-ity of experience, the authenticity of suffering."[22]

This image is not foisted upon women; rather, it is a matter of self-perception and self-representation, or so the story goes. The image is "authentic." It is "true" because it is written by a real native subject or her surrogate; it is true because it is a tale of suffering. It is a woman's own longing to escape, her own urgent plea to be liberated. It relies on the authority of personal experience, shares an insider's perspective and commands more trust and legitimacy. Often splashing images of veiled, static women on their covers, such books fetishize the veil and rein-force the stereotypes evoked by this all-too-familiar image. Written in English, they address Americans directly and are concerned with national and interna-tional security for good measure. They lure the reader by relying on a number of rhetorical ploys, literary strategies, and popular trends. They benefit from the American public's obsession with "true" tales of sordid hardship and triumphant survival. Although the central character of these works is trapped by Islamic fundamentalism, she is eventually liberated from its pernicious claws.

The figure of the trapped woman stands at the center of the ongoing national debate on Islam. "In 2001, right after the Afghanistan war [began]," wrote newspaper columnist Ellen Goodman, "the [US] president proudly declared that 'we fight for the values we hold dear' and one of those values was the freedom of women. He said, 'The central goal of the terrorists is the brutal oppression of women,' and so women's freedom was proof of our victory. 'Women now come out of their homes from house arrest, able to walk the streets without chaperones.'"[23]

The American reading public—the majority of which, according to recent statistics, is made up of women—has an unquenchable appetite for books narrated by or about Muslim women.[24] As soon as Sally Armstrong, then editor in chief of *Homemaker* magazine and one of the first journalists to focus on women under the rule of the Taliban, published an article on the subject, she received more than nine thousand letters from concerned citizens who wanted to help those women, according to publicity materials for her 2002 book *Veiled Threat*. In that one year alone, more books about Afghan women were published in the United States than in the entire history of American letters.[25] They generated great sympathy among American readers. In contrast, memoirs of life in Afghanistan after the fall of the Taliban, depicting the escalating violence, the institutionalization of corruption, and the harsh living conditions for women are rare.[26]

Afghan women under the oppressive rule of the Taliban swiftly became the symbol of oppression by Islam, their plight perfectly captured by the metaphor of the prisoner without a chance at parole or reprieve, without recourse to local justice. Ironically, the Taliban themselves had seized power in the name of Islam and in order to "protect" women. In fact, it was the kidnapping and rape of two women in 1994 that marked the dawn of the movement. The violated women symbolized an invaded motherland, and Afghan men became the emasculated sons who could not protect their mothers. Mourning the decline of the cherished ideals of honor and masculinity, Mullah Muhammad Omar, soon to become the shadowy leader of the Taliban, was a village preacher who claimed God directed him in a dream to save his country. He gathered some thirty like-minded men and sixteen rifles, killed the rapists, and vowed to shelter women. Thus was the Taliban movement born; the men's lost honor was restored, and women were "protected" by being placed under something close to house arrest.[27]

Women's captivity is now such an essential part of the dominant discourse on Islam that it shows up in unlikely places. Consider Phyllis Chesler's recent book *The Death of Feminism*. More than four decades (and twelve books) after her trip to Afghanistan, the prolific author of the pioneering *Women and Madness*, published in 1973, remembers that she was imprisoned there in the early 1960s. Chesler, who had presented Afghanistan in her earlier works as an exciting place, populated by kind and good-humored people, now likens it to Iran, "a country that has been described as a 'giant prison for women.'" She refers to her departure as an "escape" and begins the fourth chapter of the book with an arresting revelation: "On December 21, 1961, when I returned from my captivity in Afghanistan, I literally kissed the ground at Idlewild Airport."[28]

The language and the plot of this chapter, titled "My Afghan Captivity," mark a distinctive shift in scenario, tone, style, and point of view from earlier versions of the same trip. Although in the introduction to *The Death of Feminism* Chesler states that she is writing about her "Afghan sojourn here at length for the first time," she had previously published at least two other full-length accounts of her experience as a young bride in a foreign land, first in a 1969 *Mademoiselle* magazine article titled "Memoirs of Afghanistan" and later in "My First Husband: Men in Iranistan," included in her 1978 book *About Men*, a psychohistorical exploration of patriarchy. She had also alluded to her visit in her 1986 book *Mothers on Trial* and in her 2003 work *The New Anti-Semitism*.[29]

Chesler's "captivity" in Afghanistan is not only a delayed afterthought, a newsworthy postscript; it is, in her words, "a cautionary tale." The author is quick to alert her readers to the serious dangers that Islam and the "primitive East" pose. "What happened to me in Afghanistan must also be taken as a cautionary tale of what can happen when one romanticizes the 'primitive' East," she counsels. "I had seen just how badly women are treated in the Islamic world. As a young bride, I had been mistreated, too—but I survived and got out. I hope that telling my story will help other Westerners understand and empathize with Muslim and Arab women (and men) who are being increasingly held hostage to barbarous and reactionary customs." And since Muslim women are, according to Chesler, "unlikely to oppose tyranny unless they are specially and persistently 'deprogrammed,'" they need to be "militarily and legally protected from domestic terrorism."[30]

Although it is hard to miss the direct correlation established here between women's captivity and the need for foreign intervention, military or otherwise, to set them free, I do not presume to know Chesler's or any other author's intentions or political agenda. Nor do I wish to challenge the accounts of their incarceration, literal or figurative, exact or approximate, prolonged or short, recent or long ago. My objective here is to concentrate on the widespread appeal of prison literature, particularly as it is exemplified by the figure of the Muslim Woman. What is it about women's captivity in the Islamic world that catches immediate attention these days? How does it relate to social dramas unfolding within American society? What impact do these images of incarceration have on popular understandings of Islam in general and of Muslim women in particular? Do they legitimize war as a charitable intervention? Even if these life narratives were published as works of fiction, we would still need to ponder why the experience of captivity is so imperative, so key to the books' unfolding plots, so indispensable to their popularity.

## A CELEBRITY IS CREATED

An early and a particularly transparent expression of the hostage narrative can be found in Betty Mahmoody's memoir *Not Without My Daughter*. The memoir, which is presented as the "true story of a desperate struggle to survive and to escape from an alien and frightening culture," invites readers to participate emotionally in the drama. "Imagine yourself alone and vulnerable," urges the marketing blurb. "Imagine yourself . . . trapped by a husband you thought you trusted, and held prisoner in his native Iran, a land where women have no rights and Americans are despised."[31] The word *hostage*, as well as its various synonyms, appears frequently throughout the book. "Were Mahtob and I prisoners? Hostages? Captives of the venomous stranger who had once been a loving husband and father?" asks Betty Mahmoody initially (42). But soon she comes to recognize that she is not the only inmate in this prison-nation. All Iranian women are prisoners like her. "Now I realized anew that these women were caught in a trap just as surely as I, subject to the rules of a man's world, disgruntled but obedient" (118).

This is the heart-wrenching tale of a mother and daughter held hostage in an alien land. The plot is simple. The Mahmoodys' idyllic life begins in America, where Betty, a divorced mother of two sons, meets Sayyed Bozorg Mahmoody, nicknamed "Moody," when she is admitted to Carson City Hospital in Michigan for migraine headaches. After three years of courtship, the Iranian-born, American-educated physician proposes to Betty, and she accepts.[32] "To give him up," writes Mahmoody, "as I eked out a comparatively dismal existence in the blue-collar world of central Michigan was an unthinkable proposition" (210). Soon after the couple's marriage "at a *masjed* [mosque] in Houston" (210), they became "members of the Islamic Society of South Texas, organized parties and celebrations to coincide with Iranian and Islamic holidays" (212). For almost eight years, Betty lived a life of luxury, "lavished with money and affection" and "loved to the point of adulation" (212). But this dream life quickly ended when husband and wife, accompanied by their four-year-old daughter, Mahtob, traveled to Iran in August 1984. The two-week vacation turned into an endless nightmare. The doting husband and devoted father metamorphosed into a selfish, brutal warden who wanted to keep his wife and daughter in Iran against their wishes. And Iranian laws were on his side. Betty, as the wife of an Iranian man, and Mahtob, as an Iranian citizen, needed the written permission of their legal guardian, Moody, to leave the country. Thus begins the eighteen-month quest of mother and daughter to set themselves free. It culminates in a perilous escape in the bitter cold through the mountains to Turkey.

"After our return to America," writes Mahmoody, "I met with Teresa Hobgood, the State Department caseworker who aided my family throughout the eighteen-month ordeal. She agrees with my strategy of telling my story in order to warn others" (419). In her second book, *For the Love of a Child*, published in 1992, Mahmoody discloses that only on her "sixth day back in the United States," Barbara Walters called her for an interview on *20/20*, which "was aired on June 20, 1986." It coincided with "Moody's birthday."[33] Rights to a film based on her ordeal in Iran were secured and, as she writes in *For the Love of a Child*, "given the growing turmoil in the Persian Gulf at the time and my association with that part of the world, publicity for the movie took off before I was ready. Suddenly every TV and radio station for miles around wanted to come to my home for an interview" (274). In spite of her mother's strong objections, Mahmoody appeared on several mainstream radio and television programs, including *Larry King, Phil Donahue, Salle Jesse Raphael,* and *Oprah Winfrey.*

The speed with which *Not Without My Daughter* was written and reached the market is amazing. Mahmoody returned to the United States in 1986, and the 437-page book was available in bookstores throughout the country in August 1987. In *For the Love of a Child,* however, the author traces the decision to write the book to the first day she stepped into Iran's "buffeting heat, heard its chorus of high-pitched voices, and saw the obedient legions of women in their flowing, black *chadors,* many with but a single eye peeking through" (13). She acknowledges that she "lacked training as a writer" and "would only be in Iran for two weeks" (14). But these details and the fact that she did not speak the Persian language were minor inconveniences. She assures the reader, "I knew I could learn a lot if I put my mind to it" (13). Soon after her return to the United States, she chose a coauthor. The choice was easy, obvious, and fast: "I knew whom I wanted: Bill Hoffer, the co-author of *Midnight Express.*"[34] Why Hoffer? "While in Tehran," explains Mahmoody in *For the Love of a Child,* "I'd heard about street demonstrations against *Midnight Express.* Though the book and the movie based on it were banned there, I wanted to write with the person who'd had such a profound effect on ordinary people in Iran—the people who'd had such total control over my own life" (23). Together, she and Hoffer completed *Not Without My Daughter* in six months, and the speed shows: the book is littered with frequent inaccuracies and glaring errors. Consider a few lines from page 67: "Another birthday soon followed, and it added to my depression. It was that of Imam Reza, the Shiite founder. On such a holy day, a good Shiite is supposed to visit the imam's tomb, but since he was buried in the enemy country of Iraq, we had to settle for his sister's tomb in Rey, the former capital city of Iran, about an hour's drive south." Imam Reza is not the founder of Shi'ism; he is the eighth imam. He is not buried in Iraq; his shrine is in Mashhad, the major center of pilgrimage in northeastern Iran. His sister's tomb is not in Rey, but in Qom.

Mahmoody was thrust into global fame, celebrated as the Outstanding Woman of the Year by Oakland University and recognized as Woman of the Year in Germany. Her alma mater, Alma College in Michigan, granted her an honorary doctorate of letters. The book sold some fifteen million copies and was translated into more than twenty languages. Selected as a Literary Guild alternate, it was nominated for a Pulitzer Prize in 1987.

The movie adaptation was released four years later, in 1991, coincidentally with the run-up to the Gulf War and Operation Desert Storm. It featured Sally Field, who was an excellent casting choice for the role of a woman whose main driving force in the drama was the protection of her endangered child. Field was already established in Americans' hearts as a dainty and self-sacrificing mother as she had played a woman who risked her life to save her daughter by donating her kidney in *Steel Magnolias* (1989). Later, the Iranian villain of *Not Without My Daughter* replaced with a serial killer in *Eye for an Eye* (1996), she was to hunt down the man who had murdered her innocent daughter. Mahmoody, too, was now established as an advocate for children. She became the president and cofounder of One World for Children, an organization "designed to promote understanding between cultures and to offer security and protection to children of bi-cultural marriages."[35]

## IRAN AS THE TERRORLAND

*Not Without My Daughter* conveyed with great passion a primordial and reciprocated love between mother and child. It also dramatized and brought widespread and vital attention to an important national and international problem: custody battles and child abductions, especially when the parents are citizens of different countries or practitioners of different faiths. The harrowing image of a four-year-old girl abducted by her father in a foreign and unwelcoming land imparts a vivid and powerful message. We, the readers, identify more and more with the narrator as the sole protector of an innocent and vulnerable child. Impressed with her courage and fortitude, awed by her perseverance and struggle against the forces of evil, we empathize with her daily humiliation, her confined life, the suffering inflicted ruthlessly upon her. We fear for her life when we find her again and again "on the ragged edge of panic" (1), surrounded by cruel morality squads and family members who abuse her trust, spy on her, neglect her desperate pleas for help, and betray her. And as if these elements were not enough, this lonely woman, this faithful mother, is battered violently and regularly by a merciless husband. "My body felt like one huge bruise. Moody's blows had raised two welts on my head so large that I worried about serious damage" (102), Mahmoody writes in *Not Without My Daughter*. Even when she is not actually beaten up, she remains justifiably "wary," her "fears heightened" (197).

Mahmoody's narrative of her trip to Iran is nothing short of a terrifying version of an Alice in Wonderland journey—otherworldly and strange, but also horrific. As soon as the narrator lands in the country, she finds herself plunged into darkness and foul smell, surrounded by "spittle-laden" (24) black chadors. Later, on the way to a restaurant, she sees "an enormous, ugly rat, as big as a small cat, perched upon one of [her daughter's] white patent leather shoes" (153). She has arrived in a world of nightmares: "corpses of gigantic roaches" float out "from under the cupboard" (183); a "pool of fresh, brilliant red blood (13)" from slaughtered sheep runs in the middle of the streets; upon arrival in this strange land, a man is "capable of changing instantly from an attentive husband to a demon" (154). With a quasi-supernatural appetite and aptitude for violence, he can "rise from his own troubled slumber," fully equipped "with a knife, a piece of rope, his bare hands," or "a quick, fatal injection" (197). The inhabitants of this wondrous place are incapable of showing grace or compassion; instead, they reveal signs of genetic defects and produce "vacant-eyed deformed babies" (103) as a consequence of "inbreeding" (17). They attack their meals "like a herd of untamed animals" (15), and the food for which they appear to be "desperate" is often greasy and bug ridden (27). They exude an "overpowering stench of unwashed humanity" (38) and "are meek followers of authority" (114). The Iran that Mahmoody constructs for her readers is a country at once primitive and repressive, barbaric and oppressive. "I loathed Iran," she states again and again. It is a "backward nation" (55) where "women are slaves to their husbands" (35).

In Iran, Betty's love for her husband turns into hatred: "I actually prayed, Please God, let him be in an accident. Let him be blown apart by a bomb. Let him have a heart attack" (133). The narrator's revulsion toward her husband is paralleled by the bottomless hostility of Iranians toward the United States. She tells us that Iran has "the most openly hostile attitude toward Americans of any nation in the world" (3). This enmity, it seems, is written in the Iranian nation's collective DNA. In the pages of the book, it comes across as quasi-genetic, instinctive, timeless. There is no mention of the long history of friendship between the two nations that predated the Islamic Revolution. Nothing is said about the decades of valued alliance between the two governments before the hostage crisis. Instead, an angry sea of chest-pounding, fist-shaking mobs burn effigies of the American president, trample on the American flag, and scream anti-American slurs and "death to America" like a mantra.

Mahmoody's criticism of Iran, unbalanced though it might be, reflects her impressions of the country. Had her story been written and received as a personal memoir, a subjective opinion, an individual point of view colored by the dilemma of a mother and a wife caught in ghastly circumstances, there would be no reason to challenge its assertions. Although the narrator leaps from one man to a whole nation, from one country to a whole faith, and even though she presents exceptional, isolated, and extreme cases as systemic and interrupts her heart-rending personal narrative to dole out rancorous statements not only against her husband, the Mahmoody family, and Muslim fundamentalists, but also against an entire country, *Not Without My Daughter* nevertheless became an authoritative manual on Iran. As Roger Ebert of the *Chicago Sun-Times* remarks, if any book or movie adaptation "of such a vitriolic and spiteful nature were to be made in America about any other ethnic group, it would be denounced as racist and prejudiced."[36] The book, however, remained uncontested for the most part. The major antagonists in the book, who live in Iran, had no chance to respond to any of the accusations brought against them. Finally, in 2003, fifteen years after its publication, Moody chronicled his side of the story in a documentary produced in Finland. In this film titled *Without My Daughter,* a beleaguered father laments his slander and describes in poignant detail his desperate and unsuccessful attempts to be reunited with his daughter. "I am a beast and a criminal in the eyes of the world," says a disgruntled Dr. Mahmoody. "I have been portrayed as a liar, a woman-beater, and a kidnapper. Even the courts of law have not seen any need for my presence to divide my family and give away my belongings. I have been denied the right to see my daughter for 15 years or even to talk to her. My sin, my only sin was that I loved my child, my daughter, Mahtob." Other key players in *Not Without My Daughter* who are interviewed in the documentary, including some American friends still living in Iran, reject Betty Mahmoody's story and accuse her of fabricating much of it.[37] *Without My Daughter* attracted little attention in the United States.

THE WEST AS WONDERLAND

Although no book about Iran has achieved the phenomenal success of *Not Without My Daughter,* more than a decade after its publication a far more sophisticated version of the hostage narrative appeared on the shelves of American bookstores: Azar Nafisi's *Reading Lolita in Tehran*.[38] On the surface, the two books could not be more different. One offers little room for nuance or intro-spection, whereas the other celebrates the redemptive powers of self-reflection. The first book is sensational, a story not just of captivity, but of authorial self-mythologizing. The latter book is animated by its author's passion for literature, democracy, and human rights. It is an innovative and complex blending of vari-ous genres—memoir, biography, autobiography, literary criticism, and politi-cal tract. It honors literature as an art form that recognizes no geographical or temporal boundaries. Mixing life and art, it makes unique connections between Western novels and women's lives in postrevolutionary Iran, parallels that are persuasive and original. Whether we agree or disagree with Nafisi's represen-tation of the Iranian people, her book testifies to the transformative powers of literature.[39] Mahmoody and Nafisi approach contemporary Iran from widely dif-ferent perspectives. Unlike Mahmoody, who is an American once married to an Iranian, Nafisi (1947–) is an Iranian who studied in the United States and then returned and lived in Tehran for seventeen years, teaching in some of the most highly revered universities and establishing herself as a writer and an academic intellectual. As an insider and outsider, she offers a unique point of view. An Ira-nian by birth, she is, as the memoir remarks, "very American—like an American version of Alice in Wonderland" (175).

Canonized by First Lady Laura Bush alongside such world classics as *The Adventures of Huckleberry Finn*, *The Brothers Karamazov*, *Jane Eyre*, *War and Peace*, and *The Little Prince* in her list of "25 books to read before you're 25,"[40] Nafisi's book is the story of seven "girls" and their teacher caught in "someone else's dream" (37). The students, who come from different and at times conflict-ing ideological and religious backgrounds, are strong, intelligent, defiant, curi-ous, and cultured. They feel subjugated and suppressed by the Islamic Republic. They feel trapped.[41] Meeting once a week with their devoted teacher, they gather in her house in Tehran "in secret" to discuss "forbidden" works of Western fic-tion (39). It is not clear why a perfectly legal, sex-segregated gathering of eight women discussing Western novels that were taught in Iranian universities at the time as well as before and after that time had to be held in secret. Nafisi's private class, which met regularly every Thursday from 1995 to 1997 and had no run-ins with authorities during those two years, is nonetheless characterized as "under-ground" and "clandestine" (266).[42]

Like Chesler and Mahmoody, Nafisi depicts Iran as an open-air detention facility and equates all Iranian women with Vladimir Nabokov's Lolita, "the little entrapped mistress" of Humbert Humbert, "her rapist and jailer" (45). They are resigned prisoners of a "stern ayatollah, a self-proclaimed philosopher-king" (38) who has confiscated not only their rights, but also their identities. Here in this vast prison, women cannot feel the breeze in their hair or the sun on their skin. They can be punished for running, laughing, eating fruits too suggestively, wearing colorful socks. Just as "Lolita's image is forever associated in the minds of her readers with that of her jailer," having "no meaning" on its own and coming "to life through her prison bars" (47), they, too, are defined by their imprisonment.

Captivity is the central metaphor of Nafisi's memoir. It appears in a wide variety of contexts. In a passage reminiscent of Mahmoody's sense of entrapment in Iran, the author-narrator writes, "I had started having nightmares and sometimes woke up screaming, mainly because I felt I would never again be able to leave the country" (115). Even when she does leave and travel abroad (and she does so repeatedly), she still feels suffocated. She confides in her students "about waking up at night feeling as if I were choking, as if I would never be able to get out, about the dizzy spells and nausea and pacing around the apartment at all hours of the night" (332).

Captivity—coping with and escaping from it—is also the primary theme of the Western literature class that is the main subject of *Reading Lolita in Tehran.* "I formulated certain general questions for them to consider, the most central of which was how these great works of imagination could help us in our present trapped situation as women" (29). To further clarify the mission of the class, Nafisi notes, "We were not looking for blueprints, for an easy solution, but we did hope to find a link between the open spaces the novels provided and the closed ones we were confined to" (19). Her hope finds fulfillment. Here is her description of one student's emotions as she enters the classroom: "Mitra began to tell us how she felt as she climbed up the stairs every Thursday morning. She said that step by step she could feel herself gradually leaving reality behind her, leaving the dark, dank cell she lived in to surface for a few hours into open air and sunshine. Then, when it was over, she returned to her cell" (67).[43] If Iran is the prison, "the dark, dank cell," then the road to lasting freedom is through departure and flight.[44] Another student captures this message in a nutshell: "You set up a model for us that staying here is useless, that we should all leave if we want to make something of ourselves" (325).

Nafisi draws in her readers and asks us to fill in the gaps, to create our own imaginary world. "I need you," she writes, "I need you, the reader to imagine us, for we won't really exist if you don't" (6). She pays close attention to details, reconstructs scenes with vividness, dramatic emphasis, and an omniscient recall. Like a cinematographer endowed with photographic memory, she provides close-ups of facial expression, cadences of laughter, voices choked with tears. She pauses and rewinds "the reel to retrace" (18) various events. She records verbal exchanges as if they were the transcription of videotaped conversations. The book's narrative flow, its charmingly engaging tone, its use of some verifiable data, its depiction of familiar political figures, the abundance of details regarding certain historic events, which are anchored in identifiable places and dates, add to its trustworthiness. But what kind of narrative is it really?

In his novel *The White Castle*, the Turkish novelist Orhan Pamuk writes, "The ideal story should begin innocently like a fairy-tale, be frightening like a nightmare in the middle, and conclude sadly like a love story ending in separation."[45] *Reading Lolita in Tehran* follows this trajectory masterfully. It begins like a fairy tale, proceeds into a frightening space of repression, and ends with painful separation. Before taking the readers to that dreaded place of perennial violence associated with marauding fanatics, Nafisi transports us to the comfort and elegance of a protected space within the confines of her convivial home. The contrast between inside and outside is sharp; the intimacy obtained is haunting and exhilarating. Nafisi invites us into the enclosed space where she conducts her "secret" classes while keeping us conscious of the dangers lurking beyond the door. We step into a forbidden, secret, inaccessible world. We are welcomed as honored guests into this place of gaiety and transgression. The beautiful and snow-capped Alborz Mountains frame the windows of this classroom and are reflected in its antique mirror. Bouquets of flowers—white and yellow daffodils, roses, orchids, birds of paradise—provide a feast for the eyes. Shimmering tea is served time and again in "slim-waisted glasses whose honey-colored liquid trembles seductively" (20). Pastry, delicious food, and scrumptious conversation soothe the palette and the soul. Unlike the troubled world outside, this classroom is a warm, bright place, free from the repression that rules beyond its walls. It bursts with color, flows with sunshine, is filled with intimate and animated exchanges, beams with laughter and the promise of liberation. In this "protective cocoon," this "wonderland" (8)—the West, "that forbidden world" (39)—is turned "into something more pure and golden than anything it ever was or will be" (39). A memoir about life in the Islamic Republic of Iran and addressed to a Western audience could not begin with a more engaging invitation to its readers.

The tale of these idyllic Thursday morning classes is interwoven with a painstaking account of the Islamic Republic at its most repellent. The narrator records with precision and clarity the betrayal and the cruelties of the postrevolutionary years. She recounts the repression of independent thought, the brutality of the revolutionary guards, the ruthlessness of morality squads who enforce a regime of gender apartheid. She reports the systematic eradication of both sexes' civil liberties. She chronicles mass arrests, daily terrors, and the repeated bombings suffered during the eight-year war with Iraq. She writes about summary trials and public executions. She goes out of her way to elaborate on all forms of oppression, in particular those suffered by women. But she omits, minimizes, or dismisses the rights gained, the advances made, and the unprecedented social activism and resistance of women in Iran today. Most revealing of all is the conspicuous absence of a single reference to the achievements of Iranian woman writers—past or present, major or minor, dead or alive. It is ironic that a book revolving around the subversive nature of literature should leave out any mention of Iranian women writers, who are the epitome of subversion.[46]

It might be argued that *Reading Lolita in Tehran* is about Western literature in Iran, not vice versa. But the implications of the title are undermined by the rhetoric of the book itself, for Nafisi goes to great pains to offer a catalog of how local authors are mistreated at the hands of the Iranian government. According to her, the contemporary literary scene in Iran is notable for the imprisonment, exile, isolation, torture, strangulation, and execution of Iranian writers. She traffics in details about mysterious disappearances and writers hacked to death or "whisked away by the secret police for questioning" (226). She relates the government's attempt to murder some twenty members of the Association of Iranian Writers by sending the bus in which they were traveling down a ravine. But she ignores the literature of resistance that flourished in Iran during the period covered by her book. The fact remains that in spite of all hindrances or perhaps because of them, Iran can claim to be one of the most vibrant literary cultures in the Middle East today. Iranian writers are silenced on these pages in a way that has eluded the Iranian authorities.

*Reading Lolita in Tehran* not only is selective in its handling of facts central to the story it tells, but also skips over challenging historical facts. For instance, the slogan "Death to America" is heard time and again in both Persian and English, but the book rarely mentions the reality of the Iranian people's pro-American feelings. In a tone both familiar and authoritative, Nafisi tells her readers time and again that the legal age of marriage for girls was lowered to nine in Iran after the 1979 Revolution. The reader is also reminded that if Lolita had "lived in the Islamic Republic," she "would have been long ripe for marriage to men older than Humbert." The statement per se might be accurate, but it is misleading. It is only half the story, the part that fits the Lolita analogy. The omitted and critical half is that although the Islamic Republic lowered the age of marriage to nine, the law failed miserably. The average age of marriage for women has been consistently higher in postrevolutionary than in pre-revolutionary Iran. According to the United Nations, the mean age of marriage for Iranian women in the mid-1990s was 22.5 years. Higher literacy rates among women, coupled with high unemployment and double-digit inflation, made early marriage undesirable and impractical.

Moreover, for every key concept in the book there is also a caveat tucked safely in one corner that contradicts it. For every claim, there is a disclaimer. Take the central metaphor of the memoir: Iranian women as Lolitas. The analogy is so well established by the book that when Random House, the publisher, was choosing a cover for the book, one potential adviser, "who was a Persian photographer, suggested 'to have a woman with Lolita glasses with a chador,'" Nafisi told Richard Byrne of the *Chronicle of Higher Education.*[47] Yet in *Reading Lolita in Tehran,* Nafisi undermines the very association she evokes repeatedly. "I want to emphasize once more," she writes, "that we were not Lolita, the Ayatollah was not Humbert and this republic was not what Humbert called his princedom by the sea" (35).

The omission of inconvenient facts is aggravated by contradictory statements sprinkled throughout the text. Inconsistencies pose as evidence of the elusiveness of truth, the unattainability and inaccessibility of objective reality. A perfect example is the mysterious magician who, other than the narrator, is the most pivotal character in the book. A loyal and wise mentor, an engaged and engaging interlocutor, a voice of moderation and wisdom, a moral compass, he is first presented as a fictional character in one of Nabokov's short stories: "I went on to tell her one of my favorite Nabokov stories, called 'The Magician's Room.' At first he had wanted to call it 'The Underground Man.' It was about a gifted writer and critic whose two great loves had been fiction and film" (33). The magician is later defictionalized and depicted as "genuine" (337)—in fact, a cherished companion who lives in Tehran: "What I did not tell Yassi that day was that Nabokov's magician, the man who was as dangerous to the state as an armed rebel, did not exist—or, at least, not in fiction. He was real and lived less than fifteen minutes away from where she and I were sitting, aimlessly stirring our long spoons in the tall glasses" (34). Finally, the magician is refictionalized at the end of the book. "Was he real? Did I invent him? Did he invent me?" Nafisi writes in the epilogue (341). No wonder Paul Allen of *The Guardian* calls the magician a "presiding genie" in Nafisi's life.[48]

Sifting through paradoxes is part of the literary experience, one of the reasons readers go back to a text again and again, searching for clues and glimpses of the truth. Such rearrangements, such subtle reconstructions of the paradoxical nature of reality, constitute part of the magic and mystery of great literature. But how is the reader to sift through such deliberate narrative contradictions that exist in *Reading Lolita in Tehran*? Where does the truth end, and at what point does fiction begin? Are we, the readers, to consider the magician a figment of Nafisi's or Nabokov's imagination? Is he a man living in Iran, or is he a fictive, composite character? Is he of ink and paper or of flesh and blood? Or should facts never get in the way of a good story? As Goli Emami, a close friend of Nafisi who is portrayed affectionately as the "bookseller" in the memoir, told Karl Vick of the *Washington Post*, the magician "too has the benefit of some cocktail of fact and fiction intermingled."[49]

This "cocktail of fact and fiction intermingled" permeates the entire book. The students and the friends, for instance, like the magician prove to be no more than "characters" in a novel. In "the author's note," Nafisi acknowledges that she has "made every effort to protect friends and students, baptizing them with new names and disguising them perhaps even from themselves, changing and interchanging facets of their lives so that their secrets are safe." Why disguise people, many of whom have already left the country, from themselves? Isn't that deliberate blurring of the boundaries between the fictional and the real what novelists do? Before leaving Iran, Nafisi tells the magician that she intends to write a book about her experience in the Islamic Republic. "Lady," he instructs her, "we do not need your truths but your fiction" (338). Nafisi seems to have taken the magician's advice to heart. *Reading Lolita in Tehran* reads like great fiction. Perhaps that is why the book carries a different subtitle in England. Rather than a "memoir in books," it is marketed there as "a story of love, books, and revolution."

## THE APPEAL OF HOSTAGE NARRATIVES

In a review essay on books about Iran, Patrick Clawson, senior editor of *Middle East Quarterly*, writes, "And what becomes established in the Western mind as the realities about Iran may not bear any resemblance to what careful scholarship demonstrates. Therefore, a good rule of thumb for learning about Iran is to read the obscure scholarly books and ignore anything that sells well."[50] And Leslie Schunk writes, "It is symptomatic of our times that many of us serious readers are not encouraged but, to the contrary, are put off by learning a book has won a Pulitzer Prize . . . and/or is a popular book club selection and/or has been on the *New York Times* list of bestsellers for 110 weeks."[51] But, of course, popular books wield great power by touching the hearts and souls of Americans, especially at a time when the stories they believe in can become guidelines for the country's foreign policy. The authors of hostage narratives speak to massive audiences not only through their books, but also via radio and television interviews, articles and opinion pieces published in major newspapers and magazines, and the publicity attending their prestigious awards. Their books find their way to public libraries, high school classrooms, and college courses.

It is ironic that these depictions of Iranian/Muslim women as lifelong prisoners should be so popular in the United States, when one considers that the Land of the Free now imprisons three times more women than any other nation. Thanks to the incarceration boom during the past two decades, the United States is now the world's number one jailer, with more than 2.2 million people behind bars. Although incarceration rates have slowed somewhat in recent years, they still continue to climb at a steady pace, having nearly quadrupled since 1980. As a 2006 report from the National Council on Crime and Delinquency states, "The U.S. has less than 5 percent of the world's population, but over 23 percent of the world's incarcerated people."[52] "According to the Justice Department," wrote Marie Gottschalk in April 2008, "7 million people—or one in every 32 adults—are either incarcerated, on parole or probation or under some other form of state or local supervision."[53] Senator Jim Webb (D–Va.), who in 2007 held a set of hearings on mass incarceration in the United States, noted in his opening remarks that "the United States has embarked on one of the largest public policy experiments in our history, yet this experiment remains shockingly absent from public debate."[54] Given these figures, which have not attracted due attention, one wonders if the interest in Muslim women's supposed lifetime imprisonment is a denial or a projection of a harsh American reality. Does the hostage narrative titillate and comfort? Does it make the massive US penal system seem normal and necessary and less daunting?[55]

Perhaps, but there are undoubtedly other factors at play in the popular appeal of hostage narratives. The authors of these narratives spin engaging and suspenseful yarns, replete with love, betrayal, and intrigue and spiced with raids, bombings, and executions. They alleviate the anxieties of their time by reflecting them, reaffirm the values of society by meditating on their loss, validate subtle and not so subtle stereotypes and misperceptions. They write in accessible language free from academic jargon and complicated theories. With the help of experienced coauthors, skilled ghostwriters, powerful agents, and accomplished editors, the authors in effect reel in the unsuspecting reader with a number of rhetorical devices and literary strategies.

Consider the issue of familiarity. The hostage narrative is highly reminiscent of an indigenous American literary genre, the captivity narrative, which was popular from the seventeenth to the nineteenth century. The plot in such books was often a simple series of reversals. The protagonist, usually a woman, was nabbed by Native Americans, who took her from a life of comfort and freedom into harsh confinement and rough living. Whether the innocent prisoner walked unwittingly into the trap or was abducted by force, she always endured extraordinary torments, which she faced with unusual courage and resolve. In the end, the forces of good won out, and the victim returned home to tell her tale of survival, which was all the more riveting for being true. These stories alleviated the anxieties of their time by reflecting them. Reaffirming the values of society by meditating on their losses, they were among America's first indigenous literary forms and became some of its first best sellers.

Today, autobiographies, memoirs, and travelogues are some of the most popular kinds of books published in the United States. Self-narration, it seems, is an acknowledged right, a favorite American pastime. Even those who do not want to write a book about their lives make personal statements on bumper stickers and license plates; they tattoo them on their bodies; they reveal their lives on talk shows or Webcams linked to Internet sites such as YouTube and Facebook; they participate in and eagerly watch reality TV; they bare their souls for mass consumption.

Public confessions of misfortune and hard-earned redemption, even from characters with ambiguous moral or legal status, seem to fascinate Americans. The more unbearable the suffering, the better the sales; the more sordid or horrific the experience, the greater the potential for commercial success. Consider James Frey's calculated announcement in the first line of *A Million Little Pieces:* "I am an Alcoholic and I am a drug Addict and I am a Criminal."[56] Frey could not publish his story as a novel. Seventeen different publishers rejected his manuscript. Astonishingly, however, when he labeled it a "memoir," abracadabra! it was picked up by a premier publishing house, Doubleday. As "nonfiction," it sold millions of copies and was praised for its openness and candor. Three years later and only after the veracity of some sections was questioned, Frey admitted to having embellished some of his personal experiences and to having fabricated others. Only 18 out of 432 pages of the book are in dispute, he told Larry King. "This is an appropriate ratio for a memoir," he thought. Kathryn Harrison has a point when she writes, "We love stories of overcoming hardship; really, the only way to improve on them is to multiply the hero's woes."[57]

The real appeal of hostage narratives, however, is the American reading public's hunger for detailed and accessible information about the Islamic world, in particular that which transcends politics and goes beyond the headlines. So what is there to read?

Although the number of books published in the United States has increased steadily, the twenty-five-billion-dollar publishing industry is dominated by a few conglomerates driven by an obsession with blockbusters. The not-so-lucrative business of translating books from other languages into English, a cornerstone of intercultural communication and better understanding among nations, has no real place in such a market.[58] The number of translations, regardless of genre, has dropped steeply in the past two decades. According to a study conducted by the National Endowment for the Arts, of the 12,828 books of fiction and poetry published in the United States in 1999, only 297 (2.3 percent) were literary translations. Of these, 72 percent were from western and eastern Europe. Only 18 translated titles were of Middle Eastern origin. In 2004, only a scant 2.62 percent of all books published were translated from other languages. By comparison, 29 percent of all books published in the Czech Republic and 25 percent in Spain were works of translation.[59] And in Iran, of a total of 38,546 books published in the country in 2004, 23 percent, or 8,976 books, were translations, a ratio consistent with previous years.[60] The conversation between the reading public in the United States and the rest of the world has become more like a monologue.

This is why Maryam, the Iranian American protagonist of Anne Tyler's novel *Digging to America,* regrets that "Americans read only American literature."[61] On the face of it, her statement seems implausible, especially given all the mixing and interdependence entailed in globalization. Strictly speaking, it is not even true. For starters, Maryam's compatriot, Jalal al-Din Rumi (1207–73), has been a best-selling poet in America for the past two decades, as attractive or meaningful to Americans as Walt Whitman or Shakespeare in terms of the number of books sold.[62] Some 730 years after his death, the Muslim mystic continues to mesmerize American readers with his message of love and religious tolerance. And in the US academy, an avalanche of books and articles about Muslim societies are produced in several disciplines and from a variety of perspectives. Yet—and this is where Maryam has a point—poets, academics, and the small number of translated books reach a limited readership, whereas popular books wind up in the hands of millions.

### NECESSARY DISTINCTIONS

Tales of captivity, alas, have become incorporated into our collective consciousness and literary imagination. Their large-scale publication is a by-product of modernity and associated with the appearance of the prison as a form of punishment central to modern penal systems.[63] In book after book, in one anguished account after another, men and women from eastern Europe, China, and Africa as well as from the Middle East, Asia, and the Americas have lamented a long list of atrocities and indignities suffered in captivity. They have described dark dungeons, brutal interrogations, forced confessions, public recantations, mental torments, muzzled voices, blindfolded eyes, tortured and maimed bodies. They have depicted massacres in secret jails and the brutalities of solitary confinement in terms as vivid as the recorded experiences of Russians detained in the Soviet gulag and Jews locked up in Nazi concentration camps.

There are also an increasing number of prison memoirs by Muslim men and women, even though the latter are by and large new to the enterprise (starting with Zaynab al-Ghazali [1917–2005] in Egypt and Ashraf Dehghani [1948–] in Iran).[64] In recent years, however, more and more women, often religious, political, and human right activists, have written in candid detail about the pains and privations of living behind bars. Yearning for freedom and justice, they portray themselves as imbued with a spirit of survival, resistance, even hope. Far from being willing convicts, passive victims in need of special and persistent deprogramming from abroad, they succeed in pushing against the boundaries that contain them, tearing down walls, crossing frontiers, sprouting wings, flying with courage through their texts.

On the surface, women's prison memoirs and hostage narratives share certain commonalities. Born out of a desire to refuse erasure, both categories cathartically recount traumatic experiences and share personal tales of survival and liberation. Both genres present gripping tales, a form of protest against imposed stillness and invisibility. Underneath the seeming similarities, however, the two genres are as different as pomegranates and dates. Whereas prison memoirs are often an eloquent testimony to women's agency, courage, and defiance, hostage narratives trivialize or contradict, in impact if not in intent, women's attempts at subversion, resistance, and self-assertion. Though prison memoirs depict fiery protagonists who have inserted their agency and voice in the public discourse, hostage narratives revolve around helpless, voiceless, and powerless victims. Whereas prison memoirs have their roots in women's increased, albeit contentious access to the public arena and admittance to the world of politics, activism, and opposition, hostage narratives neglect women's important and unprecedented presence in the public sphere.

Marina Nemat, author of the best-selling *Prisoner of Tehran,* who was forcibly married to a prison guard and had to convert to Islam to do so, explains why she decided to publish her heartrending testimonial in 2007, after keeping silent for a quarter-century.[65] "This is my way of paying back, because it is the story of political prisoners of Iran," she told Tavis Smiley in May 2007. "But this is a story that has never been told. Thousands of innocent people were killed in those prisons and nobody knows." Contrary to Nemat's claim, memoirs by female Iranian political prisoners, before and especially after the Islamic Revolution, are in fact numerous.[66]

I do not mean to suggest that all life narratives emerging from Iran or the Islamic world and published in the United States during the past three decades are intentional or unintentional propaganda, tainted testimonials, objects of political co-optation and market commodification. On the contrary, several life narratives do not fit the mold of hostage narrative. They are important documents of historical value. They subvert expectations and refute stereotypes. They speak truth to power and not always from the safe distance of the Diaspora. They are repositories of often unrecorded and important matters. Although such books rarely break into the mass market, they nonetheless provide vital cross-cultural engagement and understanding.[67] They counter the hostage narrative in various ways.

One such example is the memoir of Shirin Ebadi (1947–), the 2003 Nobel Peace Laureate and Iran's first female judge, who was demoted soon after the Islamic Revolution to the position of clerk in the same court over which she had presided for more than a decade.[68] As a political prisoner, she was locked up with drug addicts and prostitutes. She fought for her rights before the 1979 Revolution and has continued doing so since then. Hers is a voice that has refused to be silenced even by death threats.[69] Despite the obstacles she has faced, or perhaps because of them, she continues her struggle in the courtroom, in the public square, in the country, and now in exile. And she chronicles the details of her trials and tribulations in her memoir. Although the atrocities she suffered inside and outside prison provoke the reader's sense of outrage, *Iran Awakening: A Memoir of Revolution and Hope* is ultimately a story of resolve and, as its title indicates, of hope and awakening.[70] In it, Ebadi describes her sense of hopes betrayed by a revolution that she, along with millions of other Iranians, had supported. Nevertheless, the memoir refuses to cast its narrator in the role of a helpless victim awaiting liberation. To the contrary, it calls attention to her and other women's unprecedented social activism; their presence as lawyers, human rights activists, teachers, and students; their attainment of leadership positions; their active participation in politics and nongovernmental organizations; their vigorous involvement in art, publishing, and sports.

Ebadi's portrayal of Iranian women deviates from images prevalent in the United States. She avoids entanglement in the perennial veiling/unveiling

debates. She does not use the litany of oppression so familiar to Western readers. She challenges the idea that human rights, democracy, or women's rights are
inherently incompatible with Islam. She rejects vengeance and violence and recommends sustained dialogue instead. She maintains again and again that Iran's
salvation must come from within. She does not evade the issue of the hostage
crisis, but, unlike authors of hostage narratives, she provides more of a context,
including the avalanche of causes and effects set in motion by America's 1953
intervention in Iran's internal affairs.[71] Ebadi believes books such as hers provide an "opportunity both for Americans to learn more about my country and
its people from a variety of Iranian voices, and for a better understanding to be
achieved between our two countries."[72]

Bahiyyih Nakhjavani's novel *La femme qui lisait trop* (The Woman Who
Read Too Much) also defies prevalent stereotypes of the Iranian woman and
contradicts the general trend.[73] The book is poetic in its language, philosophical
in its outlook, scholarly in its respect for facts. It contravenes several literary
genres in order to invent a new one as it tells the gripping and well-researched
tale of a nineteenth-century Iranian woman. In order to appreciate Nakhjavani's achievement in this novel, which is inspired by and dedicated to Tahirih
Qurratul'Ayn, one has first to evaluate the challenges she has undertaken. How
does one translate myth into life in order to tell the story of such a woman? How
does one capture the timbre and texture of Tahirih's fearless voice in a language
that is at once accessible and befitting? How does one convey the audacity of
her eloquence, the intensity of her conviction, the violence of her murder at
the age of thirty-six? How, moreover, does a writer of the twenty-first century
resurrect the world of women in nineteenth-century Iran? Rather than shying
away from these hurdles, Nakhjavani finds a narrative strategy commensurate
with the woman she is writing about and a structure particularly suited to the
subject matter she explores. She brings to bear upon the historical legend of
Tahirih a multiplicity of perspectives while simultaneously showing the ways
in which this woman breaks all stereotypes. She approaches the central protagonist from the point of view of several women as well as significant men
among Tahirih's contemporaries, through whose eyes we see her sometimes as
a failed wife and a heartless mother, other times as a brilliant scholar and poet,
now as a challenger of Islamic jurisprudence, an appropriator of the pulpit, a
daring scriptural interpreter, but then as a heretic, a harridan, and a whore.

Nakhjavani reproduces texts of gossip, a running commentary of hearsay, a chorus of women's voices that interface and interfere with the actual story and by so doing create the multiple perspectives necessary to interpret the life of a woman ahead of her time.

Nakhjavani successfully navigates between the extremes of prejudice and idolatry that have marked the telling of Tahirih's life. She encompasses in this multilayered portrait the demonization and the sanctification, the slander and the worship, the fascination and the terror that have marked the representation of this protagonist over the past 160 years. She humanizes a legend while revealing the mythic dimensions of each and every human being. She strips off veils of hagiography and slander that have surrounded Tahirih's life.[74]

In *Persepolis I* and *Persepolis II*, Marjane Satrapi celebrates the Iranian people's history of resistance, subversion, and rebellion as much as she bears witness to the miseries and injustices caused by political and religious dogmatism.[75] Satrapi mixes black-on-white graphic designs to portray the reality of life in pre- and postrevolutionary Iran as a complex web of paradoxes, a vibrant mix of contradictions. She depicts competing narratives of womanhood and manhood coexisting side by side in Iran. She shows how soon after the 1979 Revolution women were segregated in classes from the elementary school to the university and had to observe an obligatory dress code, but to be "fair" she adds in *Persepolis II*, "If women faced prison when they refused to wear the veil, it was also forbidden for men to wear neckties (that dreaded symbol of the West). And if women's hair got men excited, the same thing could be said of men's bare arms. And so, wearing a short-sleeved shirt was also forbidden."[76] The graphic memoirist illustrates women who demonstrate, disobey oppressive laws, confront the regime as best they can, get jailed and executed. She also portrays them dancing, drinking, dating, throwing wild parties, listening to forbidden music. "Our behavior in public," concedes the narrator, "and our behavior in private were polar opposites." Conscious "of the contrast between the official representation of my country and the real life of the people, the one that went on behind the walls,"[77] Satrapi takes her readers behind walls and veils to show them how Iranians—male and female—deploy ingenious strategies to cross and defy imposed rules and regulations. The Iranian women she depicts are not held captive by their faith, by the regime, or by men in segregated spaces, underneath the veil. She captures the intricacies of a society in transition and of women on the move.

232 • PRISONERS AWAITING LIBERATION

In the short introduction to *Persepolis I*, Satrapi declares she wrote her memoir in order to rectify misconceptions about Iran. Since the Islamic Revolution, she states, "this old and great civilization has been discussed mostly in connection with fundamentalism, fanaticism, and terrorism. As an Iranian who has lived more than half my life in Iran, I know this image is far from the truth. This is why writing *Persepolis* was so important to me. I believe an entire nation should not be judged by the wrongdoings of a few extremists. I also don't want," continues Satrapi, "those Iranians who lost their lives in prisons defending freedom, who died in the war against Iraq, who suffered under various repressive regimes, or who were forced to leave their families and flee their homeland to be forgotten. One can forgive but one should never forget."[78] Disturbed by the prevalent disinformation, Satrapi told Robert Chalmers of the *Independent Times:* "There's this misconception in the West that every Iranian is a scum, that all men force women into marriages, then beat them, and that everybody is a fanatic. It's like arguing that Western society is typified by the inquisition."[79]

## DIVERSIFYING THE POOL OF INFORMATION

In his acceptance speech for the 2005 Nobel Prize in Literature, Harold Pinter said: "In 1958 I wrote the following: 'There are no hard distinctions between what is real and what is unreal, nor between what is true and what is false. A thing is not necessarily either true or false; it can be both true and false.' I believe that these assertions still make sense and do still apply to the exploration of reality through art." As a writer, Pinter said, he stands by his earlier judgment. "But as a citizen," he cannot. "As a citizen, I must ask: What is true? What is false?"[80] We live in times that, to use Pinter's terms, call upon ordinary citizens to pay unusual attention to the truth and falsehood of what they are told and what they read. But these are times, as in Pinter's case, that call upon the artist as citizen or the citizen in the artist to carry an even heavier burden in determining what is true and what is false.

Perhaps the question as to whether hostage narratives are fiction or nonfiction would be irrelevant in a different context. But books hailed as authoritative windows onto the Islamic world carry political as well ethical responsibilities.[81] Because so many people take these richly imaginative works for truth, their production, reception, and consumption raise not only literary but also moral questions.[82] Within this context, then, it is legitimate to ask how they are received. Who promotes them? Who funds them? Who co-opts them and why? Perhaps we should question distortions of truth and betrayals of history as well as the politics of publishing and image making. Perhaps we should ask why we are so easily seduced by plots that resemble fairy tales, with monstrous wardens on one side and helpless prisoners on the other. We live in a time when women's oppression has the power to attract immediate and passionate attention and ironically to prepare the public to accept policy options that they would find otherwise unpalatable—a time when, in Azar Nafisi's words, "some politicians use human rights and, in the case of Muslim societies, women's rights for their own political convenience, without any real commitments."[83]

The issue of truth in life narratives is clearly fraught with complications. Even so, there remains a difference between fiction and nonfiction, between a novel and a life narrative, between lapses of memory and the willful manipulation of facts, between narrative choices based on the exigencies of plot and speaking untruth in the service of power. Meticulous management of information—omitting or changing or exaggerating or cherry-picking cultural and historical facts—carries with it an ethical burden. In several of these testimonials, a compassionate desire to safeguard other people's security, to "protect" family and friends, precludes the need for verifiability or identification. Plural and unsourced narrators, rumors, and speculation are mixed and matched with historical facts and choreographed as nonfiction. Readers are caught in a double-bind. How can they possibly require the verification of facts and identities if it would put the lives of innocent people in danger?

But shouldn't an autobiographer, unlike a novelist, be limited by facts and the need for accuracy? Does not nonfiction and its implicit contract between the reader and the writer—of truth seeking and truth telling—demand an effort to adhere to an objective standard of accuracy? To what degree must a writer deny the reader necessary documentation before a book has to be called fiction? And if a work is categorized as nonfiction, at what point does the unspoken covenant with readers demand that it relinquish the liberties afforded by fiction? All writers of life stories have to reconstruct the truth according to their points of view, but that is not the same as fictionalizing it.

Even if these memoirs and autobiographies were promoted as largely fictional rather than nonfictional, we would still have to ask why they so consistently convey a particular ideological vision and depict Muslim women as prisoners. As citizens of an increasingly polarized world, "a world in which people are bombarded with ideologically loaded texts from morning to night,"[84] we, the readers, cannot afford to suspend critical judgment and accept as fact deliberate manipulation of lives and histories. We need to question the distortions of truth, the betrayals of history, the disparagement of scholarship, the politics of publishing. We need to examine the seductiveness and political function of tales of captivity, sustained and supported by official power, recognized by the mass media, authenticated by hostage narratives. Should we diversify our pool of information so that, far from being the "captive" she is portrayed to be, she would be recognized as a moderating, modernizing force, a seasoned negotiator of confined spaces, a veteran trespasser of boundaries, walls, fences, cages, blind windows, closed doors, and iron gates?

# EPILOGUE

## *Words as Ambassadors of Peace and Beacons of Hope*

Remember, O sword,
You are the younger brother, the latter-born
Your triumph, however exultant,
Must one day be over,
In the beginning was the word.

—HILDA DOOLITTLE, "The Walls Do Not Fall"

Let me add only that stereotypes are easier to shrug off if yours is not the culture being stereotyped; or, at the very least, if your culture has the power to counterpunch against the stereotype.

—SALMAN RUSHDIE, "Outside the Whale"

### KILL A CAT, TAME THE SHREW

There is a well-known Iranian proverb that recommends, "Kill a cat in the nuptial chamber." Why murder and mayhem in a space of love and romance? I pondered for years. How is the slaying of a cat related to wedding rituals? I wanted to know. Why bloodshed at the threshold of matrimony? I knew the message of violence in this adage, even if targeted at a cat, was justified as a necessary form of intervention, a piece of advice to the newlyweds. But, then, what kind of a heterosexual relationship did the proverb condone by normalizing carnage and bloodshed? To whom was it addressed anyway? Was it directed to the bride or to the groom? What kind of a social order did it perpetuate? In a culture that values proverbs and believes them to be the condensed wisdom and experience of generations of revered forefathers and foremothers, what was the lesson implied in this old axiom?

235

Like most Iranian proverbs, this one, too, has a story behind it. It is said that a certain shrew of a woman known for her aggressive nonconformity had driven away all potential suitors in spite of her wealth and beauty. She was disobedient, headstrong, and ill tempered; she had a long, sharp, nagging, and scolding tongue; she had a stormy nature and a domineering disposition. No one wanted to suffer her bed, let alone her companionship. She was a *saliteh*, the Persian equivalent of a "shrew," and who wants to marry a *saliteh?* Well, perhaps only a bully. For, eventually, a man known to be a tyrant became increasingly intrigued by the challenge as well as the financial gains of marrying this woman. He volunteered to tie the knot with her in spite of all the warnings of family, friends, and well-wishers. He assured everyone that he knew exactly what he was doing and arranged for a cat to be taken to his nuptial chamber. After the wedding ceremony was over, and as soon as the newlyweds were alone in their bedroom, the groom looked in the direction of the cat and said, "Go fetch me a glass of water." The unsuspecting animal meowed in blissful ignorance. He added threat to his request. "Did you not hear me?" he said in a raised voice. "I told you to go get me a glass of water." The defiant cat flicked her tail but did not budge, so the clearly annoyed alpha man took out his dagger and without any hesitation beheaded the heedless creature.

Undisturbed by his unprovoked violent act, holding the bloodied weapon in his hand with great pride, intoxicated by his unmitigated power, the groom-turned-executioner looked at the terrified and speechless bride and repeated his command with a shrill note in his euphoric voice. "I want a glass of water," he said triumphantly. In a calculated manipulation of her ears and fears, showing no sign of remorse, never raising his hands to her, he had exerted his superiority and established her subjugation. He wanted to instill fear through the spectacle of a pitiless killing. And he succeeded. He had the wherewithal to acquire power and had thus earned the right to be obeyed. Trapped in an enclosed space with a remorseless murderer, fearing for her life, the startled bride succumbed to her husband's taming machinations. She promptly delivered a glass of water. And thus the pattern was set. Forced into submission, the shrewish woman metamorphosed into a gentle and submissive wife. She had no option—at least, not for now. The groom had established his masculine authority right from the start. Female recalcitrance was bent into submission, male supremacy recognized, and marital "harmony" assured in this household. Blessed be the Lord.

What earlier seemed like an extreme folly soon became the envy of a whole town. One man, known as a *zan zalil,* a softy, a pushover, was delighted with the awe-inspiring rumor about the bully and his bride. He had suffered his bossy wife long enough, and the new bride's unquestioning accommodation of her husband was what he had desperately desired for himself. "Enough is enough," he grumbled under his moustache. "Besides," he thought to himself with great joy and a sense of relief, "that's easy. Why in the world did I not think of it all these years?" He was in fact a bit annoyed with himself. "But better late than never," he whispered with glee in his eyes. Swiftly and cheerily he equipped himself with a huge table knife, and as soon as he reached the bedroom, he asked his pet cat to get him a glass of water. He did his best to sound serious and dictatorial. Listening carefully to her husband's newly found audacity, the wife smiled a big, knowing smile. "My man," she said undaunted and impervious, "you've got to kill the cat in the nuptial chamber, not after years of married life." Looking him directly in the eye and bossing him around in her customary fashion, she added: "Now, my friend, if you're thirsty, get yourself up and go fetch a glass of water. And leave that poor cat alone."

"Kill a cat in the nuptial chamber," then, is a taming instruction, entwined in desires and designs for dominance.[1] Although it is, for the most part, a lesson to husbands on how to discipline their wives right from the beginning, especially if they happen to be rebellious and wayward, it can also be viewed as a roadmap to the establishment of any form of dominance. To achieve the dignity of a "husband," the proverb seems to suggest, a man has to tame his wife at the very threshold of matrimony. While he trains and domesticates her, he will consolidate his authority and sovereignty not only within the household—his "little commonwealth"—but also beyond. For a man's house is his castle, and as another Persian proverb makes clear, "The nuptial night is not unlike the dawn of royal reign." In William Shakespeare's play *The Taming of the Shrew,* the husband is quite explicit about this: "Thus have I politically begun my reign," Petruchio, the tamer, announces with smugness after he has confined his bride, deprived her of food and sleep, and mistreated her. A tamed Kate finally proclaims, "Thy husband is thy Lord, thy life, thy keeper / Thy head, thy sovereign; one that cares for thee."[2]

The Persian word for "shrew," *saliteh,* comes from the same root as *salteh* and *saltanat:* dominance, kingship, and regency. *Saliteh, salit, saltanat,* and *salteh* not only derive from the same root, but also remarkably find a link in this proverb. Persian dictionaries define a *saliteh* as a woman who is boisterous and disobedient, long-tongued and blabbermouthed, fiery and obdurate. She causes trouble by dominating her husband. She produces a surplus of undesirable noises and demands. She does not remain within her assigned role, demeanor, or space. As an unyielding woman, she is denigrated in numerous aphorisms, warned against repeatedly. It is said, for instance, that a *saliteh* is the husband of her man and a dog without a leash. It is recommended to avoid three things in life: a wall that might collapse, a *saliteh,* and a rabid dog. But those very same attributes that are condemned and feared in women are condoned and encouraged in men. They are, in fact, indispensable to masculinity. According to the same dictionaries, a *salit* (the masculine form of *saliteh*) is a man who is eloquent, well built, sharp, and in control over himself and those around him. He knows how to protect his turf, tame his wife even if she is a shrew, and establish his dominance.

The violence committed in this proverb can be viewed as a reflection of the political structure of Iran, even though politicians and political movements—right, left, or centrist; religious, fundamentalist, or secular—have rarely assessed or condemned that violence. A man–woman abusive relationship has been most difficult to address or alter. Perhaps it is heard about so often that no one pays attention to it any longer. Perhaps it is seen so much that it is no longer witnessed. Whatever the reasons, gender-based violence is a major impediment to achieving a culture of mutual respect and responsibility. Furthermore, what the bully does not seem to consider and the narrative eulogizing his nasty behavior does not caution against is the simple truth that although he did not lay his hands on her, he bruised her soul, battered her trust, mutilated their relationship. Moreover, the "tamed" learns how to turn into a "tamer." In due time and as soon as circumstances allow it, she will become the one to entrap, cage, confine within the bounds of honor, anxiety, possessiveness, gossip, slander, sexual guile, dependence. Different forms of violence—active and passive, immediate and delayed, physical and emotional—thus become the normal currency of social exchange.

Putting aside for the moment the dubiousness of such strategies and the cultural anxieties of the bedroom, especially those of the nuptial night, which have a central importance in Iranian literature and society, this didactic proverb engages more than gender relations. It takes place in the nuptial chamber, a space at the interstices of public and private domains: private because it is the time and place of the first sexual intimacy between newlyweds, the consummation of their marriage; and public because it is a sanctuary closely scrutinized by the bride and groom's families. Classical Persian literature abounds in graphic, often erotic descriptions of the nuptial chamber.[3] These narrative retellings, even if issued from the pen of men and rooted mainly in male desire and satisfaction, focus mainly on love and passion. The story of the bully, however, is all about power and domination. It not only teaches how to establish male supremacy but also reconfirms a culture of governance through sheer violence and brute force.

The gratuitous violence perpetrated in the bridal room and the strategies implemented by the groom to deal with real or perceived problems prepare the ground for and maintain the politics of repression. Regardless of whose point of view we adopt—that of the murdered cat, the groom-turned-murderer, the bride–turned–crime witness; friends and relatives of the newlyweds who hear about the grisly tale, or all Iranians who use the proverb and pass it on from generation to generation—the adage tolerates and in fact condones the attainment of women's (or other subordinates') compliance through aggression and hostility. Although in Iran cats are known to be wily, deceptive, ungrateful, and hypocritical, the particular cat in this story has committed no crime at all. She has done nothing wrong. The murder of the cat is a perfect example of misguided cruelty, justified as a means to cow the young bride into compliance, even if only temporarily. It remains unavenged. Worse yet, it leads to the death of negotiation as a viable form of resolution. A vicious circle thus begins. Tyranny and violence beget tyranny and violence. They become standard strategies of social surveillance. Swords replace words.

### TELL A TALE, TAME THE SERIAL KILLER

There is another Iranian model of the nuptial chamber taming of a spouse—in this case, the spouse who is a serial killer. It is the plan adopted by Scheherazade, the high priestess of storytelling. Like the cat slayer, Scheherazade volunteered to marry a shrewish spouse against the advice of family, especially her father. She knew she was entering into the nuptial chamber with a man known to be not only unruly and wicked but also driven to murderous revenge. The groom, King Shahriyar, had been betrayed by his queen and had vowed never again to be cheated by a woman. Having concluded that only a dead wife is a loyal wife, he had the adulterous queen executed and subsequently married a virgin every night, only to have her killed off the morning after. His power was so absolute that he could kill countless innocent virgins, who were not even granted the dignity of their proper names in the royal inventory. Scheherazade refused to be complicit in the sultan's vindictive fury. Although she did not have to struggle for survival and was immune from the king's murderous schemes, she did not remain silent or tucked away in her safe place. She did not look the other way, did not pursue the policy of silence, which is itself a form of complicity. She did not leave the king to his antics. To the contrary, she engaged in public service of the highest order without a single act of violence. She left the opulent and secure palace of her father—the grand vizier—at a time of national crisis. She put her life at risk to save the lives of other innocent and helpless women, who, like the murdered cat, were massacred unjustly. Hers was social activism, political intervention of the most effective—and bloodless—kind.

Before entering the nuptial chamber, like the bully, Scheherazade relied on all the strategies and tactics she knew and gathered all the weapons she had at her disposal. But, unlike him, she did not romanticize violence. Instead of taking a dagger and an innocent cat along, she took another woman—her sister—and her tales with her. She had faith in sisterhood and the healing power of words. She was wise enough to know she could not solve the crisis at hand by using the same kind of thinking that had created the crisis in the first place. She knew the futility of fighting injustice through violent means. For one thousand and one nights, under the looming threat of having her head chopped off, she dazzled the wife-killing groom with her storytelling. Through words, she transformed the claustrophobic space of murder and mayhem to one of magic and mystery. Instead of resorting to the gruesome language of violence, without shedding a drop of blood, she depended on words as ambassadors of peace and beacons of hope.[4] And she succeeded—not temporarily, but lastingly. She cured a murderer without resorting to murder.[5]

Scheherazade calmly and convincingly defied death by weaving tales. She began every storytelling session with a succinct and simple yet paradoxical phrase, "Yeki bud, yeki nabud": "There was one, and there wasn't one." Who could listen to such an inspired opener for one thousand and one nights and not be transformed by its infinite wisdom? Scheherazade summoned all her diplomatic know-how, all her storytelling techniques, all her diagnostic and healing skills. She knew trust building was key to her enterprise. Her tales, like Babushka dolls, were always pregnant with another tale. They didn't have tidy endings. They avoided pigeonholing, stereotyping, imprisoning. They opened vistas of beauty, adventure, romance, but also ambiguity. They appeased creepy monsters, prevented intruders from executing their evil designs, showed the infinite complexity of human nature, punished an unfaithful husband or an adulterous wife without blaming the whole gender for the mistake of one. It was through these powerful aphrodisiacs that Scheherazade succeeded in turning confrontation into cooperation, in having the sultan cease his bloodletting. She led him to a twilight zone where certainty and doubt lived in peaceful coexistence, where absolutes no longer ruled supreme, where there was room for ambiguity. She destereotyped his mind and populated his universe with heroes and villains of both genders. Good or bad was not the monopoly of any one group. In the end, Shahriyar—a paragon of political power, the king of kings, the shelter of the universe, God's shadow on earth—had to admit that a woman who personified powerlessness and vulnerability had made him doubt his "kingly power." "O Scheherazade," he told her lovingly, "you made me regret my past violence towards women and my killing of innocent girls." Marital harmony was finally established in this household, too. Words replaced swords.

### ENTER THE GARDEN, BREAK THE CIRCLE OF VIOLENCE

I do not mean to suggest that in Iran only women understand and deploy the formidable power of words. Iranians—male and female, literate and illiterate, young and old—have a most reverential, even sensuous relationship with words, especially with written words. We kiss books. We carry them in miniature forms in our purses, in our pockets, in lockets around our necks. We decorate books with art forms and adorn our New Year and wedding spreads (*haft seen* and *sofrey-e aghd*) with books. We treat our favorite writers and poets as cultural icons. We name our streets and children after them. We go on pilgrimage not only to the shrines of our saints, but also to those of our venerated literary figures.[6] We hold literature almost sacred and give a quasi-scriptural dimension to poetry. We have given one poet, Shams-ed-din Muhammad Hafez, the nickname "Lessan-ol-Ghayb," Voice of the Unseen; and we call another, Jalal al-Din Rumi, "Mawlana," our Master. We believe poets can reveal hidden truths, propose answers to the enigma of life, offer us tools to think with, feel with, and predict the future with. Our blogosphere is replete with poetry.[7] The walls of our prisons and hospitals, like those of our trenches and foxholes, have poetry inscribed on them.[8]

I do believe, however, that because women have been more confined in their lives and more constrained in their movements, they have had to rely more on words to heal, to change the balance of power, to achieve their goals, to negotiate, to seek relief and release, to find an outlet for their creativity. Perhaps because they are excluded from positions of "public" power, they have had to adopt different strategies to ensure their right and their survival. Perhaps once trapped within walls, they have had little alternative but to escape through words. That is exactly what Scheherazade did. Through the magic of words, she reversed the relationship of domination and subordination. She became the narrator, he the narrated; she the active agent, he the passive and addicted subject; she the captor, he the willing captive; she the one in control, he the one controlled. Without her verbal dexterity, she could very well have been one of the many beheaded and nameless virgins.

Women have had to use words as their weapon of choice, their magic carpets, their wings. Rab'ee, the first Iranian woman known to have written poetry more than ten centuries ago, could be locked up for having the impudence to fall in love with a slave, Bakhtash, but her words could not be put under lock and key. She dipped her fingers in her own slashed veins and memorialized her love by inscribing her poems on the walls. Tahirih Qurratul'Ayn could be held under house arrest, but she macerated herbs in her mouth and wrote her green words with a reed taken from the mats beneath her feet. She could be executed in the dark of night, thrown into a well, but her words could not be buried six feet under. Her inspiring words have remained alive against all odds and spring up in inspired moments. Women could be confined and restricted, but not their words, at least not completely, not eternally.

Scheherazade herself is a case in point. According to the frame story of One Thousand and One Nights, the tales of this consummate storyteller had never reached the ears of anyone other than her own family members. Like the storyteller herself, they were kept private and privatized. Their place was inside the house, away from the eyes and ears of outside audiences. So how, then, were her spellbinding tales disseminated? King Shahriyar presumably "summoned chroniclers and copyists and bade them write all that had betided him with his wife, first and last." The stories told by the king and written down by his scribes came to thirty volumes, which diligently the "King laid up in his treasury." Later, yet another "wise," "keen-witted," and "just" ruler is credited with the task of bringing to light those hidden treasures. He "found in the treasury these marvelous stories and wondrous histories" and "bade the folk copy them and dispread them over all lands and climes." Had it not been for the "wisdom," "keen-wittedness," and "justice" of two separate male rulers and untold number of male scribes, we are led to believe, Scheherazade's stories would have been erased from any written expression. They would have been covered up like her voice and kept out of circulation like her body. At best, she would have been identified as a paragon of purity and loyalty: the talented wife of King Shahriyar, the clever daughter of the grand vizier, and the devoted mother of the three sons she gave birth to in rapid succession, "one walking, one crawling and one sucking."[9]

Of course, this is not the whole story. Scheherazade's tales circulated from mouth to mouth, from generation to generation, from mothers to daughters before they were written down at some point, probably sometime between the ninth and the fifteenth centuries, when the writing pen was mainly in the hands of men, just as the public square was increasingly monopolized by them. Otherwise, how can one explain that this woman who "had perused the books, annals and legends of preceding Kings, and the stories, examples and instances of bygone men and things," this erudite, wise, and witty woman who "had collected a thousand books of histories relating to antique races and departed rulers," did not write down her own mesmerizing tales? Why did such an accomplished teller of tales, who had scrutinized "the works of the poets and knew them by heart" and "had studied philosophy and the sciences, arts and accomplishments," need to rely on male scribes for the recording of her stories?[10] *One Thousand and One Nights* does not answer these questions but portrays Scheherazade as being at the mercy of male rulers and scribes, indebted to them, in need of their mediatory role, beholden to their writing skills. And herein is the difference between Scheherazade and her literary progeny. Iranian women have appropriated the writing pen and broken the spell of their physical and literary quasi-invisibility. No longer consigned to immobility of body and voice, no longer immured physically or verbally, they have written their bodies and their voices into circulation. Like their foremother, they have rejected violence and challenged the very foundations of their society through words. Like her, they have inserted their message of hope and temperance in the turbulent history of their land. Unlike her, however, they have become their own scribes. They have rejected the traditional partitioning of physical and literary spaces.

For the past 160 years, Iranian women writers have struggled for mobility of body and voice. And today, whether women teach or study in institutions of higher education, congregate in offices, mosques, nongovernmental agencies, or conferences and study groups; whether they appear in front of cameras or direct films from behind it; whether they communicate through books and articles or paintings or plays or keep in touch through blogs and online forums and information networks; whether they ascend the ladder of government or vote in unprecedented numbers, they are more mobile than ever before. And they are refusing to relinquish their newly acquired spaces. Never before in the written history of Iran have women moved so far outside the framework preordained by their culture, reaching beyond the traditional fields in action and imagination. Never before have they been as present in the public square and the public discourse as they are today. Animated by a dizzying, dazzling sense of movement, they have emerged as a formidable civic force to be reckoned with. One might even argue that they have been at the center of a bloodless, nonviolent revolution that has shaken the very foundations of Iranian society. Although this revolution does not correspond to traditional definitions of a revolution, it has nonetheless fundamentally transformed the country's social structures, redefined masculinity and femininity, modified the balance of public and private power. It has been a turnabout, a reallocation of physical and discursive spaces, a redistribution of authority and resources.

Women writers have indeed led the way not only toward literary liberation, but also toward gender liberation. The Campaign for One Million Signatures, an initiative to change discriminatory laws, has fittingly adopted as its motto a line from the mid-nineteenth-century poet Tahirih Qurratul'Ayn, who claimed the freedom of movement in her life and her most anthologized poem: "Face to face, and street to street." The female nightingale has not only found her way into the Iranian garden, remapping the country's cultural, visual, literary, and political geography, but also projected an inspiring presence on the world stage. The jailbird has scaled new heights, found its way to the mountaintop, and morphed into the Simurgh, the Iranian phoenix. Listen to her sing as she warns bullies and tyrants that although poets, writers, and filmmakers can be detained, their aspiration for democracy and gender equity cannot be put behind bars; that although artists can be denied the right to move about freely, art cannot be handcuffed, arrested, jailed, murdered.

> My poems are my sword.
> They are mightier than any sword.
> Though they can cut deep,
> My weapon is not for bloodshed.
> I will tell nothing but the truth
> Even if it costs my head.
> Fear of death will not stop me
> From marching on.[11]

*Notes*

*Works Cited*

*Index*

# NOTES

1. "Yeki bud, yeki nabud" is followed by "Gheyr az khoda hich kas nabud," which means "Other than God, there wasn't one." Although the appearing/disappearing act takes on a new meaning with this closure, the paradox remains the same.

2. Farzaneh Milani, *Veils and Words: The Emerging Voices of Iranian Women Writers* (Syracuse, NY: Syracuse Univ. Press, 1992).

3. Fazlollah Garakani, *Tohmat-e Sha'eri* (Accused of Being a Poet) (Tehran: Alburz, 1977), 7. Unless otherwise noted in citations, translations of quotes as well as of verse and prose extracts are mine.

4. Banu Mahvash, *Raz-e Kamyabi-ye Jensi* (The Secret of Sexual Satisfaction) (Tehran: n.p., 1957); Malakeh E'tezadi, *E'terafat-e Man* (My Confessions) (Tehran: n.p., 1956); and Taj al-Saltaneh, *Khaterat-e Taj al-Saltaneh* (Taj al-Saltaneh's Memoir), edited by Mansureh Ettehadiyeh and Sirus Sa'advandiyan (Tehran: Nashr-e Tarikh-e Iran, 1982). For the English translation of Taj al-Saltaneh's memoir, see *Crowning Anguish: Memoirs of a Persian Princess from the Harem to Modernity*, edited by Abbas Amanat, translated by Anna Vanzan and Amin Neshati (Washington, DC: Mage,1993).

5. Although I do consider the writing of a Persian cookbook a major contribution, I don't believe Mr. Golestan did.

6. Janet Malcolm, *The Silent Woman: Sylvia Plath and Ted Hughes* (New York: Vintage, 1995), 9.

7. The dramatic fate of a movie by the Syrian American director Moustaffa Akkad also attracted my attention. A multi-million-dollar project, *Mohammad, the Messenger of God* was the first filmic biography of the Prophet. Beginning in the year 610, when Prophet Mohammad receives his first revelation, it follows his rise as the spiritual and political founder of Islam. The director, himself a Muslim, took extra precaution not to offend Muslim sensibilities. He submitted his script to Islamic scholars to be checked for historical accuracy and orthodoxy. More important, he had made sure not to impersonate Prophet Mohammed. The title character never appears in *Mohammad, the Messenger of God*. He is never seen or heard. No actor plays his role. We see people address him but never see him talk. We see the head of his camel, but not him riding the camel. We see his sword, but not his hand holding the sword.

Despite these cautionary measures, the premiere of the film in March 1977 was halted by a small band of American Muslims who took 132 hostages in three Washington, DC, buildings for thirty-eight hours. (For detailed descriptions of these events, see *New York Times*, Mar. 10, 1977, and *Time*, Mar. 21, 1977.) One reporter was shot dead; four people were wounded. The gunmen found the film sacrilegious and demanded its immediate banning. The film was pulled on its opening day. To forestall further protest, the Prophet's name was removed from the title. The new title was simply *The Message*. Nevertheless, the opposition was not appeased. There were demonstrations and bomb threats. A riot broke out in Pakistan. All Islamic countries, except Libya, banned the film. The grand sheik, Abdel Halim Mahmoud of Al Azhar University in Cairo, captured in a nutshell the major objection to the film. "The Koran is revelation," he announced, "and the life of the Prophet is a divine commentary on that revelation. The idea of them being portrayed by others is particularly offensive" (Richard Schickel, "What Sparked It," *Time* 109, no. 12 [Mar. 1977], 17).

Which others, I wondered, make the portrayal of the Prophet so particularly "offensive"? Who is and who is not allowed to offer commentaries on divine commentaries? What else lies at the core of this heretical violation of propriety? After all, the massive body of reports, the hadith, presents a more comprehensive biography of the Prophet Mohammad than any other man of his time or any prophet who preceded him. Second in authority only to the Qur'an, these biographical reports form an important part of Islamic canonical law. For fourteen centuries, the study of Mohammad's life has been and continues to be a crucial part of a Muslim scholar's education.

Barbara Johnson writes about biography, "There are always at least two people competing for control over the story of a life. Sometimes they are the biographer and the subject, sometimes the biographer and the Guardians of the subject's estate" (introduction to part four, "Whose Life Is It, Anyway?" in *The Seductions of Biography*, edited by Mary Rhiel and David Suchoff [New York: Routledge, 1996], 119). In the Islamic world, the clerics, the official scholars, have had total control over the biography of the Prophet Mohammad. As guardians of his "authentic" biography and its "approved" commentary, they have disallowed anyone to appropriate their role. The film director and the camera, the storyteller, the painter, and the religiously untrained biographer are not permitted to intrude into the telling of lives. That would make them surrogate priests.

8. In *Veils and Words*, I argue that life narratives in their Western sense are rare among Iranians, especially among Iranian women. I maintain that a barrier as forbidding as a veil has covered private selves and forbade self-revelation. This cultural context, I thought at the time I wrote this book, values and strongly institutionalizes a sharp separation between the inner and the outer, the private and the public. It is not conducive to the development of personal narratives and their generic uncovering and display of the self. Marvin Zonis contends, "Autobiography and biography are not yet part of the genres of literature in the Middle East" ("Autobiography and Biography in the Middle East: A Plea for Psychopolitical Studies," in *Middle Eastern Lives: The Practice of Biography and Self-Narrative*, edited by Martin Kramer [Syracuse, NY: Syracuse University Press, 1991],61). In his biography of Prime Minister Amir-Abbas Hoveida, Abbas Milani compares the New Testament and the Qur'an with regard to each religion's views on life narratives and states, "The gospels, as the fount of Christianity, are essentially composed of four, sometimes conflicting, biographical

narratives. . . . In the Koran, on the other hand, the world and the word are created to show the glory of God. The prophet Mohammed, about whose life very little is offered and no ambiguity is tolerated, enters the narrative only to carry out the commands of his lord" (*The Persian Sphinx* [Washington, DC: Mage, 2000], xi).

## INTRODUCTION

1. See Denise Spellberg, *Politics, Gender, and the Islamic Past: The Legacy of 'A'isha Bint Abi Bakr* (New York: Columbia Univ. Press, 1994).

2. Neil Mac Farquhar, "Backlash of Intolerance Stirring Fear in Iran," *New York Times*, Sept. 20, 1996.

3. Fatima Mernissi, *Dreams of Trespass: Tales of Harem Girlhood* (New York: Addison-Wesley, 1994), 242.

4. See Lois Beck, "Women among Qashqa'i Nomadic Pastoralists in Iran," in *Women in the Muslim World,* edited by Lois Beck and Nikki Keddie, 351–73 (Cambridge, MA: Harvard Univ. Press, 1978); Erika Friedl, *Women of Deh Koh: Lives in an Iranian Village* (Washington, DC: Smithsonian Institution Press, 1989); Erika Friedl, "Sources of Female Power in Iran," in *In the Eye of the Storm: Women in Post-Revolutionary Iran,* edited by Mahnaz Afkhami and Erika Friedl, 151–67 (Syracuse, NY: Syracuse Univ. Press, 1994); and Mary Elaine Hegland, "Political Roles of Aliabad Women: The Public-Private Dichotomy Transcended," in *Women in Middle Eastern History: Shifting Boundaries in Sex and Gender,* edited by Nikki Keddie and Beth Baron, 215–30 (New Haven, CT: Yale Univ. Press, 1991).

5. The juxtaposition of a philosopher who defiantly proclaimed, "I think, therefore I am," with a novelist who created a dreamer who lived in an imaginary world is itself a symptom and an expression of modernity.

6. Milan Kundera, *The Art of the Novel,* translated by Linda Asher (New York: Grove Press, 1986), 6. "As God slowly departed from the seat whence he had directed the universe and its order of values, distinguished good from evil, and endowed each thing with meaning, Don Quixote set forth from his house into a world he could no longer recognize. In the absence of the Supreme Judge, the world suddenly appeared in its fearsome ambiguity; the single divine Truth decomposed into myriad relative truths parceled out by men. Thus was born the world of the modern era."

7. Miguel de Cervantes Saavedra, *The Adventures of Don Quixote,* translated by J. M. Cohen (New York: Penguin Books, 1950), 168. After a number of misadventures, a fatigued and weary Sancho tells his master, "For several days lately I've been thinking how little profit is gained from wandering after the adventures which your worship seeks in these wastes and at these crossroads." But Don Quixote is convinced that "a knight must wander through the world, on probation as it were, in pursuit of adventures" (165).

8. Michel Foucault, *Discipline and Punish: The Birth of the Prison,* translated by Alan Sheridan (New York: Vintage Books, 1995), 11.

9. Rita Felski, *The Gender of Modernity* (Cambridge, MA: Harvard Univ. Press, 1995), 10.

10. Although mandatory veiling and unveiling are legitimate concerns, the rather obsessive focus on the issue by non-Iranians and some Iranians is in sharp contrast to the way women activists inside Iran view it. For instance, it is remarkable that the One Million Signatures Campaign in Iran, initiated by Iranian women's rights activists to demand an end to legal discrimination against women, does not concentrate solely or even predominantly on veiling. The campaign was officially launched in August 2006.

11. In *Snow,* Orhan Pamuk captures with breathtaking precision how veiling has become a divisive issue and in the process taken women and even men as pawns in local, national, and international politics. An Islamist converses with the director of the Institute of Education, who has banned head scarves in schools in the fictive city of Kars, before he assassinates the director:

—Of course, the real question is how much suffering we've caused our womenfolk by turning head scarves into symbols and using women as pawns in a political game.

—How can you call it a game, sir? When that girl who had to choose between her honor and her education—what a pity—sank into a depression and killed herself, was that a game?

—You're very upset, my boy. But has it never occurred to you that foreign powers might be behind all this? Don't you see how they might have politicized the head-scarf issue so that they can turn Turkey into a weak and divided nation?

—If you'd let those girls back into your school, sir, there would be no head-scarf issue. (*Snow,* translated by Maureen Freely [New York: Alfred A. Knopf, 2004], 43)

12. The veil has assumed totemic status. Here are some of the major arguments presented for donning it: divine commandment: proclamation of faith; Qur'anic injunction: symbol of Islamic devotion; sign of modesty; means of safety and protection (it shields women from harassment, rape, and commodification of their body); beauty; equalizer of all women regardless of their social or economic status; economical; practical; mysterious and mystifying; indigenous; commands respect; serves as a power suit; sartorial symbol of tradition; visual signifier of urbanity; mark of social distinction; standardized; rite of passage to womanhood; anticolonial; anti-Pahlavi; anti-Western; saves men from women's sexuality; invisible sense of power; theatrical; fashion statement; symbol of political Islam; saves women from the sexual instincts of men in the streets; saves women from ceaseless competition with other women regarding their displayed beauty; offers protection to the skin from sun and wind; serves as a visual signifier of femininity; instrument of immobilization. In *Dreams of Trespass,* Mernissi writes: "The haik (the veil) was probably designed to make a woman's trip through the streets so torturous that she would quickly tire from the effort, rush back home, and never dream of going out again" (118). The very contradictory nature of this list illustrates how the veil can function as a powerful metaphor with totally dichotomous assertions and applications. For instance, whereas it is argued that the veil beautifies a woman, it is also claimed that it frees her from the tyranny of beauty or the beauty industry.

For me, the veil is associated primarily with the dignified grace and magnanimity of my grandmother. My poem, "Mulberry and Chador" captures this feeling:

She would spread her chador
under the mulberry tree, and gently
hit the branches with a long pole.

Sitting on the edge of her cotton chador
Giddy with joy I'd watch
the mulberries drift and dance
like fattened snowflakes
into my cupped receiving hands.

Harder, grandma, I would plead,
hit harder, and she'd laugh, and say,
"We can't hurt pregnant trees,"
and twirl her wand into its blizzard
of decades, oceans I've yet to travel
beyond the hem of her mulberry-studded dreams.

13. The desire to confine women to the domestic sphere is not limited to Islam. In Genesis, Rabbah 8:12, we read: "The man must master his wife, that she go not out into the market place, for every woman who goes out into the market place will eventually come to grief."

14. See Fatima Mernissi, *The Veil and the Male Elite: A Feminist Interpretation of Women's Rights in Islam* (Boston: Addison-Wesley, 1992).

15. For an interesting analysis of the complex relations between modernism and identity and how they intersect with the veiling/unveiling debate in Turkey, see Nilufer Gole, *The Forbidden Modern: Civilization and Veiling* (Ann Arbor: Univ. of Michigan Press, 1996); for a multilayered historical novel on the head scarf debate in Turkey, see Pamuk's *Snow*.

16. Regarding Turkey's modernization, Orhan Pamuk provides a detailed account of its setbacks in his various novels. In an article written soon after the tragic events of September 11, 2001, and titled "The Anger of the Damned," he sums up his views in a nutshell: "The members of the wealthy, pro-modernist class that founded the Turkish Republic reacted to resistance from the poor and backward sectors of society not by attempting to understand them, but by law enforcement measures, prohibitions on personal behavior, and repression by the army. In the end, the modernization effort remained half-finished, and Turkey became a limited democracy in which intolerance prevailed" (translated by Mary Isin, *New York Review of Books* 48, no. 18 [Nov. 15, 2001], available at http://www.nybooks.com/articles/archives/ . . . /the-anger-of-the-damned/.

17. Women have yanked off their veils or threatened to do so in order to thrust men into action or to register their protest. For instance, when the Sufi saint Mansur Hallaj was charged with heresy and hanged in A.D. 922, his exasperated sister shocked everyone by appearing unveiled in public and declaring she saw no reason to veil herself anymore. "I see no real men around me," she announced to shame the unmanly men who allowed the execution of her brother.

18. The veil now carries negative connotations in the West. *Masking, disguising, concealing, hiding, camouflaging* are some of the most common synonyms used to describe it. Perhaps that is why the Barbie doll never adopted the veil. Sold in more than 140 countries around the world, the queen of the international toy market has assumed many different nationalities. Her multiethnic wardrobe has never included the veil, though.

19. In contrast, in modern publications the Muslim woman seems to be identified by the veil. Moroccan sociologist Fatima Mernissi writes: "The French and German publishers of my books always insist on having the word 'harem' on the cover and a photo of a veiled woman. When I protest, they tell me that this makes it sell better, even if the contents of the book contradict this image. It is time to unveil women on the covers of books that sell in the West" (*Islam and Democracy: Fear of the Modern World*, translated by Mary Jo Lakeland [London: Virago Press, 1993], 187 n. 10).

20. "Every man who prays or prophesies with his head covered dishonors his head, but every wife who prays or prophesies with her head uncovered dishonors her head, since it is the same as if her head were shaven. For if a wife will not cover her head, then she should cut her hair short. But since it is disgraceful for a wife to cut off her hair or shave her head, let her cover her head. For a man ought not to cover his head, since he is the image and glory of God, but woman is the glory of man. For man was not made from woman, but woman from man. Neither was man created for woman, but woman for man. That is why a wife ought to have a symbol of authority on her head, because of the angels" (I Cor. 11:4–10, English Standard Version translation).

21. For representation of Muslim women in the West, see Mohja Kahf, *Western Representations of the Muslim Woman: From Termagent to Odalisque* (Austin: Univ. of Texas Press, 1999); and Faegheh Shirazi, *The Veil Unveiled: The Hijab in Modern Culture* (Gainesville: Univ. Press of Florida, 2001).

22. Latifa, with Shékéba Hachemi, *My Forbidden Face: Growing Up under the Taliban: A Young Woman's Story* (London: Virago, 2002), 40.

23. Zoya, with John Follain and Rita Cristofari, *Zoya's Story: An Afghan Woman's Struggle for Freedom* (New York: Harper Collins, 2002), 209.

24. For women's association of the harem with incarceration, see, for instance, Fatima Mernissi's *Scheherazade Goes West: Different Cultures, Different Harems* (New York: Vintage, 2001).

25. Quoted in Gillian Whitlock, *Soft Weapons: Autobiography in Transit* (Chicago: Univ. of Chicago Press, 2007), 87.

26. Pamuk, *Snow,* 43.

27. Helena Andrews, "Muslim Women Don't See Themselves as Oppressed, Survey Finds," *New York Times,* June 8, 2006.

28. I started talking late in my childhood, and when I finally did, it was a jumbo-mumbo sort of a language. At the time, it was believed quail's eggs help children who cannot quite talk, so my grandfather brought me those tiny, little eggs in his turban. The poem "Turban/Nest" memorializes his magic and mystery:

His turban was the nest
Where my first words

Like my first memories
Were hatched.
The scene is etched on my life.
The doorbell rings
And in anticipation of his visit
I ran to the door.
My three-year-old hands can't reach the knob
I jump and jump again
And the door does not budge
I have to wait for a grown-up to free me.
As I finally see him enter
I hide in the welcoming folds of his brown abaya
And hold on to his foot to stop the world.
The world stops.
Later, much later
A lifetime of a cherished memory later
He bends down
And gently, ever so gently
Invites me out of my fortress
And as he reaches in the labyrinthine recesses of his black turban
—His magician's box—
I throw open the gates of my eyes
As my grandfather produces
Not a bird, but a bird's egg
—Key to my locked tongue
Treasure in my memory-trove.

29. "J. K. Rowling Interview: Transcripts about Snape," available at http://www.whysnape .tripod.com/rowlingtranscript.htm.

30. Quoted in Joan McKinney, "Cooksey: Expect Racial Profiling," *Advocate*, Sept. 19, 2001.

31. The publication of these twelve cartoons in Denmark in 2006 triggered violent, even deadly riots in more than a dozen Islamic countries. The controversy surrounding the cartoons addresses three troubling but interconnected issues. First, they reflect the social drama unfolding within Europe itself, mainly the presence of a large number of Muslim immigrants within its tightly knit communities. Second, the cartoons draw attention to the most volatile issues of concern within the Islamic community itself: violence, the representation of Islam in the West, and gender relations. And last, they focus on three of the most contentious symbols of strife between the Islamic and the Western worlds: the turban, the veil, and the sword or its modern counterpart, the bomb.

Bemoaning a culture of fear perpetrated by the "war on terror" in America, Zbigniew Brzezinski writes,

Government at every level has stimulated the paranoia. Consider, for example, the electronic billboards over interstate highways urging motorists to "Report Suspicious Activity" (drivers in turbans?). Some mass media have made their own contribution. The cable channels and some print media have found that horror scenarios attract audiences, while terror "experts" as "consultants" provide authenticity for the apocalyptic visions fed to the American public. Hence the proliferation of programs with bearded "terrorists" as the central villains. Their general effect is to reinforce the sense of the unknown but lurking danger that is said to increasingly threaten the lives of all Americans. ("Terrorized by 'War on Terror,'" *Washington Post*, Mar. 25, 2007)

32. Women writers have been at the forefront of this transformation shaking the foundations of Iranian society. They have inserted and asserted their presence in the public sphere. They have rejected the silent whispers in the privacy of their homes and refused to disappear into blank pages. Exercising increasing control over how reality is defined, they have redefined their own reality.

33. Sadeq Hedayat, *The Blind Owl*, translated by D. P. Costello (London: John Calder, 1957); Hushang Golshiri, *The Prince*, translated by James Buchan (London: Vintage, 2005).

34. Golshiri, *The Prince*, 28; subsequent citations are given as parenthetical page references in the text.

35. Fakhr eddin Shadman, *Taskhir-e Tammadon Farrangi* (Possessed by Western Culture) (Tehran: Majlis, 1947); Simin Daneshvar, *Savushun* (Persian Requiem) (Tehran: Kharazmi, 1969); Gollam Hossein Sa'edi, *Dandil* (Tehran: Javaneh, 1966).

36. Jalal Al-e Ahmad, *Plagued by the West*, translated by Paul Sprachman (Delmar, NY: Caravan Books, 1982), 70.

37. Jalal Al-e Ahmad, *Weststruckness*, translated by John Green and Ahmad Alizadeh (Lexington, KY: Mazda, 1982), 80.

38. Most Iranians thought the shah was manipulated by women around him, in particular by his twin sister, Princess Ashraf Pahlavi, but he insisted that not a single woman had ever influenced him.

39. Nikki R. Keddie, "Women and 30 Years of the Islamic Republic," *Payvand's Iran News*, Feb. 9, 2009, available at http://www.payvand.com/news/09/feb/1097.html.

40. In 1975, the illiteracy rate for women in Iran was a staggering 90 percent in rural areas and 45 percent in urban settings. The current nationwide literacy rate for women between the ages of fifteen and twenty-four is 97 percent. For the statistics, see the UNICEF Web site at http://www.unicef.org/infobycountry/iran_statistics.html.

41. The Persian language is the fourth most commonly used language in the blogosphere. Even President Mahmood Ahmadinejad has his own blog—and not only in Persian, but also translated into English, French, and Arabic.

42. For fascinating interviews with six of the forty-seven women who nominated themselves for president in the 2001 campaign, see Shahla Haeri's documentary film *Mrs. President: Women and Political Leadership in Iran* (2002), distributed by Films for the Humanities and Sciences.

43. In "Public Life and Women's Resistance," Heideh Moghissi writes: "The official statistics on the increased rate of divorce, often discussed in the Majles [Parliament], and the alarming increase in the number of suicides self-burning, indicate both women's suffering and discontent and their protest. According to the Director General of Iran's Forensic Medicine, in 1990 a total of 50 women died in Tehran as a result of self-burning. The figure reported for the first six months of 1991 was 40 deaths" (in *Iran after the Revolution: Crisis of an Islamic State,* edited by Saeed Rahnema and Sohrab Behdad [London: I. B. Tauris, 1996], 254).

44. Azar Nafisi, "Don't Ban Dan Brown," *The Guardian,* Nov. 25, 2006, available at http://www .azarnafisi.com/censorship.guardian.pdf. See also Azar Nafisi, *Reading Lolita in Tehran: A Memoir in Books* (New York: Random House, 2003).

### 1. ENCLOSED BODIES, TRAPPED VOICES, FRAMED IMAGES

1. [Abu Muhammad] Nizami-ye Ganjavi, *Layla and Majnun,* translated by Dr. R. Gelpke (Boulder, CO: Shambhala, 1978), 145.

2. Peter Chelkowski, *Mirror of the Invisible World: Tales from the Khamseh of Nizami* (New York: Metropolitan Museum of Art, 1975), 66.

3. In Orhan Pamuk's masterpiece *My Name Is Red,* the protagonist, Black, like Majnun, is punished for the unrestrained and open expression of his love for his cousin Shekure. Black's uncle and Shekure's father explains the Majnun-like punishment dispensed to the reckless lover in the following terms: "Black's affliction was the overwhelming passion of an ill-fated youth who had free access to our house, who was accepted and well liked in our home and who had the opportunity actually to see Shekure. He did not bury his love, as I hoped he would, but made the mistake of revealing his extreme passion to my daughter. As a result, he was forced to quit our house completely" (translated by Erdag M. Goknar [New York: Alfred A. Knopf, 2001], 24). Black, like Majnun, chooses exile and leaves Turkey for twelve years.

4. Nizami-ye Ganjavi, *Layla and Majnun,* 81.

5. For a study of insanity as a masculine recourse, see Kaveh Safa, "Madness as Masculine Prerogative in *Layla and Majnun,*" paper presented at the Shifting Boundaries conference, University of Virginia, Apr. 1995.

6. Nizami-ye Ganjavi, *Layla and Majnun,* 22.

7. Abol Qasem Ferdowsi, *The Tragedy of Sohrab and Rustam,* translated by Jerome Clinton (Seattle: Univ. of Washington Press, 1987), 17.

8. Chelkowski, *Mirror of the Invisible World,* 31.

9. According to Gayane Karen Merguerian and Afsaneh Najmabadi, "The pervasive and multiple lives of the Yusuf and Zulaykha story in so many genres of Islamic literature (in the broadest meaning of that term) do not simply arise from its religious sanction and its Qur'anic power. On the contrary, the story draws its attraction in part from its ability to travel between genres, and, in its travels, moves from being a story of a prophet, to a story about the guile of women, to a love story, to a moral tale. Through its citation in the Qur'an; in the books of commentary, history, mythohistory,

and ethics; in the mirror of princes; in love poetry; and in popular tales, it has come to saturate the cultural construction of gender in Islamic societies" ("Zulaykha And Yusuf: Whose 'Best Story'?" *International Journal of Middle East Studies* 29 [1997], 487).

10. As Julie Scott Meisami mentions, *Vis and Ramin* "has acquired international repute as the Persian analogue of the story of Tristan and Yseult. The love triangle is substantially the same (an aging king, his young bride, and her lover—here, the king's brother)" (*Medieval Persian Court Poetry* [Princeton, NJ: Princeton Univ. Press, 1987], 86).

11. Fakhr ed-Din As'ad Gurgani, *Vis and Ramin*, translated by George Morrison (New York: Columbia Univ. Press, 1972), 111. For a new and wonderful translation of this book, see Fakhraddin Gorgani, *Vis and Ramin*, translated by Dick Davis (Washington, DC: Mage, 2008).

12. Abdol Rahman-e Jami, *Yusuf-o-Zulaikha* (Yusuf and Zulaikha), edited, abridged, and translated by David Pendlebury (London: Octagon Press, 1980), 55.

13. Chelkowski, *Mirror of the Invisible World*, 22.

14. Geraldine Brooks, *Nine Parts of Desire* (New York: Anchor Books, 1995), 15.

15. Assia Djebar writes: "There is a traditional story told about the love between the prophet Muhammad and Zainab, the most beautiful of his wives. A story born from a single look. Zainab was married to Zaid, the adopted son of the Prophet. One day, the latter needed to speak with Zaid. And so he approached his tent. Zainab told him that Zaid was not there. She hid herself behind a tapestry, but a 'gust of wind lifted the curtain' and the young woman, scantily dressed, became visible to Muhammad, who retired, distraught. Zaid then sets Zainab free again. But Muhammad will have to wait until a Koranic verse intervenes, making the union with a former wife of an adopted son legitimate" (*Women of Algiers in Their Apartment*, translated by Marjolijin de Jager [Charlottesville: Univ. Press of Virginia, 1992], 153 n. 3).

16. Gurgani, *Vis and Ramin*, Morrison trans., 60.

17. Nizami-ye Ganjavi, *Layla and Majnun*, 53.

18. Jami, *Yusuf-o-Zulaikha*, 38.

19. Ibid., 81.

20. Nannies also appear frequently in contemporary women's writing. Taj al-Saltaneh, Simin Behbahani, Mahshid AmirShahi, and Simin Daneshvar, among many others, have talked extensively about nannies. The nannies' role in this body of writing, however, is quite different from their function in classical romances. In modern literature, nannies are mainly upholders of the status quo or village women who are loving and nurturing. At times, they are negatively portrayed. For instance, even though Taj al-Saltaneh loved her nanny as a child, she came to believe that their close relationship blighted any chance for a close bond to develop between her mother and herself (Taj al-Saltaneh, *Taj al-Saltaneh's Memoir*, 115). Simin Behbahani reminisces about her nanny in her autobiographical sketch: "Perhaps I owe this good health to the milk of that village wet-nurse who had two white, soft, warm udders instead of breasts, and nurtured me abundantly from those fountains of sweetness" ("We Await the Golden Dawn," in *A Cup of Sin: Selected Poems*, translated by Farzaneh Milani and Kaveh Safa [Syracuse, NY: Syracuse Univ. Press, 1999], xvii; for the original in

Persian, see "Ta Tolou'i Tala'i Chashm be Rah Darim," *Nimeye Digar* 2, no. 1 [Autumn 1993], special issue on Simin Behbahani, guest editor Farzaneh Milani: 169).

21. Although nannies were given parental responsibilities in upper-class and aristocratic families, their noteworthy presence in classical romances is neither confined to maternal roles nor accidental.

22. From antiquity to the Middle Ages, the figure of the nanny appears in many literary works of both the East and the West. The Spanish *alcahueta*, the Indian *sakhi*, the Middle Eastern *ajuz* (the crafty old woman in such popular tales as *The Thousand and One Nights* and *The Forty Parrots*), and the European go-between not only create both thematic and narrative possibilities but also form a fascinating East–West link from the early 1300s on. Some of the most formative and vital characters in early Western courtly literature depend on the nanny for the unraveling of the action. See Leyla Rouhi, "A Comparative Typology of the Medieval Go-Between in Light of Western-European, Near-Eastern, and Spanish Cases," Ph.D. diss., Harvard Univ., 1995.

23. William L. Hanaway, "Formal Elements in the Persian Popular Romances," *Review of National Literature* 2, no. 1 (Spring 1971), 158.

24. Abol Qasem Ferdowsi, *The Shahnameh of the Persian Poet Firdausi,* translated by James Atkinson, Esq. (London: Routledge, 1976), 56.

25. In her book *From Darkness into Light: Women's Emancipation in Iran,* Badr ol-Moluk Bamdad calls nannies "brokeresses" and writes: "The semi-imprisoned women, who had to stay in the house from dawn to dusk and seldom went out of doors, inevitably needed contacts with the outside world. These needs were met by brokeresses. . . . It was thanks to the brokeresses that the harem women could keep themselves quite well informed about events in the city and circumstances of other families. All considered, these walking and talking newspapers were a boon to the prisoners behind the harem walls" (translated and edited by F. R. C. Bagley [Hicksville, NY: Exposition Univ., 1977], 13).

26. Gurgani, *Vis and Ramin,* Morrison trans., 105.

27. Jami, *Yusuf-o-Zulaikha,* 18.

28. Gurgani, *Vis and Ramin,* Morrison trans., 84.

29. Ibid., 153.

30. Fatima Mernissi, *Beyond the Veil: Male–Female Dynamics in a Modern Muslim Society* (New York: Wiley, 1975), 5.

31. Dick Davis, "Introduction," in *The Legend of Seyavash,* by Abol Qasem Ferdowsi, translated by Dick Davis (London: Penguin, 1992), x.

32. Jami, *Yusuf-o-Zulaikha,* 637.

33. Islami Nudushan, "Tragic Figures in *Shahnameh,*" *Ettela'at,* Dec. 3, 1997.

34. The word *qayd* itself seems to be shifty. It can be positive, negative, even divine. It seems to assume its significance from its context. *Qayd* etymologically has a variety of meanings: "deceit," "fraud," "stratagem," "treachery," "warfare," "plotting mischief," and "applying a remedy," among others, illustrate its large semantic field (F. Steingass, *Persian–English Dictionary* [London: Routledge and Kegan Paul, 1977]). *Qayd* can even be a divine attribute. In the Qur'anic chapter in which the Egyptian ruler admonishes his wife and utters the often repeated verse 29, "Indeed your guile is

great," verse 76 links *qayd* with God, who "did devise a plan for Joseph." "There are at least thirty-four uses of the Arabic root K.Y.D. in the Qur'an, and a number of them refer to God's action," writes Shalom Goldman in *The Wiles of Women/The Wiles of Men* (New York: State Univ. of New York Press, 1995, 48).

35. Abdol Rahman Jami, "Yusuf-o-Zulaikha" (Yusuf and Zulaikha), in *Masnavi-ye Haft Owrang* (Seven Thrones), edited by Morteza Modaress Gilani (Tehran: Sa'di, 1958), 90.

36. Ferdowsi, *The Legend of Seyavash*, 18, 27.

37. See "Who Is Jahika?" in Katayoun Mazdapour, *One Thousand and One Nights' Delilah the Trickster*, new rev. version (Tehran: Rowshangaran, 1995).

38. In sura VII:19, Satan whispers to both Adam and Eve, and in sura 20:118 "Satan whispered to him saying, 'Adam, shall I point thee to the Tree of Eternity, and a Kingdom that decays not?'" (*The Koran Interpreted*, translated by Arthur Arberry [New York: Collier, 1995]).

39. Ibid., sura 20:119.

40. Orania Fallaci, *Interview with History*, translated by John Shepley (Boston: Houghton, 1977), 272.

41. Shahrnush Parsipur, *Sag va Zemestan-e Boland* (The Dog and the Long Winter) (Tehran: Amir Kabir, 1976), 156.

42. Forugh Farrokhzad, "Confession," in *Divar* (Wall) (Tehran: Amir Kabir, 1971), 70; for the sake of brevity in poem citations, I give only translated titles rather than both the original and the translation.

43. Aristotle, *History of Animals*, in *Works of Aristotle*, vol. 4, edited by J. A. Smith and W. D. Ross (Oxford, UK: Clarendon Press, 1910), 9.1.608b.

44. Murasaki Shikibu, *Tale of Genji* (New York: Random House, 1983).

45. Jean-Jacques Rousseau, *Emile or On Education*, translated by Allan Bloom (New York: Basic Books, 1979), 371.

46. Mary Wollstonecraft, *A Vindication of the Rights of Woman* (New York: Norton, 1967), 218.

47. Maureen Dowd, "Libido Games," *New York Times*, Mar. 18, 1998.

48. Although the nanny is not wanting in personality, character, or agency, not much ink is spilled to depict the details of her personal life. Is she married? Does she have children of her own? Is she literate? Has she ever been in love? Does she have a family, passion, or desire of her own? These questions are rarely addressed in these romances. It would be fascinating to rewrite these stories from the nanny's perspective and to rescue her from her objectification and eventual invisibility.

49. In spite of their key roles and their indispensable services to the most popular heroines in the Persian literary pantheon and to the authors who created them, nannies have been neglected for the most part in critical studies of Persian literature.

## 2. THE BONDS OF BEAUTY

1. Farzaneh Milani, "Lipstick Politics," *New York Times*, Aug. 19, 1999; Katherine Butler, "Lipstick Revolution: Iran's Women Are Taking on the Mullahs," *The Independent*, Feb. 26, 2009,

available at http://www.independent.co.uk/news/world/middle-east/lipstick-revolution-irans-women-are-taking-on-the-mullahs-1632257.html; Azadeh Moaveni, *Lipstick Jihad: A Memoir of Growing Up Iranian in America and American in Iran* (New York: Public Affairs, 2005).

2. Nancy Etcoff, "Why It Pays to Be a Babe," *Cosmopolitan* (Mar. 1999), 60. See also Nancy Etcoff, *Survival of the Prettiest: The Science of Beauty* (New York: Doubleday, 1999).

3. Deborah Rodriguez, with Kristin Ohlson, *Kabul Beauty School: An American Woman Goes Behind the Veil* (New York: Random House, 2007), 294, 288. "All women want to be beautiful," writes Rodriguez. "That is the bottom line. In the United States, women dress to attract the male and impress the female. In contrast, for Afghan women there is no necessity to attract men because marriages are arranged and the mingling of men and women is forbidden. Consequently, Afghan women dress for themselves, to impress other women, and to show their financial status. In Afghanistan, a beautiful woman is worth her weight in gold" (294).

4. "Ask anyone," writes Erica Goode, "it is better to be beautiful. To be a 'dish,' a 'knockout,' a 'babe.' To be an object of desire. To be the kind of woman who can silence a chattering room with a toss of her hair" ("Life's Wrinkles, Some of Them Ugly, Afflict the Beautiful, Too," *New York Times,* June 13, 1999). Many "studies have shown that people considered attractive fare better with parents and teachers, make more friends and more money, and have better sex with more (and more beautiful) partners" (Geoffrey Cowley, "The Biology of Beauty," *Newsweek,* June 3, 1996, 62). Nancy Etcoff has suggested that not only do "parents respond more affectionately to physically attractive newborns," but even infants at three months of age gaze "longer at attractive faces than at unattractive faces" (*Survival of the Prettiest,* 24).

5. As Ani DiFranco says in the "32 Flavors" song, "God help you if you are an ugly girl / course too pretty is also your doom / cause everyone harbors a secret hatred / for the prettiest girl in the room" (*Not a Pretty Girl* [Righteous Babe Records, 1995]). Nevertheless, the penalties confronted by unattractiveness are often exorbitant. Toni Morrison writes with breathtaking precision in her first novel, *The Bluest Eye,* about the costs that may attend ugliness, especially in a woman, by tracing the journey of her protagonist, Pecola Breedlove, to insanity. "Long hours," writes Morrison, Pecola "sat looking in the mirror, trying to discover the secret of the ugliness, the ugliness that made her ignored or despised at school, by teachers and classmates alike" ([New York: Pocket Books, 1970], 39). With regard to men, it has been suggested that it is often their height that is rewarding. "As study after study has shown," writes Natalie Angier, "tall men give nearly all the orders, win most elections, monopolize girls and monopolies, and disproportionately splay their elongated limbs across the cushy unconfines of first-class cabins. By the simple act of striding into a room, taller than average men are accorded a host of positive attributes having little or nothing to do with height: a high IQ, talent, competence, trustworthiness, even kindness" ("Short Men, Short Shrift: Are Drugs the Answer?" *New York Times,* June 22, 2003).

6. Andrea Dworkin, *Woman-Hating* (New York: Dulton, 1974), 113.

7. Susan Bordo, "Material Girl," in *Unbearable Weight: Western Culture, Feminism, and the Body,* 245–75 (Berkeley and Los Angeles: Univ. of California Press, 1993).

8. Butler, "Lipstick Revolution."

9. Plastic surgery has found its way into modern Persian literature. In a poem about face-lifts, Simin Behbahani writes:

I gave my face to the scalpel
to make it young perhaps,
to make it an object of admiration
in the eyes of everyone.
The heart with a pretty face thirty years ago
wants the same now in its old age.
    "I Gave My Face to the Scalpel" (in *A Cup of Sin*, 9).

10. Elaine Sciolino, "Iran's Well-Covered Women Remodel a Part That Shows," *New York Times*, Sept. 22, 2000.

11. Fatema Soudavar Farmanfamaian, "Haft Qalam Arayish: Cosmetics in the Iranian World," *Iranian Studies* 33, nos. 2–4 (Summer–Fall 2000), 298.

12. Salman Rushdie, *Shame* (New York: Vintage, 1983), 34.

13. Shahrnush Parsipur, *Zanan bedun-e Mardan* (Women Without Men) (Tehran: Noqreh, 1989), 50.

14. Remarkably, although it has been argued that the veil frees women from the tyranny of beauty and fashion or the commodification of their bodies, it has also been claimed with equal conviction that the veil enhances feminine beauty.

15. In "Three Essays on the Theory of Sexuality," Sigmund Freud notes that "the progressive concealment of the body which goes with civilization keeps sexual curiosity awake." He further remarks that he has no doubt "the concept of 'beautiful' has its roots in sexual excitation and that its original meaning was 'sexually stimulating'" (in *The Freud Reader*, edited by Peter Gay [New York: Norton, 1989], 251.). This chapter does not engage the origins of the experience of beauty or its psychoanalysis.

16. An estimated twenty-five hundred feet of material goes into the making of Kiswah, which weighs around five thousand pounds.

17. Barbara Freyer Stowasser, *Women in the Quran, Traditions, and Interpretation* (New York: Oxford Univ. Press, 1994), 29.

18. Quoted in Hamid Dabashi, *Close Up: Iranian Cinema, Past, Present, and Future* (London: Verso, 2001), 88.

19. Quoted in Zohreh T. Sullivan, "Iranian Cinema and the Critique of Absolutism," in *Media, Culture, and Society in Iran: Living with Globalization and the Islamic State*, edited by Mehdi Semati (London: Routledge, 2008), 193.

20. Iraj Mirza, untitled poem, in *Divan* (Collected Poems) (Tehran: Mozafari, n.d.), 128–39.

21. This poem is not only about a man seduced by and seducing a veiled woman, but also about competition among men—a central issue in the institution of veiling. Although physically absent,

the husband is a vital presence in the poem. The reader might not learn much about the veiled woman's personal life. Her marital status, however, is underlined.

22. For another reading of this poem, see Afsaneh Najmabadi, "Veiled Discourse—Unveiled Body," *Feminist Studies* 19, no. 3 (Fall 1993), 510–11.

23. Jalal Al-e Ahmad, *Occidentosis: A Plague from the West*, translated by R. Campbell, edited by Hamid Algar (Berkeley, CA: Mizan, 1984), 70.

24. Ali Shari'ati, *Fatemeh Fatemeh Ast* (Fatemeh Is Fatemeh) (Tehran: n.p., n.d.), 78.

25. Ali Shari'ati, *Zan* (Woman) (Tehran: n.p., 1983), 76.

26. Some of Hedayat's books have been banned inside the country in recent years. Robert Tait writes, "Publication rights have been withdrawn for *The Cock*, a novel by Ebrahim Golestan, an Iranian writer based in Britain, and for all works by Sadegh Hedayat, a pre-revolutionary novelist and commentator whose books are renowned in several European countries. Some Iranian writers have vowed to withhold future books for publication" ("Bestsellers Banned in New Iranian Censorship Purge," *The Guardian*, Nov. 17, 2006). But as Faraj SarKouhi maintains, "Some of Hedayat's works were banned from being published even before this newly raised fever of censorship, but the efforts made last year by numerous publishers and family members of Hedayat regarding the republication of an uncensored version of the novel *The Blind Owl* once again failed to clear the barricade of censorship" ("Iran: Book Censorship the Rule, Not the Exception," Radio Free Europe/Radio Liberty, Nov. 26, 2007). And Hedayat's official Web site has a list of his books published in significantly altered forms, among which is *The Blind Owl*.

27. Hedayat, *The Blind Owl*, Costello trans., 67.

28. Sadeq Hedayat, *Buf-e Kur* (The Blind Owl) (Tehran: Amir Kabir, 1973), 68.

29. Hedayat, *The Blind Owl*, Costello trans., 103.

30. Hedayat repeatedly argued that his two favorite writers, Khayyam and Kafka, resorted to the past as a refuge and a shelter from their society. In *Payam-e Kafka* (Kafka's Message), he writes: "It should not be forgotten that when Kafka desires to portray the essence of a human being, he must resort to images from ancient society" ([Tehran: Amir Kabir, 1963], 47). In his introduction to *Songs of Khayyam*, he reiterates the same point: "From Khayyam's angry laughter and allusions to Iran's past, it is apparent that he hates the brigand Arabs and their vulgar ideas from the bottom of his heart" (quoted in Leonard Bogle, "The Khayyamic Influence in *The Blind Owl*," in *Hedayat's "The Blind Owl" Forty Years After*, edited by Michael C. Hillman [Austin: Univ. of Texas Press, 1978], 89).

31. Sadeq Hedayat, *Nayrangestan* (Tehran: Parastu, 1965), 18.

32. Hedayat, *The Blind Owl*, Costello trans., 24; subsequent citations to this translation are given as parenthetical page references in the text. Many passages in *The Blind Owl* that evoke a nostalgic revival of the Zoroastrian era are mingled with strong anti-Islamic statements. In the narrator's own bitter words, "As for mosques, the muezzin's call to prayer, the ceremonial washing of the body and rinsing of the mouth, not to mention the pious practice of bobbing up and down in honor of a high and mighty Being, the omnipotent Lord of all things, with whom it is impossible to have a chat except in the Arabic language—these things left me cold" (91).

33. In his critical analysis of *Vis-o-Ramin* (Vis and Ramin), Hedayat objects to some of Gorgani's historical distortions and indiscriminate confusion of pre- and post-Islamic observances, such as the portrayal of Zoroastrian women wearing the veil. Hedayat was convinced veiling is strictly an Islamic institution (Sadeq Hedayat, *Neveshtehay-e Parakandeh* [The Scattered Writings] [Tehran: Amir Kabir, 1965], 494).

34. Elton Daniel, "History as a Theme of the Blind Owl," in Hillman, ed., *Hedayat's 'The Blind Owl' Forty Years After*, 77.

35. Sadeq Hedayat, *Parvin, Dokhtar-e Sassan* (Parvin: Sassan's Daughter) (Tehran: Amir Kabir, 1963), 7. "Early into the night before last, our army attacked yours by surprise near the Suran River," says an Arab to Parvin, "they battled fiercely and the Iranians fought courageously till death" (49). Hedayat locates the time and setting of this final revolt "in the midst of Arab-Iranian war around the year 22 of hegirat, in the city of Rey (raga), near Tehran of Today" (7).

36. For an English translation of this short story, see Sadeq Hedayat, "The Doll Behind the Curtain," in *Sadeq Hedayat: An Anthology*, translated by Ahmad Karimi-Hakkak, edited by Ehsan Yarshater, 127–36 (Boulder, CO: Westview Press, 1979); the quotations given in the chapter are from this translation and are cited parenthetically by page number in the text.

37. Differing standards of feminine and masculine beauty ideals continue to produce gender differentiation. The toy industry, for instance, still replicates the boundary that divides men and women. The "girls section," often pink in appearance, consists mainly of dolls and feminine accessories, such as makeup and clothing. On the blue side, there is an abundance of cars, trucks, and a whole array of weaponry. Each section can have its own color code and semantic field as well. The pink is associated with the inside, nurturing, and beauty. The blue—the color of the sky—has its distinct lexicon: war and speed, among others.

38. "Perhaps women were once so dangerous that they had to have their feet bound," writes Maxine Hong Kingston (*Woman Warrior: Memoirs of a Girlhood among Ghosts* [New York: Vintage, 1989], 19).

39. Bound feet and the toe shoes of ballerinas standing on point look astoundingly similar. Generally speaking, even today, ballerinas wear toe shoes, but male dancers rarely do.

40. Feng Jicai, *The Three-Inch Lotus*, translated by David Wakefield (Honolulu: Univ. of Hawaii Press, 1994), 2.

41. Why, then, did the painful practice of foot binding last so long? Why did successive attempts to abolish it in China meet with failure? What strategies succeeded to finally eradicate it? As early as 1642, penalties were imposed on practitioners of foot binding. Three years later the law had to be rescinded. In 1847 and more than half a century later, in 1911, two new interdictions were issued. No legislative challenge seemed to be strong enough to pose a serious threat to the institution, at least not until an anti-foot-binding movement developed nationally and a sizeable number of people denounced the practice. By the twentieth century, however, "Natural-Foot" societies sprang up throughout China. They identified foot binding as a crippler of half of the country's population and recognized its eradication as a benefit to women and for the whole country. Bound feet no longer signified beauty or status; rather, they were now considered symbols of decadence, oppression,

impracticality, and undesirability. And when the issue changed from a strictly legislative mandate or the nation-state's interest to include a woman's basic rights, when the narrative that depicted feminine beauty changed, foot binding was successfully abolished in 1949, the year the Communists took over.

42. For a detailed portrayal of these beauty contests, see Jicai, *The Three-Inch Lotus.*

43. Dorothy Ko, *Cinderella's Sisters: A Revisionist History of Footbinding* (Berkeley and Los Angeles: Univ. of California Press, 2005), 189.

44. Over the course of a life, the "foot will flex, stretch and contract some 300 million times, yet remain functionally intact. With every step it will bear weight of 125 to 200 pounds, a cumulative total of some 1,000 tons a day, and 25 million tons over a lifetime. And in that span it will carry the average person anywhere from 150,000 to 250,000 miles" (William Rossi, *The Sex Life of the Foot and Shoe* [Hertfordshire, UK: Wordsworth Editions, 1977], 65).

45. In "Consequences of Foot Binding among Older Women in Beijing, China," Steven R. Cummings, Xu Ling, and Katie Stone maintain, "Women with bound feet were more likely to fall, less able to squat, and less able to stand up from a chair without assistance than women with normal feet. . . . Women with bound feet are infrequently seen on city streets. They tend to stay indoors and in residential alleys not commonly visited by tourists" (*American Journal of Public Health* [Oct. 7, 1997], 1677).

46. Quoted in Mary Daly, *Gyn/Ecology: The Metaethics of Radical Feminism* (Boston: Beacon Press, 1978), 142.

47. Ko, *Cinderella's Sisters,* 232.

48. Patricia Buckley Ebrey, *The Inner Quarter: Marriage and the Lives of Chinese Women during the Sung Period* (Berkeley and Los Angeles: Univ. of California Press, 1993), 41.

49. For Yexian, the Chinese Cinderella, see Dorothy Ko, *Every Step a Lotus: Shoes for Bound Feet* (Berkeley and Los Angeles: Univ. of California Press, 2001), 27–28.

50. Although a remarkably thin Barbie might look quite different from the voluptuous fertility goddesses, "A low waist–hip ratio is one of the few features that a long, lean Barbie doll shares with a plump, primitive fertility icon." In other words, "if our ideas of size change from one time and place to the next, our taste in shape is amazingly stable" (Cowley, "The Biology of Beauty," 66).

51. Doll collecting is the second-most-popular collecting hobby in America (the first is stamp collecting). Dolls are not inconsequential playthings. They can assume an important role in disseminating values, beliefs, and norms. They reflect attitudes about childhood, roles for men and women, and family values. Dolls were first used in rituals and ceremonies and endowed with religious or cultural significance. It was not until A.D. 1700 that the word *doll* was used for a toy. Manufactured dolls were often for adults. It was in 1820 that baby dolls began to be mass-produced for girls. Barbie collecting has spawned a whole industry. Barbie at one time had her own personal museum—the Barbie Hall of Fame in Palo Alto, California. She has a devoted army of dealers, restorers, auctioneers, convention organizers, marketers, display box designers, appraisers, and groupies. A growing publishing industry revolves around her. Authorized and unauthorized biographies, oral-history projects, poems and artworks inspired by her, and scholarly books proliferate.

52. There was one year, 1970, when after eleven years of standing tirelessly on her toes, her tiny feet flattened out. But this did not last long. The next year Barbie returned to her more familiar and popular pose: on tiptoe. Shaming all shoe fetishists, she owns a large and amazing variety of footwear.

53. Etcoff, *Survival of the Prettiest*, 12.

54. Linda von Wartburg, "Like Cinderella's Sisters, Many People with Diabetes Squeeze Big Feet into Small Shoes," *DiabetesHealth,* Jan. 1, 2008, available at http://www.diabeteshealth.com/read/2008/01/01/5592.html.

55. The German sex doll "Bild Lilli" was conceived as a playgirl by the German cartoonist Reinhard Beithien for the daily newspaper *Bild Zeitung* in July 1952. Lilli, the cartoon character, became a sensation. Three years later, in 1955, a three-dimensional doll replaced the cartoon. She proved to be a big hit and a successful business venture. Ruth and Eliot Handler, the original owners of Mattel Corporation, the manufacturer of Barbie, saw the three-dimensional Lilli during a trip to Germany, liked her, and bought all the rights to her.

56. Whereas the government in Washington worries about the nuclear threat from Iran, government officials in Tehran worry about the cultural threat from Barbie, Batman, and Spider-Man. Iran's prosecutor general Ghorban Ali Dori Najafabadi warned Iranian officialdom in 2008 about the "culturally destructive" impact of Batman, Spider-Man, Harry Potter, and Barbie on Iranian society. "The irregular importation of such toys, which unfortunately arrive through unofficial sources and smuggling, is destructive culturally and a social danger," he stated in a letter to Iran's vice president Parviz Davoudi. He continued: "The displays of personalities such as Barbie, Batman, Spider-Man and Harry Potter . . . are all warning bells to the officials in the cultural arena" ("Iran Calls for Ban on Barbie Doll," *BBC News,* Apr. 28, 2008, available at http://www.news.bbc.co.uk/2/hi/7371771.stm). So who are these culturally lethal foes?

Mattel Inc.'s Barbie doll has already been deported from Iran once before. With great fanfare and much publicity, the Islamic republic deported Barbie in 1996. This was part of an ongoing campaign to purify the native culture of all vestiges of Western values. Compared to the Trojan Horse, Barbie was considered a powerful agent of corruption and a serious threat to Islamic values. To indoctrinate Iranian children properly and assert local values and ideals, Barbie was replaced—quite unsuccessfully—by an "indigenous" and fully covered doll named "Sara." What Barbie flaunted, Sara would cover. If Barbie wore indecent clothes, Sara would be a symbol of modesty and morality. If Barbie's companion was her boyfriend, Ken, Sara would be accompanied by her brother, Dara. If Barbie was obsessed with looks and thinness, Sara, it was claimed, would develop her mind and be appreciated for who she was rather than how she looked.

With the veil as her most defining feature, Sara would islamicize beauty by rejecting the "Barbie Look," a Euro-American standard of beauty. She would not only reject the universalism and homogenizing forces of Western beauty, she would also assert an independent Islamic/Iranian identity.

But Barbie didn't stay away from Iran; she returned, accompanied by two unrelated masked men: Batman and Spider-Man. The inclusion of these male characters in the list of "warning bells" to the Islamic Republic is no coincidence. Masculinity has been a highly charged concern of the Iranian regime since the Islamic Revolution in 1979.

57. Cindy Jackson, *Living Doll* (London: Trafalgar Square, 2002).

58. Bordo, *Unbearable Weight,* 168.

59. Naomi Wolf, *The Beauty Myth: How Images of Beauty Are Used Against Women* (New York: Anchor, 1992), 10.

60. Mary Pipher, *Reviving Ophelia: Saving the Selves of Adolescent Girls* (New York: Ballantine, 1995), 12.

61. Joan Jacobs Brumberg, *The Body Project: An Intimate History of American Girls* (New York: Random House, 1997), xxiv.

62. *Aladdin* (directed by Ron Clements and John Musker, 1992).

### 3. *PARDEH NESHIN,* OR "SHE WHO SITS BEHIND THE SCREEN"

1. Ali Akbar Dehkhoda, *Loghat Nameh Dehkhoda* (Tehran: Tehran University Press, 1959), no. 7, 202.

2. The word *mahram* fittingly signifies a person who has access to women's quarters and is a confidant. Likewise, *pardeh bargereftan* and *pardeh bardashtan* mean "to lift a curtain" and "to divulge a secret."

3. M. Ali Issari, *Cinema in Iran, 1900–1979* (Metuchen, NJ: Scarecrow Press, 1989), 60.

4. Quoted in ibid., 388.

5. Quoted in Reza Tahami, "Iranian Women Make Films," *Film International Quarterly* 2, no. 3 (Summer 1994), 4.

6. Mohsen Makhmalbaf, "Limbs of No Body: The World's Indifference to the Afghan Tragedy," *Monthly Review* 53, no. 6 (Nov. 2001), 57.

7. In 1998, the Iranian Parliament considered a law to segregate health services. "In the early 1980s, Ayatollah Khomeini, the supreme leader (Imam) of Iran, said that the physical examination of female patients by male gynecologists violated religious rules. Although it was not possible to suspend the licenses of all male gynecologists, no new male residents were accepted into the specialty from that time, and the number of male gynecologists is dwindling. The country has also begun introducing female-only hospitals that men are not permitted to enter" (Dr. Pijman Azarmina, "In Iran, Gender Segregation Becoming a Fact of Medical Life," *Canadian Medical Association Journal* 166, no. 5 [Mar. 5, 2002], 645).

8. Salman Rushdie, *Midnight's Children* (New York: Avon, 1982), 19.

9. Issari, *Cinema in Iran,* 40.

10. Ja'far Shahri, *Tarikh-e Ejtema'iy-e Tehran dar Gharn-e Sizdahum* (The Social History of Tehran in the Thirteenth Century) (Tehran: Rasa, 1990), 391.

11. In her seminal article on male spectatorship, "Visual Pleasure and Narrative in Cinema," Laura Mulvey argues that "the place of the look defines cinema. . . . Going far beyond highlighting a woman's to-be-looked-at-ness, cinema builds the way she is to be looked at into the spectacle

itself" (*Visual and Other Pleasures* [Bloomington: Indiana Univ. Press, 1989], 26). My focus here is not on how the representation of women is in effect a function of men's desire, how they serve as an object of male fantasy, what voyeuristic pleasures are embodied in the unraveling of scenes, or how a scene is composed or organized for the male gaze. I am simply referring to the religiously unlawful look—for men and women alike.

12. Abdelwahab Bouhdiba, *Sexuality in Islam* (London: Saqi Books, 1989), 37.

13. A rare but telling example is the story of an old respectable clergyman who refused to leave his home after the compulsory unveiling act of 1936. "He finally died at his house without ever going outdoors during all those years. Reza Khan [Reza Shah Pahlavi] had compelled women to be unveiled and [the man] regarded it as forbidden to cast his eyes upon unveiled women" (Gh. Haddad Adel, "Clothing and the Secret of the Self," *Mahjubah* 3, nos. 4–6 [Aug.–Oct. 1983], 62). A more recent example is the widely circulated joke in Iran after Anousheh Ansari, the Iranian-born female business executive, went into space as a private explorer in 2006. Muslim clerics, it was rumored, "were refusing to look into the sky for the moon so that they could announce the beginning of Ramadan because they feared seeing the amateur astronaut without her veil" (Nazila Fathi, "A Tourist in Space Becomes a Star in Iran," *New York Times*, Oct. 25, 2006).

14. Quoted in Mernissi, *Beyond the Veil*, 141.

15. Sheikh Zabihollah Mahalati, *Kashf-ol Ghorur ya Mafased-ol Sofur* (Learning about Vanity or the Evils of Unveiling) (Tehran: Askari, 1959), 9.

16. Ayatollah Ali Moravveji, *Feqh dar A'iney-e Cinema* (Islamic Jurisprudence in the Mirror of Cinema) (Tehran: Howzey-e Honari, 1999), 82.

17. According to Sarah Graham-Brown, "The Ottoman Sultan issued a decree in November 1900 banning the importation and sale of certain kinds of photographs. He specifically mentioned the following kind of photographs: 'bearing the names of God or Muhammad; pictures of the Kaaba or any other images relating to the holy city of Mecca; Muslim buildings and ceremonies; and portraits of women'" (*Images of Women* [London: Quartet, 1988], 45).

18. Moravveji, *Islamic Jurisprudence*, 82.

19. Halaleh, the strong-minded lead woman in the film *Takhteh Siyah* (Blackboard, 2000) by Samira Makhmalbaf, articulates the importance of the mother–son relationship in Iranian culture. "My heart," she says, "is like a train wagon which many people get on and off at every station. There is, however, one who never gets off, and that is my son."

20. *Abi-o-Ravi* (Abi and Ravi, 1930) was the first Iranian feature film. A silent, black-and-white comedy, it was about men, made by men, and intended for men.

21. This objection to women's acting was not restricted to Iran. For instance, the first Syrian feature film made in 1928 was reshot at great expense with a German replacing the Muslim actress. The ulama, writes Elizabeth Thompson, "protested to French censors against the performance of a Muslim woman as the heroine, despite her family's approval" (Elizabeth Thompson, *Colonial Citizens: Republican Rights, Paternal Privilege, and Gender in French Syria and Lebanon* [New York: Columbia Univ. Press, 1999], 202).

22. Simin Behbahani, *Ba Ghalb-e Khod che Kharidam?* (What Did I Buy with My Heart?) (Tehran: Sokhan, 1996), 177.

23. In his movie *Nassereddin Shah Actor-e Cinema* (Once upon a Time Cinema, 1992), director Mohsen Makhmalbaf depicts the Qajar king, who has some eighty-four wives and concubines, as falling madly in love with Golnar.

24. Saminejad had a minor role in a second movie, another talkie directed by Sepanta, *Shirin and Farhad* (1934).

25. "Bombay Films for Persia," *Evening News of India,* Aug. 31, 1935.

26. "The Black Eyes," *Bombay Chronicle,* Aug. 4, 1935.

27. "Iranian Film Enterprise," *Times of India,* Aug. 13, 1935.

28. Dr. F. Dowlatshah, "Chance Encounter: Surprise Meeting Evokes Memories of Childhood," *Persian Heritage* 2, no. 6 (Summer 1997), 39–40.

29. "From Roots to Clichés," *Tavoos* (Peacock) 7, nos. 5–6 (Autumn 2000–Winter 2001): 284–93.

30. Sepanta significantly chose two of the most popular and highly revered Iranian romances for his films. *Shirin and Farhad* depicts the love of the Iranian king Khosrow Parviz for the beautiful Armenian princess Shirin and his betrayal of Farhad, the sculptor who is his rival for Shirin's affections. *Layli and Majnun,* based on a legendary love story, revolves around the poet Qays's love madness for his childhood classmate Layli. Qays becomes intoxicated with love to the point of insanity—hence his nickname, "Majnun" (the Mad One)—which prevents him from being united with the woman he loves. Sorrow stricken, he leaves the company of men. After much agony and wandering, he dies and is united with Layli only in death.

31. Carolyn See, "A Family—and a Country—Torn Apart," *Washington Post,* Oct. 13, 2006.

32. Nahid Rachlin, *Persian Girls* (New York: Tarcher/Penguin, 2006), 43, 96.

33. Shusha Guppy, *The Blindfold Horse: Memories of a Persian Childhood* (Boston: Beacon Press, 1998), 169.

34. Shahla Lahiji, "Portrayal of Women in Iranian Cinema: An Historical Overview," *Iran Bulletin* (n.d.), available at http://www.iran-bulletin.org/art/CINEMA2.html.

35. Ibid.

36. Hamid Naficy, "Islamizing Film Culture in Iran: A Post-Khatami Update," in *The New Iranian Cinema: Politics, Representation, and Identity,* edited by Richard Tapper (London: I. B. Tauris, 2002), 27.

37. Even today, there are no movie theaters in Saudi Arabia, where the production or public viewing of films is prohibited. The Taliban banned cinema as soon as they came into power.

38. Farrokh Ghaffary, "History of Cinema in Persia," in *Encyclopaedia Iranica,* edited by Ehsan Yarshater (New York: Bibliotheca Persica Press, 1991), 5:fascicle 6, 571.

39. The appearance of a woman who ran, chased animals, and played an active, lead role in Bahram Beyzai's film *Bashu, the Little Stranger* (1989) is a watershed in postrevolutionary Iranian cinema. In the absence of her husband, who is fighting in the Iran-Iraq War, Nai lives with her

children in a rural northern village. As a farmer, she can ill afford immobility. By force of circumstances, she is unfettered by spatial constraints.

40. Hamid Naficy, "Veiled Vision/Powerful Presences: Women in Post-Revolutionary Iranian Cinema," in *Life and Art: The New Iranian Cinema*, edited by Rose Issa and Sheila Whitaker (London: National Film Theatre, 1999), 45.

41. Hamid Naficy, "Islamizing Film Culture in Iran," in *Iran: Political Culture in the Islamic Republic*, edited by Samih Farsoun and Mehrdad Mashayekhi (London: Routledge, 1992), 179.

42. Ayatollah Ruhollah Khomeini, "Address at Bihisht-I Zahra," in *Islam and Revolution: Writings and Declarations of Imam Khomeini*, translated and annotated by Hamid Alghar (London: KPI, 1985), 258.

43. Quoted in Dabashi, *Close Up*, 182.

44. Donald Clarke, "Moving Pictures," *Irish Times*, July 30, 2001.

45. Tahami, "Iranian Women Make Films," 4.

46. Elaine Sciolino, *Persian Mirrors: The Elusive Face of Iran* (New York: Free Press, 2000). 249.

47. Quoted in Leslie Camhi, "Daughter of Iran, Shades of Her Father," *New York Times*, Feb. 21, 1999.

48. In the film *Farrari* (Runaway, 2001) by Kim Longinotto and Ziba Mir-Hosseini, the officials in charge of a house of refuge for runaway girls in Tehran repeatedly warn their residents against the dangers of leaving home. "All men are wolves," cautions one woman. "Thieves will be happy to cut up a runaway girl for her organs," says another.

49. Comparing the mingling of men and women to the proximity of fire and cotton is not Gorban Ali's invention. It appears in several literary texts as well. For instance, Yusuf, tricked into a meeting with Zulaikha, the woman who passionately loves him, implores her to let him go. "It distresses me," he tells her, "to be alone with you and hidden from view; for you are a blazing fire, and I am a wisp of dry cotton" (Jami, *Yusuf-o-Zulaykha*, Pendlebury trans., 80).

50. When Sheila Johnston asked director Samira Makhmalbaf about the mythical significance of the recurring image of the apple, he said: "The apple in Iranian poetry is the symbol of life and knowledge, as in the biblical story of Adam and Eve. . . . We have a similar story in the Koran. But I found this element in the children's own world, I didn't just invent it. Everyone was so worried about their future, but when I looked at them they were just eating apples and enjoying life. So I decided to keep the apples in the narrative to the end" (Sheila Johnston, "Quietly Ruling the Roost," *Sight and Sound* 9, no. 1 [Jan. 1999], 18).

51. A remarkably similar scene is depicted in the movie *Aladdin*. The first time Jasmine, the lead female character, leaves the palace, she picks an apple from the cart of a fruit vendor and gives it to a boy. Little does she know the punishment for her "stealing" act might be the chopping off of her hand.

52. Samira Makhmalbaf has openly identified with the twin girls. She told Irene Matthews, "I could be these girls. . . . These girls could be me" (quoted in Irene Matthews, "The Apple," *International Journal of Humanities and Peace* 17, no. 1 [2001], 102). And she commented elsewhere, "I think I was drawn to the story because it's about the relationship between fathers and daughters.

And we [Samira and Mohsen Makhmalbaf] are trying to resolve that relationship too, because we are father and daughter as well" (quoted in Johnston, "Quietly Ruling the Roost," 20).

53. Quoted in Johnston, "Quietly Ruling the Roost," 18.

54. Quoted in Camhi, "Daughter of Iran, Shades of her Father," 21.

55. Quoted in Johnston, "Quietly Ruling the Roost," 20.

56. In a sex-segregated society, men and women experience, albeit to different degrees, spatial restrictions. The first vignette ends with Hassan watching, from behind bars, the departure of his childhood friend. Both the prisoner-to-be and the warden-to-be are bound by the prison.

57. Constance Bacon, "Festival 2000: 36th Chicago International Film Festival," formerly available at http://www.chicagofilmfestival.com/news/interview_dayibecameawoman.html.

58. Regarding the open-endedness of the last scene, director Meshkini told Constance Bacon: "I don't try to make a judgment or provide a resolution for the audience. Because different audiences may have different resolutions. Even in my country, they may have different conclusions. If a woman fights, she may get somewhere—she may get the freedom. But if it is happening in Afghanistan, probably the woman will go back home and that's the end for her. That's the end for the woman. In another country maybe something else will happen" (quoted in ibid.).

59. Iranian films that feature cross-dressing in their plots range from the comedy *Adam Barfi* (Snowman, 1995, directed by Davoud Mirbaqueri) to the serious *Baran* (Rain, 2001, directed by Majid Majidi) and include such diverse titles as *Offside* (2006, directed by Ja'far Panahi); *Dokhtaran Khorshid* (Daughters of the Sun, 2000, directed by Maryam Shahriar); and *Dokhtar-e Tondar* (A Girl Called Tondar, 2000, directed by Hamaya Petracian).

60. With her minimalist but revelatory approach, Shirin Neshat portrays the ban on women's public singing in *Turbulent* (1998), winner of the Golden Lion at the Venice Biennial. *Turbulent*

features two screens on which two separate worlds are presented. In one, a man, masterfully performed by Shoja Azari, sings a passionate love song by Rumi, the 13-century Iranian mystic and the best selling poet in America. On the other, the gifted vocalist/composer Susan Deyhim sings in isolation to a hauntingly empty concert hall. With her body covered, her voice muffled, she patiently waits her turn. And as soon as Azari completes his song, her caged voice takes full flight. She sings to the world and the world listens. And turbulence arises. Untied to language or rules, she hums, squeals, howls, grunts, reaches for the microphone, wails, moans. With all the powers of suppressed passion, she conveys feelings more eloquent than any words, more universal than any language. Her song is a tapestry of voices, a mosaic of primal utterances. Now rhythmic, like the beating of a heart, now intense, like the voice of love, anger, or fear, now pleading, sobbing, and mournfully lamenting, now ecstatic and orgasmic, it is the song of a soul. Filled with intensity, it cannot be regulated or censored. The male singer and his all-male audience are awe-struck, transfixed into wondering silence. (Farzaneh Milani, "The Visual Poetry of Shirin Neshat," in *Shirin Neshat* [Milan, Italy: Charta, 2001], 8)

61. Although cross-dressing remains forbidden and now illegal, men and women who desire sex-change operations are paradoxically allowed to seek medical intervention. They can apply for revised birth certificates indicating their new identity. They can marry in their newly acquired gender. The Imam Khomeini Charity Foundation provides loans to those seeking and "needing" sex operations. One cleric, Hojatolislam Karimian, has suggested that changing gender when one is trapped in the "wrong" body is a human right. Reliable statistics regarding the total number of sex transitioners in Iran today are hard to come by, but one physician in Tehran claims to have operated on more than three hundred men and women in the past decade. The religious authorization and subsequent legalization of transsexual operations in Iran are based on the belief that gender-identity "disorders" need to be corrected and the collapse of traditional prohibitions and classifications avoided. Like the ban on cross-dressing, these official acts want to keep the lines between the genders clearly demarcated.

62. In an interview with director Panahi, David Walsh asked: "Just so there is no misunderstanding—I don't think that the metaphor of the world as a prison is just appropriate for women, or only for Iran. I don't see it as a film merely about Iran, but about conditions everywhere. Such a metaphor does suggest that the world needs to be changed. Would you like us to draw that conclusion?" Ja'far Panahi's answer expanded the boundaries of captivity beyond gender and politics. "In my view, everyone in the world lives within a circle, either due to economic, political, cultural, or family problems or traditions. The radius of the circle can be smaller or larger. Regardless of their geographic location, they live within a circle. I hope that if this film has any kind of effect on anyone, it would be to make them try to expand the size of the radius" (David Walsh, "An Interview with Ja'far Panahi, director of *The Circle*," available at http://www.wsws.org/articles/2003/sep2003/pana-s17.shtml).

63. David Denby, "Women on the Run," *The New Yorker* (Apr. 23–30, 2001), 196.

64. Ja'far Panahi believes that an "element of masquerade is a general characteristic of all the films made in Iran. They have different layers of meanings and messages. This is what annoys the authorities" (Maryam Maruf, "*Offside* Rules: An Interview with Ja'far Panahi," June 7, 2006, available at http://www.ioendemocracy.net).

65. Quoted in Michiko Kakutani, "Piecing Together a Fragmented Poet," *New York Times*, Aug. 8, 1989.

66. Women are not the only ones bound by codes of modesty; men are, too. Indeed, it is the heterosexual/heterosocial relationship primarily that is curtailed, allowing for much more play on the homosocial level.

67. Najmeh Khalili Mahani, "Women of Iranian Popular Cinema: Projection of Progress," *offscreen.com* 10, no. 7 (July 31, 2006), available at http://www.firouzanfilms.com/ . . . /NajmehKhalili_WomenOfIranianPopularCinemaProjectionOfProgress.html.

### 4. BADASHT AND SENECA FALLS

1. According to Mohammad Reza Tahmasbpoor, "Photography and its various forms emerged in Iran three years after its emergence in Europe (i.e., in 1839 in France). The first photographs,

in the form of daguerreotypes, were made during the reign of Mohammed Shah Qajar by Nikolaj Pavlov (one of the young Russian diplomats) in Dec 1842. Nâser-od-din Mirza, a thirteen-year old prince, during Mohammed Shah's reign, can be counted amongst the first to have his image preserved in daguerreotype form, and his interest in this new and exciting science was aroused" ("Early Photography in Iran," n.d., available at the Kargah.com Iranian Artists' site, http://www.kargah .com/history_of_iranian_photography/early/index.php?other=1).

2. The same is true about the male Babis. In rare instances when reference is made to them in a text without vilifying them, they are not mentioned by name or identified. For instance, Hushang Golshiri writes about a cruel scene of torture of Babis in his masterpiece *The Prince*. "The guards fall upon him, tear off his clothes, cut into him with pen knives and place candles in the wounds. Oboes are sounding. Crowds would have gathered and spat in his face. They light the candles. Two guards grip him under the arms and bring him forward. The people are clapping. From high up in the Governor's Palace, Grandfather observed the scene through field-glasses. The candles were burning and the people. . . . The candle wax must have dripped on his skin. Who was he? The seminary students would certainly have spat at him and shouted: 'Damn your filth to Hell!'" (Buchan trans., 103).

3. In her endorsement of the English translation of *Touba*, Marjane Satrapi, author of *Persepolis*, writes that it was one of the three books she took with her when she left Iran (see the back cover of Shahrnush Parsipur, *Touba and the Meaning of the Night*, translated by Hava Houshmand and Kamran Talatoff [New York: Feminist Press, 2006]).

4. Parsipur, *Touba and the Meaning of the Night*, 11, 8, 13.

5. Ibid., 13.

6. Bahiyyih Nakhjavani, *The Saddlebag* (London: Bloomsbury, 2000), 177.

7. Bahiyyih Nakhjavani, *La femme qui lisait trop* (The Woman Who Read Too Much) (Paris: Actes Sud, 2007).

8. Shoghi Effendi, "The Valiant Táririh," in *Táhirih in History: Perspectives on QurratuʾL-ʿAyn from East and West,* edited by Sabir Afaqi, Studies in the Bábí and Baháʾí Religions, vol. 16 (Los Angeles: Kalimat Press, 2004), 18.

9. Jules Bois, "Babism and Bahaism," *Forum* 74 (July 1925): 1–10.

10. Mohammad Ali Siddiqui, "Qurratuʾl-ayn: A Profile in Courage," in Afaqi, ed., *Táhirih in History,* 68.

11. According to Martha L. Root, "The book with the birth records was burned together with her other books and her clothing the day after the tragic death, so I heard" (*Tahirih the Pure*, rev. ed., with an introduction essay by Marzieh Gail [Los Angeles: Kalimat Press, 1981], 50.

12. Muhammad Iqbal (1877–1938), the philosopher, politician, and poet laureate of an Islamic nation, Pakistan, placed Tahirih in the company of Hallaj (the Sufi master) and Ghalib (a classical poet of India) in the Sphere of Jupiter in his book *Javid-Nameh* (The Song of Eternity). Published in 1932, *Javid-Nameh* is considered Iqbal's masterpiece and compared to Dante's *Divine Comedy.*

13. Abbas Amanat, *Resurrection and Renewal* (Ithaca, NY: Cornell Univ. Press, 1989), 297.

14. This information was made available thanks to the scholarship of Moojan Momen, who had access to the Baraghani family archives.

15. Tahirih Qurratul'Ayn, "From Those Locks," in *Tahirih, a Portrait in Poetry: Selected Poems of Qurratu'l-'Ayn*, edited and translated by Amin Banani, with Jascha Kessler and Anthony A. Lee (Los Angeles: Kalimat Press, 2005), 104.

16. H. M. Balyuzi, *The Bab* (Oxford, UK: George Ronald, 1974), 164.

17. For a fascinating analysis of Badasht, see Negar Mottahedeh, "Ruptured Spaces and Effective Histories: The Unveiling of the Babi Poetess Qurrat al-'Ayn-Tahirih in the Gardens of Badasht," *UCLA Historical Journal* 17 (1997): 59–81, reprinted in Afaqi, ed., *Táhirih in History*, 203–30; see also Negar Mottahedeh, "Qurrat al-'Ayn's Unveiling and the Persian Massacre of the Babis circa 1852," paper presented at the University of California at Berkeley, Apr. 1997, reprinted online at http://www.bahai-library.com/mottahedeh_mutilated_body_nations.

18. Shoghi Effendi, *God Passes By* (Wilmette, IL: Baha'i Publishing Committee, 1944), 32.

19. For a full elaboration of this theme, see Bahiyyih Nakhjavani, *Asking Questions: A Challenge to Fundamentalism* (Oxford, UK: George Ronald, 1990).

20. Lady Mary Sheil, *Glimpses of Life and Manners in Persia* (1856; reprint, New York: Arno, 1973), 85.

21. Mohammad Tavakoli-Targhi, *Refashioning Iran: Orientalism, Occidentalism, and Historiography* (New York: Palgrave, 2001), 54.

22. Bamdad, *From Darkness into Light*, 98.

23. Mernissi, *Islam and Democracy*, 9.

24. Qurratul'Ayn, "Friends Are Knocking at the Door," in *Tahirih*, 89.

25. A large tapestry at the Women's Interfaith Institute in Seneca Falls, New York, pays open tribute to Tahirih and places her in a global context. Depicted on the left side of the tapestry is the figure of Elizabeth Cady Stanton. She is resting one hand on a lectern while with the other hand she holds a piece of paper. She looks directly at the audience. Above the portrait is written: "Convention at Seneca Falls, N.Y. July, 1848," and a quotation from Stanton's first public speech is given: "Neither father, husband, brother, or son, however willing they may be, can discharge her high duties of life, or stand in her stead when called into the presence of the great Searcher of Hearts at the last day." Written underneath the portrait are the following words: "And on our banners will beat the dark storm-clouds of opposition. . . . Undaunted we will unfurl it to the gale, for we know that the storm cannot rend from it a shred, that the electric flash will but more clearly show to us the glorious words inscribed upon it, 'Equality of Rights.'"

Represented in parallel on the right side of this tapestry, standing shoulder to shoulder with Elizabeth Cady Stanton, is the figure of Tahirih, unveiled, with one hand raised and walking out from behind a curtain. We see her in half-profile, as if in dialogue with Cady Stanton. These words are inscribed above her portrait: "Conference at Badasht, Persia. June, 1848," followed by a quotation attributed to her at this gathering, whose historic significance, unlike that of the famous conference at Seneca Falls, is still largely unknown or ignored: "This is the day of festivity and universal rejoicing, the day on which the fetters of the past are burst asunder. Let those who have shared in this great achievement arise and embrace each other." Under the portrait is inscribed the caption: "Tahirih Appearing in Public Unveiled." And beneath the portrait are the last words attributed to this "Baha'i heroine" who "was executed for her religious beliefs and for championing the cause of women": "You can kill me as soon as you like, but you cannot stop the emancipation of women."

26. Library of Congress, *American Memory, Words, and Deeds in American History: Selected Documents Celebrating the Manuscript Division's First 100 Years* (Washington, DC: Library of Congress, n.d.), available at http://memory.loc.gov/cgi-bin/query/r?ammem/mcc:@field.

27. Andrea Barnes, "Women and the Law: A Brief History," in *The Handbook of Women, Psychology, and the Law,* edited by Andrea Barnes (San Francisco: Jossey Bass, 2005), 20.

28. Norma Basch, "Invisible Women: The Legal Fiction of Marital Unity in Nineteenth-Century America," *Feminist Studies* 5, no. 2 (Summer 1979), 347.

29. Quoted in ibid., 354.

30. Gretchen Ritter, *The Constitution as a Social Design: Gender and Civic Membership in the American Constitutional Order* (Stanford, CA: Stanford Univ. Press, 2006), 98.

31. According to article 5 of the Criminal Code regarding the Law of Apostasy, presented to the Parliament of the Islamic Republic of Iran in February 2008, a male apostate will be sentenced to death, and a female apostate will be imprisoned for life.

32. Peter Smith, *The Babi and Baha'i Religions: From Messianic Shi'ism to a World Religion* (Cambridge, UK: Cambridge Univ. Press, 1987), 47.

33. Quoted in Annie Londonderry, "Women on Wheels: The Bicycle and the Women's Movement of the 1890s," available at http://www.annielondonderry.com/womenWheels.html.

34. Quoted in Mo'in ed-Din Mehrabi, *Qurratol'Ayn* (Cologne: Ruyesh, 1989), 149.

35. See Nakhjavani, *The Woman Who Read Too Much.*

36. Qurratul'Ayn, "Look Up!" in *Tahirih,* 47.

37. Amin Banani, "Tahirih: A Portrait in Poetry," in Qurratul'Ayn, *Tahirih,* 5. As to what Tahirih did write, Banani believes: "What has survived of her writings is a number of theological discourses, doctrinal disputations, and polemical tracts in affirmation of her new faith written mostly in Arabic prose—and a very small number of poems, mostly in Persian" (3).

38. In a rare acknowledgment of the origins of this motto, Noushin Ahmadi Khorasani writes: "To provide the genealogy of our method in the 'One Million Signature Campaign' (that is seeking face-to-face interactions in various public spaces), it is important to recall that this method is inspired by the words of the brave poetess and campaigner for women's equal rights, *Zarrin Taj (Tahereh Qorat ul Ein),* who wrote the following couplet more than 160 years ago: If I see Thou, my beloved / Gaze-to-gaze, face-to-face / I will explain your pain / Bit-by-bit, pace-by-pace / But to see thy face / I have become the wandering breeze / Going house-to-house, door-to-door / Alley-to-alley, and street-to-street" ("The 'One Million Signature Campaign: Face to Face, Street to Street,'" translated by Shole Irani, *Payvand,* Mar. 30, 2007, available at http://www.payvand.com/news/07/mar/1352.html).

39. Butler, "Lipstick Revolution."

40. Khorasani, "The One Million Signature Campaign."

41. Quoted in Nasrin Alavi, "Women in Iran: Repression and Resistance," *openDemocracy,* Mar. 5, 2007, available at http://www.opendemocracy.net/democracy-irandemocracy/iran_alavi_4406.jsp.

### 5. ICARUS REBORN

1. I have ignored all the issues of threat and warning: the fact that the skill of the construction depended not on Icarus himself, but on his father, who had constructed the labyrinth in which the Minotaur was imprisoned, and the question of what would Daedalus have done if he had had a daughter instead of a son.

2. My unpublished poem "Icarus Reborn":

Satiated and full of fire
Drunk with his mystic ascent to light
Icarus scattered his flaming feathers to the wind.
He was not scared of death
He knew death was temporary.

Floating like snow flakes,
Dancing like whirling dervishes,
Satiated and full of fire
Icarus landed in the lush forests of Mazandaran.

The land became pregnant
And out of her longing for flames
Forugh Zaman was born—
Eternal Light.
She darted on wings
She went to the stars a thousand years away
She pursued the winds
She pushed against the walls
She went to places where no one feared the light.
She never relinquished the desire to fly.

3. I am referring to "The Sun Shall Rise" and "I Shall Salute the Sun Again" in the fourth collection, *Tavallodi Digar* (Reborn) (Tehran: Morvarid, 1963).

4. Farrokhzad, "The Sun Shall Rise," 20.

5. Farrokhzad, "Border Walls," in *Reborn*, 65.

6. [Forugh Farrokhzad], "Confession," *Omid-e Iran*, no. 10 (1955), 14–15, 20, 25.

7. Throughout Farrokhzad's body of poetry, there are several instances when the poetic persona is confronted with the option to choose between a safe, secure, acquiescent path and adventure. The latter is invariably her preferred alternative. In one of her exceptionally few poems with a male poetic persona, the young boy, Ali, has to decide between two different lifestyles. He can choose a protected life out of harm's way, or he can lead a life of adventure, danger, and mobility represented

by the sea. Ali moves out of the sheltered circle and joins the flowing waters (Farrokhzad, "To Ali Said His Mother, One Day," in *Reborn,* 132–45).

8. Farrokhzad, "Lovingly," in ibid., 55.

9. Farrokhzad, "Forgive Her," in ibid., 44.

10. Forugh Farrokhzad, "I Feel Sad," in *Iman Biavarim be Aghaz-e Fasl-e Sard* (Let's Believe in the Dawning of a Cold Season) (Tehran: Morvarid, 1974), 86.

11. Farrokhzad, "Only the Voice Remains," in ibid., 76–81.

12. Farrokhzad, "Let's Believe in the Dawning of a Cold Season," in ibid., 12.

13. Charles Dickens, *A Tale of Two Cities* (New York: Penguin, 2003), 5.

14. Farrokhzad, "I Pity the Garden," in *Let's Believe in the Dawning of a Cold Season,* 58.

15. For a more detailed biography of Farrokhzad, see Farzaneh Milani, "Farrokhzad," in *Encyclopaedia Iranica,* edited by Ehsan Yarshater, 9:fascicle 3, 324–27 (New York: Bibliotheca Persica, 1999). For her full biography, see Michael C. Hillman, *A Lonely Woman: Forugh Farrokhzad and Her Poetry* (Washington, DC: Mage, 1987).

16. As noted in the text, "Sin" was published along with pictures and a biographical sketch as the piece "A Bold Poet," *Rowshanfekr* (The Intellectual) 2, no. 61 (Sept. 24, 1954), 26.

17. Robert Surieu, *Sarve Naz* (Geneva: Nagel, 1967), 7.

18. According to article 180 of the Penal Code, "If a man kills his wife and/or her accomplice while in the act of adultery, he is exempt from punishment; if he kills his daughter or sister and/or their accomplices under the same circumstances, he is punishable by one to six months' imprisonment" (quoted in Hamideh Sedghi, *Women and Politics in Iran: Veiling, Unveiling, and Reveiling* [New York: Cambridge Univ. Press, 2007], 75).

19. For an early and interesting analysis of this poem, see Zjaleh Hajibashi, "Sin," in *Forugh Farrokhzad: A Quarter-Century Later,* compiled and edited by Michael C. Hillman, special issue of *Literature East and West* 24 (n.d.): 67–71.

20. Forugh Farrokhzad, "Sin," in *Wall,* 13–15.

21. Nasser Khodayar, interviewed by the author, Tehran, Nov. 2003.

22. Shojaeddin Shafa is a politician, author, and translator (of *The Divine Comedy, The Songs of Bilitis, Poetical Meditations of Lamartine,* and *The Selection of Master Pieces of the World's Poems* among many others). He was also a friend of Forugh Farrokhzad. Regarding his introduction to *The Captive,* he writes:

> When my *Bilitis* [*The Songs of Bilitis*] was published, a young woman approached me explaining that she had a book of poetry that she wished to be published. She further explained that because she was an unknown and her poems were uncensored, the publishers, though interested in publishing them, had postponed printing and had placed a condition on its publication—that she would have to have the book introduced by a well-known writer who would defend the originality of her work. She then stated that because her poems were in line with the thinking of *Bilitis* that she wanted me to write the introduction.

After reading her poetry I was convinced that another Iranian poetic genius was born. She was much greater than she perceived herself. I wrote my feeling in the introduction of her book. In the introduction I also mentioned that I believed that in a short period she would be much more famous than the author of the introduction. My writings introduced the first book by Forugh Farrokhzad, *The Captive*. A number of books followed. Her entire collection is one of the most famous and adored pieces by Iranians. It is also admired by many throughout the world who have recognized her as one of the prominent Iranian poets. ("Shojaeddin Shafa in His Own Words," *Persian Heritage* 5, no. 20 [Winter 2000], 59).

23. Shojaeddin Shafa, untitled essay, in Forugh Farrokhzad, *Asir* (The Captive) (Tehran: Amir Kabir, 1974), 4.

24. Forugh Farrokhzad, "Dar Diyari Digar" (Elsewhere), in *Javedaneh Zistan, Dar Owj Mandan* (Living Eternally, Staying on Top, edited by Behrouz Jalali, 66–117 (Tehran: Morvarid, 1996). Broadly speaking, travel abroad was rather rare for Iranian women at the time. Many Baha'i women participated in missionary expeditions throughout the world. Their travelogues, however, have remained unstudied for the most part. Prior to Farrokhzad, Mirza Khalil's wife, whose name the reader never learns, also wrote a short account of her pilgrimage to Mecca during the Safavid dynasty. As the number of women travelers increased, so did the number of their travel narratives. There might also exist unpublished manuscripts of travel narratives by Iranian women as well as accounts of travel published by Iranian women in periodicals that need to be unearthed and revived.

25. Farrokhzad, "Elsewhere," 103.

26. Ibid., 98.

27. Although Farrokhzad reached the height of her poetic achievement in her last two collections, and despite the fact that the first three collections possess a vision more limited both thematically and technically than the highly charged, nuanced later poetry, I do not see a sudden metamorphosis in the author or her work, but rather a dazzling progression. The earlier work, I believe, entails a radical reordering of value systems, attracts attention to that which has been relegated to silence or oblivion, and demands verbal and personal space denied women previously. Technically speaking, there is surely a great difference between *The Captive, Wall,* and *Rebellion,* on the one hand, and the last two collections, on the other. Farrokhzad herself told interviewers that she wished she had never published some of her earlier poems. Nevertheless, the early poetry is a necessary literary experiment that provides the key to the development of her poetic voice and technical evolution. It also closely chronicles the life of a pioneering woman in the 1950s—a rare historic document of monumental import.

28. This letter is included in Amir Esmaili and Abolghassem Sedarat, eds., *Javedaneh Forugh Farrokhzad* (Eternal Forugh Farrokhzad) (Tehran: Marjan, 1968), 14.

29. Farrokhzad, "Window," in *Let's Believe in the Dawning of a Cold Season,* 44.

30. Forugh Farrokhzad, "O! My Poems," in "Forugh Rouzhaye Khoob-e She'r" (The Good Days of Forugh's Poetry), *Zane Rooz,* 21 Mordad 1357, 54.

31. Farrokhzad, "The Conquest of the Garden," in *Reborn*, 128.

32. Farrokhzad, "Windup Doll," in ibid., 75.

33. Farrokhzad, "The Conquest of the Garden," in ibid., 127.

34. Farrokhzard, "Let's Believe in the Dawning of a Cold Season," 18.

35. William Butler Yeats, "Per Amica Silentia Lunae," in *Mythologies* (New York: Touchstone, 1998), 331.

36. Farrokhzad's relationship with Golestan, a married man, started another scandal that spread quickly in Iran's literary circles.

37. For a fascinating filmic biography of Hossein Mansouri, see the German documentary *Moon Sun Flower Game* by Claus Strigel (2007).

38. *The House Is Black* won the 1963 grand prize for documentary films at the Uberhausen Film Festival in West Germany. Only a few years after its production, however, it disappeared from the scene. For more than three decades, it was hidden in a purgatory where no masterpiece should end up. A movie lamenting captivity was itself held captive. Like its creator, however, *The House Is Black* refused to be relegated to absence and oblivion. It emerged from years of solitude, traveled through time, and found its audience. Resurfacing, its revival or, rather, its canonization began with a blast. The film was shown at the New York Film Festival in 1997. Its pioneering import acknowledged, it became the subject of numerous studies, articles, and conferences inside and outside the country.

39. Empathizing with the patients, mourning their captivity, Farrokhzad also believed the colony offered them sanctuary. It sheltered them from a cruel world, which had bullied, harassed, and banished them. It protected them from intrusive eyes and merciless judgments. It offered them comfort and community.

40. Forugh Farrokhzad, *Avalin Tapesh-hay-e Asheghaneh-ye Ghalbam: Name hay-e Forugh Farrokhzad be Hamsarash Parviz Shapour* (The First Romantic Palpitations of My Heart: Forugh Farrokhzad's Letters to Her Husband, Parviz Shapour), edited by Kamyar Shapour and Omran Salahi (Tehran: Morvarid, 2002), 248.

41. Pouran Farrokhzad, *Nimeha-ye Natamam* (Uncompleted Halves) (Tehran: Tandis, 2001), 254.

42. Farrokhzad, "The Captive," in *The Captive*, 34.

43. Farrokhzad, "Wedding Band," in ibid., 149.

44. Farrokhzad, "My Sister," in ibid., 159–60.

45. Betty Friedan, *The Feminine Mystique* (New York: Norton, 2001), 32.

46. Farrokhzad, "The Captive," 20.

47. Farrokhzad, "Sacrificed," in *Wall*, 45.

48. It is remarkable that in more than a thousand years of continuous written Persian literature, I have not come across the agonizing laments of a man complaining about the bitter clash between his role as father and the demands of his art. The choice to be a husband, a father, *and* a poet has been a masculine prerogative.

49. Farrokhzad, "Green Phantom," in *Reborn*, 120.

50. With characteristic candor, Farrokhzad told interviewers Gholam Hossein Sa'edi and Syrus Tahbaz: "I believe in being a poet in all moments of life. Being a poet means being a human. I know some colleagues whose daily behavior has nothing to do with their poetry. In other words, they turn into poets when they write poetry. Afterward, they turn into the same greedy, indulgent, cruel, short-sighted, miserable, envious people. Frankly, I cannot believe their words. I value the realities of life and when I find these gentlemen making feasts and claims—that is in their poems and articles—I get disgusted and doubt their sincerity. I say to myself perhaps it is only for a bowl of rice that they are screaming" (Gholam Hossein Sa'edi and Syrus Tahbaz, "An Interview with Forugh Farrokhzad," in *Harfhai ba Forugh* [Some Words with Forugh] [Tehran: Morvarid, 1976], 79).

51. Farrokhzad, "Let's Believe in the Dawning of a Cold Season," 30.

52. Barely thirty-two, Farrokhzad said: "I am glad my hair has turned grey, grooves have appeared on my forehead, and between my eyebrows two large wrinkles have settled. I am glad I am no longer fanciful and romantic. Soon I'll be thirty-two years old. Although being thirty-two means to have consumed thirty-two years of my share of life, in return I've found myself" (from an untitled section that gives selected letters from Farrokhzad to Golestan in Syrus Tahbaz, ed., *Arash*, [Tehran: Darakhshan, 1966], 5).

53. Farrokhzad, "Window," in *Let's Believe in the Dawning of a Cold Season*, 47.

54. Farrokhzad, "Let's Believe in the Dawning of a Cold Season," 12.

### 6. THE GYPSY POET

A shorter and slightly different version of this chapter appeared in *Iranian Studies* 41, no. 1 (Feb. 2008), edited by Farzaneh Milani: 3–17. For reference to "the old Eve," see Behbahani's poem by the same title published in *Iran Nameh* 23 (2006), edited by Farzaneh Milani, 3.

1. Behbahani, "My Country, I will Build You Again," in *A Cup of Sin*, 68.

2. Simin Behbahani was born in Tehran in 1927 fittingly to two writers who first became acquainted with each other through poetry. Fakhr-e Ozma Arghun, Behbahani's mother, had written a patriotic poem that was published in the journal *Eqdam*. Her father, Abbas Khalili, was the founder and editor of *Eqdam* as well as a prolific novelist. Upon the submission of Arghun's poem, Khalili was so moved by it that he proposed to her. They were soon married. Behbahani was the first and only child of this "poetic" union, which quickly ended in divorce. She was raised by her mother, who had a great impact on her life and work. "Whatever I have," said the poet, "had its original motivation from my mother." Her mother was, according to Behbahani, "among the wonders of her day. In an era in which reading and writing were considered sinful for women, she came to benefit from many of the fields of learning available to her. She learned Persian literature, Islamic jurisprudence, Arabic, astronomy, philosophy, logic, history, and geography under the tutelage of recognized masters who also taught her two brothers. From childhood, she studied French under a Swiss governess at home" ("We Await the Golden Dawn," in *A Cup of Sin*, xviii). Fakhr-e Ozma Arghun wrote poetry and short stories; she translated from French into Persian; she played the Tar. She was one of the founding members of the Association of Patriotic Women and an active member of the Women's

Society of Iran, both leading women's groups in Iran during the first part of the twentieth century. In 1935, she founded a journal, *Woman's Letter*. It was under the loving care of such a mother that Behbahani grew up in Tehran.

3. Behbahani's rich allusions to prophets, philosophers, writers, and characters in literature, mythology, and history as well as her Qur'anic, biblical, and Zoroastrian references make great demands on her readers.

4. Simin Behbahani, "A Portrait of the Revolution and Its Impact on Literature in the Last Twenty-Five Years," translated by Abbas Milani and Farzaneh Milani, paper presented at Stanford Univ., May 2004.

5. Percy Shelley (1792–1822) pronounced this idea in his much-quoted sonnet: "My name is Ozymandias, king of kings: / Look on my works, ye Mighty, and despair!"

6. Simin Behbahani, "Iran Today: A Poet's Vision," translated by Kaveh Safa and Farzaneh Milani, acceptance speech for the Bita Daryabari Stanford Prize for Literature and Freedom, Stanford Univ., Mar. 2008.

7. Ibid.

8. Ibid.

9. Quoted in Nora Boustany, "A Poet Who 'Never Sold Her Pen or Soul,'" *Washington Post*, June 10, 2006.

10. Ronald Hingley, *Nightingale Fever: Russian Poets in Revolution* (New York: Knoff, 1981), xi.

11. Quoted in Boustany, "A Poet Who 'Never Sold Her Pen or Soul.'"

12. Pierre de Boisdeffre, *Les poetes français d'aujoud'hui: 1940–1986* (French Poets of Today: 1940–1986), translated by Simin Behbahani as *Sha'eran Emruz Faranseh* (Tehran: Elmi, 1994).

13. Before finishing high school, Behbahani married Hassan Behbahani, a high school teacher. Though this marriage interrupted her higher education, she went on to earn a law degree from Tehran University years later. With this degree, she could have pursued a career as either an attorney or a judge, but she instead chose teaching as a profession. After twenty-three years, her marriage ended in divorce. Only a sense of obligation to her children had held it together for so long. After her divorce, Behbahani forged a very different relationship with Manuchehr Koushiar, who had been a fellow law student—a relationship characterized by "compatibility and harmony." The happy memories of this second union, with a man who devoted himself to her and her literary career, are the themes of an autobiography, *An Mard Mard Hamraham* (That Man, My Male Companion of the Road) (Tehran: Zavvar, 1990).

14. Behbahani, "We Await the Golden Dawn," in *A Cup of Sin*, xvii.

15. *Broken Sitar* was followed by *Jay-e pa* (Footprints, 1956); *Chelcheraq* (The Lamp of Many Lights, 1957); *Marmar* (Marble, 1963); *Rastakhiz* (Resurrection, 1973); *Khati ze Sor'at-o az Atash* (A Trajectory of Speed and Fire, 1981); *Dasht-e Arjan* (Arjan's Plain, 1983); *Kaqazin Jame* (Paper-Thin Vestment, 1989); *An Mard Mard Hamraham* (That Man, My Male Companion of the Road, 1990); *Kowli va Name va Eshq* (The Gypsy, the Letter, and Love, 1994); *Asheqtar az Hamishe Bekhan* (Sing More Lovingly Than Ever, 1994); *Yek Dariche-ye Azadi* (A Window to Freedom, 1995); *Ba Ghalb-e Khod che Kharidam?* (What Did I Buy with My Heart? 1996); *Az Salhay-e ab-o-Sarab* (On Years of

Mirage, 1998); *Neghare-ye Golgun* (Blood-Colored Designs, 1998); *Jay-e pa ta Azadi* (Footprints to Freedom, 1998); *Yad Ba'zi Nafarat* (A Few Persons Remembered, 1999); *Yeki, Masalan Inke* (For Instance, 2000); *Kelid-o-Khanjar* (Key and Dagger, 2000); *Ey Diyar Roshanam* (O, My Luminous Land, 2006); and *Divan-e Ash'ar Simin Behbahani* (Simin Behbahani's Poetry Collection, 2006).

16. I am grateful to my brother, Abbas Milani, who first remarked on the similarities between the Iranian and Russian poets.

17. Anna Akhmatova, "Plantain," in *Complete Poems of Anna Akhmatova*, translated by Judith Hemschemeyer, edited by Roberta Reeder (Boston: Zephyr, 1992), 254.

18. Behbahani, "An Interrupted Speech," in *A Cup of Sin*, xxvi.

19. Past recipients of the Carl Von Ossietzky Award include the Nobel Prize–winning German authors Günter Grass (1966) and Heinrich Böll (1974); the German American psychologist Erich Fromm (1986); and the Turkish humorist and author Aziz Nesin (1992). Past recipients of this award include Russian journalist Anna Politkovskaya, Israeli novelist Amos Oz, and Nigerian writer Wole Soyinka. Mehrangiz Kar, Janet Afary and Kevin Anderson, Noushin Ahmadi Khorasani and Parvin Ardalan, and Mehrangiz Manouchehrian and Azar Nafisi were awarded the Latifeh Yarshater Award. The Bita Daryabari Prize for Literature and Freedom was established in 2008 at Stanford University. Its first recipient was Simin Behbahani.

20. Kaveh Safa, "Afterword," in *A Cup of Sin*, 138.

21. Behbahani, "From the Street / Number 3," in ibid., 52.

22. Behbahani, "From the Street / Number 6," in ibid., 33.

23. Soheila Assemi, "No Fear: An Interview with Simin Behbahani, Iran's National Poet," *Gozaar*, Oct. 1, 2006, available at http://www.gozaar.org/english/interview-en/No-Fear.html.

24. Simin Behbahani, "Pine Tree," in *Yek Dariche-ye Azadi* (A Window to Freedom) (Tehran: Sokhan, 1995), 175.

25. Behbahani, "Gypsiesque 13," in *A Cup of Sin*, 75.

26. Behbahani, "A Portrait of the Revolution."

27. The speech was first published in *Rouzegar-e Now* 16, no. 9 (Oct.–Nov. 1997): 52–56.

28. Behbahani, "Gypsiesque 13," 75.

29. Behbahani, "I Can't Look," in *A Cup of Sin*, 89.

30. Simin Behbahani, "The House Is Bloody Now," in *Neghare-ye Golgun* (Blood-Colored Designs) (Los Angeles: Ketab, 1998), 19.

31. Behbahani, "Doubts, Doubts, Doubts," in *A Cup of Sin*, 86.

32. Simin Behbahani, "We Did Not Want It, but Here It Is," in *Khati ze Sor'at-o az Atash* (A Trajectory of Speed and Fire) (Tehran: Zavvar, 1981), 123.

33. Behbahani, "The Necklace," in *A Cup of Sin*, 26.

34. Behbahani, "Record! Record! Record!" in *A Trajectory of Speed and Fire*, 129.

35. Behbahani, "Our Tears Are Sweet," in *A Cup of Sin*, 28.

36. Behbahani, "Dark, Angry Arabic Script," in *A Trajectory of Speed and Fire*, 142.

37. Fatemeh, "the Radiant," is the embodiment of many virtues, including selflessness, purity of heart, and compassion. She is the daughter of the Prophet, wife of Ali, mother of the martyred

imams Hossein and Hassan (the children in her arms in the poem), and maternal ancestor of the other Shiʻa imams.

38. Simin Behbahani, "Banu, Our Lady," translated by Kaveh Safa and Farzaneh Milani, *Archipelago*, 4, no. 3 (Autumn 2000), available at http://www.archipelago.org/vol4-3/behbahani.htm.

39. Behbahani, "Iran Today."

40. Behbahani, "Gypsiesque (1)," in *A Cup of Sin*, 77.

41. Gypsies are also portrayed in the works of prominent Iranian women writers such as Forugh Farrokhzad, Jaleh Esfahani, Simin Daneshvar, and Moniru Ravanipour.

42. See Shirin Ebadi, with Azadeh Moaveni, *Iran Awakening: A Memoir of Revolution and Hope* (New York: Random House, 2006), 172.

### 7. WOMEN ON THE ROAD

1. Shahrzad Sepanlou is a talented, contemporary poet-writer and actor. In her insightful autobiographical novel *Touba* and with characteristic candor, Sepanlou reveals the conflicts of a woman who has refused to be locked up behind walls, forced into predetermined roles, hemmed in by tedious definitions of femininity. Although acknowledging the many external obstacles women writers confront in Iran, she also reflects the deep-seated inner conflicts of highly talented women who have transgressed gender, class, and literary boundaries (*Touba* [Tehran: Eshragi, 1977], 9).

2. See Farzaneh Milani, "Dance as Dissent: In Iran, the Author Enjoys a Subversive Boogie Night," *Ms.* (Spring 2004), 29.

3. As Faridoun Farrokh writes in his introduction to a collection of Goli Taraghi's short stories,

In the stories Taraghi wrote before 1980, there is a marked absence of women and, for that matter, romantic interest. A typical character in her early fiction is the male urban dweller, more specifically, a resident of Tehran, who is almost always literate and in a few cases even erudite with a touch of pedantry. In terms of social standing, these characters are predominantly from the lower scales of the middle class. They are very much the products of contemporary Iran: although they experience the joys and sorrows universal to humanity, they cannot be imagined in any dimension other than the Iranian framework constructed for them by Taraghi. Surprisingly, few if any of them are fashioned after the members of her immediate circle of acquaintance or the vast coterie of very interesting, even intriguing, individuals she associated with during the years she lived in Iran. ("Introduction," in Goli Taraghi, *A Mansion in the Sky: Short Stories by Goli Taraghi*, translated by Faridoun Farrokh [Austin: Center for Middle Eastern Studies, Univ. of Texas, 2003], 1)

4. For a translation of the autobiographical vignette "Avvalin Ruz," see Goli Taraghi, "The First Day," available at http://www.wordswithoutborders.org/article/the-first-day; quotes come from this translation. See also Goli Taraghi, *Dow Donya* (Two Worlds) (Tehran: Niloofar, 2002).

5. For a full citation of *Persian Requiem*, see note 35 in the introduction.

6. Farzaneh Milani, "Pay-e Sohbat-e Simin Daneshvar" (An Audience with Simin Daneshvar), *Alefba* (n.s.) no. 4 (Fall 1983), 155.

7. See Hassan Mirabedini, "Dastan Nevisiy-e Zanan: Gamhay-e Larzan-e Avaliy-e" (Women's Fiction: First Wobbly Steps) *Zanan* (Mar. 2007). Also see Hassan Mirabedini, "Persian Literature: The History of Female Storywriters," 2005, available at http://www.iranchamber.com/ . . . /history _female_storywriters.php.

8. Nazila Fathi, "Women Writing Novels Emerge as Stars in Iran," *New York Times*, June 29, 2005.

9. Fataneh Haj Seyed Javadi, *Bamdad-e Khomar* (The Morning After) (Tehran: Alborz, 1995).

10. Homa Sarshar, *Sha'ban Ja'afari* (Beverly Hills, CA: Naab, 2002).

11. Firoozeh Dumas, *Funny in Farsi: A Memoir of Growing up Iranian in America* (New York: Random House, 2004).

12. Quoted in Gabriele Stiller-Kern, "The Clear but Fragile Force of Writing," *Culturebase.net* (Sept. 2004), available at http://www.culturebase.net/artist.php?436.

13. Virginia Woolf, *A Room of One's Own* (New York: Harcourt, Brace and World, 1957), 113.

14. Mojdeh Daghighi, "Goft-o-gu ba Shiva Arastui" (A Conversation with Shiva Arastui), *Zanan* (July 2004), 66.

15. For a new and comprehensive study of women and Sufism in Iran, see Zahra Taheri, *Hozour Peyda va Penhan Zan dar Motun-e Sufiy-e* (The Presence and Absence of Women in Sufi Texts) (Tokyo: Research Institute for Languages, 2007).

16. When interviewed by Golbarg Bashi, Parsipur explained briefly why she was incarcerated four times. "The first time was because I publicly protested the execution of Khosrow Golsorkhi and Keramatollah Daneshiyan—they were both poets, on which occasion I resigned from the Iranian National Television. Because I believed the reasons of the state for the trial and execution of these poets were not sufficient and it was wrong. . . . At any rate, because of the circumstances surrounding this resignation, I was arrested and put behind bars for 54 days. . . . The second time it was in 1981." When some of the leading cadre of the Islamic Republic, including Ayatollah Beheshti and his comrades, were assassinated, some publications were banned, and Parsipur, her mother, and her two brothers were arrested for possession of banned materials. Although none of them was a political activist, Parsipur said, they all were

sent to prison for different reasons and periods. Mine became longer than all of them. It lasted for four years, seven months and seven days—but I was never officially charged. On two other occasions, I was arrested after the publication of my *Women Without Men*, when a Hezbollah-affiliated periodical attacked me, claiming that this story is anti-Islamic, unethical and contrary to this, that, or other things *(zede behman)*. I was arrested—I believe in the month of July of 1990. I was in jail for about two months and my family put my maternal aunt's house as collateral and bailed me out. After that I reported back to the prison in order to release my aunt's house from any collateral obligation.

(in Golbarg Bashi, "The Proper Etiquette of Meeting Shahrnush Parsipur in the United States," *Iranian.com,* July 9, 2006, available at http://www.iranian.com/Bashi/2006/July/Parsipur/index.html)

17. Shahrnush Parsipur, *Khaterat-e Zendan* (Prison Memoirs) (Stockholm: Baran, 1996), 494.

18. Parsipur's novels include *Sag va Zemestan-e Boland* (The Dog and the Long Winter, 1974); *Tajrobehay-e Azad* (Trial Offers, 1975); *Avizehay-e Bolur* (Prismatic Clusters, 1977); *Touba va Ma'nay-e Shab* (*Touba and the Meaning of the Night,* 1989, trans. 2006); *Zanan bedun-e Mardan* (Women Without Men, 1989); *Adab-e Sarf-e Chay dar Hozur-e Gorg* (Tea Ceremony in the Presence of the Wolf, 1993); *Aghl-e Abi* (Blue Logos, 1994); *Majerahay-e Sadeh va Kouchak-e Derakht* (The Simple and Small Adventures of the Tree Spirit, 1999); *Shiva* (1999); *Bar Bal-e Bad* (On the Wings of Wind, 2002).

19. Bashi, "The Proper Etiquette of Meeting Shahrnush Parsipur."

20. Shahrnush Parsipur, *Adab-e Sarf-e Chay dar Hozur-e Gorg* (Tea Ceremony in the Presence of the Wolf) (Los Angeles: Tassveer, 1993), 227.

21. Parsipur, *Prison Memoirs,* 15.

22. Ibid., 31.

23. Abbas Milani, *Lost Wisdom: Rethinking Modernity in Iran* (Washington, DC: Mage, 2004), 140.

24. Farzaneh Milani, "Pay-e Sohbat-e Shahrnush Parsipur" (An Audience with Shahrnush Parsipur), *Iran Nameh* 11, no. 4 (Fall 1993), 695.

25. Parsipur, *Women Without Men,* 33; and Shahrnush Parsipur, *Touba va Ma'nay-e Shab* (Touba and the Meaning of the Night) (Tehran: Spark, 1989), 456, my translation.

26. Parsipur, *Women Without Men,* 36.

27. Shahrnush Parsipur, *Aghl-e Abi* (Blue Logos) (San Jose, CA: Zamaneh, 1994), 234. "Why do you keep at the bottom of the ocean?" is a line from Forugh Farrokhzad's poem "Let's Believe in the Dawning of A Cold Season" (in *Let's Believe in the Dawning of a Cold Season,* 17).

28. Parsipur, *Touba va Ma'nay-e Shab,* 423, my translation.

29. Farid Ud-Din Attar, *The Speech of the Birds,* translated by Peter Avery (Cambridge, UK: Islamic Texts Society, 1998), 377; subsequent citations are to this translation. Another translation of note is Farid Ud-Din Attar, *The Conference of the Birds,* translated by Afkham Darbandi and Dick Davis (Harmondsworth, UK: Penguin, 1984).

30. Attar, *The Speech of the Birds,* 69.

31. Derek A. Scott, "Birds in Iran," in *Encyclopaedia Iranica,* edited by Ehsan Yarshater, 4:fascicle 3, 265–72 (New York: Routledge and Kegan Paul, 1989).

32. Edward Burgess, letter in Charles Burgess and Edward Burgess, *Letters from Persia: Written by Charles and Edward Burgess, 1828–1855,* edited by Benjamin Schwartz (New York: New York Public Library, 1942), 68.

33. In Western literature, the nightingale is nearly always female, perhaps in part owing to the story of Philomela. King Tereus conceived an illicit passion for his sister-in-law, Philomela. Finding

his lust unreciprocated, he raped her, cut her tongue out, and imprisoned her so that his crime remained untold. Philomela, however, was not to be silenced. She vowed to tell her story by whatever means she could. With her tongue cut out, she resorted to other forms of communication. She wove a tapestry that revealed her violent ordeal to her sister, Procne. Confronted with the exposure of his adultery and rape, an angered and exasperated Tereus tried to kill both sisters. He began to chase them, but before he could catch them, all three—the king, Philomela, and Procne—metamorphosed into birds. Tereus became a hoopoe; Procne turned into a swallow; and Philomela was transformed into a nightingale. Nightingales are also called "Philomel."

34. Shirin Neshat, the highly acclaimed visual artist, has directed a feature-length adaptation of this bold and imaginative novella.

35. Parsipur, *Women Without Men*, 56; subsequent citations to this work are given as parenthetical page references in the text.

36. Can the rape be viewed as, among others things, a warning to women that when roaming the streets, they do so at their own peril? Crime-prevention tips often list such suggestions as "use well-traveled, well-lit routes," "park in well-lit parking areas," "avoid using the same route." The focus is on the danger when women are in forbidden territories, thus perpetuating the myth that rape can be prevented through decreased female physical mobility. Living in an environment in which rape is a constant threat affects women's quality of life and their unconditional access to the public arena. It is as if women's mobility is blamed for the crime against them. Should it surprise us, then, that Mahdokht prefers to become a tree? I do not mean to suggest here that rape is all about the control of space, just as it is not only about sex. Rape is a pathological abuse of power and privacy.

37. Reza Afshari, *Human Rights in Iran: The Abuse of Cultural Relativism* (Philadelphia: Univ. of Pennsylvania Press, 2001), xx.

38. Mohammed Al-Urdun, "Iran's Literary Giantess Is Defiant in Exile . . . but Missing Home," *Camden New Journal*, June 19, 2007, available at Parsipur's Web site, http://www.shahrnushparsipur .com/article10.htm.

39. Mernissi, *Scheherazade Goes West*, 3.

40. Fariba Vafi, *Parandey-e Man* (My Bird) (Tehran: Markaz, 2002); see also Fariba Vafi, *My Bird*, translated by Mahnaz Kousha and Nasrin Jewell, with a foreword by Farzaneh Milani (Syracuse, NY: Syracuse Univ. Press, 2009).

41. Kate Chopin, *The Awakening* (1899; reprint, New York: Avon, 1982), 82. The full sentence is: "The bird that would soar above the level plain of tradition and prejudice must have strong wings."

8. READING AND MISREADING IRANIAN
WOMEN IN THE UNITED STATES

A shorter and slightly different version of this essay was published as "Women's Captivity in the Islamic World," *Middle East Report*, no. 246 (Spring 2008): 40–46.

1. For centuries, the veiled Muslim Woman had suggested a combination of tantalizing sexual promise and the mystery of a forbidden object. Now she is also viewed as a frightening threat.

2. For instance, when Margaret Atwood was asked in an interview, "You have recently returned from Cuba: What are your perceptions about Cuba? Is it really an evil place?" she responded: "Well, I have something to compare it with because I've been to lots of 'evil places.' I've been around the world twice. First time I stopped in Iran and Afghanistan. Of all the evil places we have to choose from, those are among the evilest now, I'd say. What Russians are doing in Afghanistan is pretty evil, and what Iran is doing to itself is pretty evil" ("A Conversation: Margaret Atwood and Students, Moderated by Francis X. Gillen," in *Margaret Atwood: Vision and Forms,* edited by Kathryn Van-Spanckeren and Jan Garden Castro [Carbondale: Southern Illinois Univ. Press, 1988], 235).

3. At the time of the takeover, there were seventy-one Americans in the embassy. Six of them avoided capture and eventually fled Iran on January 29, 1980. Thirteen female and African American hostages were released some two weeks after the seizure, on November 18 and 19, 1979. The remaining fifty-two were released on January 20, 1981.

4. The appetite for news on Iran seemed bottomless. In his book *Covering Islam,* Edward Said writes: "John Kifner of the *New York Times* wrote on December 15, 1979, that there was a corps of no less than three hundred Western reporters (most if not all of whom needed interpreters) on the ground in Tehran, and Col Allen on December 16, 1979, reported for the *Australian* that between them the three major American networks were spending a million dollars a day in Tehran. In addition to its bureau chief, CBS, according to Allen, 'Had a team of 23 journalists, a cameraman, audio man and film and technical experts aided by 12 Iranian interpreters, car driver and guide'" (*Covering Islam: How the Media and the Experts Determine How We See the Rest of the World* [New York: Vintage Books, 1997], 103). This circumstantial appeal was not a phenomenon unique to the coverage of Iran in the aftermath of the hostage crisis. Books, like those who write them and read them, respond to the pressing concerns of the day, especially when those concerns are perceived as crises or threats. During the Cold War, anti-Communist works were popular. After the Cuban Missile Crisis, a significant number of Latin American authors were translated into English. Following the cataclysmic events of September 11, 2001, there was an explosion of writing on Islam and the Middle East.

5. In her memoir *Persian Girls,* Nahid Rachlin discusses the impact of the hostage crisis on her life in America:

> In the United States, the yellow ribbons everywhere and constant media coverage provided a dispirited backdrop to the presidential election season. Throughout 1979–1980, the American public watched footage of Iran on a daily basis. News programs tallied the number of days Americans were held hostage. Nothing else seemed to matter to Americans, and America appeared to be a helpless giant.
>
> During this period I found that my friends who had never been particularly political suddenly became patriots and attacked Iran. Even though their anger at the hostage takers was justified, they lumped all Iranians, myself included, with them. My husband tried his best to be fair, but I was sensitive to his remarks, and, to me, everything he said sounded slanted in favor of America. When I gave readings from my work, people with

no interest in fiction came to ask questions about Iran and Iranians. One magazine, which had published several of my short stories as well as a condensed version of my first novel, rejected a story because it was "too sympathetic a portrait of Iranian characters." (241)

6. The popular ABC television program *Nightline* was inaugurated on November 8, 1979, congruent with the hostage crisis. Ted Koppel began each show, titled "America Held Hostage," by tracking the exact number of days Americans were held hostage in Iran.

7. Mansour Farhang, who served at the time as Iran's first postrevolutionary ambassador to the United Nations, resigned his position when his efforts to negotiate the release of the hostages failed.

8. In his biography of Ayattollah Khomeini, Baqer Moin writes that Khomeini said at the time to his first president, Abolhassan Bani-Sadr, "This action has many benefits. . . . This has united our people. Our opponents do not dare act against us. We can put the constitution to the people's vote without difficulty, and carry out presidential and parliamentary elections" (quoted in Baqer Moin, *Khomeini: Life of the Ayatollah* [London: I. B. Tauris, 1999], 228).

9. Simin Behbahani, "Gypsiesque (13)," in *Dasht-e Arjan* (Arjan's Plain) (Tehran: Zavvar, 1983), 43. For a translation of the whole poem, see *A Cup of Sin,* 75.

10. The short poem "Dead End," published by the celebrated poet Ahmad Shamlu in 1980 inside Iran, epitomizes the atmosphere of doom and gloom and the spirit of protest and resistance. The poet concentrates intense violence into the few lines of his poem and demands that the reader bear witness to the grisly brutality that had taken hold of his society. The violence perpetrated in the poem is staggering, the absence of compassion and tolerance and respect for individual rights alarming.

> They sniff at your mouth
> Lest you'd said: I love you
> They sniff at your heart
> It is a strange time, my love
> And they whip love by the barricade
> Better to hide love in the closet.

The thugs and the hatchet men, the victors, the tormentors, the new rulers are committed to extending their bloody control in all directions. In the thrust of their daggers, in the crack of their whips, they prove their lust for power and violence. They are executioners of light and love and freedom, assassins of the smile, enemies of elegance and beauty. They burn books and jasmine and innocent canaries:

> In this crooked dead end of cold
> They kindle fire
> Fueled with songs and poems

Don't risk thinking . . .

Roasted canaries

On the fire of lily and jasmine

It is a strange time, my love

Satan, victorious and drunk

Is celebrating our mourning.

> (Ahmad Shamlu, "Dead End," in *Taraneha-ye Kuchak-e Ghorbat*
> (Short Poems of Exile) [N.p.: Maziar, 1980], 30)

For an English translation of the whole poem and a longer analysis of it, see Milani, *Veils and Words*, 210–12.

11. Roya Hakakian, *Journey from the Land of No: A Girlhood Caught in Revolutionary Iran* (New York: Three Rivers Press, 2004), 225.

12. Farideh Goldin, *Wedding Song: Memoirs of an Iranian Jewish Woman* (Waltham, MA: Brandeis Univ. Press, 2003), 1.

13. Quoted in Larry Cohler-Esses, "Bunkum from Benador," *The Nation*, July 3, 2006.

14. In an interview with David Ignatius, President George W. Bush admitted, "One of the dilemmas facing (American) policymakers is to understand the nature, the complex nature of the Iranian regime" (David Ignatius, "Bush's Message to Iran," *Washington Post*, Sept. 15, 2006).

15. Sean Wilentz, "The Rise of Illiterate Democracy," *New York Times Book Review*, Dec. 11, 2005.

16. In spite of the fickleness of best-seller lists, certain categories of books—such as self-help texts, cookbooks, celebrity memoirs, self-improvement manuals, and redemptive life narratives of captivity and survival—have always had a better chance of finding their way to the coveted register.

17. Amin Maalouf believes that in the early twentieth century "all of Persia was living in the 'age of the American.'" He refers to Morgan Shuster, who functioned as treasurer general for eight months as "indisputably the most popular official and one of the most powerful" (*Samarkand*, translated by Russell Harris [New York: Interlink Books, 1996], 283). Howard Baskerville (1885–1909) is another American celebrated in Iran. He died fighting for democracy there.

18. Women's clothing, regardless of country or faith, has often constrained mobility. Remarkably, it has been easier to see and criticize the oppressive and immobilizing fashion of others than of the self. Lady Mary Wortley Montagu, who traveled to Turkey in 1716, recounts how harem women viewed her attire as a true prison. When she was invited to a Turkish bath, she attracted animated surprise when she undressed. "'Come hither and see how cruelly the poor English ladies are used by their husbands,' screams the lady of the house. 'You need boast indeed of the superior liberties allowed you, when they lock you thus up in a box'" (*The Letters and Works of Lady Mary Wortley Montagu*, vol. 1, edited by Lord E. Wharncliffe [London: Henry G. Bohn, 1887], 247).

19. Not all of these books are about Western women held captive in the Muslim world, and as such they fall in a different category. My intention here is to focus on the allure of *captivity* as a catchword in titles.

20. Ayaan Hirsi Ali, *Infidel* (New York: Free Press, 2007), 285, 350. *Infidel* was published in Holland under the title *My Freedom*. See also Ayaan Hirsi Ali, *The Caged Virgin: An Emancipation Proclamation for Women and Islam* (New York: Free Press, 2006); it was originally published in the Netherlands as *Die Maagdenkooi*.

21. Quoted in Whitlock, *Soft Weapons,* 90. See also Betty Mahmoody, with William Hoffer, *Not Without My Daughter* (New York: St. Martin's Press, 1991), and Jean Sasson, *Mayada, Daughter of Iraq: One Woman's Survival in Saddam Hussein's Torture Jail* (New York: New American Library, 2004).

22. Mary Wakefield, "'We Are at War with All Islam,'" *Spectator,* Nov. 28, 2007, available at http://www.spectator.co.uk/print/the-magazine/features/276476.

23. Ellen Goodman, "Will U.S. Remember the Ladies?" *Boston Globe,* Sept. 7, 2003.

24. An Associated Press poll released in August 2007 reported that among "avid readers" the typical woman reads nine books a year, whereas the typical man reads five. The gender gap was far wider in the fiction market (National Public Radio, Sept. 5, 2007, available at http://www.npr.org/templates/story/story.php?storyId=14175229).

25. These books include, among others: Sally Armstrong, *Veiled Threat: The Hidden Power of the Women of Afghanistan* (New York: Four Walls Eight Windows, 2002); Cheryl Bernard, *Veiled Courage: Inside the Afghan Women's Resistance* (New York: Broadway Books, 2002); Latifa, *My Forbidden Face*; Harriet Logan, *Un/Veiled: Voices of Women in Afghanistan* (New York: Harper, 2002); Batya Swift Yasgur, *Behind the Burqa: Our Life in Afghanistan and How We Escaped to Freedom* (Hoboken, NJ: Wiley, 2002); Dayna Curry, Heather Mercer, and Stacy Mattingly, *Prisoners of Hope: The Story of Our Captivity and Freedom in Afghanistan* (New York: Doubleday, 2002); and Zoya, with John Follain and Rita Cristofari, *Zoya's Story: An Afghan Woman's Struggle for Freedom* (New York: Harper Collins, 2002).

26. For notable exceptions, see, for instance, Sarah Chayes, *The Punishment of Virtue: Inside Afghanistan after the Taliban* (New York: Penguin, 2006), and Ann Jones, *Kabul in Winter: Life Without Peace in Afghanistan* (New York: Metropolitan, 2006).

27. See Robert Fisk, "War on Terrorism: Rise and Fall of Village Cleric Who Fought 'Criminals and Traitors,'" *Znet,* Dec. 7, 2001, available at http://www.independent.co.uk (news, world, Asia).

28. Phyllis Chesler, *The Death of Feminism* (New York: Palgrave McMillan, 2005), 20. Chesler writes later in this book that Afghanistan is "a prison, a police state, a feudal monarchy, a theocracy, rank with fear and paranoia" (81).

29. See Phyllis Chesler, "Memoirs of Afghanistan," *Mademoiselle* (June 1969): 154–60; *About Men* (New York: Simon and Schuster, 1978), specifically "My First Husband: Men in Iranistan"; *The New Anti-Semitism* (San Francisco: Jossey-Bass, 2003), 14–17; and *Mothers on Trial* (New York: McGraw-Hill, 1986), 339–42.

30. Chesler, *The Death of Feminism,* 79.

31. Mahmoody, *Not Without My Daughter,* back cover; subsequent citations to this book are inserted parenthetically by page number in the text.

32. In the documentary film *Without My Daughter* (2002, directed by Alexis Kouros), Dr. Mahmoody claims it was Betty Mahmoody who proposed to him.

33. Betty Mahmoody and Arnold Dunchock, *For the Love of a Child* (New York: St. Martin's Press, 1992), 18; subsequent citations to this book are inserted parenthetically in the text.

34. *Midnight Express*, a "true" tale of captivity, was the sensationalized story of a young American detained in Turkey who, after much suffering and violent abuse, managed to escape to freedom. Oliver Stone, who adapted *Midnight Express* into a screenplay, apologized publicly to the Turkish people for overdramatizing the story of Billy Hayes, the man who was imprisoned after he was caught smuggling drugs into Turkey.

35. See "Betty Mahmoudy," AEI Speakers Bureau, available at http://www.aeispeakers.com/Mahmoody-Betty.htm.

36. Roger Ebert, *"Not Without My Daughter," Chicago Sun-Times*, Jan. 11, 1991.

37. Alice, Mahmoody's American friend in the memoir, believes that "Betty was free to go." She also questions the veracity of the mother and daughter's hellish escape to Turkey. "It is my gut feeling," she told her interviewer in the documentary *Without My Daughter*, "that she didn't escape across the border."

38. Specific citations to this work are given parenthetically by page number in the text; for a full reference, see note 44 in the introduction.

39. In 1997, the year Nafisi migrated to the United States, her article "Imagination as Subversion: Narrative as a Tool of Civic Awareness" appeared in the anthology *Muslim Women and the Politics of Participation,* edited by Mahnaz Afkhami and Erika Friedl (58–71 [Syracuse, NY: Syracuse Univ. Press, 1997]). In this piece, as in *Reading Lolita in Tehran,* Nafisi discusses her private class. The differences between the article—its language, its description of the class, and its reading list—and the book are fascinating.

40. Ironically enough, Nabokov's masterpiece *Lolita,* the very book that lent Nafisi her title, does not appear on this illustrious list.

41. Several Iranian authors of autobiographies published in the United States have expressed feeling trapped in Iran. For instance, in *Wedding Song* Farideh Goldin recalls her mother's plea to her "to find a way to leave this hellhole." She encouraged her to "find someone" to take her away. "Don't allow yourself to get trapped here like me," she would counsel her young daughter (25). Nahid Rachlin still remembers the sense of jubilation when she left Iran for the United States. "I was leaving this home and going where I deeply wished to be. Free, free, free, I said to myself" (*Persian Girls,* 137).

42. The class, which was also dubbed a "workshop" or a "book club," was disbanded when Nafisi and her family left Iran for the United States. Five of the seven students also later moved to various Western countries.

43. Many other female narrators express this feeling of imprisonment. Latifa writes: "My head is empty of projects. Sometimes I pace round the apartment like a prisoner round his cell" (*My Forbidden Face,* 38).

44. In PEN's inaugural Arthur Miller Freedom to Write Memorial Lecture, Orhan Pamuk said, "As for those who emigrate from these poor countries to the West or the North to escape economic hardship and brutal repression—as we know, they sometimes find themselves further brutalized by the racism they encounter in rich countries. Yes, we must also be alert to those who denigrate immigrants and minorities for their religion, their ethnic roots or the oppression that the governments of the countries they've left behind have visited on their own people" (Orhan Pamuk, "Freedom to Write," translated by Maureen Freely, *New York Review of Books*, May 25, 2006).

45. Quoted in Jay Parini, "Pirates, Pashas, and the Imperial Astrologer," *New York Times*, May 19, 1991, available at http://www.nytimes.com/books/ . . . /pamuk-castle.html.

46. As surprising is the absence of any reference to Shirin Ebadi, who won the Nobel Peace Prize in 2003 for her decade-long struggle for human rights.

47. Quoted in Richard Byrne, "Peeking under the Chador," *Chronicle of Higher Education* 53, no. 8 (2006), A16.

48. Paul Allen, "Through the Veil," *The Guardian*, Sept. 13, 2003.

49. Karl Vick, "Sorry, Wrong Chador: In Tehran 'Reading Lolita' Translates as Ancient History," *Washington Post*, July 19, 2004.

50. Patrick Clawson, "Iran in Books: Review Essay," *Middle East Quarterly* 14, no. 2 (Spring 2007), 41.

51. Leslie Schunk, "Memoirs: From Scribbling into High Art," *World Literature Today* 73, no. 3 (Summer 1999), 475.

52. Christopher Hartney, *U.S. Rates of Incarceration: A Global Perspective* (Washington, DC: National Council on Crime and Delinquency, Nov. 2006), available at http://www.nccd-crc.org/nccd/pubs/2006nov_factsheet_incarceration.pdf. The report goes on, "Some individual US states imprison up to six times as many people as do nations of comparable population."

53. Marie Gottschalk, "Two Separate Societies: One in Prison, One Not," *Washington Post*, Apr. 15, 2008, available at http://webb.senate.gov/newsroom/newsarticles/04-15-2008-01.cfm.

54. Senator Jim Webb, opening statement, *Mass Incarceration in the United States: At What Cost? Hearings before the Joint Economic Committee*, 110th Cong., 1st sess., Oct. 4, 2007, available at http://webb.senate.gov/newsroom/newsarticles/04-15-2008-01.cfm.

55. Images of pervasive crime and punishment flood the US popular media, both as news and as entertainment. Some of America's most popular films have been about prison and the men and women who live there. Blockbusters such as *The Shawshank Redemption* (1994) and *The Green Mile* (1999) and hit TV shows such as *Oz, Prison Break,* and *Lock Up* document prison life.

56. James Frey, *A Million Little Pieces* (New York: Doubleday, 2003).

57. Kathryn Harrison, "Lives in the Arts," *New York Times Book Review*, Feb. 18, 2007. Frey was interviewed by Larry King on January 11, 2006.

58. In her enlightening book *The Ornament of the World: How Muslims, Jews, and Christians Created a Culture of Tolerance in Medieval Spain* (New York: Back Bay Books, 2002), Maria Rosa Menocal equates a "culture of translation" with a "culture of tolerance."

59. Aviya Kushner, "Literary Translations in America," *Poets and Writers* (Nov.–Dec. 2002), 47. Lorraine Adams, referring to the lack of interest in Arab literature in the United States, writes: "Non-fiction devoted to the Arab world may be in demand, but interest in Arab literature, even after Naguib Mahfouz's Nobel Prize in 1988, hasn't moved too far past Aladdin and Sinbad" ("Palestinian Lives," *New York Times Book Review,* Jan. 15, 2006).

60. Jascha Hoffman, "Data: Comparative Literature," *New York Times Book Review,* Apr. 15, 2007.

61. Anne Tyler, *Digging to America* (New York: Alfred A. Knopf, 2006), 170.

62. In 1998, 27 percent of a total of 15,960 books published in Iran were translated books. In 1999, the ratio was 24 percent of 20,642; in 2000, 18 percent of 23,305; in 2001, 18 percent of 30,885; in 2002, 23 percent of 32,801; and in 2003, 23 percent of 34,462. See the relevant volumes of *Karnameh-e Nashr: Fehrest-e Mozoee Ketabhay Montasher Shodeh* (Publishing Index: A Thematic List of Published Books) (Tehran: Khaneh Ketab, 1999–2003).

63. See Foucault, *Discipline and Punish.*

64. I am referring to Zaynab al-Ghazali's *Return of the Pharaoh: Memoir in Nasir's Prison* (Makefield, UK: Islamic Foundation, 1972) and Ashraf Dehghani's *Odyssey of Resistance* (N.p.: People's Fadaee Guerrillas, 1973).

65. Marina Nemat, *The Prisoner of Tehran: A Memoir* (New York: Free Press, 2007).

66. The interview with Nemat was aired on the *Tavis Smiley Show,* PBS, May 2007. For a list of Iranian prison memoirs, see http://www.utoronto.ca/prisonmemoirs/farsibooks.htm.

67. It is worth repeating here that there is also a rich body of scholarship on the Islamic world. But scholarship, it seems, has become something of a liability these days. When Hirsi Ali told her mentor, the prominent Dutch politician Neelie Kroes, that she planned to move to the United States to pursue a doctorate, she was swiftly dissuaded from doing so. Why? "Neelie said my dreams of academia were like a sinkhole; they would never go anywhere. No matter how wonderful a Ph.D. thesis I wrote, it would disappear into a file drawer. It would never shift the lives of Muslim women by an inch" (Hirsi Ali, *Infidel*, 295). Kroes, the politician, clearly knew the marketplace well. In less than two years, Hirsi Ali turned her anecdotal tale into two international sensations that passed for authoritative studies of Muslim women. Hailed as an expert on Islam, she angrily decried "infuriatingly stupid analysts—especially those who called themselves Arabists, yet seemed to know next to nothing about the reality of the Islamic world" (270).

68. Confronted with the US Treasury Department's Office of Foreign Assets Control regulation of literature from embargoed countries in 2004, Ebadi had to initiate a lawsuit, invoking rights granted even to non-Americans by the US Constitution. Whereas Ebadi had to threaten the US government with a lawsuit to be granted the right to publish her memoir, Massoumeh Ebtekar, whose memoir was submitted before the 2004 embargo and hence in principle had the right to be published in America, simply could not find a willing publisher. Ebtekar was one of the key hostage takers in 1979–80, their English-speaking spokesperson, a young woman at the time, known in the United States as "Mary." Decades later, when she attempted to publish her account of the embassy

occupation, she was rejected by some forty American publishers. (I am grateful to Fred Reed for this information.) Ebtekar was no marginal voice on the periphery of Iranian society at the time. Quite the opposite, she had become a leading political reformer, the minister of the Department of the Environment, and Iran's first female vice president in Mohammad Khatami's government. Nor is the book a one-sided justification of an unjustifiable act. In its preface, Seyyed Mohammad Mousavi Khoeiniha says that if today the individuals who stormed the American Embassy were asked whether they "would be prepared to take similar action . . . their response would be a definite 'no'" ("Preface," in *Takeover in Tehran: The Inside Story of the 1979 Embassy Capture* by Massoumeh Ebtekar, with Fred Reed [Vancouver: Talonbooks, 2000], 30.) Khoeiniha, too, was one of the hostage takers. Some publishers, including reputable houses, had dismissed Ebtekar's project as a fabrication. Others responded with indifference, polite refusal, or overt hostility. Such a book, some argued, would not be in their best interest. Finally, a small independent publishing house in Canada published *Takeover in Tehran*. The book attracted little, if any, attention in the United States, though.

69. Ebadi came across her own death sentence as she was sifting through government papers while she was providing legal council to the family of two assassinated intellectual dissidents. In an interview with Omid Memarian, Ebadi said: "When I was reviewing the 'chain murders case' as the Forouhar family lawyer, I read that the men under trial for the murders had stated in their affidavits that when they asked the minister of information, he issued them license to assassinate and kill me. Fortunately, before they had a chance to assassinate me they were arrested during Mr. Khatami's term" ("Q & A: 'I Feared I Could Be Killed in the Mayhem': Omid Memarian Interviews Iranian Noble Prize Laureate Shirin Ebadi," *IPS News,* Jan. 10, 2009, available at http://ipsnews.net/news .asp?idnews=45327).

70. For a full reference to *Iran Awakening,* see note 42 in chapter 6.

71. In her books and interviews, Marjane Satrapi reminds her audiences not to forget the fact that in "1953 the English and the Americans extinguished national democracy in my country, through a coup d'etat" (quoted in Robert Chalmers, "Marjane Satrapi: Princess of Darkness," *The Independent,* Oct. 1, 2006, available at http://www.independent.co.uk/arts-entertainment/books/ features/marjane-satrapi-princess-of-darkness-417932.html). Shirin Neshat, the internationally acclaimed visual artist, holds similar views: "When the Iranians attacked the U.S. embassy [in the 1979 Revolution], Americans were at a loss where the anger came from" because they did not know "the history behind" it (quoted in Marguerita Choy, "Filmmaker Sees Lessons in Iranian History," Reuters, Oct. 30, 2006). However one weighs the connections between the two consequential events, it is important to consider them from multiple perspectives. "Because most Americans did not know what the United States had done to Iran in 1953," writes Stephen Kinzer, "few Americans would have any idea why for some Iranians America had become 'the great Satan,' and that while U.S. grievances against Iran were valid in any international court of law, Iranians, too, have their own complaints" (*Overthrow: America's Century of Regime Change from Hawaii to Iraq* [New York: Times Books, 2006], 202).

72. Ebadi, *Iran Awakening,* 212.

73. For a full reference to *La femme,* see note 7 in chapter 4.

74. And yet although *The Woman Who Read Too Much,* written originally in English, has been translated into French, Italian, and Korean, it has not found a UK or US publisher to this date. Alberto Manguel, praising the novel as one of the best three books he read in 2007, writes, "As a consequence of the policy among larger English-language publishers of putting profit before quality, a number of first-rate writers are being kicked out of their habitual homes; several remain unpublished in the original and can only be read in translation. This is the case with the superb Persian novelist Bahiyyih Nakhjavani, whose book *La Femme Qui Lisait Trop* (Actes Sud) I read in French translation because Bloomsbury (publisher of her first books) rejected her new work." ("Books of the Year," *Times Literary Supplement,* Nov. 30, 2007). In a controversial speech at Harvard University in 1978, dissident writer Alexander Solzhenitsyn said: "One gradually discovers a common trend of preferences within the Western press as a whole. It is a fashion; there are generally accepted patterns of judgment and there may be common corporate interests, the sum effect being not competition but unification. Enormous freedom exists for the press, but not for the readership because newspapers mostly give enough stress and emphasis to those opinions which do not openly contradict their own and the general trend" ("A World Split Apart," June 8, 1978, available at http://www.americanrhetoric.com/speeches/alexandersolzhenitsynharvard.htm).

75. Satrapi's animated film adaptation of her memoir *Persepolis* won the Cannes Special Jury Prize in 2007. Satrapi shared the prize with Carlos Reygados for his film *Still Light.*

76. Marjane Satrapi, *Persepolis II: The Story of a Return* (New York: Pantheon, 2003), 75.

77. Ibid., 151, 150.

78. Marjane Satrapi, "Introduction," in *Persepolis I: The Story of a Childhood* (New York: Pantheon, 2003), no page numbers used.

79. Chalmers, "Marjane Satrapi."

80. Harold Pinter, acceptance speech for the 2005 Nobel Prize in Literature, Dec. 7, 2005, available at http://www.nobelprize.org/nobel_prizes/literature/ . . . /pinter-lecture.html.

81. "It's when truthiness moves beyond the realm of entertainment that it's a potential peril," wrote journalist Frank Rich in 2006. "It's the truthiness of all those imminent mushroom clouds," he contended, "that sold the invasion of Iraq" ("Truthiness Stages a Comeback," *New York Times,* Jan. 22, 2006). How much of the truth can be bent and manipulated in works of nonfiction? When we as readers notice fudging of facts, when we find ourselves floating in the slippery space between reality and illusion, between fact and fiction, shouldn't we begin to wonder what roles political groups have played in the production, distribution, promotion, and consumption of hostage narratives?

82. "The conditions are ripe for a hoax to emerge through Muslim and Arab life narratives in the course of the war on terror," asserts Gillian Whitlock in *Soft Weapons* (119). In recent years, there has been no shortage of fake life narratives. Some have been withdrawn from sale by the publisher, such as Norma Khouri's *Forbidden Love* (published in the United States as *Honor Lost: Love and Death in Modern Day Jordan* [New York: Atria Books, 2003]), a memoir about the author and her best friend, Dalia. The memoir tells us that the two women lived and worked together in a beauty salon in Jordan, where Dalia was brutally murdered. She was a victim of honor killing, or so the

readers are told. The only problem, however, is that Khouri had left Jordan when she was three, and such a friend as Dalia never existed. Other books have also been discredited, such as the best-selling *Burned Alive: A Victim of the Law of Men* (New York: Time Warner, 2003) by "Souad," written in collaboration with Marie-Therese Cuny. Souad, who does not speak a word of Arabic and always wears a mask in interviews and book promotions, is a Palestinian and a survivor of an alleged attempted honor killing in the West Bank. (For a detailed list of discrepancies and faux testimonials in these two books, see Therese Taylor's articles at http://www.aljadid.com/features/Burning-Question.html and http://www.palestinechronicle.com/view_article_details.php?id=13511.)

Still other book projects have been aborted before completion and publication, such as Jumana Michael Hanna's prison memoir. As Austrian historian Therese Taylor convincingly remarks, "Fake memoirs have always existed, but since the mid-1990s they have become increasingly common, and have gained a disturbing amount of influence." Referring to readers and publishers' preference for works of nonfiction, Taylor explains that it "has created a market that demands similar level of sensation and entertainment as from fiction" ("Memoirs of Deception," *Jewish Quarterly* [Spring 2007], 47). A twenty-four/seven news culture that is ceaselessly on the lookout for the unique and the extreme as well as the melodramatic and the personal attracts both brave witnesses and con artists.

Jumana Michael Hanna's prison experience is a fascinating case in point. On July 21, 2003, the *Washington Post* published a blood-curdling front-page story headlined, "A Lone Woman Testifies to Iraq's Order of Terror." It was about "a 41-year-old Assyrian Christian" woman who had contacted the new provisional government to share her graphic story of torture, sexual abuse, and repeated rapes inside an Iraqi prison on the direct orders of Saddam Hussein's son Uday. Although the government "had made it illegal for Iraqi citizens to marry non-nationals," claimed Hanna according to the story, she had the audacity to fall in love with and then marry an Indian man. For her insubordination and waywardness, she paid dearly.

Foreign correspondent Peter Finn, a "diligent and experienced reporter" (Michael Getler, "A Powerful Tale Unravels," *Washington Post,* Jan. 23, 2005) who was told by "U.S. officials before *The Post* article was published that they found her story credible," covered Hanna's chronicle of internment and abuse (Peter Finn, in collaboration with correspondent Khalid Saffar in Baghdad, "Threads Unravel in Iraqi's Tale; Story of Husband's Execution Contradicted by Relatives Who Say He Is Alive," *Washington Post,* Jan. 20, 2005). Dressed "in black, as she has been since her husband's death," the star witness, who "appeared to be deeply traumatized," told Finn that she had been incarcerated for "two years, three months, and seven days without the approval of any court of law." This is where she was "hung from a rod and beaten with a special stick when she called out for Jesus or the Virgin Mary. This is where she and other female prisoners were dragged outside, tied to a dead tree trunk, nicknamed 'Walid' by the guards, and raped in the shadow of palm trees. This is the place where electric shock was applied to Hanna's vagina. And this is where in February 2001 someone put a bullet in her husband's head and handed his corpse through the steel gate like a butcher's meat" (Peter Finn, in collaboration with special correspondents Souad Mekhemet and Hoda Lazin, "A Lone Woman Testifies to Iraq's Order of Terror," *Washington Post,* July 21, 2003). Hanna's experience personified the terror Saddam Hussein and his sons had unleashed upon perfectly innocent people, in particular women; it personalized senseless suffering and heroic survival; it traced the geography of brutality upon the anguished body and soul of a helpless woman, clad in black in mourning for her husband's unjust execution in prison; it displayed the marks of her stolen honor and dignified life. "The Coalition Provisional Authority bestowed medallions of honor on Hanna. . . . Her story became a defining parable in Washington of a world gone mad, in which dictators had been given license to terrorize their people without consequence" (Sara Solovitch, "The American Dream," *Esquire Magazine* [Jan. 2005], available at http://www.sarasolo.com/dream.html).

Eight days after the publication of this feature article, Deputy Secretary of Defense Paul Wolfowitz, who had just returned from a four-and-a-half-day visit to Iraq, testified in front of the Senate Foreign Relations Committee on Tuesday, July 29, 2003. Referring to the *Washington Post* article and its "sad story of one Assyrian Christian woman," Wolfowitz reminded the committee members that Hanna was made to "endure unspeakable torture. Her husband was executed at the academy, and his body was passed through the steel gate to her, as the article described it, 'like a piece of butcher's meat'—all because the couple had not received state approval for their marriage." To protect Hanna, US authorities moved her and "her seventy-two-year-old mother, and her two young children out of a homeless shelter and into a trailer in the Green Zone. There, for the next three months, they lived under twenty-four-hour guard, just a few feet from the office of Ambassador L. Paul Bremer, head of Iraq's Coalition Provisional Authority, in one of Saddam's palaces. Everybody in the palace knew Hanna. The soldiers photographed her in one of Saddam's golden thrones, her seven-year-old daughter, Sabr, and five-year-old son, Ayyub, perched on its gilded arms. In their free time, the Americans taught the kids how to swim in Saddam's Olympic-sized pool." The family was soon afterward given refugee status in the United States, where Hanna wanted "the same treatment" she was given in the Green Zone. "It was such a good life," she told Sara Solovitch. "They treated me like a queen" (Solovitch, "The American Dream").

Hanna's story and the crimes committed against her were so compelling that a literary agent hired Solovitch, a reporter for twenty-five years, to coauthor her memoir. The freelance writer was excited about the prospect of a lucrative book project. "I didn't have any doubt that this story would sell very well," she told David Folkenflik of National Public Radio. "It struck me that it had all the potential for being an international bestseller" (David Folkenflik, "Questions Arise on 'Post' Story of Iraqi Anguish," National Public Radio, Jan. 19, 2005, available at http://www.npr.org/templates/story/story.php?storyId=4459051). Aware of "the recent scandal involving a book called *Forbidden Love*, about the honor killing of a young Muslim woman in Jordan who had fallen in love with a Catholic army officer," Solovitch stressed to Hanna that they "couldn't risk any inaccuracy." So she began double-checking Hanna's claims and asking simple questions such as, "Was Hanna's husband dead? Was he really not an Iraqi? Did Iraqi law really prevent intermarriage with foreign nationals?" The husband, it turns out, is an Iraqi; far from being "a piece of butcher's meat," he is alive and well; there was no law prohibiting intermarriage; and neither husband nor wife was in prison for that reason. If the "Americans had spoken to Iraqi neighbors or family," writes Solovitch, "they might have learned one of the most persistent rumors surrounding Hanna": her mother had sent her "to jail, on charges of prostitution." Solovitch decided she could not write the commissioned memoir. She instead wrote an inspiring article, "The American Dream," detailing why she had refused to proceed. This was not "a story about the indomitability of the human spirit," confessed a disgruntled Solovitch, but rather a tale about "the willingness" of the coalition's "leaders to believe almost anything that fit their agenda" (Folkenflik, "Questions Arise").

Should we ask why prison testimonials command such engagement and emphatic witnessing? What is it about these tales of atrocities that attracts such national interest and lands them on the front pages of premier newspapers and in best-selling books? "Tragically," Whitlock observes astutely, "the emotional valency of testimony has little to do with the intensity of the suffering or pain that it carries, and it has everything to do with the cultural and political milieu it encounters and its capacity there to command witness" (*Soft Weapons*, 79). Perhaps, as Solovitch remarks, "Jumana Hanna's story of torture was something politicians needed, journalists were looking for and the American public expected" ("The American Dream"). Perhaps "that's why for a long time no one thought to verify the facts, which would have been easy enough" (Voice of America, "Iraqi Woman Profits from False Testimony," Mar. 3, 2005, available at http://www.voanews.com/english/ NewsAnalysis/2005-03-03-voa41.cfm). The sad consequence of these fake memoirs and memories is that, as Joseph Campbell, professor of journalism at American University in Washington, notes, "once these myths and urban legends take hold, they can be very enduring, and they can defy any efforts by scholars and journalists to debunk the myth" (quoted in Voice of America, "Iraqi Woman Profits from False Testimony"). They lodge themselves not only on the front pages of major and minor newspapers, in bookstores and libraries, in classrooms, and on radio and television, but also in the minds of countless seduced and well-intentioned readers.

83. "Azar Nafisi Replies to Hitchens et al.," Oct. 14, 2004, available at http://syndicated.live journal.com/dougireland/1916.html.

84. Scholes, "Presidential Address 2004."

## EPILOGUE

1. There are more than four hundred different versions of the "taming a shrew" story in different parts of the world.

2. William Shakespeare, *The Taming of the Shrew*, IV.i.175 and V.ii.151–52. Written around 1592, *The Taming of the Shrew* is one of Shakespeare's earlier plays. It is a comedy, focusing mainly on issues of courtship and marriage. Unlike many of his plays, it does not refer to historical figures or events. In writing it, Shakespeare was probably responding to society's fascination with spousal disputes. Renaissance marriages of the upper class were usually arranged for money, land, or power, and unhappy marriages were rarely escaped. Gender roles were entrenched, male dominance being the rule. An issue of relevance at the time was the existence of "shrews" or "scolds"—that is, unruly woman who did not display the conventional characteristics of servitude and subordination. Virtues such as chastity, shamefacedness, temperance, moderation, and so forth were of importance.

*The Taming of the Shrew* has been adapted at least seventeen times for the screen, including *Kiss Me Kate* (1953, directed by George Sydney) and the teen-oriented *10 Things I Hate about You* (1999, directed by Gil Junger), starring Julia Stiles.

3. Classical Persian literature offers several descriptions of the nuptial chamber. Here is how Jami describes Yusuf and Zulaikha's first sexual encounter: "Zulaikha suddenly saw the curtain pulled aside; and there was the unveiled moon, filling her chamber with splendor. She could not take her eyes away from Yusuf's face; and the sight of his radiant beauty transported her into ecstasy. Touched by this swooning adoration, Yusuf lifted her tenderly to the golden bed. . . . When he had feasted his eyes to his heart's content, he drew her in an embrace. . . . Quickly he sought the jewel casket in that treasure trove: it was shut with a silver lock; neither trusty guard nor traitorous intruder had ever laid a hand on it. With a glistening ruby for a key, he unlocked that casket and slipped the jewel in. To and fro his charger sped along that narrow course, until in the end it galloped itself lame." A pleasantly surprised Yusuf asks Zulaikha: "How is it that this pearl had never been pierced? Why the rose never opened in the morning breeze?" "Because," replied Zulaikha, "although the Vizier is the only man to have glimpsed my garden, he never gathered any rosebud there. . . . For my part, ever since I was a child, when I saw you in my dreams . . . I have protected it jealously from everyone else. No one has ever touched that pearl."

Zulaikha—who had lost her youth and beauty, whose graceful body was bent, her eyes drowned in tears of blood, causing her to lose her sight—is miraculously rejuvenated. Jami, one of her several literary creators, restored her youth, her vanished beauty, and her eyesight. "Her slender body became as straight as a cypress tree once more; and the wrinkles vanished from her silver skin. Youth ousted age; forty became eighteen; and her new-found beauty reached even greater heights than before." Although Yusuf and Zulaikha had known each other for decades, the passage of time seems to have impacted them differently. By age "forty," Zulaikha is "wrinkled" and "bent." Her beauty has simply vanished, whereas Yusuf has retained his "radiant beauty." To return to Zulaikha her all-too-transitory beauty, Jami, like many other Iranian writers of the classical period, turns into expert plastic surgeon. (All quotes from Jami, *Yusuf-o-Zulaikha*, Pendlebury trans., 124–27.)

Another example is from Nezami:

> Khosrow was carried to the bridal chamber to which Shirin, long wearied of the festivities, had withdrawn. When she saw that Khosrow was dazed by wine, she was angered and sent a wrinkled, hairy, hunchbacked old woman servant to him. It was a crone whom Khosrow took in his eager embrace; a crow in place of a beauty, a dragon instead of the moon. . . . The king cried out and cursed, and threw her from the chamber. Shirin, well satisfied that Khosrow was not beyond his senses, dismissed the servant and went in to him. As dawn broke, the lovers were united in a perfect love. The strength of the lion mingled with the sweetness of the rose. All that day and night, and even the next, and the day and night after that, they lingered within, until at last their joy was spent. (Chelkowski, *Mirror of the Invisible World*, 42)

Women's representation of the nuptial chamber in the past few decades contrasts sharply with that of the classical period. Mahshid Amirshahi's narrator in the short story "Labyrinth" reminisces about her wedding night:

> The room was strange and Kareem [the husband] and I were alone; I had no clear idea of what would happen next—not out of innocence or ignorance, but rather out of a lack of curiosity. What was to happen didn't matter to me. I felt absurd and I thought that our life together should begin with a different sort of feeling. "Aren't you coming to bed?" asked Kareem. "Yes," I said. "I'm coming, let me write a couple of words." I wanted to write something very poetic in my journal, something very touching. But the pen remained still in my hand for a long time and finally I wrote: "Tonight is my wedding night. I am at Kareem's house." Love making was so ugly, so graceless, so inelegant, so painful. The house was Kareem's house. My name was Kareem's name. (*Montakhab-e Dastanha* (Selected Stories) [Tehran: Tus, 1972], 159)

Houri, the protagonist of Shahrnush Parsipur's novel *The Dog and the Long Winter,* believes her mother's wedding night to be nothing worth remembering, let alone cherishing. Her mother, she writes, "had no clear memory of her wedding night. Whenever women talked about such issues in their gatherings, she listened timidly and her eyes looked more and more baffled. It seemed as if she had no wedding night at all. Had she not borne the children, it would have been possible to think of her as virginal" (155).

The representation of the nuptial night in women's life narratives is not much different from the fictive portrayal. The singer-dancer Banu Mahvash includes a tragic, almost surrealistic account of her wedding night in her controversial book *Raz-e Kamyabi-ye Jensi* (The Secret of Sexual Satisfaction). "An amazing night was my wedding night," she notes. "I shall never forget it. I vividly recall how fiercely he undressed me when we entered the room and as soon as he locked the door behind us. He ripped off my wedding gown and tore my nylons. When he held me and laid me on the bed, my head hit the board. Blood spilled all over the white sheets. Meanwhile he kept busy doing his thing. Finally, when I got out of his claws, I felt so weak that I was about to faint. He had deflowered me with an astonishing violence. Eventually, when he calmed down he started to kiss my feet and nurse my wound" ([Tehran: n.p., 1957], 60).

And here is how Gohar Kordi portrays her mother's wedding night: "When she slept with her husband for the first time, she did not resist, she did not fight. She imagined that she was with Assim [the man she loved] in order to make light the pain and discomfort. . . . From then on every time her husband made love to her she imagined Assim" (*An Iranian Odyssey* [London: Serpent's Tail, 1991], 22).

4. Perhaps Scheherazade heals the king of his obsession through stories of men and women who overcome obstacles and succeed through their patience, wits, courage, resolve, and humanity. She mingles these types of stories with those that reek with blood, flowing from the dreadful blows of swords and sabers.

Azar Nafisi remembers:

> I could not make love with him. I was scared and lonely and suddenly I felt as young as I was and not at all worldly. I wanted to go home. . . . I was afraid and genuinely sad, but he did not understand this. He took my reluctance to have sex with him as a sign that I might not be a virgin. Had he been misled? I see in my imagination one clear scene in black and white: the air is moist, his figure distinct, in a white terry-cloth robe, standing pensively by the door, smoking a cigarette. Where was I? I must have been standing next to him, explaining something, reassuring him that I really was a virgin. The next night at dinner, over the sound of laughter and festivity, he said to his youngest sister, "Tell her what to do." She turned to me sweetly—and she was ever so sweet—and said, "Just close your eyes and let yourself go. Imagine you are somewhere else. Imagine anything, imagine you are eating an omelet." I did as she said. I pretended I was somewhere else, although I could not bring myself to think of omelets. . . . But I did absent myself from my body. From then on, for decades, sex was something you did because it was expected of you, because you could not say no, because you did not care, could not care. (*Things I've Been Silent About* [New York: Random House, 2008], 177)

5. In "The Thousand-and-Second Tale of Scheherazade," Edgar Allan Poe portrays the legendary storyteller as a "politic damsel (who had been reading Machiavelli beyond doubt)." He kills off Scheherazade by the hands of her husband, King Shahriyar.

6. In his delightful book *Garden of the Brave in War*, Terrence O'Donnell writes: "From all that I know of the Iranians, I believe that in time the fanaticism of the revolution will pass. I can think of no better support for this than the nature of the Iranian pilgrimage, for though they love the flesh, they love the spirit too—perhaps not quite the contradiction that some in the West might think. And they certainly have much opportunity for pilgrimage since Iran is covered with shrines, everything from little wayside places to great edifices in the holy cities—some of the latter among the most dazzling buildings in the East. Not one of these thousands of shrines honors a soldier or a political figure. All are dedicated to either saints or poets. In the end, these, rather than bullhorns, are the voices that Iranians heed and venerate" (*Garden of the Brave in War: Recollections of Iran* [Chicago: University of Chicago Press, 1980], xi).

7. A study by the Berkman Center for Internet and Society at Harvard Law School found that "so many barbs might be uncommon in many other countries, but in Iran it is simply a reflection of a culture that so reveres poetry, where many children grow up dreaming of becoming great poets in the way many young Americans dream of a future in sports" (Neil MacFarquhar, "Iranian Blogosphere Tests Government's Limits," *New York Times*, Apr. 6, 2008).

8. During the Iran-Iraq War, remarks poet Farideh Hassanzadeh, "one journalist reported about the poetry he found in the trenches and foxholes that survived after the dead soldiers, poems like this from Forugh Farrokhzad: "Remember the flight / the bird is mortal" (Melissa Tuckey,

"Interview with Iranian Poet Farideh Hassanzadeh," *Foreign Policy in Focus: A Think Tank Without Walls*, June 12, 2007, available at http://www.fpif.org/fpiftxt/4300).

9. *The Thousand Nights and a Night: A Plain and Literal Translation of the Arabian Nights Entertainments*, 10 vols., translated by Richard F. Burton (London: Burton Club, 1886), 10:61, 10:54.

10. Ibid., 1:14.

11. Simin Behbahani, "Sword," in *Ey Diyar Roshanam* (O, My Luminous Land) (Los Angeles: Ketab, 2006), 85, poem translated by Kaveh Safa and Farzaneh Milani.

# WORKS CITED

Adams, Lorraine. "Palestinian Lives." *New York Times Book Review,* Jan. 15, 2006.

Adel, Gh. Haddad. "Clothing and the Secret of the Self." *Mahjubah* 3, nos. 4–6 (Aug.–Oct. 1983): 60–68.

Afaqi, Sabir, ed. *Táhirih in History: Perspectives on Qurratu'L-'Ayn from East and West.* Studies in the Bábí and Bahá'í Religions, vol. 16. Los Angeles: Kalimat Press, 2004.

Afshari, Reza. *Human Rights in Iran: The Abuse of Cultural Relativism.* Philadelphia: Univ. of Pennsylvania Press, 2001.

Akhmatova, Anna. *Complete Poems of Anna Akhmatova.* Translated by Judith Hemschemeyer. Edited by Roberta Reeder. Boston: Zephyr, 1992.

Alavi, Nasrin. "Women in Iran: Repression and Resistance." *openDemocracy,* Mar. 5, 2007. Available at http://www.opendemocracy.net/democracy-irandemocracy/iran_alavi_4406.jsp.

Al-e Ahmad, Jalal. *Occidentosis: A Plague from the West.* Translated by R. Campbell. Edited by Hamid Algar. Berkeley, CA: Mizan, 1984.

———. *Plagued by the West.* Translated by Paul Sprachman. Delmar, NY: Caravan Books, 1982.

———. *Weststruckness.* Translated by John Green and Ahmad Alizadeh. Lexington, KY: Mazda, 1982.

Allen, Paul. "Through the Veil." *The Guardian,* Sept. 13, 2003.

Amanat, Abbas. *Resurrection and Renewal.* Ithaca, NY: Cornell Univ. Press, 1989.

Amirshahi, Mahshid. *Montakhab-e Dastanha* (Selected Stories). Tehran: Tus, 1972.

Andrews, Helena. "Muslim Women Don't See Themselves as Oppressed, Survey Finds." *New York Times,* June 8, 2006.

Angier, Natalie. "Short Men, Short Shrift: Are Drugs the Answer?" *New York Times,* June 22, 2003.

Aristotle. *Works of Aristotle.* Vol. 4. Edited by J. A. Smith and W. D. Ross. Oxford, UK: Clarendon Press, 1910.

303

Armstrong, Sally. *Veiled Threat: The Hidden Power of the Women of Afghanistan.* New York: Four Walls Eight Windows, 2002.

Assemi, Soheila. "No Fear: An Interview with Simin Behbahani, Iran's National Poet." *Gozaar,* Oct. 1, 2006. Available at http://www.gozaar.org/english/interview-en/No-Fear.html.

Attar, Farid Ud-Din. *The Conference of the Birds.* Translated by Afkham Darbandi and Dick Davis. Harmondsworth, UK: Penguin, 1984.

Atwood, Margaret. *The Handmaid's Tale.* New York: Anchor, 1998.

Azarmina, Dr. Pijman. "In Iran, Gender Segregation Becoming a Fact of Medical Life." *Canadian Medical Association Journal* 166, no. 5 (Mar. 5, 2002): 645.

"Azar Nafisi Replies to Hitchens et al." Oct. 14, 2004. Available at http://syndicated.live journal.com/dougireland/1916.html.

Bacon, Constance. "Festival 2000: 36th Chicago International Film Festival." Formerly available at http://www.chicagofilmfestival.com/news/interview_dayibecameawoman .html.

Balyuzi, H. M. *The Bab.* Oxford, UK: George Ronald, 1974.

Bamdad, Badr ol-Moluk. *From Darkness into Light: Women's Emancipation in Iran.* Translated and edited by F. R. C. Bagley. Hicksville, NY: Exposition Univ., 1977.

Banani, Amin. "A Woman for Our Time." In *Tahirih, a Portrait in Poetry: Selected Poems of Qurratu'l-'Ayn,* edited and translated by Amin Banani, with Jascha Kessler and Anthony A. Lee, 1–30. Los Angeles: Kalimat Press, 2005.

Barnes, Andrea. "Women and the Law: A Brief History." In *The Handbook of Women, Psychology, and the Law,* edited by Andrea Barnes, 20–36. San Francisco: Jossey-Bass, 2005.

Basch, Norma. "Invisible Women: The Legal Fiction of Marital Unity in Nineteenth-Century America." *Feminist Studies* 5, no. 2 (Summer 1979): 346–66.

Bashi, Golbarg. "The Proper Etiquette of Meeting Shahrnush Parsipur in the United States." Iranian.com, July 9, 2006. Available at http://www.iranian.com/Bashi/2006/ July/Parsipur/index.html.

Beck, Lois. "Women among Qashqa'i Nomadic Pastoralists in Iran." In *Women in the Muslim World,* edited by Lois Beck and Nikki Keddie, 351–73. Cambridge, MA: Harvard Univ. Press, 1978.

Behbahani, Simin. *Ba Ghalb-e Khod che Kharidam?* (What Did I Buy with My Heart?) Tehran: Sokhan, 1996.

———. "Banu, Our Lady." Translated by Kaveh Safa and Farzaneh Milani. *Archipelago* 4, no. 3 (Autumn 2000). Available at http://www.archipelago.org/vol4-3/behbahani .htm.

———. *A Cup of Sin: Selected Poems of Simin Behbahani*. Edited and translated by Farzaneh Milani and Kaveh Safa. Syracuse, NY: Syracuse Univ. Press, 1999.

———. *Dasht-e Arjan* (Arjan's Plain). Tehran: Zavar, 1983.

———. *Ey Diyar Roshanam* (O, My Luminous Land). Los Angeles: Ketab, 2006.

———. "Iran Today: A Poet's Vision." Translated by Farzaneh Milani and Kaveh Safa. Acceptance speech for Bita Daryabari Stanford Prize for Literature and Freedom, Stanford Univ., Mar. 2008.

———. *Khati ze Sor'at-o az Atash* (A Trajectory of Speed and Fire). Tehran: Zavvar, 1981.

———. *An Mard Mard Hamraham* (That Man, My Male Companion of the Road). Tehran: Zavvar, 1990.

———. *Neghare-ye Golgun* (Blood-Colored Designs). Los Angeles: Ketab, 1998.

———. "A Portrait of the Revolution and Its Impact on Literature in the Last Twenty-Five Years." Translated by Abbas Milani and Farzaneh Milani. Paper presented at Stanford Univ., May 2004.

———. "Ta Tolou'i Tala'i Chashm be Rah Darim" (We Await the Golden Dawn). *Nimeye Digar* 2, no. 1 (Autumn 1993), special issue on Simin Behbahani, guest editor Farzaneh Milani: 169–76.

———. *Yek Dariche-ye Azadi* (A Window to Freedom). Tehran: Sokhan, 1995.

Bernard, Cheryl. *Veiled Courage: Inside the Afghan Women's Resistance*. New York: Broadway Books, 2002.

"Black Eyes, The." *Bombay Chronicle*, Aug. 4, 1935.

Bogle, Leonard. "The Khayyamic Influence in *The Blind Owl*." In *Hedayat's "The Blind Owl" Forty Years After*, edited by Michael C. Hillman, 87–98. Austin: Univ. of Texas Press, 1978.

Bois, Jules. "Babism and Bahaism." *Forum* 74 (July 1925): 1–10.

Boisdeffre, Pierre de. *Les poetes français d'aujoud'hui: 1940–1986* (French Poets of Today: 1940–1986). Translated by Simin Behbahani as *Sha'eran Emruz Faranseh* (Tehran: Elmi, 1994).

"Bold Poet, A." *Rowshanfekr* (The Intellectual) 2, no. 61 (1954): 26.

"Bombay Films for Persia." *Evening News of India*, Aug. 31, 1935.

Bordo, Susan. *Unbearable Weight: Western Culture, Feminism, and the Body*. Berkeley and Los Angeles: Univ. of California Press, 1993.

Bouhdiba, Abdelwahab. *Sexuality in Islam*. London: Saqi Books, 1989.

Boustany, Nora. "A Poet Who 'Never Sold Her Pen or Soul.'" *Washington Post*, June 10, 2006.

Brooks, Geraldine. *Nine Parts of Desire*. New York: Anchor Books, 1995.

Brumberg, Joan Jacobs. *The Body Project: An Intimate History of American Girls.* New York: Random House, 1997.

Brzezinski, Zbigniew. "Terrorized by 'War on Terror.'" *Washington Post,* Mar. 25, 2007.

Burgess, Charles, and Edward Burgess. *Letters from Persia: Written by Charles and Edward Burgess, 1828–1855.* Edited by Benjamin Schwartz. New York: New York Public Library, 1942.

Butler, Katherine. "Lipstick Revolution: Iran's Women Are Taking on the Mullahs." *The Independent,* Feb. 26, 2009. Available at http://www.independent.co.uk/news/world/middle-east/lipstick-revolution-irans-women-are-taking-on-the-mullahs-1632257.html.

Byrne, Richard. "Peeking under the Chador." *Chronicle of Higher Education* 53, no. 8 (2006): A16.

Camhi, Leslie. "Daughter of Iran, Shades of Her Father." *New York Times,* Feb. 21, 1999.

Cervantes Saavedra, Miguel de. *The Adventures of Don Quixote.* Translated by J. M. Cohen. New York: Penguin Books, 1950.

Chalmers, Robert. "Marjane Satrapi: Princess of Darkness." *The Independent,* Oct. 1, 2006. Available at http://www.independent.co.uk/arts-entertainment/books/features/marjane-satrapi-princess-of-darkness-417932.html.

Chayes, Sarah. *The Punishment of Virtue: Inside Afghanistan after the Taliban.* New York: Penguin, 2006.

Chelkowski, Peter. *Mirror of the Invisible World: Tales from the Khamseh of Nizami.* New York: Metropolitan Museum of Art, 1975.

Chesler, Phyllis. *About Men.* New York: Simon and Schuster, 1978.

———. *The Death of Feminism.* New York: Palgrave McMillan, 2005.

———. "Memoirs of Afghanistan." *Mademoiselle* (June 1969): 154–60.

———. *Mothers on Trial.* New York: McGraw-Hill, 1986.

———. *The New Anti-Semitism.* San Francisco: Jossey-Bass, 2003.

Chopin, Kate. *The Awakening.* 1899. Reprint. New York: Avon, 1982.

Choy, Marguerita. "Filmmaker Sees Lessons in Iranian History." Reuters, Oct. 30, 2006.

Clarke, Donald. "Moving Pictures." *Irish Times,* July 30, 2001.

Clawson, Patrick. "Iran in Books: Review Essay." *Middle East Quarterly* 14, no. 2 (Spring 2007): 41–50.

Cohler-Esses, Larry. "Bunkum from Benador." *The Nation,* July 3, 2006.

"Confession." *Omid-e Iran,* no. 10 (1955): 14–15, 20, 25.

"A Conversation: Margaret Atwood and Students, Moderated by Francis X. Gillen." In *Margaret Atwood: Vision and Forms,* edited by Kathryn VanSpanckeren and Jan Garden Castro, 233–69. Carbondale: Southern Illinois Univ. Press, 1988.

Cowley, Geoffrey. "The Biology of Beauty." *Newsweek* (June 3, 1996): 62.

Cummings, Steven R., Xu Ling, and Katie Stone. "Consequences of Foot Binding among Older Women in Beijing, China." *American Journal of Public Health* (Oct. 7, 1997): 1677–79.

Curry, Dayna, Heather Mercer, and Stacy Mattingly. *Prisoners of Hope: The Story of Our Captivity and Freedom in Afghanistan.* New York: Doubleday, 2002.

Dabashi, Hamid. *Close Up: Iranian Cinema, Past, Present, and Future.* London: Verso, 2001.

Daghighi, Mojdeh. "Goft-o-gu ba Shiva Arastui" (A Conversation with Shiva Arastui). *Zanan* (July 2004): 62–69.

Daly, Mary. *Gyn/Ecology: The Metaethics of Radical Feminism.* Boston: Beacon Press, 1978.

Daneshvar, Simin. *Savushun* (Persian Requiem). Tehran: Kharazmi, 1964.

Daniel, Elton. "History as a Theme of *The Blind Owl.*" In *Hedayat's "The Blind Owl" Forty Years After,* edited by Michael C. Hillman, 76–86. Austin: Univ. of Texas Press, 1978.

Davis, Dick. "Introduction." In *The Legend of Seyavash,* by Abol Qasem Ferdowsi, translated by Dick Davis, ix–xxvii. London: Penguin, 1992.

Dehghani, Ashraf. *Odyssey of Resistance.* N.p.: People's Fadaee Guerrillas, 1973.

Dehkhoda, Ali Akbar. *Loghat Nameh Dehkhoda.* Tehran: Tehran University Press, 1959.

Denby, David. "Women on the Run." *The New Yorker* (Apr. 23–30, 2001): 196–98.

Dickens, Charles. *A Tale of Two Cities.* New York: Penguin, 2003.

DiFranco, Ani. *Not a Pretty Girl.* Righteous Babe Records, 1995.

Djebar, Assia. *Women of Algiers in Their Apartment.* Translated by Marjolijin de Jager. Charlottesville: Univ. Press of Virginia, 1992.

Doolittle, Hilda. *Collected Poems, 1912–1944.* Edited by Louis L. Martz. Manchester, UK: Carcanet, 1984.

Dowd, Maureen. "Libido Games." *New York Times,* Mar. 18, 1998.

Dowlatshah, Dr. F. "Chance Encounter: Surprise Meeting Evokes Memories of Childhood." *Persian Heritage* 2, no. 6 (Summer 1997): 39–40.

Dumas, Firoozeh. *Funny in Farsi: A Memoir of Growing up Iranian in America.* New York: Random House, 2004.

Dworkin, Andrea. *Woman-Hating.* New York: Dulton, 1974.

Dylan, Bob. *The Times They Are A-Changin'.* Columbia Records, 1964.

Ebadi, Shirin, with Azadeh Moaveni. *Iran Awakening: A Memoir of Revolution and Hope.* New York: Random House, 2006.

Ebert, Roger. *"Not Without My Daughter." Chicago Sun-Times,* Jan. 11, 1991.

Ebrey, Patricia Buckley. *The Inner Quarter: Marriage and the Lives of Chinese Women during the Sung Period.* Berkeley and Los Angeles: Univ. of California Press, 1993.

Ebtekar, Massoumeh, with Fred Reed. *Takeover in Tehran: The Inside Story of the 1979 Embassy Capture.* Vancouver: Talonbooks, 2000.

Effendi, Shoghi. *God Passes By.* Wilmette, IL: Baha'i Publishing Committee, 1944.

———. "The Valiant Táririh." In *Táhirih in History: Perspectives on Qurratu'L-'Ayn from East and West,* edited by Sabir Afaqi, 15–20, Studies in the Bábí and Bahá'í Religions, vol. 16. Los Angeles: Kalimat Press, 2004.

Ellison, Ralph. *Invisible Man.* New York: Random House, 1972.

Esfandiari, Haleh. *My Prison, My Home: One Woman's Story of Captivity in Iran.* New York: HarperCollins, 2009.

Esmaili, Amir, and Abolghassem Sedarat, eds. *Javedaneh Forugh Farrokhzad* (Eternal Forugh Farrokhzad). Tehran: Marjan, 1968.

Etcoff, Nancy. *Survival of the Prettiest: The Science of Beauty.* New York: Doubleday, 1999.

———. "Why It Pays to Be a Babe." *Cosmopolitan* (Mar. 1999): 60.

E'tezadi, Malakeh. *E'terafat-e Man* (My Confessions). Tehran: n.p., 1956.

Fallaci, Orania. *Interview with History.* Translated by John Shepley. Boston: Houghton, 1977.

Farmanfamaian, Fatema Soudavar. "Haft Qalam Arayish: Cosmetics in the Iranian World." *Iranian Studies* 33, nos. 2–4 (Summer–Fall 2000): 285–326.

Farrokh, Faridoun. "Introduction." In Goli Taraghi, *A Mansion in the Sky: Short Stories by Goli Taraghi,* translated by Faridoun Farrokh, 1–8. Austin: Center for Middle Eastern Studies, Univ. of Texas.

Farrokhzad, Forugh. *Asir* (The Captive). Tehran: Amir Kabir, 1974.

———. *Avalin Tapesh-hay-e Asheghaneh-ye Ghalbam: Name hay-e Forugh Farrokhzad be Hamsarash Parviz Shapour* (The First Romantic Palpitations of My Heart: Forugh Farrokhzad's Letters to Her Husband, Parviz Shapour). Edited by Kamyar Shapour and Omran Salahi. Tehran: Morvarid, 2002.

———. "Confession." *Omid-e Iran,* no. 10 (1955): 14–15, 20, 25.

———. "Dar Diyari Digar" (Elsewhere). In *Javedaneh Zistan, Dar Owj Mandan* (Living Eternally, Staying on Top), edited by Behrouz Jalali, 66–117. Tehran: Morvarid, 1996.

———. *Divar* (Wall). Tehran: Amir Kabir, 1971.

———. *Iman Biavarim be Aghaz-e Fasl-e Sard* (Let's Believe in the Dawning of a Cold Season. Tehran: Morvarid, 1974.

———. "O! My Poems." In "Forugh Rouzhaye Khoob-e She'r" (The Good Days of Forugh's Poetry). *Zane Rooz* (21 Mordad 1357): 54.

———. *Tavallodi Digar* (Reborn). Tehran: Morvarid, 1963.

Farrokhzad, Pouran. *Nimeha-ye Natamam* (Uncompleted Halves). Tehran: Tandis, 2001.

Fathi, Nazila. "A Tourist in Space Becomes a Star in Iran." *New York Times,* Oct. 25, 2006.

———. "Women Writing Novels Emerge as Stars in Iran." *New York Times,* June 29, 2005.

Felski, Rita. *The Gender of Modernity.* Cambridge, MA: Harvard Univ. Press, 1995.

Ferdowsi, Abol Qasem. *The Legend of Seyavash.* Translated by Dick Davis. London: Penguin, 1992.

———. *The Shahnameh of the Persian Poet Firdausi.* Translated by James Atkinson, Esq. London: Routledge, 1976.

———. *The Tragedy of Sohrab and Rustam.* Translated by Jerome Clinton. Seattle: Univ. of Washington Press, 1987.

Finn, Peter, with Souad Mekhemet and Hoda Lazin. "A Lone Woman Testifies to Iraq's Order of Terror." *Washington Post,* July 21, 2003.

Finn, Peter, with Khalid Saffar. "Threads Unravel in Iraqi's Tale: Story of Husband's Execution Contradicted by Relatives Who Say He Is Alive." *Washington Post,* Jan. 20, 2005.

Fisk, Robert. "War on Terrorism: Rise and Fall of Village Cleric Who Fought 'Criminals and Traitors.'" *Znet,* Dec. 7, 2001. Available at http://www.independent.co.uk (news, world, Asia).

Folkenflik, David. "Questions Arise on 'Post' Story of Iraqi Anguish." National Public Radio, Jan. 19, 2005. Available at http://www.npr.org/templates/story/story.php?story Id=4459051.

Foucault, Michel. *Discipline and Punish: The Birth of the Prison.* Translated by Alan Sheridan. New York: Vintage Books, 1995.

Freud, Sigmund. "Three Essays on the Theory of Sexuality." In *The Freud Reader,* edited by Peter Gay, 239–92. New York: Norton, 1989.

Frey, James. *A Million Little Pieces.* New York: Doubleday, 2003.

Friedan, Betty. *The Feminine Mystique.* New York: Norton, 2001.

Friedl, Erika. "Sources of Female Power in Iran." In *In the Eye of the Storm: Women in Post-Revolutionary Iran,* edited by Mahnaz Afkhami and Erika Friedl, 151–67. Syracuse, NY: Syracuse Univ. Press, 1994.

———. *Women of Deh Koh: Lives in an Iranian Village.* Washington, DC: Smithsonian Institution Press, 1989.

"From Roots to Clichés." *Tavoos* (Peacock) 7, nos. 5–6 (Autumn 2000–Winter 2001): 284–93.

Garakani, Fazlollah. *Tohmat-e Sha'eri* (Accused of Being a Poet). Tehran: Alburz, 1977.

Getler, Michael. "A Powerful Tale Unravels." *Washington Post,* Jan. 23, 2005.

Ghaffary, Farrokh. "History of Cinema in Persia." In *Encyclopaedia Iranica,* edited by Ehsan Yarshater, 5:fascicle 6, 567–72. New York: Bibliotheca Persica Press, 1991.

Al-Ghazali, Zaynab. *Return of the Pharaoh: Memoir in Nasir's Prison.* Markfield, UK: Islamic Foundation, 1972.

Goldin, Farideh. *Wedding Song: Memoirs of an Iranian Jewish Woman.* Waltham, MA: Brandeis Univ. Press, 2003.

Goldman, Shalom. *The Wiles of Women/The Wiles of Men.* New York: State Univ. of New York Press, 1995.

Gole, Nilufer. *The Forbidden Modern: Civilization and Veiling.* Ann Arbor: Univ. of Michigan Press, 1996.

Golshiri, Hushang. *The Prince.* Translated by James Buchan. London: Vintage, 2005.

Goode, Erica. "Life's Wrinkles, Some of Them Ugly, Afflict the Beautiful, Too." *New York Times,* June 13, 1999.

Goodman, Ellen. "Will U.S. Remember the Ladies?" *Boston Globe,* Sept. 7, 2003.

Gorgani, Fakhraddin. *Vis and Ramin.* Translated by Dick Davis. Washington, DC: Mage, 2008.

Gottschalk, Marie. "Two Separate Societies: One in Prison, One Not." *Washington Post,* Apr. 15, 2008. Available at http://webb.senate.gov/newsroom/newsarticles/04-15-2008-01.cfm.

Graham-Brown, Sarah. *Images of Women.* London: Quartet, 1988.

Guppy, Shusha. *The Blindfold Horse: Memories of a Persian Childhood.* Boston: Beacon Press, 1998.

Gurgani, Fakhr ed-Din As'ad. *Vis and Ramin.* Translated by George Morrison. New York: Columbia Univ. Press, 1972.

Hajibashi, Zjaleh. "Sin." In *Forugh Farrokhzad: A Quarter-Century Later,* compiled and edited by Michael C. Hillman, special issue of *Literature East and West* 24 (n.d.): 67–71.

Haj Seyed Javadi, Fataneh. *Bamdad-e Khomar* (The Morning After). Tehran: Alborz, 1995.

Hakakian, Roya. *Journey from the Land of No: A Girlhood Caught in Revolutionary Iran.* New York: Three Rivers Press, 2004.

Hanaway, William L. "Formal Elements in the Persian Popular Romances." *Review of National Literature* 2, no. 1 (Spring 1971): 140–43.

Harrison, Kathryn. "Lives in the Arts." *New York Times Book Review,* Feb. 18, 2007.

Hartney, Christopher. *U.S. Rates of Incarceration: A Global Perspective.* Washington, DC: National Council on Crime and Delinquency, Nov. 2006. Available at http://www.nccd-crc.org/nccd/pubs/2006nov_factsheet_incarceration.pdf.

Haven, Cynthia. "Iran's Leading Poet Receives New Stanford Literature Prize." *Stanford Report,* Mar. 5, 2008.

Hedayat, Sadeq. *The Blind Owl*. Translated by D. P. Costello. London: John Calder, 1957.

———. *Buf-e Kur* (The Blind Owl). Tehran: Amir Kabir, 1973.

———. *Nayrangestan*. Tehran: Parastu, 1965.

———. *Neveshtehay-e Parakandeh* (The Scattered Writings). Tehran: Amir Kabir, 1965.

———. *Parvin, Dokhtar-e Sassan* (Parvin: Sassan's Daughter). Tehran: Amir Kabir, 1963.

———. *Payam-e Kafka* (Kafka's Message). Tehran: Amir Kabir, 1963.

———. *Sadeq Hedayat: An Anthology*. Translated by Ahmad Karimi-Hakkak. Edited by Ehsan Yarshater. Boulder, CO: Westview Press, 1979.

Hegland, Mary Elaine. "Political Roles of Aliabad Women: The Public–Private Dichotomy Transcended." In *Women in Middle Eastern History: Shifting Boundaries in Sex and Gender,* edited by Nikki Keddie and Beth Baron, 215–30. New Haven, CT: Yale Univ. Press, 1991.

Hillman, Michael C., ed. *Hedayat's "The Blind Owl" Forty Years After.* Austin: Univ. of Texas Press, 1978.

———. *A Lonely Woman: Forugh Farrokhzad and Her Poetry.* Washington, DC: Mage, 1987.

Hingley, Ronald. *Nightingale Fever: Russian Poets in Revolution.* New York: Knopf, 1981.

Hirsi Ali, Ayaan. *The Caged Virgin: An Emancipation Proclamation for Women and Islam.* New York: Free Press, 2006.

———. *Infidel.* New York: Free Press, 2007.

Hoffman, Jascha. "Data: Comparative Literature." *New York Times Book Review,* Apr. 15, 2007.

Ignatius, David. "Bush's Message to Iran." *Washington Post,* Sept. 15, 2006.

Iraj Mirza. *Divan* (Collected Poems). Tehran: Mozafari, n.d.

"Iran Calls for Ban on Barbie Doll." *BBC News,* Apr. 28, 2008. available at http://www.news.bbc.co.uk/2/hi/7371771.

"Iranian Film Enterprise." *Times of India,* Aug. 13, 1935.

Issari, M. Ali. *Cinema in Iran, 1900–1979.* Metuchen, NJ: Scarecrow Press, 1989.

Jackson, Cindy. *Living Doll.* London: Trafalgar Square, 2002.

Jami, Abdol Rahman. *Yusuf-o-Zulaikha* (Yusuf and Zulaikha). Edited, abridged, and translated by David Pendlebury. London: Octagon Press, 1980.

———. "Yusuf-o-Zulaikha" (Yusuf and Zulaikha). In *Masnavi-ye Haft Owrang* (Seven Thrones), edited by Morteza Modaress Gilani, 90. Tehran: Saʿdi, 1958.

Jicai, Feng. *The Three-Inch Lotus.* Translated by David Wakefield. Honolulu: Univ. of Hawaii Press, 1994.

"J. K. Rowling Interview: Transcripts about Snape." Available at http://www.whysnape.tripod.com/rowlingtranscript.htm.

Johnson, Barbara. Introduction to part four, "Whose Life Is It, Anyway?" In *The Seductions of Biography*, edited by Mary Rhiel and David Suchoff, 119–22. New York: Routledge, 1996.

Johnston, Sheila. "Quietly Ruling the Roost." *Sight and Sound* 9, no. 1 (Jan. 1999): 18–20.

Jones, Ann. *Kabul in Winter: Life Without Peace in Afghanistan.* New York: Metropolitan, 2006.

Kahf, Mohja. *Western Representations of the Muslim Woman: From Termagent to Odalisque.* Austin: Univ. of Texas Press, 1999.

Kakutani, Michiko. "Piecing Together a Fragmented Poet." *New York Times,* Aug. 8, 1989.

*Karnameh-e Nashr: Fehrest-e Mozoee Ketabhay Montasher Shodeh* (Publishing Index: A Thematic List of Published Books). Tehran: Khaneh Ketab, 1999–2003.

Keddie, Nikki R. "Women and 30 Years of the Islamic Republic." *Payvand's Iran News,* Feb. 9, 2009. Available at http://www.payvand.com/news/09/feb/1097.html.

Khoeiniha, Seyyed Mohammad Mousavi. "Preface." In *Takeover in Tehran: The Inside Story of the 1979 Embassy Capture,* by Massoumeh Ebtekar, with Fred Reed, 25–30. Vancouver: Talonbooks, 2000.

Khomeini, Ayatollah Ruhollah. "Address at Bihisht-I Zahra." In *Islam and Revolution: Writings and Declarations of Imam Khomeini,* translated and annotated by Hamid Alghar, 254–60. London: KPI, 1985.

Khorasani, Noushin Ahmadi. "The 'One Million Signature Campaign: Face to Face, Street to Street.'" Translated by Shole Irani. *Payvand's Iran News,* Mar. 30, 2007. Available at http://www.payvand.com/news/07/mar/1352.html.

Khouri, Norma. *Honor Lost: Love and Death in Modern Day Jordan.* New York: Atria Books, 2003.

Kingston, Maxine Hong. *Woman Warrior: Memoirs of a Girlhood among Ghosts.* New York: Vintage, 1989.

Kinzer, Stephen. *Overthrow: America's Century of Regime Change from Hawaii to Iraq.* New York: Times Books, 2006.

Ko, Dorothy. *Cinderella's Sisters: A Revisionist History of Footbinding.* Berkeley and Los Angeles: Univ. of California Press, 2005.

———. *Every Step a Lotus: Shoes for Bound Feet.* Berkeley and Los Angeles: Univ. of California Press, 2001.

*The Koran Interpreted.* Translated by Arthur Arberry. New York: Collier, 1995.

Kordi, Gohar. *An Iranian Odyssey.* London: Serpent's Tail, 1991.

Kramer, Martin. "Introduction." In *Middle Eastern Lives: The Practice of Biography and Self-Narrative,* edited by Martin Kramer, 1–19. Syracuse, NY: Syracuse University Press, 1991.

Kundera, Milan. *The Art of the Novel.* Translated by Linda Asher. New York: Grove Press, 1986.

Kushner, Aviya. "Literary Translations in America." *Poets and Writers* (Nov.–Dec. 2002): 47–48.

Lahiji, Shahla. "Portrayal of Women in Iranian Cinema: An Historical Overview." *Iran Bulletin* (n.d.). Available at http://www.iran-bulletin.org/art/CINEMA2.html.

Latifa, with Shékéba Hachemi. *My Forbidden Face: Growing Up under the Taliban: A Young Woman's Story.* London: Virago, 2002.

Library of Congress. *American Memory, Words, and Deeds in American History: Selected Documents Celebrating the Manuscript Division's First 100 Years.* Washington, DC: Library of Congress, n.d. Available at http://memory.loc.gov/cgi-bin/query/r?ammem/mcc:@field.

Logan, Harriet. *Un/Veiled: Voices of Women in Afghanistan.* New York: Harper, 2002.

Londonderry, Annie. "Women on Wheels: The Bicycle and the Women's Movement of the 1890s." Available at http://www.annielondonderry.com/womenWheels.html.

Maalouf, Amin. *Samarkand.* Translated by Russell Harris. New York: Interlink Books, 1996.

MacFarquhar, Neil. "Backlash of Intolerance Stirring Fear in Iran." *New York Times,* Sept. 20, 1996.

———. "Iranian Blogosphere Tests Government's Limits." *New York Times,* Apr. 6, 2008.

Mahalati, Sheikh Zabihollah. *Kashf-ol Ghorur ya Mafased-ol Sofur* (Learning about Vanity or the Evils of Unveiling). Tehran: Askari, 1959.

Mahani, Najmeh Khalili. "Women of Iranian Popular Cinema: Projection of Progress." *offscreen.com* 10, no. 7 (July 31, 2006). available at http://www.firouzanfilms.com/ . . . /NajmehKhalili_ WomenOfIranianPopularCinemaProjectionOfProgress.html.

Mahmoody, Betty, and Arnold Dunchock. *For the Love of a Child.* New York: St. Martin's Press, 1992.

Mahmoody, Betty, with William Hoffer. *Not Without My Daughter.* New York: St. Martin's Press, 1991.

Mahvash, Banu. *Raz-e Kamyabi-ye Jensi* (The Secret of Sexual Satisfaction). Tehran: n.p., 1957.

Makhmalbaf, Mohsen. "Limbs of No Body: The World's Indifference to the Afghan Tragedy." *Monthly Review* 53, no. 6 (Nov. 2001). Available at http://www.iranian.com/Opinion/2001/June/Afghan/index.html.

Malcolm, Janet. *The Silent Woman: Sylvia Plath and Ted Hughes.* New York: Vintage, 1995.

Manguel, Alberto. "Books of the Year." *Times Literary Supplement,* Nov. 30, 2007.

Matthews, Irene. "The Apple." *International Journal of Humanities and Peace* 17, no. 1 (2001): 102.

Maruf, Maryam. "*Offside* Rules: An Interview with Ja'far Panahi." June 7, 2006. Available at http://www.ioendemocracy.net.

Mazdapour, Katayoun. *One Thousand and One Nights' Delilah the Trickster.* New rev. version. Tehran: Rowshangaran, 1995.

McKinney, Joan. "Cooksey: Expect Racial Profiling." *Advocate,* Sept. 19, 2001.

Mehrabi, Mo'in ed-Din. *Qurratol'Ayn.* Cologne: Ruyesh, 1989.

Meisami, Julie Scott. *Medieval Persian Court Poetry.* Princeton, NJ: Princeton Univ. Press, 1987.

Menocal, Maria Rosa. *The Ornament of the World: How Muslims, Jews, and Christians Created a Culture of Tolerance in Medieval Spain.* New York: Back Bay Books, 2002.

Merguerian, Gayane Karen, and Afsaneh Najmabadi. "Zulaykha and Yusuf: Whose 'Best Story'?" *International Journal of Middle East Studies* 29 (1997): 485–508.

Mernissi, Fatima [under the pseudonym Fatna Saba]. *Beyond the Veil: Male–Female Dynamics in a Modern Muslim Society.* New York: Wiley, 1975.

———. *Dreams of Trespass: Tales of Harem Girlhood.* New York: Addison-Wesley, 1994.

———. *Islam and Democracy: Fear of the Modern World.* Translated by Mary Jo Lakeland. London: Virago Press, 1993.

———. *Scheherazade Goes West: Different Cultures, Different Harems.* New York: Vintage, 2001.

———. *The Veil and the Male Elite: A Feminist Interpretation of Women's Rights in Islam.* Boston: Addison-Wesley, 1992.

Milani, Abbas. *Lost Wisdom: Rethinking Modernity in Iran.* Washington, DC: Mage, 2004.

———. *The Persian Sphinx.* Washington, DC: Mage, 2000.

Milani, Farzaneh. "Dance as Dissent: In Iran, the Author Enjoys a Subversive Boogie Night." *Ms.* (Spring 2004): 29.

———. "Farrokhzad." In *Encyclopaedia Iranica,* edited by Ehsan Yarshater, 9:fascicle 3, 324–27. New York: Bibliotheca Persica, 1999.

———. "Lipstick Politics." *New York Times,* Aug. 19, 1999.

———. "Pay-e Sohbat-e Shahrnush Parsipur" (An Audience with Shahrnush Parsipur). *Iran Nameh* 11, no. 4 (Fall 1993): 691–704.

———. "Pay-e Sohbat-e Simin Daneshvar" (An Audience with Simin Daneshvar). *Alefba* (n.s.), no. 4 (Fall 1983): 147–57.

———. *Veils and Words: The Emerging Voices of Iranian Women Writers.* Syracuse, NY: Syracuse Univ. Press, 1992.

————. "The Visual Poetry of Shirin Neshat." In *Shirin Neshat*, 6–13. Milan, Italy: Charta, 2001.

Mirabedini, Hassan. "Dastan Nevisiy-e Zanan: Gamhay-e Larzan-e Avaliy-e" (Women's Fiction: First Wobbly Steps). *Zanan* (Mar. 2007).

————. "Persian Literature: The History of Female Storywriters." 2005. Available at http://www.iranchamber.com/ . . . /history_female_storywriters.php.

Moaveni, Azadeh. *Lipstick Jihad: A Memoir of Growing Up Iranian in America and American in Iran*. New York: Public Affairs, 2005.

Moghissi, Heideh. "Public Life and Women's Resistance." In *Iran after the Revolution: Crisis of an Islamic State,* edited by Saeed Rahnema and Sohrab Behdad, 251–67. London: I. B. Tauris, 1996.

Moin, Baqer. *Khomeini: Life of the Ayatollah*. London: I. B. Tauris, 1999.

Montagu, Lady Mary Wortley. *The Letters and Works of Lady Mary Wortley Montagu*. Vol. 1. Edited by Lord E. Wharncliffe. London: Henry G. Bohn, 1887.

Moravveji, Ayatollah Ali. *Feqh dar A'iney-e Cinema* (Islamic Jurisprudence in the Mirror of Cinema). Tehran: Howzey-e Honari, 1999.

Morrison, Toni. *The Bluest Eye*. New York: Pocket Books, 1970.

Mottahedeh, Negar. "Qurrat al-'Ayn's Unveiling and the Persian Massacre of the Babis circa 1852." Paper presented at the University of California at Berkeley, Apr. 1997. Reprinted online at http://www.bahai-library.com/mottahedeh_mutilated_body_ nations.

————. "Ruptured Spaces and Effective Histories: The Unveiling of the Babi Poetess Qurrat al-'Ayn-Tahirih in the Gardens of Badasht." *UCLA Historical Journal* 17 (1997): 59–81. Reprinted in *Táhirih in History: Perspectives on Qurratu'L-'Ayn from East and West,* edited by Sabir Afaqi, 203–30. Studies in the Bábí and Bahá'í Religions, vol. 16. Los Angeles: Kalimat Press, 2004.

Mulvey, Laura. *Visual and Other Pleasures*. Bloomington: Indiana Univ. Press, 1989.

Naficy, Hamid. "Islamizing Film Culture in Iran." In *Iran: Political Culture in the Islamic Republic,* edited by Samih Farsoun and Mehrdad Mashayekhi, 178–213. London: Routledge, 1992.

————. "Islamizing Film Culture in Iran: A Post-Khatami Update." In *The New Iranian Cinema: Politics, Representation, and Identity,* edited by Richard Tapper, 26–54. London: I. B. Tauris, 2002.

————. "Veiled Vision/Powerful Presences: Women in Post-Revolutionary Iranian Cinema." In *Life and Art: The New Iranian Cinema,* edited by Rose Issa and Sheila Whitaker, 44–65. London: National Film Theatre, 1999.

Nafisi, Azar. "Don't Ban Dan Brown." *The Guardian,* Nov. 25, 2006. Available at http://www.azarnafisi.com/censorship.guardian.pdf.

———. "Imagination as Subversion: Narrative as a Tool of Civic Awareness." In *Muslim Women and the Politics of Participation,* edited by Mahnaz Afkhami and Erika Friedl, 58–71. Syracuse, NY: Syracuse Univ. Press, 1997.

———. *Reading Lolita in Tehran: A Memoir in Books.* New York: Random House, 2003.

———. *Things I've Been Silent About.* New York: Random House, 2008.

Najmabadi, Afsaneh. "Veiled Discourse—Unveiled Body." *Feminist Studies* 19, no. 3 (Fall 1993): 487–518.

Nakhjavani, Bahiyyih. *Asking Questions: A Challenge to Fundamentalism.* Oxford, UK: George Ronald, 1990.

———. *La femme qui lisait trop* (The Woman Who Read Too Much). Paris: Actes Sud, 2007.

———. *The Saddlebag.* London: Bloomsbury, 2000.

———. "The Woman Who Read Too Much." Unpublished manuscript.

Nazif, Suleyman. "Passages from *Nasiruddin Shah ve Babiler.*" Translated by Necati Alkan. In *Táhirih in History: Perspectives on QurratuʿL-ʿAyn from East and West,* edited by Sabir Afaqi, 79–82. Studies in the Bábí and Baháʾí Religions, vol. 16. Los Angeles: Kalimat Press, 2004.

Nemat, Marina. *The Prisoner of Tehran: A Memoir.* New York: Free Press, 2007.

Nizami-ye Ganjavi, [Abu Muhammad]. *Layla and Majnun.* Translated by Dr. R. Gelpke. Boulder, CO: Shambhala, 1978.

Nudushan, Islami. "Tragic Figures in *Shahnameh.*" *Ettelaʾat,* Dec. 3, 1997.

O'Donnell, Terence. *Garden of the Brave in War: Recollections of Iran.* Chicago: University of Chicago Press, 1980.

Pamuk, Orhan. "The Anger of the Damned." Translated by Mary Isin. *New York Review of Books* 48, no. 18 (Nov. 15, 2001). Available at http://www.nybooks.com/articles/archives/ . . . /the-anger-of-the-damned/.

———. "Freedom to Write." Translated by Maureen Freely. *New York Review of Books,* May 25, 2006.

———. *My Name Is Red.* Translated by Erdag M. Goknar. New York: Alfred A. Knopf, 2001.

———. *Snow.* Translated by Maureen Freely. New York: Alfred A. Knopf, 2004.

Parini, Jay. "Pirates, Pashas, and the Imperial Astrologer." *New York Times,* May 19, 1991. Available at http://www.nytimes.com/books/ . . . /pamuk-castle.html.

Parsipur, Shahrnush. *Adab-e Sarf-e Chay dar Hozur-e Gorg* (Tea Ceremony in the Presence of the Wolf). Los Angeles: Tassveer, 1993.

———. *Aghl-e Abi* (Blue Logos). San Jose, CA: Zamaneh, 1994.

———. *Khaterat-e Zendan* (Prison Memoirs). Stockholm: Baran, 1996.

———. *Sag va Zemestan-e Boland* (The Dog and the Long Winter). Tehran: Amir Kabir, 1974.

———. *Touba and the Meaning of the Night.* Translated by Hava Houshmand and Kamran Talatoff. New York: Feminist Press, 2006.

———. *Touba va Ma'nay-e Shab.* Tehran: Spark, 1989.

———. *Zanan bedun-e Mardan* (Women Without Men). Tehran: Noqreh, 1989.

Pipher, Mary. *Reviving Ophelia: Saving the Selves of Adolescent Girls.* New York: Ballantine, 1995.

Plath, Sylvia. *Ariel.* New York: Harper Perennial Modern Classics, 1999.

"Q & A: 'I Feared I Could Be Killed in the Mayhem': Omid Memarian Interviews Iranian Noble Prize Laureate Shirin Ebadi." *IPS News,* Jan. 10, 2009. Available at http://ipsnews.net/news.asp?idnews=45327.

Qurratul'Ayn, Tahirih. *Tahirih, a Portrait in Poetry: Selected Poems of Qurratu'l-'Ayn.* Edited and translated by Amin Banani, with Jascha Kessler and Anthony A. Lee. Los Angeles: Kalimat Press, 2005.

Rachlin, Nahid. *Persian Girls.* New York: Tarcher/Penguin, 2006.

Rich, Frank. "Truthiness Stages a Comeback." *New York Times,* Jan. 22, 2006.

Ritter, Gretchen. *The Constitution as a Social Design: Gender and Civic Membership in the American Constitutional Order.* Stanford, CA: Stanford Univ. Press, 2006.

Rodriguez, Deborah, with Kristin Ohlson. *Kabul Beauty School: An American Woman Goes Behind the Veil.* New York: Random House, 2007.

Root, Martha L. *Tahirih the Pure.* Rev. ed. With an introduction by Marzieh Gail. Los Angeles: Kalimat Press, 1981.

Rossi, William. *The Sex Life of the Foot and Shoe.* Hertfordshire, UK: Wordsworth Editions, 1977.

Rouhi, Leyla. "A Comparative Typology of the Medieval Go-Between in Light of Western-European, Near-Eastern, and Spanish Cases." Ph.D. diss., Harvard Univ., 1995.

Rousseau, Jean-Jacques. *Emile or On Education.* Translated by Allan Bloom. New York: Basic Books, 1979.

Rushdie, Salman. *Midnight's Children.* New York: Avon, 1982.

———. "Outside the Whale." *American Film* (Jan.–Feb. 1985): 70.

———. *Shame.* New York: Vintage, 1983.

Sa'edi, Gollam Hossein. *Dandil.* Tehran: Javaneh, 1966.

Sa'edi, Gholam Hossein, and Syrus Tahbaz. "An Interview with Forugh Farrokhzad." In *Harfhai ba Forugh* (Some Words with Forugh), 47–79. Tehran: Morvarid 1976.

Safa, Kaveh. "Madness as Masculine Prerogative in *Layla and Majnun*." Paper presented at the Shifting Boundaries conference, Univ. of Virginia, Apr. 1995.

Said, Edward. *Covering Islam: How the Media and the Experts Determine How We See the Rest of the World*. New York: Vintage Books, 1997.

———. *Khaterat-e Taj al-Saltaneh* (Taj al-Saltaneh's Memoir). Edited by Mansureh Ettehadiyeh and Sirus Sa'advandiyan. Tehran: Nashr-e Tarikh-e Iran, 1982.

Sarkouhi, Faraj. "Iran: Book Censorship the Rule, Not the Exception." Radio Free Europe/Radio Liberty, Nov. 26, 2007.

Sarshar, Homa. *Sha'ban Ja'afari*. Beverly Hills, CA: Naab, 2002.

Sasson, Jean. *Mayada, Daughter of Iraq: One Woman's Survival in Saddam Hussein's Torture Jail*. New York: New American Library, 2004.

Satrapi, Marjane. *Persepolis I: The Story of a Childhood*. New York: Pantheon, 2003.

———. *Persepolis II: The Story of a Return*. New York: Pantheon, 2003.

Schickel, Richard. "What Sparked It." *Time* 109, no. 12 (Mar. 1977): 17.

Scholes, Robert. "Presidential Address 2004: The Humanities in a Posthumanist World." *PMLA* 120, no. 3 (May 2005): 724–33.

Schunk, Leslie. "Memoirs: From Scribbling into High Art." *World Literature Today* 73, no. 3 (Summer 1999): 475–80.

Sciolino, Elaine. "Iran's Well-Covered Women Remodel a Part That Shows." *New York Times,* Sept. 22, 2000.

———. *Persian Mirrors: The Elusive Face of Iran*. New York: Free Press, 2000.

Scott, Derek A. "Birds in Iran." In *Encyclopaedia Iranica,* edited by Ehsan Yarshater, 4:fascicle 3, 265–72. New York: Routledge and Kegan Paul, 1989.

Sedghi, Hamideh. *Women and Politics in Iran: Veiling, Unveiling, and Reveiling*. New York: Cambridge Univ. Press, 2007.

See, Carolyn. "A Family—and a Country—Torn Apart." *Washington Post,* Oct. 13, 2006.

Sepanlou, Shahrzad. *Touba*. Tehran: Eshragi, 1977.

Shadman, Fakhr eddin. *Taskhir-e Tammadon Farrangi* (Possessed by Western Culture). Tehran: Majlis, 1947.

Shafa, Shojaeddin. "Shojaeddin Shafa in His Own Words." *Persian Heritage* 5, no. 20 (Winter 2000): 59.

———. Untitled essay. In *Asir* (Captive), by Forugh Farrokhzad, 3–7. Tehran: Amir Kabir, 1974.

Shahri, Ja'far. *Tarikh-e Ejtema'iy-e Tehran dar Gharn-e Sizdahum* (The Social History of Tehran in the Thirteenth Century). Tehran: Rasa, 1990.

Shamlu, Ahmad. *Taraneha-ye Kuchak-e Ghorbat* (Short Poems of Exile). N.p.: Maziar, 1980.

Shari'ati, Ali. *Fatemeh Fatemeh Ast* (Fatemeh Is Fatemeh). Tehran: n.p., n.d.

————. *Zan* (Woman). Tehran: n.p., 1983.

Sheil, Lady Mary. *Glimpses of Life and Manners in Persia.* 1856. Reprint. New York: Arno, 1973.

Shikibu, Murasaki. *The Tale of Genji.* New York: Random House, 1983.

Shirazi, Faegheh. *The Veil Unveiled: The Hijab in Modern Culture.* Gainesville: Univ. Press of Florida, 2001.

Siddiqui, Mohammad Ali. "Qurratu'l-ayn: A Profile in Courage." In *Táhirih in History: Perspectives on Qurratu'L-'Ayn from East and West,* edited by Sabir Afaqi, 67–70. Studies in the Bábí and Bahá'í Religions, vol. 16 . Los Angeles: Kalimat Press, 2004).

Smith, Peter. *The Babi and Baha'i Religions: From Messianic Shi'ism to a World Religion.* Cambridge, UK: Cambridge Univ. Press, 1987.

Solovitch, Sara. "The American Dream." *Esquire Magazine* (Jan. 2005). Available at http://www.sarasolo.com/dream.html.

Solzhenitsyn, Alexander. "A World Split Apart." June 8, 1978. Available at http://www.americanrhetoric.com/speeches/alexandersolzhenitsynharvard.htm.

Souad, with Marie-Therese Cuny. *Burned Alive: A Victim of the Law of Men.* New York: Time Warner, 2003.

Spellberg, Denise. *Politics, Gender, and the Islamic Past: The Legacy of 'A'isha Bint Abi Bakr.* New York: Columbia Univ. Press, 1994.

Spender, Stephen. "I Think Continually of Those Who Were Truly Great." In *The Oxford Anthology of English Literature,* vols. 1–2, edited by Frank Kermode and John Hollander, 22–26. Oxford, UK: Oxford Univ. Press, 1973.

Steingass, F. *Persian–English Dictionary.* London: Routledge and Kegan Paul, 1977.

Stiller-Kern, Gabriele. "The Clear but Fragile Force of Writing." *Culturebase.net* (Sept. 2004). Available at http://www.culturebase.net/artist.php?436.

Stowasser, Barbara Freyer. *Women in the Quran, Traditions, and Interpretation.* New York: Oxford Univ. Press, 1994.

Sullivan, Zohreh T. "Iranian Cinema and the Critique of Absolutism." In *Media, Culture, and Society in Iran: Living with Globalization and the Islamic State,* edited by Mehdi Semati, 193–204. London: Routledge, 2008.

Surieu, Robert. *Sarve Naz.* Geneva: Nagel, 1967.

Tahmasbpoor, Mohammad Reza. "Early Photography in Iran." N.d. Available at the Kargah.com Iranian Artists' site, http://www.kargah.com/history_of_iranian_photography/early/index.php?other=1.

Tahami, Reza. "Iranian Women Make Films." *Film International Quarterly* 2, no. 3 (Summer 1994): 4–13.

Tahbaz, Syrus, ed. *Arash*. Tehran: Darakhshan, 1966.

Taheri, Zahra. *Hozour Peyda va Penhan Zan dar Motun-e Sufiy-e* (The Presence and Absence of Women in Sufi Texts). Tokyo: Research Institute for Languages, 2007.

Tait, Robert. "Bestsellers Banned in New Iranian Censorship Purge." *The Guardian*, Nov. 17, 2006.

Taj Al-Saltaneh. *Crowning Anguish: Memoirs of a Persian Princess from the Harem to Modernity*. Edited by Abbas Amanat. Translated by Anna Vanzan and Amin Neshati. Washington, DC: Mage, 1993.

Taraghi, Goli. *Dow Donya* (Two Worlds). Tehran: Niloofar, 2002.

———. *A Mansion in the Sky: Short Stories by Goli Taraghi*. Translated by Faridoun Farrokh. Austin: Center for Middle Eastern Studies, Univ. of Texas, 2003.

Tavakoli-Targhi, Mohammad. *Refashioning Iran: Orientalism, Occidentalism, and Historiography*. New York: Palgrave, 2001.

Taylor, Therese. "Memoirs of Deception." *Jewish Quarterly* (Spring 2007): 47–51.

Thompson, Elizabeth. *Colonial Citizens: Republican Rights, Paternal Privilege, and Gender in French Syria and Lebanon*. New York: Columbia Univ. Press, 1999.

*Thousand Nights and a Night: A Plain and Literal Translation of the Arabian Nights Entertainments, The*. Translated by Richard F. Burton. 10 vols. London: Burton Club, 1886.

Tuckey, Melissa. "Interview with Iranian Poet Farideh Hassanzadeh." *Foreign Policy in Focus: A Think Tank Without Walls*, June 12, 2007. Available at http://www.fpif.org/fpiftxt/4300.

Tyler, Anne. *Digging to America*. New York: Alfred A. Knopf, 2006.

Al-Urdun, Mohammed. "Iran's Literary Giantess Is Defiant in Exile . . . but Missing Home." *Camden New Journal*, June 19, 2007. Available at http://www.shahrnush parsipur.com/article10.htm.

Vafi, Fariba. *My Bird*. Translated by Mahnaz Kousha and Nasrin Jewell. With a foreword by Farzaneh Milani. Syracuse, NY: Syracuse Univ. Press, 2009.

———. *Parandey-e Man* (My Bird). Tehran: Markaz, 2002.

Vick, Karl. "Sorry, Wrong Chador: In Tehran 'Reading Lolita' Translates as Ancient History." *Washington Post*, July 19, 2004.

Voice of America. "Iraqi Woman Profits from False Testimony." Mar. 3, 2005. Available at http://www.voanews.com/english/NewsAnalysis/2005-03-03-voa41.cfm.

Von Wartburg, Linda. "Like Cinderella's Sisters, Many People with Diabetes Squeeze Big Feet into Small Shoes." *DiabetesHealth*, Jan. 1, 2008. Available at http://www.diabetes health.com/read/2008/01/01/5592.html.

Wakefield, Mary. "'We Are at War with All Islam.'" *Spectator,* Nov. 28, 2007. Available at http://www.spectator.co.uk/print/the-magazine/features/276476.

Walsh, David. "An Interview with Ja'far Panahi, director of *The Circle*." Sept. 17, 2003. Available at http://www.wsws.org/articles/2003/sep2003/pana-s17.shtml.

Whitlock, Gillian. *Soft Weapons: Autobiography in Transit.* Chicago: Univ. of Chicago Press, 2007.

Wilentz, Sean. "The Rise of Illiterate Democracy." *New York Times Book Review,* Dec. 11, 2005.

Wolf, Naomi. *The Beauty Myth: How Images of Beauty Are Used Against Women.* New York: Anchor, 1992.

Wollstonecraft, Mary. *A Vindication of the Rights of Woman.* New York: Norton, 1967.

Woolf, Virginia. *A Room of One's Own.* New York: Harcourt, Brace and World, 1957.

Yasgur, Batya Swift. *Behind the Burqa: Our Life in Afghanistan and How We Escaped to Freedom.* Hoboken, NJ: Wiley, 2002.

Yeats, William Butler. *Mythologies.* New York: Touchstone, 1998.

Zonis, Marvin. "Autobiography and Biography in the Middle East: A Plea for Psychopolitical Studies." In *Middle Eastern Lives: The Practice of Biography and Self-Narrative,* edited by Martin Kramer, 60–88. Syracuse, NY: Syracuse University Press, 1991.

Zoya, with John Follain and Rita Cristofari. *Zoya's Story: An Afghan Woman's Struggle for Freedom.* New York: Harper Collins, 2002.

# INDEX

323

Khaksar, Nassim, 161

Khalili, Abbas, 280–81n2

Khamene'i, Seyed Ali, 3

Khayyam, Omar, 263n30

*Khesht va Ayeneh* (Mud Brick and Mirror) (film), 86

Khodayar, Nasser, 136, 139, 140

Khoeiniha, Mousavi, 294n68

Khoi, Esmai'il, 161

Khomeini, Ruhollah (Ayatollah): on cinema, 86, 88; on gynecologists, 267n7; on hostage crisis, 205, 288n8; marriage of, 35

Khorasani, Noushin Ahmadi, 126–27, 275n38

Khosrow, 38, 299n3

*Khosrow and Shirin* (Ganjavi), 34, 35

Khouri, Norma, 295–97n82

Kiarostami, Abbas, 102

Kifner, John, 287n4

"Kill a cat in the nuptial chamber" (proverb), 235–39

Kingston, Maxine Hong, 68, 264n38

Kinzer, Stephen, 294n71

Kish Island, 97

Kiswah, 57, 262n16

Kiya, Zahra, 184–85

Ko, Dorothy, 69

Kordi, Gohar, 300n3

Koushiar, Manuchehr, 160, 281n13

*kowligari* (like gypsies), 82, 177–79, 283n41

Krishna of India, 84

Kroes, Neelie, 293n67

Kundera, Milan, 6–7, 251nn5–6

Kushner, Aviya, 293n59


"Labyrinth" (Amirshahi), 300n3

labyrinths, 38–39, 128–29, 276n1

Lahiji, Shahla, 86, 184

Lakkateh, 65, 66

*Lamp of Forty Lights, A* (Behbahani), 162

Latifa, 13, 291n43

Latifeh Yarshater Book Award, 162, 282n19

law of apostasy, 121, 275n31

laws: adultery, 277n18; inheritance, 119–20; marriage, 119–20, 136, 213, 222; property, 119–20

*Layli and Majnun* (film), 84, 269n30

legal discrimination, 23, 119–20, 244, 252n10

Leili (fictional character), 31–33, 37

*Leili and Majnun,* 32–33, 40

Leonardo da Vinci, 194

leprosy, 146–48, 279n39

"Let's Believe in the Dawning of a Cold Season" (Farrokhzad), 132, 152–53, 285n27

Lewis, Reina, 14

life expectancy, 21

life narratives: in America, xviii–xix; culture and, 250–51n8; Muslim women portrayed in, 25, 208–12; popular appeal of, 225–26; prison memoirs as, 212, 228–32; truth and falsehood in, 233–34, 295–98n82; *Veils and Words* on, 250–51n8

Ling, Xu, 265n45

literacy rate, 256n40

literature: Arab, 293n59; contemporary, 182–86, 200, 258–59n20, 300n3; courtly, 259n22; early postrevolutionary, 183, 206; embargoes on, 293–94n68; on imperiled masculinity, 18–20; masculine character of, 30; modernity and, 6–8; as public art, 30. *See also* American literature; Persian literature

*Living Doll* (Jackson), 71

*Lolita* (Nabokov), 219, 291n41

Longinotto, Kim, 270n48

*Lor Girl, The (Doktar-e Lor)* (film), 82, 83

lovemaking, 59–60

love poems, 131, 132, 136–38, 153, 280n52